Lord Aberdeen

By the same author

IT'S A BIGGER LIFE
CREOLE
THE CANNIBALS
THE GHOSTS OF VERSAILLES
LOVE AND THE PRINCESS
AND HIS CHARMING LADY
YES, MY DARLING DAUGHTER
THE FIERY CHARIOT
HOW DO I LOVE THEE

Lord Aberdeen

A biography of the fourth
Earl of Aberdeen, K.G., K.T.,
Prime Minister 1852-1855

LUCILLE IREMONGER

COLLINS
St James's Place, London
1978

William Collins Sons & Co Ltd
London · Glasgow · Sydney · Auckland
Toronto · Johannesburg

First published 1978
© Lucille Iremonger 1978
ISBN 0 00 216082 X

Set in Linotype Times
Made and Printed in Great Britain by
William Collins Sons & Co Ltd Glasgow

Contents

	List of Illustrations	6
	Preface	9
1	Scion of the Gordons	13
2	'The Travelled Thane' at Home	24
3	*'Verissima, dulcissima imago'*	33
4	'The Din of War'	46
5	The Field of Leipzig	59
6	'Heartburnings Enough'	66
7	Disappointed Hopes	76
8	*'Vive la Paix! Vive qui voudra!'*	84
9	'Most Dear and Sweet Love'	95
10	Foreign Secretary	111
11	The Years the Locust Hath Eaten	124
12	*L'Entente Peu Amicale*	141
13	The Spanish Marriages	151
14	American Problems	166
15	Cincinnatus Recalled	185
16	'Chained to the Oar'	212
17	'Odd Tempers and Queer Ways'	228
18	A Russell at Home and a Russell Abroad	239
19	To Sebastopol	252
20	'Anxiety and Suspense'	259
21	A Stormy Session	271
22	'Treachery and Deceit'	281
23	The Fall	293
24	*Procul Negotiis Non Beatus*	303
25	The Last Years	317
	Appendix: Scottish Church Affairs	327
	References	333
	Selected Bibliography	365
	Index	373

List of Illustrations

between pages 120-1

Lord Aberdeen as a young man (c. 1808) by Sir Thomas Lawrence. Reproduced by permission of the executors and trustees of the fourth Marquess of Aberdeen and Temair.

Catherine, Lord Aberdeen's first wife, by Sir Thomas Lawrence. Reproduced by permission of Mr Kenneth Garlick.

Harriet, Lord Aberdeen's second wife (c. 1823), by Sir Thomas Lawrence.

Argyll House, London. Reproduced by permission of the Trustees of the British Museum.

Haddo House, Aberdeenshire, today. Reproduced by permission of the Haddo House Choral and Operatic Society. From a photograph taken by the fourth Marquess of Aberdeen and Temair.

between pages 264-5

Mary, Lady Haddo, on her marriage in 1840, by Mrs Carpenter. Reproduced by permission of the executors and trustees of the fourth Marquess of Aberdeen and Temair.

Lord Aberdeen's Cabinet, 1854, by Sir John Gilbert. Reproduced by permission of the National Portrait Gallery.

Lord Aberdeen in 1855. From the photograph by Mayall.

Even for the most honourable of men the life of politics is no affair of saintliness. There are certain necessities, certain dark passes which a man is bound to accept because they are bound to affect him . . . A man who cannot bear lightly the weight of these imperfections proper to a political career would be wiser to keep within the sphere of private life and speculation.

François Guizot, *Mémoires*, Volume IV, p. 287.
(Translation by Woodward, in
Studies in European Conservation, p. 116)

Les malheureux ont toujours tort.

Sir John Burgoyne to Colonel Anson
(Theodore Martin, *The Life of the Prince Consort*,
Volume III, p. 193)

Preface

This is only the third biography of the fourth Earl of Aberdeen to be published since his death in 1860. The first, by his youngest son, then Sir Arthur Gordon, was published in 1894, and suffered greatly from severe abridgement made necessary in order to fit it into a series of short works on Victorian prime ministers. The second, by Lady Frances Balfour, daughter of his protégé the Duke of Argyll, written at the request of the first Marquess of Aberdeen and Temair and published in 1922, relied heavily on the first.

There is hardly an aspect of Aberdeen's public life which has not been exhaustively treated by historians, and usually, though with distinguished exceptions, unsympathetically to him. On the other hand the personality of the man himself has received little attention, and that though the Muniment Room at Haddo House, Aberdeenshire, contains material which, as the representative of the British Museum who examined it pointed out, should prove of decided interest to future historians. It has been my object to offer my readers the fruits of my researches at Haddo, while doing justice to Aberdeen's work as Foreign Secretary, and as Prime Minister during the Crimean War during which a fine reputation foundered. Even to attempt this within the limitations of space available to me presented me with a difficult task of selection, and I can only hope that I have struck the right balance.

Her Majesty the Queen gave me her gracious permission to examine material in the Royal Archives at Windsor Castle, and this has proved of inestimable advantage to me. Sir Robert Mackworth-Young, Librarian at the Castle, and Miss Jane Langton, the Registrar, were unfailingly kind and helpful. The fourth Marquess of Aberdeen and Temair gave me his enthusiastic support and encouragement in the writing of this biography until his untimely death, extending to the closing of the Muniment Room at Haddo House to all other researchers. I am glad to record, too, my gratitude to him and June, Marchioness of Aberdeen and Temair for their bounteous hospitality and warm friendship over the years. My friend from our salad days, the fifth Marquess, has not only given me the benefit of his own valuable knowledge of family history, but has taken a close and informed interest in the development of the work. To him too I owe the gift of a volume of the proof copy of Arthur Gordon's original draft of his life of his father, bound for private circulation,

9

paginated only by chapters, and containing much material excised from the published version, as well as the long-standing loan of Arthur Gordon's original manuscript diaries, and of other volumes, published but hard to come by.

I owe particular thanks to Professor W. D. Jones of the University of Georgia for reading my chapter on the American problems which confronted Aberdeen during his second foreign secretaryship; to Mr Jasper Ridley for an interesting correspondence on the Spanish Marriages question, and for his most generous offer of gleanings from his own researches in the Museo Historico in Montevideo and in the Spanish press; to Dr J. C. Macaulay, M.D., for attempting a diagnosis, with all due caution, of the interesting symptoms from which Aberdeen suffered; to my editor Mr Philip Ziegler for his expertise of every kind, not least as a brilliant historian himself, and for his unfailing patience and helpfulness; to Mr Bruce Hunter of David Higham's for being a tower of strength as always; to Professor Donald Southgate and Dr C. J. Bartlett for having read my book and given me the benefit of their specialized knowledge in their respective fields; to Mr David Farrer, friend and former publisher, for having suggested that I write this book after reading my chapter on Aberdeen in my study of prime ministers, *The Fiery Chariot*, published by Secker & Warburg.

My thanks are due also to the Duke of Abercorn; Mrs Mary Bennett, the Principal of St Hilda's College, Oxford; the late Sir Charles Petrie; Sir David Lidderdale, formerly Clerk of the House of Commons; Sir John Pope-Hennessey, formerly Director of the British Museum; the Countess of Longford, for encouraging me to undertake the work; Mr Geoffrey Treasure; Miss Joanna Gordon; Dr J. Mordaunt Crook; the Trustees of the British Museum; the British Library; the Public Record Office; the Bodleian Library; the Cambridge University Library; Mr N. H. Robinson, Librarian of the Royal Society; Mr John Hopkins, Librarian of the Society of Antiquaries; Dr James Corson, Honorary Librarian of Abbotsford; Mrs K. F. Campbell, of the Library Records Department of the Foreign and Commonwealth Office; Mr Godfrey Thompson, Librarian, the Guildhall; Mr J. M. Smethurst, University Librarian, and Miss Margaret Stephen, of the Aberdeen University Library; Mr Gordon Phillips, the Archivist, *The Times*; Mr Maurice F. Bond, Clerk of the Records, the House of Lords; and in a very special degree Mr Kenneth Jay, Branch Librarian, Chelsea Library.

I acknowledge with thanks the permission of John Murray Ltd. to quote from John Martineau's *Life of Henry Pelham, fifth Duke of Newcastle*, and of Macmillan and Co. Ltd. to quote from Professor E. Jones Parry's *The Spanish Marriages*.

For help with illustrations I owe thanks to the Rt. Hon. James Callaghan, M.P.; the Viscount Cowdray; Mr Michael Levey, Director of the National Gallery; Mr Malcolm Rogers of the National Portrait Gallery; the Department of Prints and Drawings of the British Museum; Mr. John Sunderland, of the Witt Library, The Courtauld Institute; and, especially, Mr Kenneth Garlick, Keeper of Western Art at the Ashmolean Museum, Oxford; as well as June, Marchioness of Aberdeen and Temair and the fifth Marquess of Aberdeen and Temair.

My husband, as always, gave me boundless help in every possible way during the research and writing of this book, and I am indebted to him not least for insights into the realities of politics gained during his twenty years as a Member of Parliament. To my daughter goes my warm gratitude for practical and imaginative help of every kind.

Lucille Iremonger.

Chapter 1

Scion of the Gordons

Sir Robert Peel admired the fourth Earl of Aberdeen so greatly that he 'estimated him higher than any' of all those men of exceptional talent and ability who surrounded him. The chilly and exacting Duke of Wellington, an intimate friend of his, wrote to him, 'You have only to give your attention to any subject or any business, however irksome or disagreeable to you, to do it better than others'. To the day of his death Gladstone respected – and *'loved'* – him to the point of veneration. *The Times*, in its obituary, said of him, 'Out of office he had more authority than half the Cabinet'.

Now he is little more than a name to all but a handful of historians. When, too rarely and transiently, he is summoned from oblivion, he is usually dismissed with an angry impatience. Partly this may be because there have been pitifully few to speak up for him. Even of those few hardly any have been disinterested or weighty. No party, and no interest or cabal, has found it important to keep his name green and resist assaults upon it, since Aberdeen was above all a non-party man, that *beau idéal* of the electorate. He left his papers to his youngest son and secretary, Arthur Gordon, later Lord Stanmore, subject only to the veto of his friends and colleagues, Sir James Graham and Gladstone. Again the two guardians Lord Aberdeen chose for his reputation either could not, or would not, vindicate it as he might himself have wished. Graham died soon after him. Gladstone persistently refused permission for Aberdeen's correspondence to be published. His son could only print it privately in readiness for the day that never came. Then he was rushed into writing a valuable but cruelly abridged life of his father, so that at least a well-informed friend should speak for him in a series of volumes on Queen Victoria's Prime Ministers. In the end the correspondence was presented, still unpublished, to the British Museum, by the seventh Earl and first Marquess of Aberdeen, in 1931.

So long as Arthur Gordon, armed with loyalty and the knowledge gained in his years as confidant and political secretary during the most critical period of his father's career, was alive, Aberdeen could never be unjustly attacked with impunity. His old enemy, the slippery Lord John Russell, had only to traduce him in *The Times* in the course of one of his brash and irresponsible pronouncements, for the vigilant Arthur to bludgeon him into withdrawal and apology[1]; but Arthur was not immortal. There have been few defenders to follow him.

There may, possibly, be another reason for the emotional dismissal of Aberdeen, which can extend to the abusive, by historians – that he has been a victim, in the sense elaborated by Sir Herbert Butterfield, of 'the Whig interpretation of history'.[2] As the contemporary and rival of Palmerston, who is canonized as the successful friend of radical revolution in Europe against 'despotism', he offends, and is dismissed as negligible and contemptible. In truth, as Algernon Cecil pointed out half a century ago, 'No one in [Aberdeen's] own day, unless it be Clarendon, was his equal in the practice of a certain sort of diplomacy which some of the wisest judges amongst us have come to reckon high. He understood that the first principle of international business is to dispel distrust . . .'[3] Palmerston, of course, cut a far more attractive figure than Aberdeen – jaunty, resilient, and lucky, while Aberdeen was sober, dogged, and, always, tragically unfortunate. (Courage they both had in abundance.) But there was a great deal more to Aberdeen than the pasteboard figure which subsists today of the prime minister who allowed the nation to 'drift' into the Crimean War. To quote Butterfield, 'The description of a man's characteristics, the analysis of a mind and a personality are, subject to obvious limits, part of the whole realm of historical interpretation; for it is the assumption of historical study that by sympathy and imagination we can go at least some way towards the understanding of people other than ourselves and times other than our own'.[4] It is my hope that this account of his life, which includes hitherto unpublished material, may fulfil this modest aim.

When Lady Haddo gave birth to her first son, George, in Edinburgh on 28 January 1784, she and her young husband, George Gordon, Lord Haddo, heir to the third Earl of Aberdeen, could hope for much for him. Two years before Lord Haddo had married Charlotte Baird, the sister of a distinguished general, Sir David Baird, when he was only eighteen years of age. In course of time Haddo could expect to become the fourth Earl, and inherit the vast Scottish acres and great wealth which went with the title. Long years in the future their infant son would doubtless become the fifth Earl of Aberdeen.

The Gordons were a proud and ancient family. They liked to claim descent from the Bertrand de Gourdon whose arrow had slain Richard Coeur de Lion in 1199 before the hill-top Castle of Chalus in Perigord, and whose children had settled in Scotland at the beginning of the thirteenth century. In fact the family was probably domiciled long before in the south of Scotland, whence it migrated in the fourteenth century, acquiring territory until its lands stretched from the North Sea to the Atlantic. By mid-century a direct progenitor of the little boy who had been born to Haddo and his 'Charles' was established as a laird at Haddo in Aberdeenshire. It was in the sixteenth and seventeenth centuries, however, that the family had risen to eminence. In 1682 Charles II had created the infant's great-great-grandfather Lord Haddo, Methlic, Tarves and Kellie, Viscount Formartine and Earl of Aberdeen in the peerage of Scotland, and had appointed him Lord High Chancellor of Scotland – rewards which were in fact meant as a tribute to the new peer's father. Sir John Gordon had been the first man beheaded in the Cavalier cause, and King Charles's thanks came posthumously nearly forty years later.

The first Earl had been a man of stalwart independence, and had done honour to an office which was normally a mere political sinecure. A lawyer by profession, he had not hesitated to resign the Great Seal rather than be dictated to by the King in the exercise of his duties. (As a judge, he had declared that the orders of the Privy Council, that husbands and fathers should be made responsible by fine and imprisonment for the religious opinions of their wives and daughters, and landlords for those of their tenants, could not be carried out under any existing statute; and, as a minister, had declined to propose any alteration in the law.) The fourth Earl frequently showed himself his true descendant in fearlessness and obstinacy in sticking to his opinions.

William, the second Earl, was a strong Jacobite, which may have adversely affected his own public career. Under the Treaty of Union between England and Scotland in 1707 it was agreed that sixteen Scottish peers should be elected by their fellows to serve in the House of Lords for the life of each Parliament. (The sixteen peers who were not elected were not eligible for membership of the House of Commons – a disability which would later cause the fourth Earl some anguish.) As Lord Haddo, William had been elected one of these representative peers, as Member for Aberdeenshire; but in 1714 the election was set aside – a decision which the Gordons believed had more to do with William's Jacobite sympathies than with strict adherence to constitutional propriety. He died suddenly in '45, just before joining the Pretender, and so ruining the family fortunes. He left behind him a lovely memorial in Haddo House, the family seat, designed by William Adam in 1731 to stand on the blackened ruins of the old House of Kellie, which the Covenanters had burned down.

The third Earl had been reared a Hanoverian, according to the canny custom of great Scots families of hedging their bets, and at once declared himself for George II. He was one of those 'sports' who crop up among the Gordons, of whom his nephew, Lord George Gordon of the Gordon Riots, is the most notorious. Despite an arrogance so great that he always referred to himself as 'Us', this Earl (whose mother and stepmother were both the daughters of Dukes, and one of whose sisters had married an Earl and the other a Duke) made an unconventional match. He took as his wife the sister of his mistress and housekeeper in his London house in Tilney Street, a Miss Catherine Hanson from Wakefield in Yorkshire.

'Us' also bought three great houses at a certain distance from each other – Cairnbulg, a fortress on the North Buchan coast, Ellon Castle, not far from Haddo House, and Wiscombe Park, in a Devonshire valley – and established a mistress or mistresses in each, all of them traditionally blessed with the brown eyes for which he had a weakness. At Ellon Castle, which he had bought in 1752, he lived openly with two mistresses, Mrs Dearing and Mrs Janet Forrest (the daughter of his head housekeeper), and their five children – Alexander (born in the same year as his son's third son, Alexander) and Penelope Gordon by the first; John, Charles and Isabella Gordon by the second.[5] His humble Countess was eventually abandoned, with the six legitimate children she bore him, to live on at Haddo House; but 'Us' stripped it of its treasures for the sake of his natural children, and devoted his energies to setting them up in an almost princely style. In fact these illegitimate Gordons were not a discredit to the family, and in turn produced between them a surprising number of admirals and generals.

The young Lady Haddo found the third Earl no charming rake, but an unnatural father who was assiduously depriving his legitimate heir of his birthright, and naturally enough resented his behaviour. Unfortunately she was strait-laced and suffered from what seems to have been the family failing of a lack of tact. Wellington wrote of her brother the general, Sir David, 'Baird was a gallant, hard-headed, lion-hearted officer; but he had no talent, no *tact*'. Lady Haddo expressed her opinion of her father-in-law's actions and way of life with vigour.[6] 'Us' returned this folly with open enmity and a malice which did not flag as six children quickly followed the birth of his son's heir.

The worst breaches may be healed by time; but even time was not on the side of the young Haddos. Nine years after it had begun the happy marriage was shattered.

Five miles from Haddo House stood the Castle of Gight, brooding over the woodland, rocks and cliffs of the braes of Gight and Haddo and the ravine in which the sparkling Ythan ran to plunge into its supposedly bottomless pool, the Hagberry Pot of evil repute. Catherine Gordon, mother of the poet Byron, was the thirteenth and last Laird of Gight.[7] In 1785, the year she reached her majority and came into her heritage, she married 'Mad' Jack Byron, and watched him dissipate her fortune and lose her estate within a year. In the summer of 1786 they left Gight for ever. The Haddos' heir was two years old; and watchful neighbours, observing the speedy disappearance of Catherine's inheritance, remembered the prophecy of Thomas the Rhymer:

> When the heron leaves the tree,
> The Laird of Gight will landless be.

Lord Haddo, too, remembered, and, so tradition goes, when a number of herons which had nested for years in a wood on the banks of the haunted Hagberry Pot suddenly deserted Gight and flew over to Haddo, he is supposed to have said, 'Let the birds come, and do them no harm, for the land will soon follow.' Not long after the third Earl acquired the lands and the castle for £17,850.

Thomas the Rhymer's prophecy was not yet quite fulfilled. In a yet more sinister couplet he had written:

> At Gight three men a violent death shall dee,
> And after that the lands shall lie in lea.

The first of the three whose deaths were put down to the curse was Lord Haddo, who was living at Gight with his wife and family. There are extant half a dozen different accounts of the cause of his death on 2 October 1791, ranging from the humdrum one of a heart attack, to the romantic one of the rearing of his horse at the sudden clanking of a bucket as a maid drew water from a well in the castle courtyard. Whatever the cause, after his death the castle was allowed to fall into ruin.

For Lady Haddo the death of her husband was almost the end

of life itself. There was to be no help from 'Us'. Turning her back on him and on Gight Castle, she took her seven children, the eldest of whom was only seven, and the last of whom had been born posthumously, and shut herself away in England in a state of profound shock and depression. Her eldest son George was put to school near her house at Barnet, and later on at Parson's Green. Her grief did not lighten, and four years after her husband almost to the day she too died.

This second blow left the new Lord Haddo, who had been made fatherless at seven, motherless at eleven and the head of a family of six brothers and one sister, the youngest of whom was only four. Though heir to vast wealth and property in one of the most powerful families in the north of Scotland, he was as lonely and wretched a child as could be found in the world. Today we know more than we once did of the results of parental deprivation in childhood, and no longer underestimate the long-lasting desolation of spirit caused by it. This child would forever show those marks of disturbance which are so laconically set down in the clinical notebooks of workers in the field. He would always be stiff, and icy, 'isolated', awkward and rebuffing in manner. Yet he would also be abnormally sensitive and, himself capable of giving the strongest affection, always hungry for total commitment in love. Above all he would show that extreme reaction to bereavement which is always to be expected in the childhood-bereaved.*

On the most material level the boy was without help. The third Earl, still relentless after the double orphaning of his grandchildren, steadily continued to buy estates with which to endow his illegitimate children, thus heavily eroding his eldest grandson's inheritance. As for that grandson, he disliked him and neglected him, and took pleasure in visiting his mother's 'sins' on him.

Young George Gordon, Lord Haddo, seems to have measured up manfully to his massive responsibilities. As it happened, all his own five brothers would do well, William and John becoming admirals, Alexander and Charles distinguished soldiers, and Robert a diplomat and privy councillor. Their eldest brother and surrogate father, however, could not foresee that, nor that he himself would become Prime Minister. He could only know that he was parentless and friendless, with a baleful enemy for his closest and most power-

---

* For those who would like to follow this further, my study of the childhood-bereaved, with particular reference to British Prime Ministers, a very large proportion of whom were thus deprived, may be of interest. See *The Fiery Chariot*, Secker & Warburg, 1970.

ful male kinsman. When his overtures to his grandfather went unanswered, the orphaned child of eleven turned to a friend of his parents, Henry Dundas, later Lord Melville, the most influential man in Scotland. Dundas at once took the whole family of seven Gordon orphans into his home. Alicia, the only girl, was treated as a daughter, and lived with Lady Jane Dundas for another thirty years.

Pitt the Prime Minister often came to Dundas's Wimbledon villa, and showed a keen interest in the handsome, intelligent Scottish boy he found there. George was now at Harrow. We know from a draft will in the third Earl's writing at Haddo House, made some time between 1791 and 1795, while the widowed Lady Haddo was still living, how strongly he resented her removing his heir to England. 'I likewise recommend,' he wrote, 'that my grandson Lord Haddo be partly educat[ed] in Scotland that he do not despise his owne country.'[8] Consequently he refused to pay the boy's fees to Harrow and had to be shamed into it by George's friends. So George carved HADDO on the oak panels of the fourth form room at Harrow, where they can still be seen, together with those of his cousin Byron, Peel and Harry Temple, later Lord Palmerston. George was quiet and scholarly, so much so that he laid the foundations of a wide knowledge of Italian literature and poetry and modern European history while still at school. Byron, who might have been the fourteenth Laird of Gight, and Peel, his future leader, followed him to Harrow only after four years; but Palmerston, who was fated to be his lifelong rival and *bête noire*, was only nine months younger, and passed through the school side by side with him. Friendships begun at Harrow which lasted all his life were those with Peel; Lord Althorp, later Earl Spencer; Lord Grantham, later Earl de Grey; Frederick Robinson, later Viscount Goderich, and then Earl of Ripon; and Lord Binning, later the ninth Earl of Haddington.[9]

When he was fourteen George took advantage of a provision of Scottish law which gave minors the right to name their 'curators' or guardians when they reached that age, and again showed wisdom by appointing Pitt and Dundas. From that time on he spent his holidays alternatively with one and the other. In Pitt's bachelor household the only other young person was his niece Lady Hester Stanhope. A strong attachment sprang up between the boy in his teens and the striking young woman with bright blue-grey eyes, a dazzling white skin and an excellent figure, seven years older than he. It was sweet and lasting enough to have taken the sting out of Hester's waspish tongue. In the famous *Memoirs of Lady Hester*

Stanhope recorded by her doctor, he was not mentioned. Of all her acquaintances only her brothers and Sir John Moore escaped as lightly.[10]

Soon his curators bearded his grandfather again, in order to persuade him to pay to have him sent to Cambridge, the university which Pitt represented in Parliament, going so far as to threaten to meet the fees themselves if he would not do so. Whoever paid, in October 1800, at the age of sixteen, George did go up to St John's College, and worked hard at Greek and Latin and modern history, though as a nobleman he was not only entitled to a degree without sitting an examination, but was actually precluded from sitting one. Among friends of like studious tastes whom he made there was a young clergyman Fellow of St John's, the Reverend George Downing Whittington, a devotee of Gothic architecture, and Hudson Gurney, the rich dilettante antiquarian and versifier, who was to be close to him until his death some sixty years later. More surprisingly perhaps, he enjoyed himself as an amateur actor, and a good one. He and two friends as a joke got themselves taken on by the manager of the theatre at Canterbury, acting the chief parts in Shakespeare's *King John*, and George was offered a good salary to sign on for the season.[11] He still divided his vacations between the homes of Pitt the Prime Minister and Dundas, President of the Board of Control, Secretary of War, Keeper of the Privy Seal of Scotland, Treasurer of the Navy and a Privy Councillor. He watched the battles of Fox and Pitt, and listened to Burke and Sheridan, Granville and Grey and Whitbread, moving easily in the world of politics. He was old enough too to be received in the salon of Jane Duchess of Gordon, whose husband, Alexander, fourth Duke of Gordon, was first cousin to his late father. The high-spirited, free-spoken Tory duchess, who had for thirteen years represented the opposition to the Whig Duchess of Devonshire and Mrs Crewe, was, according to *The Times*, 'if not the most adorable . . . the most powerful woman then in London'. She held sway over Whigs as well as Tories, numbered the Prince of Wales among her admirers, and married three of her daughters to dukes – one of them to that Whig of Whigs, the Duke of Bedford. In her salon, in her home in Pall Mall, so soon to be given up, George was able to mix with politicians of all factions.[12]

In 1801 George's grandfather died, unlamented by his legitimate kin at least, and at seventeen he found himself the fourth Earl of Aberdeen. He would not come into his inheritance in Aberdeenshire until he was twenty-one; and he had to decide how best to employ the intervening years.

The war with France had deprived many young men of a sight of the Continent, but now, suddenly, there was peace. By March 1802 Addington had signed the Treaty of Amiens, and a stream of Englishmen were crossing the Channel. In the autumn the eighteen-year-old Earl of Aberdeen and his tutor joined their number and made for Paris. Though still shy and rather awkward, he was now growing into an exceptionally handsome young man not unlike his cousin Byron, as may be seen from one of Lawrence's finest portraits. If his manner was chilly his warm eyes and full lips gave promise of an ardour no less burning because it was fastidious. Women seemed to recognize this. All his life he was attractive to them; and certainly he always had an eye for a beauty.

The rival strains present in the House of Gordon, of wild men who met violent ends on the battlefield or the scaffold and their long-headed and long-lived brothers, combined in him to produce an impressive personality, and perhaps the blood of his Yorkshire grandmother added a welcome new strain. Behind the diffidence lay granite determination; behind the ice, passion; behind the deliberate thought and careful utterance, quick intelligence and sure decision; and behind the genuine modesty the independence and quiet self-confidence of one who had early formed his values and set the course which he would follow to the end. He was not a man who would ever suffer much from uncertainty; and he was never to be shaken from what he believed to be right.

As Pitt's protégé this good-looking young man caused something of a stir in France. Napoleon himself, doubtless convinced that the peace would last only a short time, and that Pitt would return to power, took the opportunity of learning something of the brilliant enemy who was so intimately known to this youth. The First Consul invited him to dine at Malmaison several times, unusually, almost in private, and devoted many hours to conversation with him. Aberdeen had long been fascinated by the genius and meteoric career of his host, and now found himself spellbound by his charm and fascinated by his 'singular beauty'. 'I have often heard him say,' his son Arthur Gordon was to write, 'that Napoleon's smile was the most winning he ever saw and that his eye was wholly unlike that of any other man.'[13]

So Aberdeen at eighteen dined at the table of the 33-year-old Corsican and his Josephine, at 39 still beautiful, charming and humorous. *La Citoyenne Buonaparte* had given up the low-cut transparent dresses which had shocked her husband, and led the fashion with the soft high-waisted Empire style, wearing flowers and ribbons or jewels in her dark curls. Aberdeen would know that she had been flagrantly unfaithful to her husband, while he had been fighting in Egypt, with the mincing Hippolyte Charles. Napoleon's agonized letter to his brother Joseph had been intercepted by Nelson together with one written to Josephine from her son, which described his stepfather's misery in vivid terms. They had both been published in the *Morning Chronicle*, and had roused the British to loud guffawing. Now the two seemed happy enough, leading a bourgeois existence at the week-ends which came only at the end of the cruelly long ten-day republican week.

In this autumn of 1802 Napoleon was collecting taxes, balancing the budget, putting the bankrupt exchequer in funds, bending his mind to unravelling the knots of the 14,400 decrees passed since 1789, defending his Civil Code, improving communications, reforming the educational system, opening the schools, and reopening the churches. That April the church bells, silent for years, had rung again, and 40,000 émigrés had been granted an amnesty. That year the first pavement had been laid in Paris, the *Légion d'honneur* had been instituted, and Napoleon had forced his brother Louis to marry Josephine's daughter Hortense – a marriage which was to produce the future Napoleon III, who long years in the future would be an agent of Aberdeen's worst misfortune. That autumn, too, Napoleon accepted the Consulate for life. Already, from the early months of that year, he had been urged to become Emperor so as to establish a stable dynasty and put a stop to the increasingly frequent attempts to assassinate him.

That year, too, Russia had anointed a new Czar, an event which would prove of inestimable importance to both Napoleon and Aberdeen in days to come. In five years Czar Paul's increasing insanity had done Russia so much harm that his son had forced him to abdicate, and had then been unjustly blamed for his assassination. Remorse and guilt would torment him for life, with strange results. Alexander was none too well-balanced himself, and was already the victim of irreconcilable conflicts in an education during which he had been alternately terrorized by a despotic and disciplinarian father and indoctrinated with liberal ideas by his grandmother Catherine the Great. His tutor, La Harpe, the Swiss republican, always enthusiastic for social reform and human welfare, had dominated him in youth, still did so, and would continue to exert his influence twelve years thence. In 1802, however, Alexander, in some moods the would-be initiator of gentle liberal reforms, also spent hours planning bloody and vainglorious conquests after the style of Napoleon. The day when he would abandon the world and seek a hermit's life, leaving an empty coffin behind him to frustrate pursuit, was still far off. This Czar, Napoleon himself, and the young man of eighteen who dined at his table (undoubtedly on Chicken Marengo and an undistinguished Chambertin or Château Lafite) would play historic interacting roles which not one of them could then have envisaged in his wildest fantasies.

Chapter 2

'The Travelled Thane' at Home

At length Aberdeen left the excitements of Paris behind, and travelled on through France, studying Gothic architecture with his tutor.[1] In Italy he paused in Florence to visit Bonnie Prince Charlie's widow and her lover, the poet Alfieri. While the Countess of Albany held court at one end of the room he sat cloaked and hatted, and totally ignored, at a table at the other end. Speaking fluent Italian, Aberdeen struck up a friendship with him, and they met often before his departure. It was an episode in neat contrast to his Napoleonic experiences.

By May 1803, only fourteen months after the signing of the treaty, England and France were again at war; but Aberdeen was in neither country. He had persuaded his reluctant guardians to allow him to go on to the Levant. Accompanying the newly-appointed British ambassador to the Porte, Drummond, he touched at almost every island in the Aegean; and after spending some time at Constantinople made a long-drawn-out and often dangerous journey through Greece and Asia Minor. A protracted visit to Athens was the summit of this happy travelling, and he turned it into a triumph. There he rediscovered and excavated the amphitheatre on the hill known as the Pnyx, an achievement which added lustre to his name in certain circles for ever. The reliefs he found on the site came to England with the Elgin Marbles, and are now in the British Museum. He left his name carved on a pillar of the gymnasium at Delphi.[2] Later he was to found the short-lived Athenian Society, and bring on his head a graceless attack by Byron in his *English Bards and Scotch Reviewers.**

---

* First in the oat-fed phalanx shall be seen
The travelled thane, Athenian Aberdeen . . .
Let Aberdeen and Elgin still pursue
The shade of fame through regions of Virtù;
Waste useless thousands on their Phidian freaks,
Misshapen monuments and maimed antiques;
And make their grand saloons a general mart
For all the mutilated blocks of art . . .

24

Then Aberdeen crossed to Smyrna, and visited Ephesus, returned to Greece to explore the Morea and visit Albania, and went on to Corfu. His notes on the condition of the Parthenon and of his excavations at Ephesus and Athens are still valuable archaeological records, and he copied numerous inscriptions which would otherwise now be lost for ever. After two years he made his way home through Dalmatia, Venice, Vienna and the north of Germany.

Lord Aberdeen returned to a war-burdened England in 1804, and lived, as before, with Pitt and Melville. Across the water Napoleon and his Josephine were crowned Emperor and Empress.

In Pitt's household the bachelor was at last ruled by a woman, for his niece, Lady Hester Stanhope, now 27 to Aberdeen's 20, had been presiding there for the past year.[3] Pitt had resigned the year before Aberdeen left England because of his inability to carry Catholic Emancipation. Now back in office, he was embroiled in a thousand difficulties.

It was Pitt who commended Aberdeen to the Marquess of Abercorn, his great friend. There was no one quite like this magnifico. Extremely rich, very handsome and a notorious libertine, he was a patron of literature and the arts. He was also very shrewd, and carried great weight in the political world. He was, too, a little crazy, insufferably arrogant and as wilful as a child. Pitt, who had been his friend since Cambridge days, once said to Wilberforce, according to Aberdeen, that if Abercorn had chosen to take to public life, 'as a speaker he would have beaten us all'.[4] Pitt indeed had exposed himself to criticism by ensuring that Abercorn was made a marquess soon after his succession to his earldom and that a female cousin of his, later to be his wife, was, alone of five sisters, granted the precedence of an earl's daughter.

For young Aberdeen at Bentley Priory, Stanmore, Abercorn's seat, and the Holland House of the Tories, all was sunshine in those early days. He relaxed in the luxurious and cultivated atmosphere of the beautiful house with its renowned entrance hall by Sir John Soane, so often crossed by such gods of literature, art and the stage as Sir Walter Scott, Sir Thomas Lawrence, the Sheridans and John Philip Kemble.[5] It was an atmosphere of carefree happiness, too, which still pervades the collection of miscellaneous verses now at the British Museum, ranging from sentimental tributes to Abercorn's pretty daughters, Catherine, Elizabeth and Maria, to the comic, such as 'Lord Abercorn's Glove to Lord Aberdeen's Boot'. If, as seems likely, Aberdeen wrote 'A Proposed inscription for the entrance gate of Lady C. Hamilton's flower garden' and 'To the Right Honourable Lady Jane Gordon, an Ode on her Ladyship's

Birthday', he was an accomplished if unoriginal versifier. Two verses from the former run:

> Far from the senseless joys of crowded scenes
> Here Cath'rine waves the scientific page,
> With studious thought the fact historick gleans
> Or treads with Shakespeare's muse the buskin'd stage.
>
> Her artful hand the splendid wreath entwin'd
> Which forms the Arch of yonder verdant bow'r.
> Her tasteful eye each varied hue combined,
> Her fostr'ing care protects each tender flower.

The ode features Phoebus, the Graces, nymphs and Zephyr, and hails 'the natal day of lovely Lady Jane!'.[6]

Aberdeen was particularly welcome at the Priory because of his talents as an amateur actor, for Abercorn took much pleasure in putting on plays at Bentley Priory, and calling on his guests to perform in them. In one tragedy, in which Aberdeen took the chief part, William Lamb (the future Lord Melbourne) and his brother Frederick (later Lord Beauvale), Lawrence, Sheridan, and Aberdeen's brother Robert all also acted. Aberdeen's son noted that in that drama, in which Aberdeen played the part of a savage chief, Oronoko, he showed his complete identification with his rôle by 'weeping with real and uncontrolled emotion over the imaginary sorrows of the savage chief he personated'. Acting clearly provided a release for the passions, sternly held in check, of an otherwise 'silent, shy and sensitive' man.[7]

Soon those passions found another outlet. Aberdeen was deeply in love with the Marquess's eldest daughter Lady Catherine Hamilton, an acknowledged beauty, as proud, fiery and gay as her father, but with a natural charm all her own. The forlorn and wooden young man was enchanted by her. Lady Catherine too had had a disturbed childhood. Her mother had died twelve years after her marriage, in the same year as Aberdeen had lost his father, when Catherine was still a child, and her father had remarried almost at once. After seven years that marriage had been dissolved by Act of Parliament, and Abercorn had taken a third and rather difficult wife. The girl who had come through such choppy seas would understand Aberdeen's feelings of insecurity, and be glad to rest on the total devotion and fidelity which he offered her.

Naturally spontaneous and lively, Catherine could also be haughty. Lawrence jested that he would have made his fortune if he had dared to paint her as the embodiment of scorn as she stood, her head turned away, holding out her arm while the Prince of Wales, whom she abominated, fastened an armlet above her elbow.

Soon the two were betrothed, and something of the adoration Catherine felt for her lover was reflected in Melville's letter written to Aberdeen on visiting the Priory shortly afterwards.

Priory, July.

'My dear Lord,
    . . . I find Lady Catherine is really one among ten thousand, and . . . I don't find that any part of *all* the good I had heard of her has been exaggerated. I think her one of the most natural and most pleasing people I ever saw, and I am persuaded, though on so short an acquaintance, that she has one of those happy natures that, the more undisguised they are, must become the more attaching . . . She has perfectly complied with your desire . . . and met me at least half-way – but what I honour her for is the honesty with which she shows her regard for you without either mystery or affectation . . . I trust nothing will happen to detain you long – I never saw any person's presence more desired than yours is here.'[8]

Aberdeen came of age on 28 January 1805, and Catherine and he were married on the 28th July following. Abercorn had looked to him for handsome settlements, insisting on his daughter's being 'maintained in the style of splendour she had always been us'd to, which was proper for her rank in life', and Aberdeen had expressed willingness to do all in his power, but had said 'that his Brother[s] and Sister must be provided for', and he must give financial aid to Melville in his trouble 'before anything else could be thought of'.[9]

His twenty-first birthday had marked another event of major importance for Aberdeen. At last he had visited those estates which he had not seen since he was a child of eight, and entered into his inheritance.

For him, whose roots were now struck deep in the south, and who had for many years been enjoying the highest standard of living, both physical and intellectual, the homecoming was a rude shock. His promised land seemed a tree-less, ugly wilderness, his house a near-ruin, the people of his demesne a Caliban-like crew, and the lairds of the neighbourhood a collection of self-satisfied boors. He had not complained of the rigours or dangers of his travels; but he flinched from making his life permanently among men who ate raw turnips for dessert in winter and harnessed their women to the plough. He was not amused when they goggled at the sight of his umbrella and begged him again and again to open and shut it for them.

At first Aberdeen wanted only to flee this disappointing land. In his wretchedness he even thought of cutting the entail, and when that was not to be done considered becoming an absentee landlord. He did not see any beauty in Haddo House, half-hidden by stacks of fuel and timber sheds leaning against its deteriorating walls, and with peat-moss stretching from its door to the distant deer-park. In the end he decided to bend his head to the yoke. Over the years to come he drained, he built, he planted trees. Fields of corn shone in the sun, new schools rose for the children, solid farm buildings delighted the farmers. In the first ten years he laid out nearly £3000 in improvements. The bleakness gradually went from the scene. When the time came for him to die, more than half a century later, he would leave behind him the majestic memorial of fourteen million trees and would have spent sixty thousand pounds on improvements. Long before then he would have been accepted by the rough, crude Highlanders originally so suspicious of their young laird from the south – the softening of an attitude expressed by the old family huntsman with traditional caution when he declared that the young Earl would have been a fine man 'gin they hadna ta'en him to England and spoiled his education'.

Aberdeen and his Catherine were absolutely happy. 'Beware the love of a Gordon', runs an old saying, referring to the jealous and demanding nature of Gordon affections. The natural ardour of Aberdeen's blood was increased by his yearning for a wife and a home. He had lived with strangers since the age of eleven, and had had no family except younger siblings. Now the orphan's consuming need for total commitment lapped his Catherine in a burning and exclusive passion. Luckily for him his charming girl had a heart and a need as great as his own. During their honeymoon summer months of 1805, while Napoleon's *grande armée* stood ready at Boulogne to invade England, only Pitt was really allowed within the magic circle of their lives. Yet even they, self-absorbed, must have been stirred by Trafalgar, fought three months after their marriage. That winter Harriet Cavendish noted, at Bentley Priory, the Aberdeens 'played at spillikins with their arms round one another's necks'.[10]

By then, tragedy had overtaken Melville as First Lord of the Admiralty. After an enquiry into naval administration he had been convicted of malversation by the Speaker's casting vote, and his name erased from the roll of the Privy Council. In the Chamber Pitt had pulled his hat over his eyes to hide his tears. Not till 1806 would Melville be impeached in the Lords and found guilty of negligence, but acquitted of the charge against him.[11] In 1805 Pitt himself was still powerful and kind, and he persuaded the young people to rent Melville's Wimbledon villa (which the ruined Melville could no longer afford) and become his neighbours at Bowling Green House in Putney. He promised Aberdeen an English peerage in the next session of Parliament, and clearly meant to give him high office in the near future. Aberdeen stood on the threshold of a glittering career. Then, six months after Aberdeen's marriage, and five days before he reached his 22nd birthday, Pitt died.

That death shook the nation, but it devastated Aberdeen. He began a private diary the next day, and poured into it his dismay and despair at 'the dreadful calamity'.[12] He had to leave Wimbledon for a while, and lay awake night after night, seeming to see Pitt before his eyes. Pitt had been succeeded by Grenville and his Ministry of All the Talents. The promised United Kingdom peerage was now out of reach, and with it had evaporated any hope of speedy and satisfying political office based on the Lords.

'This is my birthday,' he wrote on January 28 in his diary, the day after the House of Commons had debated the question of a public funeral and a monument for Pitt: 'my prospects are miserably changed since last year. Lord Melville and Mr Pitt, my only friends, both gone. Had Mr P. lived I should certainly in the summer have got my English peerage, as he promised Lord Melville I should be the first created. I must now depend on myself, but I am determined never to renounce the principles Mr Pitt has taught me, or to become dependent on Government. I pray God to grant me abilities and honour to steer through all difficulties'.[13] That day his sister Alicia, as Lady Melville wrote from Bath, 'made all the servants get drunk for your sake', drinking his health.[14]

Aberdeen made one desperate effort to catch at a handhold for himself by offering to replace Pitt in his Cambridge University seat, on the grounds that (though disenfranchised elsewhere as a Scottish nobleman who was not a representative peer in the Lords, and could not sit in the Commons) as he had a university vote he might qualify as a candidate. The Vice-Chancellor wrote to say that he did not. Yet Viscount Palmerston, an *Irish* peer, born in the same year as Aberdeen, and inheriting his peerage at the same early age of seventeen, was able to contest the same seat, and as a Tory, in the by-election. It must have seemed to Aberdeen, literally, the luck of the Irish. At least Palmerston was not elected, and at least Aberdeen had only to wait for the first dissolution of Parliament before he reached twenty-one to be elected a representative peer of Scotland and take his seat in the House of Lords.[15]

For, deprived of his English peerage, and hope of the Cambridge seat, he was determined to become a Scottish representative peer. Within a month of Pitt's death he had approached Lord Grenville to ask whether he could be considered for any vacancy in the representation.[16] In the General Election of 1806 Aberdeen embarked on a most bitterly-fought campaign of canvassing among the Scottish peers, with Melville as his manager, working hard and passionately for success, the heavily pregnant Catherine by his side. Abercorn entered wholeheartedly into the fray, sending letters of advice, horse-trading wherever he could, bringing himself to 'write to Lord Mansfield, though I didn't much like it' for his vote,[17] and cheering on his son-in-law with 'Huzza! Aberdeen for ever!'[18] On 4 December 1806 he was safely elected, though his Whig friend Lady Holland recorded in her own journal, 'The Scotch Peers elections have gone well; Lord Melville was cruelly disappointed, he expected to carry four, and only carried 'Lord Aberdeen'.[19] Within a fortnight Aberdeen had taken his seat on the Tory side of the House of Lords,[20] though he seems not to have made his maiden speech until the following April, during the debate on the change of administration.[21]

Catherine shared everything with him, and her love for Haddo exceeded his own. She went there with him even when he feared for her health on the long cold journey to Scotland, travelling in easy stages of forty miles a day; and even though her father trembled for her when she departed for what he considered the Arctic Circle. The postscripts she put on her husband's letters to Lord Abercorn are full of the breathless gaiety of perfect happiness.

'Dear Papa,' she wrote, on 27 September 1806, during her first visit, 'You need not believe one word of what Lord Aberdeen says about this place, for I assure you that there is nothing to complain of, I never was so surprised in my life as when I first saw it, for I had been told so much about it by everybody, that I expected a thing not fit for a human being to live in, placed in the middle of a barren, bleak moor, without a tree or anything near it but a bog, instead of that I saw a great many very good trees about the house, which is not regularly beautiful on the outside but very comfortable on the inside, from the windows you see nothing but trees, and in this fine weather it is as cheerful as possible. It is really very strange that everybody should have thought it despressing [*sic*], they said it was useless to do anything but build for that we never could make it tolerable, but with a good chair and sopha or two and new curtains to the drawing room, I do not wish for anything better – and what do you think I have got two little tame fawns.'[22]

For his part Aberdeen got on amazingly well with his difficult father-in-law, who seemed almost to defer to his son-in-law in matters of taste. A year after his marriage we find Abercorn consulting the young man of 22 about his cherished plans for a beautiful private theatre he proposed that William Wilkins should design, which, he says, 'will, I hope, please you'.[23] His letters to Aberdeen are full of affection.

Lady Catherine bore a daughter a year for three years – Jane in 1807, Caroline in 1808, and Alice in 1809.

Meanwhile Aberdeen was not politically inactive. Within a month of Pitt's death he had had 'much conversation' with Castlereagh, deciding on the best line for opposition. They plumped for moderation, with frequent meetings at dinners in order 'to cement the party out of the House'[24] – a party now not only leaderless but full of dissensions.[25] So Castlereagh, Canning, Abercorn, Hawkesbury and others who had been of Pitt's party during his lifetime met at dinners, which might number as many as twenty-five, usually at White's, and the young man kept in touch with thought and action at the highest level. He was very close to the distressed Melville, supporting him when, though acquitted, he proudly refused to take office under Portland, and to Harrowby, who, with a distinguished career behind him, had become Pitt's Foreign Secretary in 1804, and had later remained in the Cabinet as Chancellor of the Duchy of Lancaster. There were twenty-two years between them, but Aberdeen always got on well with older men, and they met as friends. Lady Harrowby was devoted to him and he to her.

Soon launched in the Lords, Aberdeen looked about anxiously for some rewarding post. (By then his brothers were nearly all, in theory, off his hands – William a naval lieutenant, Alexander and Charles lieutenants in the 3rd Foot Guards (later the Scots Guards), and John a midshipman.) He was not a frequent speaker, and was certainly no orator,[26] but from the beginning seems to have won golden opinions. Before long some handsome offers were made to him.

In early 1807 Lord Douglas, later the tenth Duke of Hamilton, who had been made a privy councillor and appointed Russian

Ambassador on the Whigs taking office in 1806, was recalled on the change of ministry. Although Aberdeen was only just 23 he was offered the opportunity of succeeding a man both experienced and distinguished, as well as sixteen years older than he – clear and impressive evidence of the high estimation in which he was held, and that despite the effective loss of both his enthusiastic and imposing patrons. To his friend of Cambridge days, George Whittington, he wrote: 'Respecting myself, I am offered the Russian Embassy, it being determined that Lord Douglas is to return. This, you must allow, is arduous, and I think I should prefer a mission of less importance. Unfortunately Constantinople, which I should like better than any place in Europe, is now shut up. But all this is a matter for mature deliberation'.[27]

After reflection Aberdeen turned down the post, and, in the same spring, was offered the appointment of British Minister to Sicily in succession to Drummond, with whom he had travelled to the Porte in 1803 – fourteen years older than he, and with six years' ambassadorial experience behind him. At the time Sicily was a post of considerable importance. Canning wrote to him, on 27th April, that 'the question of your succession to Mr Drummond is merely a matter of time, and depends upon circumstances which had not occurred when first I communicated with Lord Melville, which I will explain to you whenever I see you. Your succession to Mr Drummond when he comes home I consider as fixed, on my part at least, and subject only to your own decision'.[28] In fact Aberdeen had asked for this post, supported by Melville,[29] and Drummond wrote to him at length about the state of affairs in Sicily. Eventually Aberdeen refused, giving as his reason that it had been decided to deprive the new ambassador of much of the control over the Sicilian government which his predecessor had enjoyed. Lord Abercorn, however, was strongly opposed to Aberdeen's accepting the ambassadorship, and he is thought to have yielded to his father-in-law's pressure 'somewhat against his better judgement'.[30]

In 1808 Aberdeen, at 24, was made a Knight of the Thistle, the order a Scotsman is proudest to wear; and elected a Fellow of the Royal Society. Then, in 1809, at 25, he was again offered the post of British Ambassador to Russia, and again refused it.

Chapter 3

'Verissima, dulcissima imago'

In 1810 the shadows of tragedy began to close about Aberdeen once more.

The months from July 1810 to February 1812 formed one of the most important periods in Aberdeen's life, and we know a good deal about his thoughts and actions during them. He was obviously working hard to make his mark, and not without effect. On 12 February 1811 he moved the address to the Prince Regent;[1] and, though in June he opposed Lord Donoughmore's motion on the Roman Catholic petitions for relief, he declared his conviction 'that a time would come when the Catholics would ultimately succeed'.[2] From the beginning he tried to make the most of his information from the front. In the summer of 1810 his brother Alexander, after his blooding at Corunna, had just joined Wellington as his ADC in the Peninsula, and Aberdeen persuaded him to write to him once a week and in diary form if possible, while he replied once a fortnight giving him family, national and social news and details of what he was doing in Parliament. Charles, four years younger than Alex, was also one of Wellington's ADCs. We learn a great deal about Aberdeen from his dealings with his brothers.

During these years the young Aberdeen – who in 1810 was still only 25 – continued to act the disciplinarian, if generous and affectionate, father to his ready-made family, doling out advice more freely than money, and insisting on regular reports from all, by letter or in person. By that year Robert was appointed attaché to the British embassy in Persia. Aberdeen was always ready to help John or William to get a ship by, in his own words, 'badgering . . . a great deal' their rear-admiral and Lord of the Admiralty, Yorke,[3] and, when he failed him, threatening to complain to Liverpool himself 'unless the thing is done'.[4] He went direct to the Commander-in-Chief of the Army, the Duke of York, to rescue Charles from the results of what he himself castigated as his indecision, indolence, obstinacy and quarrelsomeness.[5] He pulled strings wherever he could, always willing to try again when his brothers were dissatisfied with their lot or sinking under their difficulties. They were usually, in Aberdeen's eyes, 'infamously treated', and he himself 'infamously used', when the best was not produced for them.[6] Tenderly concerned for their health, he sent for Charles when Alex reported him poorly, writing that 'it would be unpardonable if he is in the state you mention to sacrifice him to any false notions of honour'. He even consented to Charles's decision to resign his commission, to the violent disapprobation of his sister and brothers, and his own embarrassment, since Charles had already been ordered to embark. In the end he got Charles home, and sent him to Cheltenham for a long cure.[7] By 1812 a fully-recovered Charles set off as ADC to the commander-in-chief of the troops in Ireland.[8] At that stage it certainly might not have seemed likely that both John and William would become admirals and Charles a colonel of the Black Watch and a KCB. Indeed, John would still be causing embarrassment at the ripe age of 55. Only Alex and Robert seemed to give no trouble at all. Alex was the flower of the family, and Aberdeen had a particular place in his affections for him, though Alex embarrassed him by ordering expensive scabbards and living above his allowance. Aberdeen supplied him with boots, books and most things he asked for, even promising to scrape acquaintance with Lady Wellington at Tunbridge Wells on his behalf.[9]

Alex was a brave and keen soldier, and soon won his way into Wellington's special favour. There were numerous signs of kindness from the great man, with whom he would share the dangers of every battle in Spain, Portugal and France, and Wellington made him a present of a fine Andalusian horse taken from a dead French officer at the battle of Talavera to replace his own, which had been shot under him.[10] Alex found Wellington a chilly man, all the same.

'You ask me how I am with him,' he wrote in May 1811, from Quinta, near Elvas. 'I assure you I have every reason to be flattered with my situation, and have vanity enough to believe that no young man ever had more to say to him than myself, and believe I am the only one in his family [his company of ADCs] who has never had an ill-natured word from him; and I assure you in the field and in action I have the greatest possible cause for satisfaction in the manner in which he treats me. However, enough of this, he is a man without a *heart*.'[11]

Much to Alex's discomfiture, his brother insisted in being given precise details of the most secret nature concerning the campaign and the officers. He made use of his information in the Lords, and, doubtless, privately, but he testily assured Alex that he had nothing to fear from any lack of discretion on his part.

The following extracts from letters give some indication of the kind of pressure Aberdeen thought proper to exert, and of the relationship between the brothers. It must be remembered that Alexander was absolutely dependent on his brother for funds. Indeed, when he eventually got a company of his own his diplomat brother Robert rejoiced with him mainly on the score that he would at last be financially independent.

Aberdeen wrote to Alex on 10 October 1811, very sharply, as follows:

'You talk of writing things that you had better let alone, and give opinions of individuals as if they had been extorted from you, and say you do not mean to answer such questions in future, etc. etc. Now I am aware from your situation that what you tell me is in confidence, and so I have considered it, and have always used great discretion in shewing or quoting any parts of your letters. But I must say that if your correspondence is not to continue of this unreserved description, I am very indifferent whether you write or not. The newspapers will give me just as accurate accounts of the movements and positions of the armies, if that is all you mean to send.'[12]

To this blistering communication Alex replied on November 27, from Fuènte Ginaldo:

'Of opinions of affairs in general and of Lord W's plans you cannot . . . be much surprised at my sometimes dwelling upon discretion. When I tell you that Lord W. often expatiates to me upon the impropriety of officers' letter-writing, and believes that things have been made publick which he wished not by some of those about him writing to their friends, and when in addition to this I tell you that excepting his secretaries who know what is going on from his own correspondence and papers, I am exclusively the only person who is on such a footing with him as to enter into conversation upon the affairs of the Peninsula, and frequently talk of plans and movements before even he has decided upon them, and when his opinions are then given to me as a friend, feeling myself so situated, I think you might excuse any difficulty I may have expressed about too fully giving my opinions upon our operations . . .

'I know not whether Lord Wellington is aware of the service I rendered him at El Bodorn but he has frequently said publickly at his table that had it not been for me he should have been taken prisoner. This came from himself first and not from me; it is a fact is known, and was seen by many on that day, and the act of my saving him from the same fate took place more than once. But you do not know Lord Wellington's private character. He has no idea of gratitude, favor or affection; and cares not for anyone, however much he may owe to him and find him useful.'[13]

If Lord Aberdeen used the information with which Alex supplied him to good purpose, since his main interest was in foreign affairs, Wellington did not overlook the advantages of having an ADC with a direct line of communication to a member of the upper chamber, a supporter of the government, and one with the ear of men of influence. 'Lord Wellington always asks me what you say about things at home,' Alex said in another letter.[14] He had his bulletins too, to exchange, for Aberdeen kept his brother informed of the situation in Parliament as well as of the feelings in the country at large, and especially about reactions to the Peninsular campaign, now at last proving successful. The King's serious attack of madness, the possibility of a regency having to be established, the worries of the ministers concerning the Prince's Whiggish tendencies, all enliven Aberdeen's letters with dramatic detail very frankly expressed.[15]

On 13 February 1811, soon after the Regency Act was passed, he wrote delightedly of his triumph: 'Yesterday the Regent's Speech was delivered by Commissioners to Parliament. In consequence of the earnest entreaties of Lord Liverpool I moved the address. I had great reason to be satisfied with myself; and to be sure there never was anything like the compliments of Lord Grenville'.[16] The approval of an ex-Prime Minister and the Minister for War and the Colonies made up somewhat for the bad reporting in the newspapers, which he sent to Alex. His mind was stubbornly directed to shining in politics, and he still resisted efforts to divert him into the diplomatic service. By April 9 he had turned down two more missions abroad. 'You may probably have heard of my having been offered diplomatic appointments,' he wrote to Alex. 'Lord Wellesley pressed me very much to go to America or to Constantinople. On consideration I refused both.'[17]

By June 8 he sent him a lengthy outline of a speech of eulogy of his on Wellington's conduct at the battle of Fuentes de Onoro. Doubtless this too was intended for Wellington's ears or eyes.[18] By 4 February 1812 he reported, 'We had the Catholick question the other night in the House of Lords. I spoke for about 40 minutes, and was very well satisfied with myself, and had every reason to be so with what others said of me'.[19] Aberdeen, we know from his son, 'was, from the first, a steady advocate of Roman Catholic emancipation'.[20] If Creevey was right when he wrote to his wife later that year that Colonel Alexander Gordon was 'in constant correspondence with both Grey and Whitbread', writing depressingly of Wellington's danger and of certain and speedy defeat – and as a close friend and political ally of both Grey and Whitbread Creevey probably was right – this was almost certainly not known to Aberdeen, and would have caused him some distress if it had been. Creevey warned his wife, 'Of course you will not use this information but in the most discreet manner'.[21]

Not content with Alex's military exploits, Aberdeen tried to get him a seat in parliament. By the end of 1811 Perceval had given encouragement that he might get Alex in for Weymouth, undoubtedly as a pledged government supporter, but had 'rather committed himself, in promising his assistance to another man'.[22] By the New Year of 1812, however, Aberdeen had to write that this 'early and secure place with the assistance of the family and the government', proved to be very expensive, as well as having the drawback that 'it was absolutely necessary that the candidate should go down' – that is, appear.[23] So, at the best, Charles, and not Alex, would have to be elected. The idea was abandoned. By May the unbalanced Bellingham had shot Perceval in the lobby of the House of Commons, and by June Liverpool was Prime Minister.

Not all Aberdeen's dealings with his brothers were on such a lofty plane. He was capable of encouraging – indeed, of pestering – his two soldier brothers to engage in some barefaced smuggling on his behalf. This man of very sensitive honour seemed to regard such exploits as well within those permitted for people in their position. The following extracts from his letters to Alex tell their own tale.

25 July 1810
'You must keep the plate with your own baggage, unless you have any friend in a Man-of-War to take it as the duties are so enormous.'
The Priory. 23 August 1810
'Do not forget the plate; but do not send it by any common vessel or it will certainly be seized.'
Brighton. 1 December 1810
'Charles is not yet arrived. I have expected him a long time. I trust he will be careful about landing the plate, for if it is seized, no duty will get it out, as by law it must be destroyed and melted.'
Argyll House. 13 February 1811
'You have heard of the calamity about the Plate, and I fear there is no chance of getting it released. It was very ill managed,

for God's sake be more careful. I told you frequently that the greatest caution must be used, and yet Charles says he never knew that it was contraband. It ought to be given in charge to some naval officer on whose prudence you can depend. I should like anything fit for a sideboard that is highly wrought and embossed with figures, animals, flowers, etc. . . .'

Argyll House. 4 June 1811

'If you get me more plate, let it be *large* and *round*, with *very* richly embossed borders. If it is *very finely* wrought *indeed*, I do not mind if it is oval – but for God's sake be careful about it and do not let us get into such a scrape as Charles. Poor fellow, he has been very hardly used.'

And, finally,

Tunbridge Wells. 26 August 1811

'What do you mean to do with the handsome piece of plate which you have got for me? When you send it pray let it be by a person who can get it on shore safely. Sew it up in some leather or canvas.'

Aberdeen's piece of plate cost him £20.[24]

So Aberdeen had much on his mind in 1810 and 1811, ranging from determined efforts to advance the careers of all his brothers, as well as his own, to the minor adventures of a little gentlemanly smuggling. By November he and Catherine were expecting their fourth child, and hoping that this time he would have his heir. Her brother, Viscount Hamilton, had not been well, and was recovering from a bad cold at Brighton where the Aberdeens were also staying. His wife Harriet, too, was pregnant. On the 17th of November Aberdeen wrote to Alex, 'Hamilton and his wife are here, he is going on well. She is with child, and indeed will be confined in I believe about two months. She is rather well looking as you know, but certainly one of the most stupid persons I ever met with'.

On December 1 Aberdeen writes unhappily to his brother to tell him of Catherine's having for no apparent reason had a miscarriage and lost her son half an hour after his birth.[25] Catherine had always been delicate, with a tendency to tuberculosis, and constant child-bearing had probably weakened her. Soon after this miscarriage she began to slip away from Aberdeen; but at first he did not realize what was happening. He reported her as 'quite recovered', and said that they had been 'very gay' at the Priory and had seen 'many people'.[26] He continued to write to Alex spirited accounts of the doings in parliament and in the nation. It was not until the end of April that Catherine was reported as 'extremely unwell with an inflammation of the lungs'.[27] From then on her health was a constant source of anxiety. They could not go to Scotland, and did not know what was the matter with her. She had no pain, but was weak, with a slight cough, and a very fast pulse. He tried to persuade her to go to Lisbon for the winter months, but she had 'a great repugnance to leave the country', which proved 'invincible'.[28] By October 10 he was rebuking Alex irritably for his lack of understanding of why he had not written to him.

'The fact is, that I seldom write to anyone, except frequent accounts of Lady Aberdeen to Lady Abercorn and Lady Manners. Her health is in such a state that I am obliged to attend to her nearly all day, and when not actually occupied with her, it is not easy for me to think of anything else . . . She is much the same as she has been for some time past, perhaps a little better, but frequent bleedings have made her very weak. Charles and Lady Maria [her sister] are with me.'[29]

By November 25 his sister Alicia had come to live with them at their London home, Argyll House, in Argyll Street (now superseded by the London Palladium), 'in order to be at hand to nurse Lady A.'.[30] By the end of December four doctors, including the royal physician Knighton, were in regular attendance, and Aberdeen had sent for 'a doctor from Scotland who is said to have performed wonders'. He stayed three weeks with the patient, but proved a disappointment. 'What medicine can do will be done – I pray God the result may repay our cares,' he wrote, as he realized at last what he might have to face.[31]

On 4 February 1812 Aberdeen wrote his last letter to Alex of this period. He reported that his wife was getting weaker but not suffering much pain.[32] His Catherine died on 29 February 1812. They had been married for only seven years. He was still only 28.

It must have been with a fearful heart that Aberdeen saw the tragedies of the previous generation repeated for himself and his children. After nine years of marriage his mother had been left with seven children, the eldest of whom was seven; and after seven years of marriage he had been left with three children, the eldest of them five, the second four, and the third three years of age. His mother had had six boys and a girl. He had had three girls and a dead boy. The memory of his mother's inconsolable grief for his father when he had reached the impressionable age of seven would be strong in him as he mourned his own wife.

Catherine's death was a devastating blow to her young husband. His son Arthur Gordon would say that the sunshine went out of his life for ever.[33] From the day of Catherine's funeral to his own death nearly fifty years later, Aberdeen wore mourning for her, and never took her rings from his finger.[34] Queen Victoria, who would be his devoted friend and neighbour in years to come, would react to the loss of her own husband in similar fashion. Those were times for much panoply in mourning. Yet it was universally agreed that the Queen's reaction was so exaggerated as to be shocking; and so, it was felt those many years before, was Aberdeen's.

He was convinced that Catherine's ghost came to him almost daily. For more than a year he recorded her appearances in Latin. '*Vidi*,' he wrote, 'I saw her.' Again, '*Vidi sed obscuriorem*, I saw her, but not so distinctly.' Then, '*Verissima, dulcissima imago*, The reallest, sweetest vision,' and '*Verissima tristissima imago*, The truest, saddest vision,' and '*Tota nocti vidi, ut in vita*, I saw her, just as she was in life, all through the night.' To the end of his life his lost love haunted him, and when, even in late old age, he tenderly murmured long passages from the Italian poets or dreamed fondly over Petrarch's sonnets it was an open secret that he was remembering her.[35]

In that year in which Catherine died Aberdeen refused yet another mission, this time to the United States. Her death seems to have quenched his enthusiasm for the hurly-burly of political life. In August he wrote to Alex from Haddo, 'Having got over the first shock, and dreadful it was, of coming here, I feel very little inclined to mix in the world. If the children continue well, it is possible I may stay a good while'.[36] He was turning again to intellectual and cultural pursuits. He had set his heart on being made a trustee of the British Museum and was angry enough to write to his brother that he had given Liverpool a piece of his mind and was 'disgusted' when someone else was elected instead, 'because it is an employment that squares with my general pursuits, but as for politics and political jobs, I have done with them, it is not my intention to ask for a peerage, and I hope so to regulate my mind as to view with indifference any number of new creations that may be made'.[37] His friend Harrowby offered to surrender his trusteeship in Aberdeen's favour, perhaps out of sympathy for his desolate state; but soon another trustee died, and Aberdeen, though refusing to 'say a word after having been so ill-treated', was elected. The concern he had shown was in marked contrast to his almost apathetic attitude towards ambassadorial posts.[38]

However, before long Aberdeen began to raise his head, and show a little more interest in the outside world, though he was still suffering so much from shock late that year that Lord Granville Leveson-Gower 'complained' of his 'unceasing conversation' – unusual in a singularly reserved young man.[39] It is possible too that he was pressed for money. By 14 December 1812 he was writing to Alex, who had sent in a draft for £100 on Coutts's Bank, that he was already overdrawn there by £300;[40] and by 9 February 1813 he was talking of offering to sell Argyll House for £17,000 though it was worth £20,000.[41] Perhaps the fees demanded by the eminent doctors who had attended Catherine had been formidable. Certainly his expenses at Haddo for tree planting and other improvements were considerable. At any rate, when in the spring of 1813 Castlereagh asked him to undertake a mission to Vienna to try to persuade Austria to break with France he toyed with the idea. Then he relapsed into apathy, finding various reasons for refusal. From Castlereagh's point of view the most cogent was that Aberdeen was unwilling to undertake the mission unless the British Cabinet would agree to supply money in lieu of the troops which the treaty of alliance would bind the parties to keep in the field, and which Great Britain could not provide. The Cabinet had not agreed to this stipulation.[42]

Most cogent for Aberdeen himself, however, may have been more personal grounds. He did not want to leave the country, or abandon his three motherless little girls.[43] And already, surprisingly, only a year after Catherine's death, he was thinking of taking a new wife. In fact, Aberdeen was again head over heels in love, while not for a moment ceasing his terrible mourning for his first wife.

Now he was anxious to marry Anne, daughter of Lord and Lady George Cavendish.[44] The choice may seem a little unexpected for one with his Tory background, but, according to his son, he was 'one of the most constant *habitués* of Holland House', and 'formed a part of the intimate society which gathered round the Duke of Devonshire, Lord Lansdowne and other Whig magnates'.[45] This was surprising from the ward of Pitt and Dundas, and Abercorn's son-in-law, and indeed Lord Abercorn was adamantly opposed to the marriage, precisely because the Cavendishs were Whigs, and he wanted no Whigs in his family. Lady George Cavendish too was sceptical of Aberdeen's motives, believing him to be seeking a *mariage de convenance*; but she did him an injustice.

In this situation Lord Aberdeen found one friend, his sister-in-law Lady Maria Hamilton. He seems to have transferred much of the devotion which he had felt for Lady Catherine to her sister, who was very like her. The ardour of his affection for her was remarked on as exceptional by his own family, and it is hard to

41

say whether he loved her only as a sister or rather more. Perhaps even he was not quite sure of exactly what his feelings were towards her. There could have been no question of marriage between Lord Aberdeen and his sister-in-law, for the Church would have none of such marriages. Nearly sixty years later, and after his death, the Lords would still be throwing out the Deceased Wife's Sister Bill, though by then public feeling was strong enough for there to be riotings and the waving of red flags about it in London. To one of Aberdeen's temperament the mere knowledge of such a taboo would have acted as a powerful deterrent. On the other hand, he was a passionate man, very attractive to women. Altogether Aberdeen seems to have been in a curious state of mind, yet one not incomprehensible. He had suffered a shock from which he would never recover in the death of his idolized wife – in his eyes 'the most perfect creature ever formed by the power and wisdom of God.'[46] Desolated at 28, and emotionally demanding, he must have hoped for some consolation, or, at least, alleviation of his intense loneliness. If to the onlooker it is at times difficult to decide whether he was more in love with Anne Cavendish or with Lady Maria Hamilton, what is never in doubt is that not only could no woman ever take the place of his dead wife, but that he had no intention that any woman ever should do so.

Lady Maria, at any rate, was proving a true friend to him in his lover's difficulties. She was acting as his go-between in opposition to the wishes of her autocratic father. We can today share the private thoughts and feelings of the young man in the summer of 1813, for he set them down most vividly in a letter to her which has never before been published, writing from Argyll House on 29 July 1813.

'My dear Lady Maria,

'I have received your letter this morning; but before I answer it, I must relate something of an event connected with the same subject. We arrived in town on Monday, and on Tuesday the Duke asked me to sup at Devonshire House after the opera. That evening I had been with Castlereagh and went to D. House when it was over, rather early.

'After looking about me for some time quite alone the door opened, and in walked Lady H. and Anne! From mere awkwardness I went up to them, indeed it could not be avoided. I was received more cordially than ever, which encouraged me to persevere. Lady H. and she sat at a small supper table with a space between them; it was not to be resisted, so I placed myself.

Lady H. turned to her neighbour, and during the whole supper, and it was very long, Anne continued to talk with great empressement on very interesting subjects; charming and catechising me in an unusual manner. This was the more difficult as from the small size of the table it was necessary to do it almost in a whisper, and she seemed to wish not to be heard – you may believe that I did my best; and I am quite certain with effect, her look and manner incontestably evinced it. I do not recollect that I ever made a greater exertion.

'The only other woman at the table was Lady Harrowby, with whom Robert [Aberdeen's brother] sat. She did nothing but watch us, in such a manner as would have frozen me at another time; had not this opportunity been so favourable, I never could have endured the appearance we made.

'Now is not all this most extraordinary? I never can believe that she is playing the heartless game of a regular coquette; it is impossible – what am I to think! My sanguine nature has led me to hope that your last letter to Lady H. may have had some little effect; for she said that she had heard from you that morning. She also said that she should write to you yesterday; I hope to God she may, for there will be just time for me to hear from you after you receive it. I should tell you the Duke saw us at supper and appeared delighted.

'Now for your letter; and first of *Robert* . . . Lady H. had rather an odd conversation with him yesterday. She talked a great deal about my marrying, and blamed my notions of a *mariage de convenance* etc. etc. Now really, if Anne understands my views in this way, it is impossible to wonder at her reluctance, or that of her family. This should be cleared – I feel capable of entertaining sentiment for her more ardent and pure than I believe she is likely to meet with. I am more and more struck with the rectitude of her principles and the nobility of her character.

'Do I not sacrifice, or at least impair, the attachment of the best friends I have had (the Harrowbys) on her account? I give up a person whose innocence of character, whose amiable qualities, whose regard for myself, whose beauty, all conspire to make me love her. What further proof would she have?

'Most undoubtedly, as long as I live, I shall believe that I have seen human nature under a form in which it never before existed. My heart must be more than metaphorically cold before this feeling can ever be changed or forgotten. Yet if I am not wholly mistaken in the character of Anne, she will not have to complain of the want of enthusiasm and devotion.

'Yet I partly agree with you in your observations. I owe it to myself not to encourage a pursuit which is to lead only to disappointment and vexation. We will allow some time for reflection on her part, and something for the assistance which I hope Lady H. will give me. But, really, after what I have heard of Lady H. saying about *convenance*, caution and timidity in her is not to be wondered at.'[47]

The letter leaves us with several queries unanswered. 'Lady H.' was almost certainly the redoubtable Lady Holland, an old friend of the Duke and Duchess of Devonshire and of Lady George Cavendish. As early as December 1793 she recorded in her diary that she had recently passed all her mornings and evenings with the Duchess of Devonshire, and that she went to Court with Lady George Cavendish. Unfortunately, because of a very trying experience in childbirth, she abandoned her journal just when it might have yielded some interesting details on Aberdeen's courtship of Anne Cavendish. However, she had recovered sufficiently by July 1813 to have been present at the supper party.[48]

It is not easy to understand why Aberdeen thought that this courtship would cost him 'or at least impair', the friendship of 'the best friends I have had', the Harrowbys. That Lady Harrowby, the innocent, amiable and beautiful, was hostile was evident from her watching them whispering together 'in such a manner as would have frozen me at another time'. It is possible, of course, that their objections, like Abercorn's, were politically based, despite the fact that they too dined at the Duke of Devonshire's table, and that Pitt's Foreign Secretary might have been as opposed as Abercorn to Whig alliances. It might account for the embarrassment Aberdeen clearly felt at offending his Tory friends and looking for help to Lady Holland. Whether or not she was conscious of such reactions, Anne Cavendish, according to Aberdeen's son Arthur, returned his affection, but rejected his proposal.[49]

That letter was written twelve days before Aberdeen's departure overseas. By then he had at last been persuaded by Castlereagh to undertake what one of his severest critics has called 'as important and responsible a mission as had been sent out from Britain during the war'.[50] So highly was Aberdeen thought of that he wrote to Abercorn on July 16, from Haddo, 'The urgency of Castlereagh himself as well as the entreaties of the other ministers are so great that it would be affectation to refuse'.[51] Imploring Lady Maria to help keep his children from being spoiled ('Do not let them be stuffed with eatables of any sort, or admired to their faces'), and to 'be just to Lady Abercorn with all her faults', he sailed away from his new love. He went, he said, 'to certain vexation and, from all that I can learn, probable disappointment'.[52]

William Lamb's younger brother, Frederick, went with him as Secretary of Embassy, and he had arranged that his brother Robert should be attached to him.[53]

Chapter 4

'The Din of War'

The fate of Germany, indeed the whole outcome of the war, might depend on the man chosen at this juncture to persuade the Austrian Emperor and his dominating Chancellor to co-operate enthusiastically in an actively aggressive policy. The man Castlereagh and the Prince Regent selected for this delicate mission was not yet 30, with negligible diplomatic experience, and far from fluent French. That Aberdeen was an aristocrat and Abercorn's son-in-law were probably less important to Castlereagh, the devoted admirer and protégé of Pitt, than the fact that Aberdeen was an enthusiastic Pittite.[1]

Aberdeen went reluctantly, insisting, despite his amateur status, on being on a footing of equality with other negotiators, and stipulating that his stay would be for only a few months except at his express desire.[2] Since Austria had not yet openly declared herself, he had to leave England on August 10 without any official rôle. His instructions were given in general terms, and he was left a wide discretion. What he was precisely told was that the English Cabinet would not rest satisfied that any peace which did not confine France within her natural borders (that is, the limits of the Pyrenees, the Alps and the Rhine) would provide adequately for the tranquillity and independence of Europe, and was willing to fight on with the allies to ensure that. However, if the powers which were more immediately involved preferred to settle for a less satisfactory arrangement rather than risk prolonging the struggle, then Britain would acquiesce subject to certain conditions.

These were the fulfilment of her undertakings to restore Sicily, Portugal and Spain to their real monarchs, and the surrender of Norway to Sweden. Secondly, without laying down exact details, the Government made clear its anxiety to set up some counterbalance to France's power in central Europe and its readiness to co-operate in the re-establishment of an independent Holland. Thirdly, it was categoric in its insistence on the restoration of Hanover.

Lord Aberdeen was empowered to authorize insurrections against the French in the Tyrol and in Northern Italy.[3] He was to sign a treaty with Murat, the usurping King of Naples, in conjunction with Austria. If Murat gave active co-operation against Napoleon he would be guaranteed compensation elsewhere in Italy. If it was not possible to get him to agree to this, in a separate and secret despatch Aberdeen was empowered to try to persuade Murat to join the allies at the price of leaving him on his throne. However, the bargaining was to be hard, since the British Government made it clear that it would much prefer to find Murat another kingdom and restore Naples to the Bourbon King Ferdinand of Sicily.[4] Murat and his Neapolitan army had of course gone with Napoleon to Moscow.

Lord Aberdeen's frame of mind was almost doleful, as he wrote to give his news to his sister-in-law, Lady Maria Hamilton, and his unhappiness was not only because of the lady he was leaving behind him: 'The feebleness of the Austrian Government is dreadful, and I am too late. But I will do my best and act honestly where little honesty has been seen; I pray God may protect my endeavours'.[5]

Small wonder if the magnitude and delicacy of the task, and its seeming hopelessness, oppressed him. Yet Castlereagh's optimism, evident in the contents of the secret despatch, was more realistic. That document shrewdly assessed Austria's position, pointing out that it was in her interest, more so even than in that of the other great continental powers, to ensure the general safety. Despite her close family ties with Napoleon, she was (both because of her geographical position and because of her recent line of policy) likely to become 'the first object of his future enterprise and resentment'.[6] Aberdeen was ordered to urge Metternich strongly to consider the unusual circumstances which at that time might combine to help the Austrian monarchy against France and restore it to its former position in Europe.

Those circumstances the despatch set out as: a powerful British army, combined with a Portuguese and Spanish force of about 90,000 men in all in the Pyrenees, threatening France on one of her most vulnerable frontiers; a large Russian army, encouraged by successes against the enemy, advancing to the heart of Germany with the object of liberating her from her oppressor; the burial of the traditional jealousy between the Austrian and Prussian courts in a sense of common danger, with Prussia anxious to unite herself with her former enemy against the common foe; 'the extraordinary feature' of a large Swedish army actually already in the north of Germany and ready to act against Napoleon under the command of one of his most celebrated generals, Bernadotte; and yet another powerful army in the south of Italy, similarly led, and ready to come out against Napoleon if Austria moved to open hostility. 'Surely then,' the despatch urged, 'it is not too much to assert that such means have never before existed, so if the occasion is allowed to pass away without effectually turning them to the salvation of Europe they may never again be placed within our reach.'[7]

Armed with this remarkably prescient and able document Aberdeen set off. He was headed for Vienna, but was ordered to visit the headquarters of the allied armies on his way. In the troubled state of Europe he had to take a circuitous route. He sailed from Yarmouth in HMS *Cydnus* on August 10, and landed at Gottenburg in Sweden on August 14. Crossing Sweden for about 300 miles, he went across the Baltic from Ystadt to Stralsund, and from there pursued his still very indirect route through Berlin, Breslau and Glatz to Prague.

In truth, Aberdeen was, as he had feared, already 'too late', but not in the sense he intended. Two days after he set sail, and two days before he landed, that is, on August 12, Austria had declared war on France. The result he had been sent to achieve had come to pass before he had arrived on the scene.

What, then, had occurred to bring Austria into the war?

From December 1812 Napoleon had been dealing with conscious deceivers in Austria. The Emperor Francis of Austria had accepted the rôle of double-crossing patriot in preference to that of a father who put his daughter's happiness before his country's. Napoleon, feeling that the earth was slipping dangerously beneath him, had begun to press for a meeting, and Metternich's first proposal had been for an armistice between France and Prussia.

It had been in the map-room of the Marcolini Palace that the final scene of the drama had been played out. Pointing to the map of Europe, Metternich had claimed for Austria not merely Illyria but northern Italy; for Russia, all Poland; and for Prussia, the left bank of the Elbe. He had stipulated that the Confederation of the Rhine must also be dissolved. He had demanded that Napoleon should abandon all interests in Spain and Switzerland and the Netherlands. Napoleon had reacted violently, and had accused Metternich of insolence, treachery and blackmail. He could not, he said, believe that his father-in-law had agreed to such an 'outrage'. Fresh from two major victories, he was being asked to abandon the greater part of all his proud conquests gained since 1800. What was more, Metternich was laying it down that if Napoleon would not agree to his terms Austria would join Russia and Prussia in their war against France. If he failed to accept them he would be fighting three great continental powers, and at a time when the campaign in Spain had turned into catastrophe. Desperately Napoleon had tried to bargain. They had argued for eight hours. At the end had come the celebrated exchange. 'Let me tell you something,' Napoleon had said grimly. 'You won't make war on me.' Metternich had replied in icy confidence, 'You are lost, sire'.[8]

Metternich was right, and Napoleon had underestimated his power. The Czar Alexander and Frederick William of Prussia, as well as Francis, were under Metternich's thumb. The next day the treaty which he had organized at Reichenbach was signed with Russia and Prussia. In the Treaty of Reichenbach the terms which Metternich had put to Napoleon in the Marcolini Palace had been baldly restated, with the ultimatum that if Napoleon had not accepted them by July 10 Austria would declare war on him. The only change in that position of stalemate had been that the deadline had been extended to August 10 – the day Aberdeen sailed from England.

On August 12, while Aberdeen was half-way across the ocean, Austria had declared war on France.

Now the French faced three separate foes: an army of 230,000 Austrians under the corpulent ex-diplomat Schwarzenberg in Bohemia; an army of 100,000 Prussians and Russians under Blücher in Silesia; and an army of 100,000 Swedes and Russians under Bernadotte in and around Berlin.

Metternich had grown more and more friendly towards Britain as Austria had come closer to taking the plunge into war. After the declaration British subsidies at once became a matter of great importance. Metternich realized too that he would have to take Britain's interests, and even her prejudices, into serious consideration.

Britain had been affronted by the Reichenbach Treaty between the three countries. In the phrase of Sir Charles Stewart, Castlereagh's half-brother and the ambassador to Prussia, she considered it 'a very strange proceeding' that such a treaty should have been signed by Russia and Prussia only a few days after the completion of the subsidy treaties with Britain, which had bound them not to negotiate separately and to communicate all matters of policy to each other.[9]

However, when Austria had been forced into war Britain had decided to forgive her. Metternich was in the advantageous position which he had so cunningly worked for. He had no treaties to explain away, since only Russia and Prussia had signed at Reichenbach. Still, he was uneasy about the impact which his conduct would have undoubtedly made on Britain. He began to put it about that he had all along intended to join the allies but had been forced to adopt his devious methods because of the unhappy situation in which his poor country found herself.

Half his mission, then, had been completed before Lord Aberdeen set foot on land. A very important half, however, remained, and he pressed on with his journey.

From Ystadt Aberdeen wrote the first of his almost daily letters to Lady Maria.[10] Then, as there was no English ship to be had, he took passage in a dirty and unseaworthy Swedish packet bound for Stralsund. Passing through Pomerania, he arrived at Strelitz to find the people up in arms and incensed against the French. The frontal attack against the enemy on which the Czar had insisted had been successful, the French were on the run and the Crown Prince of Prussia advancing to the Elbe. However, that very evening the tables were turned, and the allies had to fall back. Aberdeen and his party continued their journey through the beautiful countryside, and towards evening heard that the French were on the way to Berlin and that a battle was expected. This experience set the pattern for the alarums and excursions and contradictory reports to which he would eventually become accustomed though never quite reconciled.[11]

Next day, a Monday, at about seven o'clock in the morning, they reached Berlin. There Aberdeen made up his mind to snatch a few hours' rest, though he noticed that there was already a great deal of bustle and confusion in the town. He learned that the French army was rapidly approaching, and that the troops were only 'about twelve or sixteen English miles' from Berlin. The Crown Prince had taken up his position near Potsdam, and at any moment battle would begin. The noise of cannon fire was heard, estafettes hurried to and fro, officers galloped through the streets, and crowds gathered in the public squares and meeting-places. He 'wished very much' to remain at Berlin until the fate of the city had been decided by the battle which had perhaps already begun; but it was his duty to continue on his way to Prague, for if the French were victorious they would cut him off from Frankfort.[12]

None of his future colleagues were in Berlin, so he could not ask for their advice. The British ambassador to Prussia, Stewart, with whom he was going to work closely, was in Prague. When he called on the Commandant of the town, General l'Estocq, he was told firmly, 'I think you may now go in safety. Tomorrow, I will not answer for it'. Aberdeen decided to set off for Frankfort. He reached it at two o'clock next morning, not without incident. The rest of the journey was punctuated by frequent spills and narrow escapes from French outposts. The first 'capsize' occurred as they made their way along the Oder to Grossen through immense forests of pine and beech, and Aberdeen suffered concussion, which left him with a persistent headache and a painful reaction to light. It was not until the 26th that Aberdeen arrived at Breslau, and there he wrote, 'For the first time [I] have gone to bed, being completely worn out'. That was all the rest he permitted himself before pressing on at full speed to the Imperial headquarters. Soon he and Frederick Lamb decided to leave the cumbrous main party and its 24 horses.[13]

As things turned out Aberdeen need not have fled Berlin after all. In his next letter, written at Prague on September 1, he rejoiced at the city's safety, and gave the credit to the Prussians and their commander the Crown Prince. Stirring and strange sights met his eyes as he rattled through the fine countryside on the frontiers of Silesia and Bohemia, among them large bodies of Cossacks on their way to join the Russians; but he was most astounded by 'a body of several hundred Asiatick Tartars', armed with bows and arrows, and carrying light spears. 'They have the Chinese face,' he observed, 'and are exactly like the fellows one sees painted on tea-boxes.'[14]

Meanwhile Aberdeen had been out of touch with events of the greatest importance. As he pressed on blindly he heard rumours that the conferences at Prague were at an end; that the armistice Napoleon had signed at Plaswitz was over; and, finally, and late enough, that Austria had declared war on France on August 17. (The declaration had actually been made five days earlier, but it had not been published in Prague until then.) He also picked up the information that the Emperor of Austria and his minister Metternich were with the army at their headquarters near Teplitz. There he would be brought up to date on all that had been happening since he had left England.

On the day after Aberdeen had landed at Gottenburg and begun his 300-mile journey through Sweden – Napoleon's 44th birthday, on August 15 – the French Emperor had left Dresden. Faced with the 230,000 Austrians under Schwarzenberg in Bohemia, the 100,000 Prusso-Russians under Blücher in Silesia, and the 100,000 Swedish-Russians in the Berlin area under Bernadotte, and with

51

only 300,000 men to deploy against 430,000, he had decided to attack each force separately. First he drove Blücher and his Prussians and Russians across the River Katzbach. He had left Macdonald (son of a Scottish clansman from the Isle of South Uist, and one of his best generals) in charge, and returned to Dresden to face Schwarzenberg and a strong force of Austrians. On August 26, the day on which Aberdeen had reached Breslau and fallen into bed exhausted from lack of sleep, the mighty two-day battle of Dresden had been launched. Next morning, while Aberdeen, refreshed, had been sitting with pen and paper re-living for Lady Maria's benefit the events of his journey, Napoleon, drenched to the skin and weak with diarrhoea, had been directing his troops in the pouring rain. Before he collapsed and retired to bed he had achieved a stupendous victory against the allies, with his 120,000 men defeating their 170,000 and (according to the account, at any rate, which he sent to his Marie Louise) taking 25,000 prisoners, 30 flags and a great many guns. Unhappily for him, however, his triumphs were personal ones. His marshals were being beaten everywhere else – Oudinot at Gros-Beeren by Bernadotte, Macdonald on the Katzbach by Blücher, and Vandamme at Kulm. Napoleon had dashed after Blücher to try to mend matters but the enemy had melted away before him, refusing battle.

By September 1, indeed, though Aberdeen was telling Lady Maria from Prague of the allies' defeat in the attack on Dresden, he was also able to give her news of 'a complete victory gained over Vandamme, whose corps is cut to pieces, and himself a prisoner'. He went on soberly, 'Our real difficulties are only beginning. The Emperor of Austria is either at Lann or Teplitz. He and Metternich have been sleeping on straw'.[15] He reached Teplitz the next day, September 2. But that one day's journey from Prague to Teplitz was dreadful to him, and would never be forgotten as long as he lived. In his own words to Lady Maria he set down his reactions:

'The near approach of war and its effects are horrible beyond what you can conceive. The whole road from Prague to this place was covered with waggons full of wounded – dead and dying – the shock and disgust and pity produced by such scenes are beyond what I could have supposed possible at a distance. There is much splendour and much animation in the sight, yet the scenes of distress and misery have sunk deeper in my mind. I have been quite haunted by them.'[16] To the six-year-old Jane, resolutely putting such scenes out of his mind, he wrote tenderly, 'My dearest Jane, although I am very far from you, I hope that you do not forget me. I think of you and Caro and Alice a hundred times every day. I am not able to say when I shall see you again, but I hope it will not be very long . . . you must be very good and mind what is said to you, and when I return I shall love you more than ever'; and he promised to find 'something pretty to send you'.[17]

The allied sovereigns, their ministers, and the diplomatic agents accredited to them, were gathered in the small Bohemian town of Teplitz. It was bursting at the seams with the strains put on it to accommodate two emperors, the King of Prussia and a dozen princes, as well as the staffs of all the various armies. Aberdeen shared his quarters with one of the princes, but even princes came pretty low on so splendid a register, and they were wretchedly lodged. For miles around, the lines of the vast armies of the allies were spread out in a daunting array. A large French force occupied rising ground within three miles of the town. For most of September Napoleon made repeated visits, conscious that his presence turned brave men into heroes. The allies themselves recognized this, and preferred to engage his marshals and avoid him whenever possible.

Now at last Aberdeen had come face to face with the two men who would be of enormous importance to him during the coming months. Perhaps to his surprise, he liked Metternich at once. By the time he closed his letter to Lady Maria on September 6 he had also met 'his' emperor, Francis II of Austria, and had been received as ambassador. 'In an audience of considerable length,' he wrote with some arrogance, 'I have had every reason to be satisfied with him.'[18]

That Aberdeen should have found the Emperor Francis a sympathetic character was not particularly surprising. But one might have expected the young man who declared his 'feeling approaching contempt' for 'the whole diplomatic profession in general'[19] to have cordially disliked the man so feared and mistrusted by English statesmen. The smooth and glossy Metternich was 40 when Aberdeen, at 29, first met him. With his frizzy light hair, inquisitive muzzle, long smiling mouth and alert eyes, he seemed very foxy. Neither tall nor good-looking and with a strong nasal drawl, he had in his thorough Germanic way worked hard to perfect an ease of manner and an obvious charm. His wide reading, his collections of various *objets d'art*, his dilettante's knowledge of Italian opera and of the sciences were his stock-in-trade, as were his considerable amateur talent on the violin, his fluency in languages and his drawing-room wit. His career could hardly be spoken of in the same breath as that of Napoleon, who was only four years older.

Yet it had been brilliant, for he had become Austrian ambassador in Paris at 33, and after three successful years there had left to replace Austria's foreign minister and become virtual ruler of his adopted country for the next forty years. The fact that he was devoutly religious had not prevented him from having many mistresses, among them, it was rumoured, Napoleon's sister and Murat's wife, Caroline Murat. Behind the smiling face and the social chatter was an obsessional and humourless man, limited, enormously conceited, fanatically sure of himself. Lord Liverpool disliked him, observing that he regarded politics as 'finesse and tricks'; and Talleyrand, himself a master of deception, called him the great liar who never deceived.

Although Austria had declared war on France without any encouragement from him, Aberdeen had yet to settle the terms of the treaty at Teplitz. The treaty provided that Austria was to keep an army of upwards of 150,000 men, and that Great Britain should pay her a subsidy of a million pounds. In return for this Austria would agree not to make peace with Napoleon except by common accord. Aberdeen wanted to press for more, hoping that Austria would agree to fight on until Britain's own particular aims had been achieved. If she did so she would be committing herself further than Russia and Prussia despite her treaty of alliance with those powers. (They were mutually committed only to prosecuting the war until Germany was liberated and Hanover restored to Great Britain.) Aberdeen wanted Austria not only to enter into her treaty of concert and subsidy with Britain but to undertake not to conclude any peace with France which did not guarantee the complete independence of Spain, Holland and Italy. If he could induce her to do so, Prussia and Russia might follow her lead.

Metternich was agreeable; so the next step for Aberdeen was to try to arrange a Treaty of General Alliance to be signed by Austria, Russia and Prussia to begin with, and by other powers as they came into the war against Napoleon. Here he found himself up against the prevailing deep suspicion of Austria's real attitudes and motivations in any action she took. No one believed that Metternich was anti-French, certainly not the British ambassadors to Russia and Prussia, Lord Cathcart and Sir Charles Stewart. In fact, for nineteen years he had nursed a secret determination to overthrow the French republicans who had reduced him and his family from the status of the lesser German nobility to that of penniless refugees.

Aberdeen was swift to realize that Metternich's actions had created a very satisfactory situation for the allies. Not only were the Austrian Emperor and King Frederick William of Prussia now declared enemies of Napoleon, but there could be no turning back for them since Napoleon would never forgive what he considered their betrayal. Aberdeen believed that Austria was working hard to achieve Napoleon's extinction before she herself was wiped out, but he had a difficult task convincing his Government of this. Castlereagh had great confidence in his sound judgement; but it was at war with the Foreign Secretary's preconceptions about Metternich, whom he did not know except by repute.

Before long the general mistrust of Metternich led to some odd results. The Czar asked Cathcart not to let Metternich know that England had agreed that Austria would act as mediator in the event of peace talks being arranged. Cathcart agreed, and then he and the Czar's representative, Nesselrode, persuaded the newly-arrived Aberdeen to fall in with their policy. So it came about that, although in his first communication to Metternich he was dealing with the terms of peace required by England, Aberdeen too withheld the information. He at once regretted this lack of candour, and not only because he was by nature frank.[20] His father-in-law had charged him to be straightforward, since honesty was the best policy.[21] After all, Aberdeen wrote to Castlereagh, even if concealment had been desirable, Metternich could hardly fail to discover what was afoot, seeing that it was already known to the Courts of Russia, Prussia and Sweden. Aberdeen went to Metternich and made a clean breast of things, including the reason for his silence – a move not calculated to endear him to Cathcart and Stewart.[22] To his relief Metternich received the information blandly, if with 'some surprise'.[23] This episode, skilfully handled by Metternich, marked the beginning of the surprisingly close relationship which developed between these two superficially very different, if not inimical, characters.

From St James's Square on September 1 Castlereagh had written to Aberdeen of having received the Austrian declaration of war, and commented that Napoleon seemed to have for once been out-manoeuvred, since he had gambled on Metternich and lost. He would not be sending Aberdeen any official instructions 'until all chance of further *pourparlers* are extinguished in the din of war'. He gave Aberdeen authority, however, to convey the strong approval of the Prince Regent and his Ministers of Austria's behaviour.[24]

Aberdeen had serious matters to reveal to Castlereagh, and a few days after reaching Teplitz he set them out in a despatch marked *Private*. He was horrified by the jealousy and ill-feeling he found all about him, and above all fearful of what the divided command of the army might lead to. He saw that the authority of the Commander-in-Chief, the Austrian ex-diplomat Schwarzenberg, was little more than nominal. Every plan had to be approved by all the different sovereigns before being acted on, and the resulting delays were infinitely damaging. Aberdeen reported that, only the day before, a vital movement of the main Austrian army directed at Napoleon's flank had been delayed for 48 hours because the Czar would not agree to it. Spite and jealousy were evident in pettier questions also, such as the Austrians' resentment at the Czar's award of the Grand Cross of the Order of St George to his own general, Barclay de Tolly. Should the Czar be made Commander-in-Chief of the allies, as he longed to be? Or should all sovereigns be deprived of any authority and one man be given supreme power? Should the armies be separated? That had in fact already virtually taken place. Aberdeen was convinced that only some great success could now weld the allies together into a useful whole.[25]

Aberdeen agreed with Metternich that every proposal for peace should be welcomed and the whole odium of war thrown on to Napoleon. Prepared as he was to bargain with Murat and persuade him to join the allies, even at the cost of leaving him on his throne, Aberdeen was surprised and disappointed to find that he was actually in Dresden, commanding the cavalry for his brother-in-law, Napoleon. The flashy innkeeper's son had been Napoleon's trusted friend and stand-by since the beginning of his career. His name was a by-word for flamboyance, but also for a superb physical courage. Unfortunately behind the peacock plumes and the braggadocio was a weak, greedy man dominated by an ambitious termagant of a wife. Despite all the rewards heaped on them by Napoleon, he and Caroline were eaten up by resentment at not being on the throne of Spain. Perhaps it had been in Caroline's bed that Metternich had learned of her husband's weaknesses, on which he now sought to play.

By September 14 Metternich had revealed the details of Murat's volte-face. Napoleon had pressed his brother-in-law to join him in Dresden on the pretext that he was on the point of settling a general peace with Austria. Murat had arrived the day before the armistice had been concluded, and Napoleon had at once clapped him under arrest. Murat had agreed to command the cavalry on condition that Napoleon would offer reasonable peace proposals as soon as possible. Notwithstanding 'this singular transaction',[26] as Aberdeen called it, Murat had sent an agent to Metternich from

Dresden to assure him that his troops would observe the strictest neutrality, and that not a man of them would leave Naples, and had begged Metternich to continue the negotiations. Metternich had replied that Murat must either come out into the open as an independent, or transfer his authority to someone who could treat on his behalf.

Despite this lofty stance Metternich had kept in touch with Murat, in effect continuing the negotiations while refusing to do so. He had expressed his conviction that Murat would be joining the allies before long if Napoleon's luck gave out. Now Metternich not only asked Aberdeen's help in this arrangement, but he asked him for proof in writing of his own power to negotiate in the form of a confidential written statement setting out the precise extent of his own 'authority and disposition to treat' with Murat.[27]

This was a great deal to ask; and at first Aberdeen demurred, refusing to put so delicate and secret a matter in writing. Metternich persevered and at last Aberdeen gave way, exceeding his instructions by assuring Metternich in writing that Great Britain would have no objection to Murat's retaining the throne of Naples. After all, Aberdeen wrote in troubled explanation to the Foreign Secretary, Castlereagh himself had ordered him to pursue the Murat question hand-in-hand with Austria and to defer to her wishes.[28] Aberdeen was evidently far from sure that he had done the right thing. He was, in fact, at a very low ebb at the time, for good reason. 'The worst of it is,' he wrote to Lady Maria next day, 'I am extremely unwell. I have had a severe attack of cholera morbus; it is still bad, but I hope it is better than it was.'[29] He was bothered enough about Castlereagh's reaction to write again four days afterwards to the Foreign Secretary's younger brother. Under cover of giving Stewart details of the military situation he took care to emphasize that there was no danger of a real commitment to Murat. Metternich, he declared, had acted with the greatest caution and prudence – 'He will draw Murat step by step, and not produce any communication until we have him fully pledged . . . I wish Castlereagh knew this, as perhaps he may be alarmed by the bare statement of what has already taken place'. Stewart might be relied upon to see that his brother Castlereagh did know it.[30]

All these worries and troubles had to be dealt with in a state of extreme discomfort, and as time went on things seemed to grow worse.

Aberdeen was depressed by the increasing difficulty of his work, concerned at the slow progress of the treaty, anxious to be home, and fretful at the impossibility of abandoning a task which seemed to be just beginning instead of almost over. 'The Baltic will not be passable after November,' he complained to Lady Maria, 'and will be very unpleasant then.' Worst of all was the human suffering by which he was surrounded: 'The horrible thing is the wounded of all nations. It quite haunts one day and night; such dreadful objects in every variety of misery.' As for his own troubles, he said that he would refrain from cataloguing his hardships and privations 'at this abominable place, where we literally run the risk of being starved, and where the horses die of hunger daily by dozens. I hope to God we shall soon change our quarters; yet I know of no better town in the neighbourhood, and we must be near the enemy'.[31]

Writing to his friend Lord Harrowby, who was then President of the Council, Aberdeen's picture was more trenchant still. For the third time he referred to the haunting effect of the scenes he witnessed daily.

'The wonder is how we exist at all in this vile hole, with scarcely anything to eat, and that of the worst kind. Surrounded by such multitudes of the living and dead, human and brute, the air is pestilential. Novice as I am in the scenes of destruction, the continual sight of the poor wounded wretches of all nations is quite horrible, and haunts me day and night. Walking in a sort of shrubbery belonging to a house in the town, I stumbled over a great heap of arms and legs which had been thrown out of a summer-house in which they had been cut off: this is a pleasant incident, of a more interesting nature than you are likely to meet with in your walks at Sandon.'[32]

Over forty years later those scenes, and his reaction to them, would have a grave bearing on the course of English history.

Chapter 5

The Field of Leipzig

Whether from deliberate policy or not, from the moment of his arrival Aberdeen was flattered and pampered in a thoroughly invidious way which was certain to offend Cathcart and Stewart. He wrote to Lady Maria that the distinction with which he was treated by the Austrian Emperor was 'quite unheard of in the annals of this stiff and proud Imperial Court'.[1] He dined and supped with him every day and sat at his right hand. Unlike most people, Aberdeen genuinely liked the Emperor, seeing through his 'awkward and rather foolish manner'.[2] The 45-year-old Francis, who looked like a horse, with his long bony chinless head and loose Hapsburg underlip, had come to the throne of the Holy Roman Empire at the age of 24. A mediocrity terrified of his great responsibilities, he had clutched for guidelines at religion, patriotism and the divine right of kings.

Francis's one exceptional endowment did nothing to solve his major problems. According to Frédéric Masson he was so over-sexed as to be a danger to his wives. His first wife had survived only two years, his second had borne him thirteen children in seventeen years before succumbing, and he had immediately re-married. He would outlive Maria Ludovica Beatrix, implacable foe of Napoleon, and marry a fourth time. It was this Francis to whom Marie Louise, daughter of his second wife, had written when her marriage to Napoleon was first proposed, pleading with him not to force her into it, and who had not even replied to her letter. Aberdeen, however, accepted that Francis was a broken-hearted father bitterly torn between daughter and country, and did not suspect that Marie Louise was happy in her marriage and dreaded the thought of war between her country and her husband's. He saw only a Francis sincerely concerned for her interest and safety, and admired him for what he took to be his Roman virtues. He believed, rightly, that Francis was anti-Bonapartist and that if his daughter were safely back in Vienna he would feel himself well rid of his son-in-law. The day was yet to come when Francis would unleash the one-eyed seducer Von Neipperg with instructions to distract Marie Louise from thoughts of joining her husband in exile 'by any means whatsoever', and would silently accept the humiliation and solitary imprisonment of his grandson, the tragic young King of Rome. As far as Britain's interests were concerned, however, Aberdeen had assessed Francis's attitude quite correctly.

Nothing much happened that September while the allied headquarters remained at Teplitz. Reinforcements were arriving from every corner of the Austrian Empire. Now Bavaria broke with France and brought 30,000 men over to the allies, endangering Napoleon's communications and exposing his right flank. Aberdeen, delighted, was sure that this could decide the fate of Germany and set Europe free, and that other states in the Confederation of the Rhine would quickly follow Bavaria's example. He gave all the credit for this to Metternich's wisdom and moderation. On the other hand the English cavalry were in dire straits, having run out of ammunition, and Aberdeen was fretting that he had had no instructions concerning Italy, although the Tyrol was 'up', and Switzerland and Italy 'open to us'.[3]

With the coming of October things grew more exciting. By then the allies outnumbered the French by three to one. General Bennigsen arrived with his fine well-equipped Russians, who were to stay at Teplitz while the main army went on by Comotau, Marienberg, Zwickau and Gera, and light corps advanced to Saalfeld and Erfurth, scene of the Czar's historic second meeting with Napoleon. The allies' overall plan was to try to manœuvre Napoleon out of the line of the Elbe or to get between him and his supplies. On October 1 Aberdeen wrote to Castlereagh and gave him, unusually, a breakdown of the military situation. Napoleon was said to have left Dresden three days before, and to have set up his headquarters in Leipzig with 100,000 men. The Commander-in-Chief, Schwarzenberg, was determined to avoid a pitched battle and to concentrate on harassing the enemy, but the Czar and Blücher were thirsting for blood. Between Dresden and Peterswade on the Teplitz road there were 30,000 men; at and near Freyburg 15,000; at Meissen and Torgau 30,000. Unless the forces on the Teplitz road turned out to be more than the estimated 30,000, the plan was to attack with Russians or Austrians. The French had about 50,000 men on the move as a rearguard, and they were expected to arrive on the Saal at some time between October 10 and October 16.[4]

What Aberdeen did not know was that by early October Napoleon, always against defensive warfare, had thought up a plan of attack – a brilliant, risky undertaking in the grand tradition of his most daring exploits. He would march on Berlin, take it, and sweep on into Poland, thus cutting off the Russians. However, his marshals were afraid of the dangers involved, and everything was held up while he argued with them.

The allied armies had already marched on Dresden and Leipzig in pursuit of the retreating French by the time the Emperor of Austria decided to make a move to join them. Aberdeen was the only diplomat of any nationality whom he kept constantly with him. From Comotau Aberdeen wrote to Lady Maria a description of the tense atmosphere as the allies waited for battle to begin: 'We are on the eve of great events. A general battle is expected today or tomorrow. If the different armies act in concert as it is intended they should, the issue cannot be doubtful'.[5]

That was on October 8. The battle of Leipzig would not begin until October 16.

On October 9 Aberdeen reported to Castlereagh that the army had advanced in a direct line towards Leipzig, near which Prince Schwarzenberg had set up his headquarters. The Prince Royal of Prussia and General Blücher had advanced towards the same point and the two allied armies had nearly converged. In the meantime General Bennigsen and his Russians had driven the French from their entrenchments at Giesshubel, and had advanced towards Dresden on the highway from Teplitz. No one had any idea of Napoleon's position or intentions.[6]

On October 14 Aberdeen left Comotau in snow and cold for Marienberg. That day Napoleon, furious with his craven marshals, abandoned his plan to march on Berlin. While the allies waiting opposite his lines had grown more and more nervous at the incomprehensible delay, he had sat on a sofa sunk in black gloom for two whole days, and had then given up. By that time the allied armies were closing in on him, Blücher to the north and Schwarzenberg on the south, with the object of outflanking Dresden. Napoleon had ordered his troops to fall back 60 miles north-west to Leipzig. There he would engage.

Meanwhile Aberdeen travelled on over abominable roads full of muddy holes, running through a mountainous fir- and beech-forested area. When he reached the pretty and friendly little town of Marienberg on the 15th he was lodged in apartments just vacated by the Emperor but found nothing to eat except black bread and potatoes.[7] Hungry and strung up, he wrote that night that he was expecting the armies to have clashed before he closed his letter. In fact there was yet another day to be lived through before that happened.

The whole journey, which would take him from Teplitz to Leipzig, and again from Leipzig to Frankfort, was despite its horrors a magical, never-to-be-forgotten experience. It was made on horseback through impressive scenery. Aberdeen's diplomat brother Robert, on his way to England with the news of the accession of Bavaria to the alliance, accompanied him part of the way; and Metternich rode beside him. The subtle charmer of forty and the good-looking young Scot of thirty rapidly became intimate, sharing dangers and discomforts, and once losing their way and sleeping in a hayloft. Aberdeen was convinced that the prevailing attitude to Metternich was misguided. Once, on September 23, he had had a moment of doubt, and had written to Castlereagh, 'Metternich continues to be as cordial and as confidential as possible. I think this man must be honest; yet it may be, after all, that he is only a most consummate actor. I will be sufficiently cautious, but I will also retain the favourable opinion of him until I see some good ground to change it'.[8] His doubts soon blew over. He was impatient with Stewart's suspicions. Soon for him Metternich could do no wrong.

On October 16 Aberdeen rode through a magnificent defile, following the Austrian Emperor's tracks to Chemnitz. It was a silent journey for his sole companion was an Austrian dragoon who could speak only German. As they rode wordlessly on at daybreak the sharp noise of their horses' hooves was joined by the sound of gunfire. All day it continued, growing louder as they neared Chemnitz. What they heard, though they did not realize it, was the noise of two thousand guns, thundering away in the greatest artillery exchange which had ever taken place. The battle of Leipzig had begun and would continue for sixty hours.

As Aberdeen had been leaving Comotau Napoleon had been arriving at Leipzig. There, south-east of the town, on the slight rise called Gallows Hill, he had taken up his headquarters, set up his farmhouse table in a stubble field, nailed his map to it so that the wind should not blow it away, and commanded a great fire to be lit close by. He had in fact 177,000 men to pit against the allies' 257,000, and his plan was first to attack Schwarzenberg's Austrian army to the south, and then Blücher's Prusso-Austrians to the north. While Aberdeen was still riding on the muddy road between Marienberg and Chemnitz he was preparing to open battle; and at dawn he had given the signal. From then on he had watched disaster overtake him. The allies' guns had wrought havoc in the French lines; and then Schwarzenberg had attacked in four columns. Napoleon had thrown in his celebrated Old Guard, but even they had failed to break the Austrians.

Then to his horror Napoleon had seen Blücher appearing to the north, long before he was expected, and attacking his left wing. The country was flat, and there was no room for stratagems, especially as all his forces were engaged. Numbers and gunpower told, as they must, and by evening Napoleon had lost 26,000 in killed and wounded. The Russians, the Prussians, the Austrians, the Swedes and some German States, including the Saxons, had bested Napoleon in the first day's fighting of the Battle of the Nations. The next day was Sunday, and both armies rested except for sporadic bursts of shellfire.[9]

That day Aberdeen posted on to Zwickau in the rain. His way went through very pretty country which reminded him of England, but the people fled before him, for he boldly preferred to wear a red coat and be taken for a soldier, and they had heard of Cossack atrocities.[10]

At Altenburgh on October 18, Aberdeen at last had news of the battle of Leipzig. On the opening day, the 16th, he heard, it had been 'most sanguinary . . . still more obstinate and bloody' even than the battles of Lutzen and Bautzen.[11] The deadlock at day's end was confirmed. On Sunday afternoon Napoleon had seen long lines of enemy troops advancing on the far horizon. He was watching the Russian General Bennigsen at the head of 50,000 men to the south and Prince Bernadotte with 60,000 more to the north. On the Monday morning, while it was still dark, he had moved his headquarters to a tobacco mill on high ground and had closely watched the enemy movements. Bernadotte had attacked first. In the midst of the fighting 3000 Saxons had deserted to the allies. Napoleon had thrown in his Old Guard again, and deployed 5000 cavalry against the Swedes and the turn-coat Saxons, and had routed them. The French had fought fiercely and bravely, but they were tired men, and the allies were fresher and more numerous. By evening of that long day another 20,000 Frenchmen lay dead and Napoleon's ammunition was nearly exhausted. The invincible leader faced a personal defeat, and he decided to withdraw to avoid annihilation.

That evening, while Aberdeen at Altenburgh was writing to Lady Maria of the wounded men he had seen on the road he had travelled, Napoleon went to Leipzig. All that night and all next morning he directed his weary soldiers across the one bridge left over the River Elster while troops on the old city wall held off the enemy. Only when the main part of his army was safely across had he snatched a nap in a mill on the left bank. Final disaster had overtaken him as he slept. Colonel Monfort had been ordered to blow up the bridge as soon as the enemy came in sight. He had left his post, and a corporal had blown it up before time, with 20,000 Frenchmen marooned on the left bank. Some had swum across, some had been drowned, and 15,000 had been taken prisoner.

For Napoleon the battle of Leipzig had been total catastrophe. In its four days the French had lost 38,000 men in killed and wounded and 30,000 prisoners. The Saxon troops had abandoned him, and he and his men were alone in their retreat across Germany.

At Altenburgh Aberdeen was getting news of a decisive victory. 'The enemy is followed up, and I trust will suffer,' he wrote triumphantly. 'We have not lost less than 30,000 men, exclusive of Blücher and the Crown Prince . . . Bonaparte made offers of negotiation, which have been rejected for the present. I shall go to Rotha tomorrow, and perhaps to Leipzig.'[12] The allies had in fact lost 55,000 men.

So ended the battle of Leipzig. With victory confirmed, Aberdeen's joy outweighed all other reactions – at first. 'The most brilliant prospect opens,' he wrote. 'If we go on with tolerable prudence, we must have him to the Rhine very soon.'[13]

'Our success has been complete . . .' he wrote contentedly from Rotha, where Francis still had his headquarters. 'Poles and Germans come over in great numbers, and the retreat of the French is conducted in great disorder.' The false King of Saxony had thrown himself on the allies' mercy, and had joined the cavalcade of the three sovereigns in their triumphant entry of the city of Leipzig on October 20, only to be made a prisoner of war next day. The Emperor of Austria had been received with acclamation.[14]

Aberdeen himself went into Leipzig more quietly. There his feelings of joy at the victory evaporated. With Humboldt the Prussian Minister he rode over the field of Leipzig, an experience more terrible than anything which had gone before. It inspired him with a revulsion so powerful that he filled his letters home with details of the horrible sights and sounds he was forced to see and hear. Nor did the journey from Leipzig to Frankfort do anything to harden him. All the way, as he rode over dangerous roads through incomparable scenery, he saw appalling sights. At Hanau the allies had cut off Napoleon's line of retreat to the Rhine, and a fierce battle had taken place, ending in the rout of the allies.

Hanau reduced Aberdeen to silence, even to Lady Maria. From there on November 5 he could write only: 'I will spare you the description of the road, and the appearance of the field of battle at the gates of this town. The town itself is half-burnt, and the rest is a charnel-house'.[15]

The Emperor Francis was received with great joy. But all the illuminations, all the parades, even the compliment so gracefully paid to Britain when the Austrian military band played 'God Save the King' before his quarters, could not keep Aberdeen's mind from dwelling on these horrors. Sadly he journeyed to Frankfort behind the Emperor, and abstractedly watched his happiness at the magnificent triumphal entry. Metternich, too, was elated. 'I have come to Frankfort like the Messiah, in order to free sinners,' he exulted. Not so Aberdeen. He was already a very different person from the young man who had left England less than three months before.[16]

Chapter 6

'Heartburnings Enough'

It was not only the sovereigns and their armies who were eaten up by jealousy. Aberdeen's colleagues Cathcart and Stewart were full of rancour towards the stiff young man with little French, no experience, a very good opinion of himself, and no desire to defer to them.[1] They clearly hoped that he would make a resounding failure of his mission, and their resentment grew greater as they saw him receiving treatment at the Austrian Court in embarrassing contrast with that meted out to the senior ambassador at the Russian one.

Aberdeen cared for his colleagues as little as they did for him. He described Cathcart to his father-in-law as a 'man of very moderate talents, stiff, pedantic and difficult', and Stewart as 'scatter-brained, obstinate and wrong-headed'.[2] He was determined to remain on good terms with Castlereagh's beloved younger brother but, he told Abercorn, 'I have been deceived in him two or three times, and in cases which have contributed to affect my opinion of him materially'.

It is easy to blame Aberdeen for some share of the unhappy situation which soon developed between him and his colleagues; and some historians have not scrupled to lump him with them as merely one of a jealous and quarrelsome trio. However, anyone who has experienced the relentless malevolence of the small-minded who consider themselves threatened may pause before condemning him too facilely.

These flowers of the aristocracy made a strange pair, and invited the ridicule of the foreigners. That caustic diplomat, the Chevalier Friedrich von Gentz, Metternich's secretary, described them as 'real caricatures of ambassadors, whose whole behaviour is an epigram on England'.[3] Both Earl Cathcart and Sir Charles Stewart were passionately dedicated soldiers, specifically chosen for their posts because of their military ardour. Since Francis of Austria, unlike the Czar and the King of Prussia, chose not to lead his troops into battle, Aberdeen's civilian status was no disadvantage to him at his Court; but it accounted to some extent for his colleagues' attitude. Lord Cathcart's distinguished military career was behind

66

him, and he was now an easy-going old tortoise. Admirably phleg-
matic in a crisis, he was irritatingly secretive and self-important
about everyday trivialities. He had been despatched to Russia as
soon as war broke out between that country and France with wide
instructions, which included some overlap of Aberdeen's present
responsibilities. During the dramatic three months' campaigning
in Russia in 1812 he had devoted a good deal of effort to trying
to induce the Czar to conciliate Austria, and firmly believed that
he had good reason to distrust Metternich. Since he had arrived
at allied headquarters in March he had been doing his best to
encourage the Czar to resist Metternich's insistent demands for
peace talks.

Castlereagh's half-brother, Stewart, also had a successful military
career behind him, and in 1807 had been Under-Secretary for War.
To him his ambassadorship was a *pis aller*. Wellington had refused
him, despite all pressures, a cavalry command in the Peninsula,
doubtless because he was deaf, short-sighted, flamboyant, vain,
indiscreet and rash – very much the stage Irishman, always fighting
and getting into scrapes. He had said himself when appointed to
his post in April that he felt 'devilish nervous' about his task.[4]
Both men were chief intelligence officers to the armies affected by
their Courts, and both lived for a taste of warfare. (Stewart never
forgave Cathcart for leaving him behind at his desk to deputize for
him while he went off to enjoy the battle of Lutzen. At Bautzen
he would fight happily, and receive 'a contusion' which would
keep him from riding for three weeks.)[5] Stewart's mistrust of
Austria was even greater than Cathcart's, because of his experience
of Metternich's disingenuous behaviour in the past. To see Aberdeen, as they believed, enmeshed by that spider, and eagerly putting
forward his policies, was offensive enough to the two ambassadors.
It was intolerable when sovereigns to whom they were accredited,
following the lead of Austria's Emperor, began to show exceptional
favour to this, diplomatically and militarily speaking, unlicked cub.
To crown it all, the Commander-in-Chief himself, a soldier who
should have known better, rapidly joined the admirers of the
greenhorn civilian, and took him into his confidence, actually allowing him a say in his military councils.

Austria's desire to treat was still very suspect, and now Metternich appeared to have Aberdeen in his pocket, with the concomitant
danger that a too-easy peace might be hastily made and Europe
left exposed to another damaging attack by Napoleon. In the
intoxicating aftermath of victory the ambassadors found it particularly irritating to find Aberdeen strongly urging that peace should

be made at once, and on moderate terms, and arguing that it was the humiliation of a proud France which would bring future and inevitable danger to Europe. That, after all, he pointed out, was what had come to pass only twenty years before. Those were heady days, with Bavaria and Würtemberg joining the allies, the Confederation of the Rhine being dissolved, Holland in revolt, Denmark submissive, Murat defecting, and the French being driven out of Spain. Neither Cathcart nor Stewart was in any mood to leave France her 'natural limits', merely depriving her of all the conquests which her Emperor had gained for her. Yet they were denied any say in the matter, and had to endure Nesselrode's giving Aberdeen precedence over them, and conferring with him (instead of with Cathcart, as was proper) on the Treaty of General Alliance, the arrangements with Denmark, the future operations of the allies, and the proposals made by Napoleon. In fact, of all the English ministers only Aberdeen was informed of those terms, or of the proposals to Denmark. Even worse, it was only at Aberdeen's request that this information was later passed on to Lord Cathcart.

Aberdeen would have been more than human if he had not to some extent savoured this treatment, at least as far as Stewart was concerned, for that gentleman had already dealt him a rather mean and cruel blow on the field of Leipzig. The Austrian general Count Merfeldt had been taken prisoner, and Napoleon had sent him back on parole bearing peace proposals to the Austrian army. Merfeldt had made contact with Sir Robert Wilson as English military representative at the Austrian headquarters. With cannon firing all about him, Wilson had made full notes of the vital interview and had then handed this supremely important document to his ADC with orders to deliver it direct to Aberdeen. Unfortunately for Aberdeen the ADC was a brave blundering fool, so anxious to return to the battle that on sighting Stewart he at once handed over the document and galloped off. To him one ambassador was as good as another.

Fresh from capturing a battery at the head of the Brandenburg Hussars, Stewart at once sent off a despatch to his brother Castlereagh, passing on the information without any mention of Aberdeen. That same evening he compounded his disingenuousness by saying nothing to him when they met in Leipzig. Not until the messenger had got well on his way with his despatch did he break silence and give Aberdeen the document which had been meant for him. Stewart received the Government's warmest thanks and a substantial reward. Aberdeen was left with nothing but a grievance. Arthur Gordon (who thought it better not to name Stewart in his biography of his father) clearly shared Aberdeen's long and burning resentment, but praised his father for his self-control and lack of bitterness. At the time Aberdeen made no reference to the incident, strenuously maintaining a façade of friendliness until long afterwards. Even then he merely added a mild postscript to a cordial letter. 'I hope you repent of your silence to me at Leipsic; it was not fair or friendly, and I am sure could not have been deserved by me.'[6] At least this was hardly the behaviour of a hotheaded and quarrelsome young man.

Perhaps such iron self-control proved more of a strain than he bargained for, for it was soon after Leipzig that Aberdeen first gave signs of wanting to be relieved of his post. Plaintive sighings for home gave way to serious efforts to wind up his work and depart. It was at this time too that the first note was struck in a letter to Lady Maria of his concern for the state of her health. Yet Aberdeen's real work was only beginning, and was to prove long and anxious.

The allied sovereigns would remain at Frankfort for more than a month from early November. Even more kings, generals and statesmen were congregated there than had been at Teplitz, perhaps more than had ever before been gathered together in Europe. At a dinner for two dozen Aberdeen would estimate that three-quarters of those present were sovereigns and their relations, and list their glittering titles, down to and including the newly-created Prince Metternich. Yet he was bored with them all. 'I have seen all the great men who at a distance are imposing,' he had already written to Lady Maria, 'but I think little of most of them.'[7] The Russian generals he stigmatized as barbarians or dull dogs or over eighty. The city too had lost its appeal for him. When he had first arrived he had been impressed by it and glad of the luxuries it provided. But the excitement of a coachman's asking, on being told to drive to the Emperor's, '*Which* Emperor?' had palled, and the trumpets and tinsel of daily military parades and reviews quickly became monotonous.[8] Aberdeen went often to the opera, and daily dined grandly at Metternich's with a chosen few, but as they ate at three o'clock the day was 'terribly shortened'. His groom and horses had arrived from England, so he could ride for an hour every day, and the Czar's two pretty sisters had come to brighten the scene for him somewhat; but he was overworked, overtired, and worried by the rapid spread of an outbreak of fever in the city.[9]

Now Aberdeen obstinately pursued his objective: a quick, secret and moderate peace. The utmost secrecy was to his mind essential, and if the war was to be brought to a speedy end the demands made must be acceptable. To Napoleon's grudging offer after Leipzig to surrender the Elbe and make other unspecified sacrifices the allies had replied merely by renewing battle. Nonetheless, Metternich, Nesselrode and Aberdeen had gone into conference on the peace terms, and had produced the Frankfort Proposals. Nesselrode wanted to pitch the allies' demands high and negotiate downwards. Aberdeen wanted to state the lowest and most palatable terms and stick to them. Metternich shared his view, discussing with the Count de St Aignan, a French diplomat and soldier who had been captured at Leipzig, possible bases of negotiation, and assuring him that if Napoleon would accept a France bounded by the Alps, the Rhine and the Pyrenees, and agree to the absolute independence of Germany, Spain, Italy and Holland, he had reason to believe that England would not interfere with France's freedom to trade, and that she would be 'reasonable' about maritime rights – Britain's cherished freedom of the seas, the right to board neutral vessels as a belligerent, about which Castlereagh had written on July 14 to Cathcart, 'Great Britain may be driven out of a congress, but not out of her maritime rights'.[10] When putting the terms in writing St Aignan had twisted Metternich's assurance into a formula to the effect that 'Great Britain was ready to recognize the liberty of commerce and navigation which France had the right to claim'. Aberdeen has been much blamed for not rejecting the formula out of hand, though he made verbal reservations about it; and for not raising the vital question of Antwerp or the subsidiary questions of Sicily and Norway. The fact that his assent was, in his words, 'perfectly unofficial' has not saved him.[11] It is true that had Napoleon immediately and unconditionally accepted the Frankfort Proposals he might have retained his throne and secured a peace such as Metternich at least desired, but the reply he sent on November 18 was ambiguous, merely acknowledging the communication and suggesting a conference. A few days later his Foreign Secretary Maret was succeeded by Caulaincourt, who was known to be in favour of peace. In a Note of December 5 Caulaincourt accepted the Frankfort Proposals, agreeing to the *bases generales et communes qui ont été communiqués par M. de St Aignan*.

This was an achievement; but it had been brought off by Nesselrode, Metternich and Aberdeen alone. St Aignan had not been allowed to see the two emperors, and the whole negotiation had been concealed from both Cathcart and Stewart. Every indication of Aberdeen's character suggests that his chief motive for concealment was fear that their intransigence would ruin the negotiations, and not merely, as Harold Nicolson, following Webster's lead, suggested, 'that he was seeking, as young diplomats so often seek, to score a personal success behind the backs of his more experienced colleagues'.[12] Aberdeen was too self-torturingly determined to live up to the highest ideals of public service, too scornful of disingenuousness, and too intelligent to descend to low and foolish machinations – the more so since he had himself recently paid a high price as the victim of similar tactics. When Cathcart and Stewart were informed they exploded in wrath. Cathcart at once tried to have a clause inserted to the effect that the war should be carried on without further negotiation. Aberdeen succeeded in mollifying him, but Stewart was at Hanover with Bernadotte, and threatened to resign when the news reached him. Stewart's resentment was not lessened when the Prussian Chancellor, Hardenberg, asked him to convey to his Government Prussia's request that Aberdeen should be appointed sole British plenipotentiary in all matters affecting the alliance in general. Austria and Russia had already made the same request, but had sent it more discreetly through their ambassadors in London. This time Stewart behaved well, even gracefully, bearing witness to Aberdeen's success and his weighty influence with the ministers of all the allied powers.

Stewart was nonetheless convinced that Aberdeen was selling the pass both for Europe and for England. In his despatches he insisted that Aberdeen had omitted points from the proposals sent to Napoleon which were of the utmost importance to his country. Disappointingly for him, Castlereagh and the Cabinet underwrote Aberdeen's actions. Further, they delivered a snub to Stewart, curtly telling him that he did not appreciate the difference between a basis of negotiation and the terms of a definitive treaty. Aberdeen was assured that he had 'HRH the Prince Regent's full approval of the part he had borne in these delicate and momentous discussions', and that the British Government was willing to treat on the bases which he had proposed.[13]

It seemed an important triumph for Aberdeen over his detractors, and a great blow struck for a satisfactory and lasting peace in Europe – that is, if Castlereagh was right in thinking that Napoleon would abide by the peace terms. On the other hand, Castlereagh privately made it crisply clear to him that he was far from satisfied with the bases of the peace proposals offered. He did not care for the vagueness about Holland's future frontiers, the inclusion of British maritime rights (despite Britain's veto) as a fit subject for discussion, and the absence of any mention of vital British objectives. In all this he suspected the hand of Metternich, and feared that it was directed to a rapid and unsatisfactory compromise peace, which would be bound to set the British public by the ears. He at once ordered Aberdeen to make a formal protest against the inclusion of the all-important maritime rights on the agenda; and he drafted it himself. He also insisted on sticking out for the old limits, as opposed to the natural ones, for France, as Cathcart desired; the complete overthrow of Napoleon instead of a dignified agreement with him; and a precisely expressed reference concerning the establishment of a barrier for the protection of Holland. He was caustic about the need to destroy 'that arsenal',[14] Antwerp, which Aberdeen had tacitly recognized as a French port.

At Frankfort, while arranging the peace negotiations, Aberdeen was kept at full stretch, for he was also occupied with the liberation of Holland, where the French had been expelled, and of Switzerland, where there was a question of inciting a revolution and restoring the old cantonal government in time to greet the allies marching through on their way to France. Then there was the bringing of Denmark into the alliance, achieved entirely because of Aberdeen's firm stand against Russia, Prussia and his own government, since Castlereagh was more anxious to fulfil his reluctantly-given guarantee to Bernadotte than to help Denmark. Not least of Aberdeen's many complicated tasks was the clearing up of the murky Murat situation, and the arranging of an armistice between that strange character, who had at last defected from Napoleon after Leipzig, and the British army in Sicily.

Unfortunately all was not harmony between Aberdeen and his government. Too often he was convinced that he was right and they were wrong. There had been the disagreement as to how best to deal with Denmark; but this was as nothing compared with what the Emperor Francis, Metternich and Aberdeen now believed to be the very invidious treatment meted out to Austria by England. As Francis and Metternich grew more and more aggrieved, Aberdeen wrote with an increasing and somewhat surprising testiness to Castlereagh. Once he objected to an 'outrageous compliment' having been paid to the Czar in a speech of the Prince Regent's, which did not 'suit the taste of the successor of the Caesars'. He complained too of Castlereagh's having lumped Austria and Bavaria together in the same sentence, to the great offence of 'the proudest Court in Europe'. 'Really these sallies undo all that I am labouring to accomplish,' Aberdeen wrote tartly on December 4. 'God knows there are heartburnings enough to allay, and the task is not easy. I do my best, but tell you plainly a few more instances of such odious preference will go far to loosen the very foundations of the coalition.' This was strong language to use to a Foreign Secretary, however patient and tactful.[15]

Throughout November Aberdeen had been struggling with the peace terms. Napoleon, not yet on his knees, was pressing that the line of the French frontier towards Holland and Piedmont should be left for future discussion. For the sake of preserving secrecy Aberdeen had not only made Nesselrode and Metternich agree that St Aignan was not to see either of the emperors before leaving, but had dissuaded them from publishing a proclamation on the grounds that it would only irritate Napoleon. While working for peace in these ways Aberdeen was also setting up an alternative 'bold and gigantic plan', which was to involve 400,000 men in the south.

All this involved work enough for ten men, and Aberdeen might have been forgiven for not concerning himself with the problems of individuals. The Wilson incident is revealing in many ways, perhaps most of all as an illustration of his almost suicidal loyalty to those he counted as friends.

Major-General Sir Robert Wilson, British Commissioner on Schwarzenberg's staff at Leipzig, was a brave and energetic soldier, whose virtues were heavily overshadowed by a political fanaticism, which many thought distorted his war reports and made him unreliable. Aberdeen was not of their number, and his horror was great when Wilson was suddenly replaced by an inexperienced young man, Lord Burghersh, the son of Lord Westmorland. Believing that this switch 'bordered on the ludicrous',[16] he bombarded Castlereagh with imperative demands to send the new-comer packing, preferably to the army in Italy, and leave Wilson where he was. Worse, Aberdeen went to Burghersh and told him that 'it would be more for his own comfort as well as for the good of the public service that he should go to Italy'. In vain, he wrote to Castlereagh, since, 'as Burghersh informed me, he would be damned if he did'.[17]

Castlereagh dug in his heels. Burghersh was to stay. It was Aberdeen's turn to be snubbed; and this reverse affected him strongly. The day after writing a long and painful letter to Castlereagh in very emotional phraseology he again rushed to pen and paper to demand permission to go home. Until then he had been prepared to see things through. Now, sick at heart, he felt that Castlereagh had lost confidence in him.

The enormous strain was telling on him. Not only was he over-worked, but for some time he had been worried about decisions he had taken concerning matters of unparalleled importance which he either knew or feared would be displeasing to Castlereagh. He had gone against his Government's wishes about Denmark; had crossed swords with his colleagues about peace with France; had pushed for a total reversal of attitude as between Austria and Russia. The 'bold and gigantic plan' for an invasion of France, which he was organizing, was also undertaken against his colleagues' wishes. At first Stewart and Cathcart had not wanted to make peace; now they were against a vigorous attack. Yet it must be promoted with the utmost celerity, vigour and ruthlessness in order to be effective. The lover of peace, tender as a girl to human suffering, was in the ironical situation of mounting a great war offensive against the will of his militaristic colleagues. It was hardly surprising if his normal calm and balance were somewhat disturbed.

It was unfortunate, however, in view of the general attitude towards Metternich, that it was he who provided the reason for Aberdeen's second, almost angry, letter to Castlereagh. Replying to a despatch critical of the Austrian, which touched him closely just when he was relying on Metternich to help complete the Treaty of Alliance by being his intermediary with the Czar, he wrote: 'Do not think Metternich such a formidable personage; depend upon it, I have most substantial reasons for knowing that he is heart and soul with us; but, my dear Castlereagh, with all your wisdom, judgment and experience, which are as great as possible, and which I respect sincerely, I think you have so much of the Englishman about you as not quite to be aware of the real value of foreign modes of acting'.

This was not the tone best calculated to please the vain and touchy, though determinedly patient, Castlereagh. 'He is, I repeat it to you,' Aberdeen went on, 'not a very clever man. He is vain; but he is a good Austrian. He may, perhaps, like the appearance of negotiation a little too much, but he is to be trusted.'[18]

Now, feeling increasingly rejected, Aberdeen tried to hold Castlereagh to his original promise to release him when he wished to go, insisting, 'You know my bargain'. If Castlereagh needed him in the future for negotiation then, he hinted, he would be glad to stay; but he did not want to remain merely for the waging of war. 'Parliament has met,' he wrote, 'and although I am not a regular performer, that is the scene, after all. To assist you, I would do this, or almost anything else, but I lean towards home.' He added, 'Stewart and Cathcart have their stars and crosses. My rewards are at home, which, if no other, are at least great in the renewed love of my friends, and I trust your approbation'.[19]

In all his letters he quoted the flattering reactions of horror of those around him to the thought of his departure, but still he hoped that he might be allowed to travel home once the Elbe was opened. To Lady Maria he revealed that he actually hoped to be in London by the end of January, though he warned her that this was very uncertain, and asked her not to mention it. To her too, and to her alone, he opened his heart about his feelings of resentment towards Castlereagh, saying, 'But if my stay is prolonged, it will be more on account of the very unusual kindness and desire of the Emperor and the principal persons here, than from the wishes of ministers at home'.[20]

Chapter 7

Disappointed Hopes

Aberdeen's private life had not been prospering.

At first the excitement and variety of his new life had helped to ease his lover's heartache, but while he was still at Leipzig his brother Charles had arrived bearing letters which reawakened his hopes. Anne Cavendish's mother was toying with the idea of him as a husband for her daughter after all. 'Only let this rise into reasonable hope,' he wrote to Lady Maria, 'and I fly to England.' He asserted his strong belief that Anne Cavendish was favourably disposed towards him, and he lamented the fact that he was unknown to Lord and Lady George Cavendish.[1]

By October 31 he had again relapsed into despair. Writing from Smalhalden, he said, 'After all, I am decidedly of opinion that the affair had better be brought to a speedy conclusion. It will never do for me to torment myself here, and linger in uncertainty at home'. He felt that he had got himself into an intolerable situation, and should extricate himself as soon as possible. 'If you can,' he pleaded with Lady Maria, 'for God's sake take some means with Ly. H[olland] to clinch the matter at once if possible, and then if the worst arrives – I will try what pride, philosophy and commonsense can effect – I wish to return to England either perfectly free or with those just hopes of success which would make my return prosperous.'[2]

At Frankfort the English were thinning out, and there were 'no alarms, no cannonades, and even no new kings. I believe we have exhausted the whole stock',[3] he wrote wryly. It was duller than ever.

Nothing seemed to be going quite right for Aberdeen. In the capitulation of Dresden certain conditions had been agreed which Schwarzenberg was not prepared to ratify. Aberdeen believed it foolish to try to jog back, however justifiably, thus inviting criticisms. His advice was not taken. Time would prove him to have been right, but that could be no comfort to him at the time. Then, Cathcart and Stewart were growing more and more hostile to his great initiative against France.

It was towards the end of November that he had written to Lady Maria to complain that he had not heard from her for a long time.

76

Her last letter had been dated a month before. His anxiety was clear, and in sending her 'a repetition of my love and interest' he hoped that she was going on well and that the visit she had paid to Brighton had done for her all that she had wished. For himself, he was kept on tenterhooks by 'this dreadful fever', which had laid low two of his servants, and which now looked like achieving a death rate on the scale of the plague itself.[4]

Aberdeen seemed to have lost all joy in his work, to which he referred as 'my slavery' or 'the drudgery to which I am condemned'.[5] He had lost some of his self-confidence, too, and was nervous about his decisions concerning Denmark. 'I had been led to do a good deal in this business,' he wrote to Castlereagh, 'but I hope not injudiciously.'[6] He had thought up a plan of going home as a sort of leave of absence. That would take him home, but leave it open for him to come back if Castlereagh objected to his staying in England. Still, the day after writing to Lady Maria so dolefully, Aberdeen was throwing his cap in the air at the triumphant conclusion of the Treaty of General Alliance. Scribbling from Metternich's room to catch the courier, he could not resist directing some pretty sharp jibes at Castlereagh for his mistrust of Metternich:

'It is with the greatest satisfaction that I announce to you the realisation of my promises regarding Metternich. He is just returned from an interview with the Emperor of Russia. The Treaty of General Alliance *will positively be made forthwith*. The difficulties have not been few or slight, but Metternich has made a point of bringing your unjust suspicions of Austria to shame. Now, pray observe, these are not fine words only, but *facts*, and pretty important too. I wait for your *amende honorable*.'

It was a pity that in his elation at this achievement Aberdeen had made a bad slip. He had agreed to the request made by the Czar that the Treaty should be executed in London. 'Farewell,' he ended his triumphant letter to Castlereagh. 'I hope everything meets with your approbation. As far as I am able to perceive, there is no just reason to complain.'[7]

He was wrong. In no time at all, and in a very chastened mood, he was once more addressing himself to the Foreign Secretary: 'I was so happy in the thought of its being done anywhere, that I, perhaps, too eagerly caught at the proposed agreement of its being signed in London'.

Cathcart and Stewart had been making the most of the opportunity with which Aberdeen had presented them. Cathcart had informed Aberdeen that in some of his despatches to him Castle-

reagh had laid it down that the Treaty should on no account be
sent back to London, and Stewart had come out strongly against
the whole proposal as unsatisfactory. So Aberdeen wrote again in
mortification, 'I have told Metternich that he must undo everything
which he had fixed with the Emperor Alexander'.[8] In doing so he
had almost fallen out with Metternich.

His brief taste of happiness having gone sour, Aberdeen again
turned his eyes towards home. Now that the Treaty was settled he
could see no reason for staying on, and believed that any complica-
tions would be better sorted out by a few talks face to face than
by the exchange of a thousand despatches. After all, the Russians
were sending Pozzo di Borgo over to England for that reason. Pozzo
was in fact principally concerned to gain the British Government's
agreement to alter the project of the alliance so as to allow for
discussion with the French about subsidies and colonial conquests.
He also had instructions to press for fuller representation of the
British point of view, asking that one person should be designated
to represent Britain at headquarters with authority to make important decisions.[9] Metternich's letter to Wessenberg, the Austrian
ambassador in London, particularly stressed this. Aberdeen himself
would know nothing of all this until Pozzo di Borgo had left on
December 6, and did not suspect, as Cathcart did, that Metternich
was playing the traitor, and was as much responsible as the Czar
for the rejection of the Treaty of General Alliance.

Impatiently, almost peremptorily, Aberdeen demanded his recall,
and seemed about to take matters into his own hands. 'I have now
only to request that you will have the goodness to give directions
for a frigate to receive us, Pozzo and myself . . .' he wrote coldly.
'Pray have the goodness to give the orders as soon as you receive
this letter, for although it is *possible* we may be detained, it is
most probable that we shall set out in a very few days.'[10]

To Lady Maria he said firmly that he had 'nearly determined to
go to England immediately'. Whether he came back, as the two
emperors wanted, 'must be decided by what I find in England'.
Then, anxiously and tenderly, he writes of her, 'Not a word of
news from you; I am quite sick with hope long deferred. I cannot
imagine what has happened. I trust you are well and happy'.[11]

The revolutions which had been fomented in Holland and
Switzerland were progressing well, he told her. In short everything
was prospering for the allies. The end, so long predicted by Talleyrand, had come for Napoleon. It was difficult to express the delight
with which he looked forward to the moment of meeting them all
again. However, he ended on the same anxious note, 'Yet I shall

not go to England without apprehension'.[12]

Deep concern about his future prospects was oppressing him, for he found himself in a situation of bitter conflict. Pozzo di Borgo was bearing with him to England the joint request of the three allied powers that Aberdeen should be appointed as the English negotiator of the bases of negotiation to which Napoleon had agreed, as he was acceptable to all of their Governments. Should his own Government be equally pleased with him he would be honoured by the appointment which, despite his disclaimers, he coveted. He had already made it clear that he would gladly remain in Europe if he were made sole negotiator, but not otherwise.

He was to be disappointed. On December 5 Lord Castlereagh had decided to leave for the Continent and confer on the spot with the allied sovereigns and their ministers.

By December 4 Cathcart and Stewart were no longer the only ambassadors with 'stars and crosses'. The Emperor of Austria had given Aberdeen the Order of St Stephen – 'a very different thing', he could not resist saying to Lord Abercorn, 'from the Russian St Andrew and the Prussian Black Eagle', and he pointed out that Wellington was the only other Englishman on whom it had ever been conferred.[13] On the other hand, at home Abercorn was raging at the invidious treatment which had been meted out to his son-in-law, and by implication to the Emperor Francis, to Metternich and to Austria. In the setting out of the instructions for the Treaty of General Alliance Cathcart had been named first. Aberdeen told his father-in-law that the English ministers had intentionally given Cathcart precedence in order to show favour to the Czar. 'But I can as little permit this on the part of the Emperor of Austria as on my own,' he wrote haughtily. 'It may produce the most mischievous effect.'[14]

The slap in the face to him was made worse since Cathcart and Stewart had not even been present during the making of the Treaty. The fact that Aberdeen was not to be allowed to finish the job would put him in a still more embarrassing position. It was not unreasonable that Castlereagh should add his considerable weight to the efforts to weld the allies together for a final conclusive push. But Aberdeen, after all his hard work, and the triumphant success of his mission, had been given every reason for hope, and now he was sick at heart.

From Freyburg Aberdeen wrote to Harrowby. It was Christmas Eve, and he was certainly hankering for home and his children, which may explain his urgent and almost angry tone. Since last writing he had been rapped over the knuckles for wanting to abandon his post, and had been told that it would be a nuisance if he did so. He told Harrowby of his having written to Castlereagh to state his intention of going home at once, but of having later decided to stay a little longer.

'It is a little hard after so very explicit an understanding as I had with Castlereagh before leaving London that I should be blamed for profiting by that understanding,' he wrote, and added that it was possible that his going might be an inconvenience but that he had never imagined that he would have to remain until it was a matter of indifference whether he stayed or went.[15]

Then he came out strongly once again with the main point. There was only one thing important enough to keep him where he was, and that was for him to be in charge of the negotiations with Napoleon, whenever they began. That was the crux of the matter; and he stated it baldly: 'As I was informed both by Metternich and Nesselrode that they had expressed a wish I should be charged with this affair, it appeared probable that such a joint application might be worth attending to, at any rate. If not, it became doubly incumbent on me to go home when so very different an opinion was entertained by the two leading powers here and my own Government'.[16]

Then at last he frankly admitted that he would very much like to be given the task, and that he felt he deserved the promotion and the prominence which it would bring him. Until then he had played second fiddle. Now he wanted to be first.

'I confess,' he wrote, 'that the importance of the charge, and a kind of feeling that I should act well with those employed in the great work of negotiation led me to desire, even ardently, that after having in appearance played a second[ary] part through the war, I should at least possess a prominent situation before the conclusion of peace, if ever it should take place. Castlereagh knew of this long since; but the question is very much changed now. Private reasons make me much more indifferent to anything of this kind and proportionately anxious to go home.'[17] The situation at home had indeed changed, and in a way which deeply affected him. On December 5 Abercorn had written to him, 'But alas my dear A! You must prepare yourself for the chance of never seeing poor Maria again! . . . she has returned [from Brighton] too evidently very few stages of her last. I will not for both our sakes enter further on this subject'.[18] Now Aberdeen opened his heart to Harrowby. 'To you who know how small a share of my mind is occupied by political events of any description I may confess that the alarming account of Lady Maria's health is a motive of action stronger than all others. If it be true that she is not destined to survive more than a few months I solemnly declare to you that I had rather be the means of contributing to her happiness and tranquillity during the dreadful time than preserve the crown on the Emperor's head.'[19]

He begged Harrowby to try to understand and help him in his grief and anxiety: 'For God's sake lay aside your character of minister. As my friend recollect what I have enjoyed and what I have suffered. See the person nearest in blood, worthy in every respect to be the sister of the most perfect being whom God in his power ever created – see her reduced to the state in which she is, and then, following the dictates of your own heart, tell me what on earth can stand in competition with her claims on my love and attention. I know she desires to see me again; and I am sure you are not the person to blame me for listening to such a call, for I am sure you can appreciate it. I have only within these two days known the real situation, and have not before felt thus strongly, although always desirous of going home'.[20]

It was indeed a situation full of agonizing conflicts. The sister-in-law for whom he had a more than usually ardent affection was dying, and had asked for him; and he wanted to go to her. Yet he was torn between the natural ambitions alive in his heart and this call. So he temporized, even in the midst of his grief-stricken out-pouring to the older man, and added, 'As I have expressed myself decidedly on the subject of negotiation, and as a delay might be most pernicious, in the event of Castlereagh's demanding my services they shall still be given'. Nevertheless he was adamant that he would not stay unless he received the desired promotion, and he insisted, 'There can be no possible reason for my continuing the routine of business at this Court if there should be no such reason to detain me'.[21]

That, then, was his mood on Christmas Eve 1813. On January 17 Aberdeen again wrote to Harrowby. By then he was making the best of the decision to send Castlereagh to Europe, writing, 'I have now determined not to do the thing by halves, but to stay as long as I can to be of use to Castlereagh'.[22]

It had not, however, been suddenly done. It was on December 15 that he had first learned of Lady Maria's serious illness. His anguished letter to Harrowby had been written two days later. On December 15, too, he had written to Lady Maria herself from Karlsruhe, where he had just arrived, 'It must appear rather extra-ordinary to you, as it certainly does to me, that while I think of nothing but going to England, and write to you of nothing else, still I am increasing the distance of my journey; and every day adds to the difficulties when I begin to retrace my steps . . . The fact is that I must wait for despatches from Castlereagh, and while I am here it is as well to be placed where the duty can best be done. However, I confidently trust it will soon be over, and that I shall still be able to join you by the end of next month'.[23]

He was then on the road to Switzerland, ready to take up his quarters at Freyburg, so as to be able to negotiate with the Swiss without violating their neutrality.

Instead of hurrying home as he wished to the woman he knew to be dying and who had sent for him, Aberdeen moved forward with the allied armies to the French frontier. Helpless to ease the prolonged agonies of which he knew only too well from dreadful experience, he could only write almost daily. His letters to her of this period are so detailed and personal that they take almost the form of a journal; and, harassed though he was, he made them as leisurely, as interesting and as entertaining as it was in him to do. Thus we can read today what he thought of the Germans and their Emperor, of the Black Forest, of noble 40-mile-long avenues of walnut trees, of the picturesqueness of castles poised on every eminence, of the pleasure of buying presents of engravings of old Heidelberg for her, and of the gigantic tun kept in the castle's cellars – 'a barrel able to contain two hundred thousand bottles of wine'.[24] He shared his life, his thoughts and his heart with her, as if both she and he had all the time in the world.

On December 18 he was still, he told her, hoping that the next messenger would bring him his release despite the Emperor's threats to refuse to receive any other ambassador and his own growing suspicions that he would be asked to remain. 'Farewell, dearest Lady Maria,' he wrote from Freyburg; 'I will not suppose it possible that I should be out of England by the end of next month. Take care of yourself, and for God's sake exert yourself as much as possible not to increase that state of nervous irritability from which you suffer so much.'[25]

Meanwhile he continued to address her as if she were well and active, and he still sought her help with his wooing. Two days before Christmas he sent her a note for 'Lady H.' from Freyburg, trying to express his feelings 'on the subject of which we have said so much', and assuring her that he still hoped to be in England before the end of January.[26] On Christmas Day he wrote again, 'I am certainly provoked about this affair'. He pressed her, ill as she was, to get the whole question sorted out and settled for him. 'It is probable my return to England may not be distant, but, my dearest Lady M., I must know quickly how it stands, both as to the present and the future in order that I may act accordingly. It will never do to return on any other footing.' Could she, he begged, '*really* ascertain' how the matter stood?[27]

Yet on Christmas Eve, the night before, he had made his decision to stay on for as long as Castlereagh needed him. In the end he would not sail for England before April, and Lady Maria would die without seeing him again.

Chapter 8

'Vive la Paix! Vive qui voudra!'

So Castlereagh left for Europe. Great decisions as to peace and war, and his cherished project for a Grand Alliance, were about to be taken. The Foreign Secretary was concerned too about the ever-worsening relations between the powers, which, in the event of Napoleon's collapse, could grow into dangerous conflicts for supremacy in Europe. The quarrels between the allies had been growing alarmingly during the three weeks which Aberdeen had spent at Freyburg. No sooner had he smoothed one out than another had erupted. At one stage things had gone so far that the sulky Czar had called in his troops and threatened to withdraw them altogether from active service.

Switzerland's neutrality had been the bone of contention. The allies had come to an agreement to violate it, and then the Czar's conscience had pricked him. He had announced that he would take the entry of Austrian forces into Switzerland as a declaration of war against Russia, had refused to go any further towards coming to terms with Napoleon, had fallen out with Nesselrode, and had moved his headquarters nearer the front to Langres. When the allied discussions began at Basle the Czar was sulking there, the angrier because his stand for principle was a costly one. Metternich, in his foxy way, did not attempt to dispute the principle, relying on the Czar's agreeing in the end. Aberdeen simply tried to keep the allies together, and followed Metternich's lead, since that at least allowed them to continue their march. He had himself seen the Swiss agents at Frankfort and had disbursed money to foment a revolution – just the kind of cloak-and-dagger rôle which he found most uncomfortable.

The revolution in Switzerland was fomented and effected, the old cantonal governments restored, and the new government invited the Austrians to pass through Switzerland. The Czar had given no more trouble. This dangerous quarrel between the allies was, however, only one more warning to Aberdeen of a perilously explosive situation.

On January 19 Castlereagh arrived at Basle after a grim and icy journey, determined to have it recognized that Aberdeen's admissions about maritime rights at Frankfort were indeed, as he had claimed, 'perfectly unofficial' and unauthorized, and that the allies were not to discuss such questions at any conference, as well as to establish the General Alliance with essential safeguards. The continentals were excited at the arrival of the first senior English representative ever to attend the allied councils, and gave him a noteworthy reception. It must have given Aberdeen a somewhat jaundiced pleasure to see Castlereagh, the glacial and hard-headed, rapidly abandoning his former prejudices and thawing under Metternich's practised charm. Not only was he completely converted concerning Metternich's character – with much the same reservations as the younger man had had – but he was quickly won round to a sober appreciation of his policies, both in the past and for the future. Now he saw them less as the machinations of a dishonest man than as the brilliant and patient ruses of a superb diplomat whose life was dedicated to preserving his country's existence and against all the odds maintaining her in a position of power. A personal friendship would last until Castlereagh's suicide in 1822, and frequently and profoundly influence European diplomacy. For the present its immediate effect was that another chance was given to Napoleon to make peace.

At first Castlereagh had intended to conduct the peace negotiations himself. He had given Aberdeen to understand that if he did decide against doing so he would hand over to him so that he could complete the work which he had begun at Frankfort. For ten days Castlereagh thought things over. Those ten days must have seemed endless to Aberdeen, for he was very conscious of the invidious position in which he had been placed. 'Castlereagh has not made up his mind how the negotiations shall be conducted,' he wrote to Abercorn, 'and I am bound to wait for his decision. I think it most probable that he will manage it all himself, in which case I think he will scarcely have treated me fairly in not coming to a decision sooner, because my departure at this moment cannot but be misunderstood.'[1] Not to put too fine a point on it, Aberdeen feared it might seem as if after inspecting things on the spot the Foreign Secretary had dismissed his plenipotentiary.

When Castlereagh and Metternich, armed with their own basic agreements, moved off to Langres from Basle in the last week of January to meet Alexander, they found him more prepared to talk. It took Castlereagh rather longer to make a friend of the Czar than of Metternich, and he was nervous of his crazy and erratic schemes and the effect they might have on the Alliance – which he was achieving no more readily than Aberdeen had done. However, on

January 29 the four powers signed a protocol providing that the war should be continued under the command of Schwarzenberg, but that armistice negotiations should be held simultaneously with peace talks at Châtillon, and that after peace had been arranged a congress should be held at Vienna to settle any matters left outstanding. It was a compromise, but a satisfactory one.

The preliminary conference was opened at Châtillon at the beginning of February. Unfortunately it did not live up to expectations.

Aberdeen had been left to cool his heels until January 29. Not until then did Castlereagh decide that, since neither Prince Metternich nor Count Nesselrode, the respective ministers for Austria and Russia, proposed to act as negotiators, it would be unsuitable for him to do so for Britain. He then made a move to fulfil his promise to Aberdeen to appoint him sole British plenipotentiary. The dramatic denouement is best related in Arthur Gordon's words, which are all the more telling since he was no lover of extravagant language.

'But when this became known to Lord Cathcart and Sir Charles Stewart, as well as the fact that Lord Aberdeen attended meetings of the ministers of the four powers, from which they were excluded, their discontent was so violent, and seemed likely to have such prejudicial consequences, that Castlereagh was induced to hesitate, and begged Lord Aberdeen (while himself remaining "the sole efficient person, to make all reports, to be the sole mouthpiece and generally the negotiator") to consent that Lord Cathcart and Sir Charles Stewart should act along with him as assistants in "a sort of cabinet". Castlereagh told Lord Aberdeen that, although one of the disappointed negotiators was his own brother, he should have thought nothing of their dissatisfaction had it not been for the opportunity of serious mischief which might be given by the insinuation that the appointment of the ambassador to Austria as the sole English plenipotentiary showed a disposition to disregard the interests of Russia and Prussia, and begged Lord Aberdeen, in language of the most earnest entreaty, to agree to an arrangement which he could not require, and could hardly expect him to accept.'[2]

This put Aberdeen in a very difficult position. (In his own words, he found this 'a very bad arrangement and very disagreeable', and felt that the affair was 'not the more pleasant from the nature of my colleagues'.)[3] His tendency was always to bite the bullet rather than create a scene for the sake of securing his own advancement, as Stewart and Cathcart so constantly did. At any rate, to the distress of many of his friends, he gave way and agreed to do as

Castlereagh asked. Abercorn was among those who felt that he had let them down, as well as himself, by being too pliant. He impatiently dismissed Lord Castlereagh's explanations as mere excuses, and blamed Aberdeen for 'playing into Lord Castlereagh's and his brother's hands'. He added grimly, 'All praise will be arrogated by Lord Cathcart and his extensive connections, and blame and unpopularity you will studiously be made to share'.[4]

Lord Aberdeen, however, in his son's opinion, had no option but to accept the situation. He would, as things stood, be doing the real work, and taking on the chief conduct of the negotiations. He would be sacrificing the credit for it, some reputation and his just reward. He would also be harnessing himself to two captious team-mates instead of directing the operations on his sole responsibility. He went to the conference at Châtillon, moreover, with little faith that peace would be the outcome.

On February 3 the negotiators arrived, and on February 5 they went into conference with the French plenipotentiary, Caulaincourt. Alexander was a great admirer of this former French ambassador to Russia and close friend of Napoleon's, which augured well. The allies' terms, however, had hardened considerably since the conference at Frankfort of the previous November, when Napoleon had still been confident of victory, and had turned down their offer to leave France her natural frontiers. Now they were unwilling to let her have more than her 1792 limits. Unexpectedly Caulaincourt proved willing to meet these stringent demands. Indeed he was desperately anxious to persuade his master to accept them. But Napoleon would be sacrificing not only the conquests he had gained for France, but those won by her revolutionary armies before he had come on the scene. Far from providing France with a greater Empire, he would be responsible for diminishing the one he had inherited. It was not a role he could tolerate.

A factor unknown to the allies was affecting these discussions. After the battle of La Rothière Napoleon had given Caulaincourt *carte blanche* to sign any agreement with the allies which might slow up their advance and gain time for him. Caulaincourt was anxious to speed up an agreement before these special powers, reluctantly given, were revoked. So, much to the surprise of Aberdeen and the other allies, things went along smoothly. After the second conference Aberdeen felt able to assure Castlereagh that the French government were genuinely anxious for peace.

By the time the conference got off to a good start the armies of the allies were well into France, and Holland and the Low Countries in full revolt. There was no doubt that terms for a preliminary treaty would have been decided on, and the preliminary treaty itself signed, at the next conference, the third. So much was this the case that when Aberdeen asked Castlereagh how Caulaincourt's pacific overtures were to be greeted, Castlereagh sent him a historic note.

'My dear Aberdeen, we must sign. Certainly we must sign. We shall be stoned when we get back to England, but we must sign – Yours ever, C.'[5]

Drama was never long absent, however, and once again the Czar supplied it. On the morning of February 9, to Aberdeen's surprise and high indignation, the Russian plenipotentiary was ordered to go no further with the negotiations without fresh instructions. Excited by the victory of La Rothière, the Czar had suddenly decided that he did not want to treat with Napoleon after all. Always anxious to revenge the rape of Moscow in 1812, he preferred to press on with total war, march into Paris, and leave the choice of a French sovereign to an elective assembly there. Aberdeen was very suspicious of his motives, fearing 'a dark intrigue' of Russian aggrandizement, at the end of which a packed assembly would elect Bernadotte King of France.[6] The Emperor Francis of Austria categorically refused to have anything to do with this idea. He was, he declared, quite prepared to help dethrone his daughter's husband if the welfare of Europe made such a step necessary and if a fitting peace was otherwise unobtainable. He was not prepared to do so for the benefit of a French adventurer. If Napoleon was to be deposed he did not intend to treat with any sovereign of France except Louis XVIII. The Austrians would make a separate peace rather than act in concert with the Czar.

Francis need not have concerned himself, for the Czar was doomed to fail in any case. Napoleon checkmated his move. In the ten days since La Rothière he had gained a series of brilliant victories, and soon the allied forces looked more like being beaten out of France altogether than marching in triumph into Paris. The disconcerted Czar see-sawed between manic optimism and black despair, while Napoleon regained his buoyancy and his superstitious belief in his incredible luck. Thus when, on February 17, the conferences were renewed, Caulaincourt was far less ready to accept the terms than he had been a week before. The Czar's change of front had put the allies in a most awkward position.

Caulaincourt himself was by then in a different and far more vulnerable situation. Napoleon had revoked his full powers, and now Caulaincourt had to refer everything back to him before signature. The allies did not know this, but they stuck to their demands, and their determination was rewarded. The terms agreed were the 1792 limits, and the abandonment by Napoleon of all direct or indirect constitutional influence as King of Italy, Protector of the Confederation of the Rhine, and Mediator of Switzerland. Caulaincourt protested at the unpalatableness to Napoleon of the phraseology used, particularly in the article requiring the abolition of the slave-trade by France, which could 'never be tolerated by a great people, who are not yet in a situation to be insulted with perfect impunity'.[7]

Negotiations were resumed; and a draft treaty was agreed among the allies. Then once again the Czar threw a spanner in the works. According to Castlereagh, writing to Aberdeen on February 25, his vacillations bordered on the unbalanced, 'at one time too proud to listen to anything, at another so impatient to be delivered from the pressure of our enemy as to make our propositions at Châtillon almost ludicrous'.[8]

As Castlereagh's laconic little note had said so clearly, one of the greatest hurdles on the road to peace with Napoleon was the unpopularity at home of any such move. Aware of this, Aberdeen undeviatingly encouraged Castlereagh to pursue his aim, knowing how unlikely it was that any successor of his would do so. As to the terms of peace, he believed them unobjectionable, and felt that insistence on the limits of ancient pre-revolutionary France as a basis and *sine qua non* instead of her natural boundaries should satisfy the Foreign Secretary. 'As to making war against the man, it may become necessary, but must be hopeless so long as the people adhere to him,' he declared.[9]

In his desire for peace he was driven on by dread of what the mutual jealousies might bring forth. It was on February 28 that he wrote to Castlereagh that the enemy himself was less a source of danger than those self-destructive animosities, and that he could not too often labour 'the real state of the minds of those weak men by whom Europe is governed'.[10] Success might possibly bind them together, but adversity meant certain dissolution.

After Caulaincourt had kept everyone waiting for ten days he was given an ultimatum and another ten days' grace, while the conference was suspended. The plenipotentiaries could do nothing but wait in the midst of a hostile population. The French peasants were actually taking to arms and the townsfolk at Châtillon were going out in packs to hunt down stragglers and shoot them. By February 28 they had killed about forty Austrian soldiers between Châtillon and Dijon. 'They appear to be most enraged in the immediate neighbourhood of this place,' wrote Aberdeen in an almost jolly mood, 'and we are advised not to go far from the gates. The Mayor has published a most touching address to the inhabitants on our behalf, from which one would almost imagine them anthropophagi, and [that they] required much persuasion to prevent them from devouring us.'[11]

It was not until March 10 that Caulaincourt presented himself to the conference, and then only to bring a long list of objections to the allies' proposals. This time, however, he was facing a body of men who were far more united than before. On March 1 Castlereagh, by a combination of firmness, persuasiveness and bribery by huge subsidy, had succeeded in getting the four powers to sign the Treaty of Chaumont and it had been published the day before. They had entered into the sought-after Grand Alliance against Napoleon, to continue in force until twenty years after the war's end. There would be no separate peace treaties. They had also entered into a solidarity pact by which the four signatories guaranteed mutual security; and it was understood that those guarantees might later be extended to other European nations, including those freed from the French yoke. The Netherlands and Switzerland would be independent. A German confederacy of sovereign states would be established. The old order would be restored as far as possible in Italy. The Bourbon dynasty would re-ascend the Spanish throne. Finally, the allies had undertaken to keep in close contact with each other by meeting at intervals, and had decided that the first such congress would be held in Vienna. It was Castlereagh's grandest hour.

By March 10, too, Blücher had won the battles of Craonne and Laon, which were decisive in swinging the war to the allies, and in opening up the way to Paris. By then, too, the Czar and Castlereagh had come together in trust and liking. Castlereagh noted on March 5 in words ironically reminiscent of Aberdeen's in like circumstances, 'His Imperial Majesty now encourages me to come to him without form. I see him almost every day, and he receives me with great kindness and converses with me fully on all subjects'. Ironically, since the very sages who castigate Aberdeen for naïveté and weakness in succumbing to such flattering attentions from the Emperor Francis, Metternich and the Czar praise Castlereagh fulsomely for his skill in achieving valuable personal relationships as a foundation for future diplomatic association.

So Caulaincourt and his list of objections, though he fought as doggedly at Châtillon as Napoleon had done in the field, had short shrift. When the list was thrown out he substituted another one of the concessions which Napoleon was prepared to make – a list,

Aberdeen was convinced, drawn up not by Napoleon but by Caulaincourt himself at Châtillon.[12] This too was thrown out; and on March 13 he was given a 24-hour ultimatum to accept or reject the terms submitted to him, or to put up a counter-proposal. After some fencing Caulaincourt produced his counter-proposal within 48 hours. The plenipotentiaries also found this unsatisfactory, and rejected it. On that note the conference ended. On March 21 Aberdeen returned to allied headquarters. Four days later Caulaincourt accepted the allied terms as they stood.

It was too late. The allies' march on Paris had begun.

The allies had truly intended to make peace, at any rate at the earlier stage of the talks. In England the Government were less enthusiastic; but they too had been prepared to sign, and as late as March 21 Lord Liverpool had written Aberdeen a memorable letter:

'Peace, if it comes, will be most unpopular in this country. If it can be obtained, however, upon our own terms, I shall not fear the result. We shall have played a straight game, and it is a problem, to say the least, what may be the ultimate consequence of embarking in the war upon a new principle. We must not, however, lower our terms.'[13]

Ten days earlier Aberdeen's friend Lord Harrowby had written to him in chattier but no less convincing vein:

'If your terms were yesterday accepted we shall feel that we ought to be more glad than we are . . . Whatever other demerits we *blocks* may have, we have at least the merit of jogging on side by side with great cordiality. We shall all swing together whenever your signature at Châtillon, or elsewhere, brings us to the gallows, for nothing but "no peace with Bonaparte" is to be heard from Land's End to Berwick.'[14]

So Aberdeen's policy, to which he was unswervingly dedicated, of making peace was very unpopular in the country at large, and far from popular with his political friends. It had been accepted and adopted, none the less. Castlereagh had acted as he would himself have done, trying to preserve allied unity for the sake of peace, and turning to war again only when Napoleon had made any alternative impossible. In all this Castlereagh had worked hand in hand with Metternich.

Right up to the end of the Châtillon conference, Aberdeen, the negotiator, had been proceeding on the basis that when peace was made Napoleon would be reinstated as Emperor. When the negotiations ended in failure he, with others, began to consider a Bourbon restoration. Napoleon had played his cards badly. In view of his intractability the allies felt no compunction about making a new plan for Europe, perhaps without him.

There were various possibilities. Neither Austria nor the English Tories would entertain the thought of setting up another French republic. All the allies, including Francis of Austria, were unenthusiastic about establishing Marie Louise as regent for the King of Rome, who would become, in due course, the Emperor Napoleon II. Suddenly the Bourbons were in favour, even with Metternich. Public opinion in England was still violently against Napoleon. Liverpool himself, on hearing that Bordeaux had come out for the Bourbons, ordered Castlereagh to abandon any plans of making peace with him. The British opened negotiations at once with the Comte d'Artois, brother of Louis XVIII. The Czar, on the other hand, would have nothing to do with a Bourbon restoration. He had abandoned his plan to put Bernadotte on the throne of France, but he thoroughly disliked Louis XVIII, and would have much preferred to see his old friend-and-enemy, Napoleon, there.

Whatever the attitude of the bloodthirsty English, Aberdeen believed that the French wanted peace above all, and that their longing should be used in England's interest. 'We must show that the return of the Bourbons will bring peace,' he wrote from Dijon on March 29, 'and that without their return it is not attainable, in consequence of the ambition of Bonaparte.'[15] He also believed that, once convinced of that, the French would tolerate any prince or pretender who could promise them peace. He admitted that on this score he had changed his mind, but maintained that his principles and objectives were the same. In twelve years the lad who had been honoured to dine at the table of the First Consul had become the man who could have a say in whether to tumble him from his throne.

On March 30 the Czar led the victorious allied armies into Paris. Castlereagh and Metternich, determined not to be involved in the internal affairs of France, remained outside the city. The Emperor Francis, too, invidiously placed as the father of the absent Empress, stayed away. Talleyrand took charge of the Czar, and organized a national appeal to Louis XVIII to return to France as sovereign. On April 11, by the Treaty of Fontainebleau, Napoleon would receive the Island of Elba in exchange for his Empire.

On April 4 Aberdeen, at Dijon with the Austrian Emperor, Castlereagh and Metternich, had received the news of the capture of Paris and of the enemy's defeat on the same morning. 'All the principal personages from all the allied nations' had been dined by him, and they had worn the Bourbon white cockade.[16] 'The first toast I gave was Louis XVIII,' he recorded. But although he was now backing the Bourbons Aberdeen could not regard their restoration as anything but temporary. When the allies had entered Paris they had been given a welcome which had startled them, *'Vive la Paix! Vive les alliés! Vive qui voudra!'*[17]

It took six or seven weeks to conclude the peace treaty with France; and the first Peace of Paris was not signed until May 30. Most of Britain's main interests were secured. Only the immediate abolition of the slave-trade was not achieved.

Lord Aberdeen had accompanied the army to Paris as one of the plenipotentiaries for the settlement of the general treaty of peace. As Castlereagh was there his rôle in the negotiations could only be a subordinate one. Irked at being thus demoted among those with whom he had worked on a very different footing, he grew impatient once more to return to England. Castlereagh again overbore him, and he reluctantly remained in Paris until the treaty was signed.

It was an unhappy time for him. Equally disgusted with the insolence and treachery of Napoleon's generals and friends, with those who cried *'Vive Napoleon! Vive l'Empereur!'* within earshot of the King's carriage, and with such as Fouché who criticized the allies for leaving France too strong, he could hardly wait to put them all behind him.[18] While he waited he visited the Louvre frequently, and pleaded successfully that the works of art Napoleon had looted from foreign cities should remain in Paris rather than suffer the risk of damage from further journeyings. The French had hidden them in the cellars of the Louvre, cynically displaying bad copies to the public.[19]

As soon as the treaty was signed he set off for England, taking it with him in his carriage. His complex and exhausting task had been done and, he believed, well done. In the particularly difficult circumstances of being appreciated and lauded by strangers while blamed and nagged by colleagues he had soldiered on valiantly. He had remained to see ideas, attitudes and policies for which he had been consistently rebuked largely adopted and successful, but had then had to watch the rewards being bestowed on others.

He had left England on 10 August 1813. He arrived back on 31 May 1814. He had been away for under ten months. He had undergone a baptism of fire. He had been indiscreet, made errors of judgement, sometimes trusted too much. But no disaster had come of such shortcomings. Murat had not been given the kingdom of Naples, and Castlereagh had wiped maritime rights from the agenda. The shy, reluctant and inexperienced young man who had embarked on his formidable task had to his credit achievements which were considerable and even remarkable. The opinion of the late Professor R. W. Seton-Watson was that he had 'had only less influence on the final settlement than Castlereagh and Wellington'.[20] He returned from those ten months a changed man. Forty years thence, as Prime Minister of England, he would see the nation for which he was responsible being sucked into another great war. His motives and his actions in those vital days would be of the utmost importance, and the experiences of the young Aberdeen during these grim ten months profoundly and dramatically affected his country's history.

Chapter 9

'Most Dear and Sweet Love'

When Aberdeen arrived in London on 31 May 1814 he found that
Argyll House had not been made ready for him, and went straight
on to Lord Harrowby's house in Grosvenor Square.* There he
heard that Viscount Hamilton, Catherine's brother and heir to the
Abercorn marquesate, had died three days before. After five years
of marriage Harriet, whom Aberdeen had found 'rather well looking . . . but certainly one of the most stupid persons I ever met
with', was left alone with her two sons, James, three, and Claud,
ten months, and a daughter, Harriet.[1]

Aberdeen was still hoping that Anne Cavendish would consent
to marry him. Now, however, Lady Maria was dead and he had
no one to help him. He was affected too by his formidable father-
in-law's opposition to the Whig connection. Arthur Gordon suggested that this 'strong-willed despot'[2] actually misled Aberdeen
about the attitude of the Cavendishs to his proposal of marriage,
so Aberdeen did not repeat it. Still rather bruised, though he was
given a United Kingdom viscountcy and made a privy councillor
in June in recognition of his ambassadorship, and feeling rejected
in both personal and public spheres, he was in a particularly
vulnerable state.

What Abercorn wanted was a match between his son's widow
and his daughter's widower. His son's and his daughter's orphans
would be united in the bosom of one family, in which he would
still be the patriarch. In theory it was an admirable arrangement,
especially with so kind and dutiful a son-in-law in whose hands
to place Abercorn's new heir, James, the infant Lord Hamilton,
and one which would remove all misgivings about an unsuitable
husband for Harriet and stepfather for his grandchildren.

Fortune smiled on Abercorn's plans, for Harriet was already in
love with the handsome Aberdeen, and, it is said, pursued him
shamelessly. Too tender-hearted not to be racked with sympathy
for her and her orphaned children, and too fond of his own little

* Now number 44.

daughters not to wish to give them a new mother, Aberdeen also had no heir, as his father-in-law would not fail to remind him. Even so it is on record that Abercorn had a good deal of trouble with his son-in-law before he finally got his way.[3]

It was while Napoleon was making his escape from Elba and advancing towards Paris that these family tangles were being unravelled. On 8 July 1815 Lord Aberdeen and Lady Hamilton were married at Bentley Priory. Less than a month before, Aberdeen's brother, Lieutenant-Colonel Sir Alexander Gordon, by then a KCB and holder of ten medals (including the Gold Cross with three clasps for his services at the battles of Salamanca, Vitoria, Pyrenees, Nivelle, Alva, Orthes and Toulouse), had been mortally wounded at the battle of Waterloo while actually expostulating with Wellington about the danger to which the Duke was exposing himself.[4] The Duke, roused from sleep at about three in the morning, 'to go and see poor Gordon', who was dying in another room in the same inn at Waterloo, had found him already dead.[5] In the very hour of his triumph the 'man without a heart' had sat down to write to Aberdeen of the death of the most favoured of all those 'gay fellows',[6] his ADCs, and his letter is still cherished at Haddo House.

Brussels June 19th 1815

'My dear Lord

'You will readily give credit to the existence of the extreme grief with which I announce to you the death of your gallant brother, in consequence of a wound received in our great battle of yesterday.

'He had served me most zealously and usefully for many years, and on many trying occasions, but he had never rendered himself more useful, and had never distinguished himself more than in our late actions. He received the Wound which occasioned his death when rallying one of the Brunswick Battal[ns] which was shaking a little; and he lived long enough to be informed by myself of the glorious result of our actions to which he had so much contributed by his active and zealous assistance.

'I cannot express to you the regret and sorrow with which I look round me, and contemplate the loss which I have sustained, particularly in your brother. The glory resulting from such actions so dearly bought is no consolation to me, and I cannot suggest it as any to you, and his friends; but I hope that it may be expected that this last one has been so decisive as that no doubt remains that our exertions and our individual losses will be rewarded by the early attainment of our first object. It is then that the glory of the actions in which our friends and relations have fallen will be some consolation to us for their loss.

'Believe me my dear Lord
                    Yours most sincerely
                              Wellington

'Your brother had a black horse given to him I believe by Lord Ashburnham, which I will keep till I hear from you what you wish should be done with it.'[7]

Sir Walter Scott would immortalize the hero's end in his poem 'The Fall of Sir Alexander Gordon', and Aberdeen would cherish a copy of it, and leave behind drafts of the inscription on the monument which his family raised on the battlefield in memory of Sir Alexander – the only British monument on the field of Waterloo, commemorating in English and French this most gallant of soldiers. 'In testimony of feelings which no language can express,' it reads, 'a disconsolate sister and five surviving brothers have erected this simple memorial to the object of their tenderest affection.'[8] A replica was raised, too, at Haddo House.

It was a very emotional time, and the whole Gordon family, despite their mourning, must have been stirred by the excitement of Napoleon's arrival in Paris on June 20, his forced abdication in favour of the King of Rome on the 21st, and the entry of Louis XVIII on July 8, Aberdeen's wedding day. Only two days before Napoleon had thrown himself on the mercy of England, and on the very day had sailed for Plymouth in the *Bellerophon*.

The following year Harriet gave Aberdeen his heir George, Lord Haddo, the year after that she produced another son, Alexander, and the year after that a daughter, Frances. Two more sons, Douglas and Arthur, who was named after Wellington, would be born in 1824 and 1829.

However lukewarm Aberdeen had been about the marriage, he meant to make a success of it. In fact, he seems to have approached it in much the spirit with which he had attacked his disappointing inheritance. His conscience was clear, and he gave Harriet his heart, or as much of it as he could. He was a generous husband, and an affectionate one, anxious to share his life, and nearly all his thoughts, with her. It soon became clear, however, that Harriet was disappointed and resentful. Despite his pleas, and in unhappy contrast to Catherine, who had gone with him notwithstanding her yearly pregnancies, she refused to go to Haddo. Stubbornly Aberdeen set out every summer on his uncomfortable and expensive week-long journey,* travelling eighty miles a day, to live like a bachelor, as often as not with one or two of his bachelor brothers, John, Charles and William, while Harriet enjoyed vague ill-health among the attractions of Brighton. Rising early, he might do seven to nine hours' hard physical labour like tree-planting, or take walks about the estate for up to seven hours. A fine mile-long avenue already stretched from the house to a hill on the eastern side, and a large artificial lake smiled where there had been bog; new roads ran everywhere; and there were flower-beds and terraces. On the nine hundred farms substantial new farmhouses and granite outbuildings rose. Woods were beginning to flourish. There were always more mosses to be drained and wastes to be planted. Now, too, Aberdeen laid out a new garden, paying £1200 for the foundations, and built a hothouse for an estimated £2000. Indoors he erected two staircases and carried out alterations. 'I can tell you,' he wrote to Harriet on 6 September 1822, 'that if I have ten years more I shall make this really a fine place.' He established pheasants, and shot them, and partridges, and fat bucks. He caught trout in the Ythan. He paid off debts, and tried to collect heavy arrears on the £22,000 annual rent-roll. He gave up wine, and lived on a cold partridge for breakfast and a hot one for dinner at 6.30. The two captains fell asleep immediately afterwards, 'sulky' John silently, 'good humoured' William snoring 'vociferously', and Sir Charles played his flute in his bedroom to the discomfiture of Aberdeen. Uncomplainingly he suffered in silence, and himself only went to bed exhausted at midnight. He wrote daily letters to Harriet, insisting on his love for her and how much he needed her in his bed; but he dismissed her 'aches and pains' as not being 'anything of consequence'. She had to be nagged into replying, and in their letters the word 'dismal' re-echoes miserably.[9]

In London it was the same. Harriet often left him alone at Bentley Priory or Argyll House to nurse his three daughters by Catherine, who were frequently ill. He took their pulses and their temperatures, administered calomel, James's powder and salts, consulted doctors, and clutched at advice.[10] When he was away he wrote to Harriet, begging her 'to paste down the windows of Alice's

---

* Even in the 1840s, as Jarnac found, an autumn journey to Haddo from London, making all possible speed, took five days, and involved 'sur mer la tempête, sur terre les ouragans de neige'. (Révue des Deux Mondes, Vol. XXXIV, p. 446.)

room with strong paper, as I remember to have seen done at Carlton House. There is no occasion for them ever to open, as there is a little closet with a window in it, which when opened will sufficiently air the room. Perhaps strips of cloth nailed down will be better than paper, in consequence of the wet'. The lady from Chelsea who shut up her (fortunately robust) six sons and one daughter in the house from mid-November to mid-February, only letting them out on fine days, seemed wise to him.[11] According to family legend, during the winter the three girls, then fifteen, fourteen and thirteen, worked at embroidering splendid, dark, full curtains for the long windows of the dining-room at Haddo House. To this day the delicate stitches bear witness to the innumerable hours which must have been spent on them. His fourth daughter, Frances, was then only four.

Husband and wife were still too much apart in 1820. That year the doctors began to speak of tuberculosis, and contemplated even more severe confinement for his daughterss than the lady from Chelsea – from the beginning of November to the beginning of April. His own letters to the thirteen-year-old Jane were poignant and tender, for she was very ill; but her stepmother wrote to her in a vein which was either obtuse or cruel. She emphasized the lingering and dangerous nature of the child's illness, piously suggested that God might make her recover, and added, 'but the probabilities I am bound to say appear against it'. She then told Jane plainly that she was going to die, ordered her not to dwell on it, and signed this remarkable document cheerfully, 'Bless you, my dearest, H. Aberdeen'.[12]

The marriage would last for eighteen years; but it proved full of pain for them both. Harriet's own son Arthur, while conceding that she was a strikingly handsome woman, would say with chilly precision that 'the new Lady Aberdeen had not the dazzling beauty of her predecessor, nor was she her intellectual equal'.[13] He claimed, however, that she was devoted to her husband and that they grew closer with the years, which was a pleasant way of glossing over the deep and long-lasting difficulties which strained their relationship. Aberdeen's new wife was a passionate and not very attractive personality, especially when contrasted with that unspoiled charmer, his first.

Lord Abercorn had made his arrangements none too soon, for he died less than three years after the marriage. He left Aberdeen a large share of his personal property and named him as guardian of the infant Marquess. Soon after, by royal licence dated 13 November 1818, Aberdeen adopted the surname of Hamilton-

Gordon, 'as a last memorial of his respect for the memory of his late father-in-law, John James, Marquis of Abercorn, KG'.[14] For the next sixteen years the Priory would be Lord Aberdeen's home.[15] It was a great asset to him, for, as it was close to London, he was able to entertain there a constant stream of useful and distinguished people from the worlds of literature, art and public life. In October 1813 he had written to Abercorn from Gera, 'On the whole it is the place I like best in the world. My own place in Scotland has many charms, but not of so powerful a kind'.[16] He would go to Haddo House only in the summer; but an obsessive love for it had begun to take root.

Aberdeen could not but be aware that something was very wrong with his marriage. In September 1822, lonely and depressed by Harriet's refusal to join him even for the glittering occasion of the King's visit to Scotland, when he learned that Castlereagh had had a mental breakdown and had cut his throat, the shock was great to him.[17] The trouble lay in Harriet's resentment of his attentions to his own daughters. She had seen from close quarters how well Aberdeen could love a woman, and must have yearned for what he had given to her dead sister-in-law. But Aberdeen had never had any intention of allowing her into his innermost heart. There only one woman reigned and would reign until his death. Even when he had thought of marrying his Whig lady he had written to Lady Maria, 'Most undoubtedly, as long as I live, I shall believe that I have seen human nature under a form in which it never before existed. My heart must be more than metaphorically cold before this feeling can ever be changed or forgotten'.[18] Now his extravagant mourning for his dead wife continued unabated, and he made no attempt to conceal his sense of irreparable loss. Stung by this contemptuous rejection of her love, as she must have seen it, Harriet reacted violently. She lashed out, seeking to wound him where he was most vulnerable, behaving like the traditional stepmother towards his three lovely but fragile daughters, Jane, Caroline and Alice, who were all he had left to remind him of Catherine.

In the event it was Aberdeen's second child, Caroline, and not Jane, who first died of tuberculosis, after long suffering. His love and concern for his two remaining girls, Jane and Alice, became feverish. Instead of growing kinder, Harriet seemed to be driven almost out of her mind at the sight of this dogged and fearful devotion. So tigerish and irrational did she become at this period that her behaviour was often abnormal. Aberdeen found himself in a nightmarish situation. His two surviving children needed him as never before, yet the woman whom he had sworn to love and cherish seemed to have become a monster who demanded that he turn his back on them. Before spite, pettiness and neurosis he was always at a loss. In trying to combat them he continued to use the arguments by which he set store – reason, Christianity, loving-kindness, self-respect – but unavailingly. The story is painful – a classic example of the your-children-and-my-children-and-our-children syndrome frequent in modern divorce situations, with overtones reminiscent of Grimm's fairy-tales – but it gives an unexampled opportunity of appraising the man. The letters which he wrote to his wife from Haddo at this time illumine him as no public records can do. The private man was also the public man.

The issue which brought matters to a head in 1822, seven years after his marriage, was, ludicrously enough, that his eldest daughter, fifteen-year-old Jane, had at one time been guilty of bullying her little Hamilton cousins. Harriet was insisting that legal steps should be taken to ensure that if she died Jane would have no control over her cousins and stepsisters. I reproduce here extracts from three letters, hitherto unpublished, which her husband wrote to her. They are kind, reasonable, and above all just. Aberdeen even agrees that Harriet is entitled to her pound of flesh if she wishes to exact it. But he uses some strong words, 'hatred' and 'bitterness' among them, and does not fail to threaten that she will lose his love if she persists in her demand.

On 30 August 1822, the day after the King had re-embarked for England, he wrote from Haddo House:

'My dearest love,

'. . . The whole is so strange and unaccountable that when I view the thing deliberately I can scarcely think it possible . . . My whole wish and desire are confined to one word – "Be kind." If you answer in substance "I hate your child, and therefore I cannot be kind," you must not be surprised if I am not quite satisfied. When you say that if you were to behave to Jane for a week precisely as you do to Harriet [her daughter] I should not like it, I can only say that if you punished her ten times a day in the severest manner, so that it arose from the same maternal regard, I could have no objection. The feelings of tenderness which accompanied the severity would be quite sufficient, whether the act itself was judicious or not.

'But what I have to complain of is the declared and avowed hatred of a stepmother. Now when I married you, although I certainly had no right to expect that my children would meet

101

with equal love, yet I had good reason to suppose that they would never be regarded *with indignation and disgust*. When you tell me that it is all my own fault; that I have always been unjust to you on this subject; and that I do not view it impartially; the case remains exactly the same. Your hatred is just as cruel and unnatural.

'I say this in the supposition of all your opinions of character being perfectly correct, and that you are not influenced by prejudice. But I think if I were to assume the existence of all these bad qualities in one of your children, and then justify myself by this for my feelings of hatred, it would not meet with your acquiescence. I do not require a tenth part of the love for my children which I willingly accord to yours; I only ask for as much as I should have felt for them if I had never beheld you . . . Dearest, I write in sorrow, but not in anger; on the contrary, at this moment my heart turns towards you swelling with love and tenderness. God bless you, ever your most affec.

A.'[19]

Ten days later he wrote again in answer to a letter from her which has not survived.

'My dearest love . . . The first thing that strikes me is, even if everything you say about Jane is perfectly accurate, that my happiness and her welfare are sacrificed merely to a spirit of resentment. For it cannot be pretended that she tyrannises over and oppresses your children now. If I admit that she may, a child herself, have exercised a sort of dominion over those who were younger, the thing is not uncommon, and is sure to cease with childhood; it ought not to be viewed in the light in which you see it; and it would not be more unreasonable in me to consider the tyranny of James and Claud [her sons] over George [their son] in the same way.

'You speak of her influence over me. I know when such a notion has taken possession of the mind how impossible it is to combat it; but how is this influence shown? Has she had the art to make me hate your children? Or what has she accomplished by it? I can only solemnly protest against its existence.

'I am aware that *your* children are in some degree the innocent cause of your hatred of *mine*; but I trust I should always be too just to visit them with resentment for it. You really give way too far to these feelings which every sense of religion and duty ought to check – I would add, which sentiments of love might soften . . .

'You mention my anxiety about Alice. I am really aware of no other than was dictated by an opinion of her weakness and delicacy. Surely the narrow escape she has had from death, if she be destined to escape at present, may in some degree have justified it. I have lost one, under circumstances which I shall not easily forget, and if ever you are placed in a similar situation you will perhaps learn how to feel for me.

'You have also mentioned the possibility of your death, and what you should feel in leaving your children exposed to the influence of one whom you believe to hate them. But here too I must implore of you to place yourself in my situation. My life may be terminated as speedily as yours; and just think how the bitterness of that moment would be increased by the conviction of my leaving mine, not exposed to an influence, the operation of which is more than doubtful, but to an open undisguised hatred on the part of her who is bound by every tie to cherish and protect them.

'But, really, when you speak of this influence, and when I examine my own feelings about your children, and know that I would give my right hand to serve them, that I love them, and have the same interest and pride in them as if they were my own, it seems most marvellous to me . . . Feeling as I do towards your children, and ardently desiring to hold you to my heart, and to repose in your arms full of love and confidence, it is quite vexatious to think that anything should arise which admits of control to diminish that happiness . . .'[20]

Harriet was not to be moved, though in his next letter he sends her partridges, again speaks of the joy of holding her in his arms, and ends, 'As you like to hear it, and in the hope that it will make up for other matters, I will tell you, most dear and sweet love, I love you most ardently and long to kiss and embrace you ten thousand times'.[21] Three days later he is writing again, stiffly and very firmly indeed.

'As you make your request seriously, I will only say that although I am not conscious of the possibility of its being neces-sary – nor is it any great mark of your confidence – I have no hesitation in declaring that it shall not only be strictly executed to the letter but that the spirit of it shall pervade every considera-tion connected with the subject. In making this declaration, I do it with the solemnity of all that is most sacred and binding on

103

man. I will just add that the first part of your request shall be granted the instant you please to put it in execution. If you wish it to be done, you have only to say so.

'And now, my love, if my fate should be that which you have anticipated for yourself, how am I to diminish its bitterness? To whom am I to look, and what promise can I exact? Alas! I can only trust that my death may soften the cruelty of those feelings which have hitherto been proof against every other consideration.

'You tell me in your letter that I must be reasonable, and not suppose that Jane's happiness is what we are to live for only, which seems to you to be the case now. Is this fair, is this just, is it kind? Really, her happiness is scarcely in question. My object is to remove the hatred of a person in the situation of a mother for one who is in the situation of a child. Is this unnatural, or is it unreasonable?'[22]

That was on September 20. Two years after that letter was written Jane died. She was eighteen, and had just come out. Her illness lasted for only a few hours. Now his eldest child, who as a little girl of seven had been deeply distressed at his leaving her for the Napoleonic campaigns, the 'dearest Jane' to whom he had written such frequent and loving letters, the 'lovely Lady Jane' of the birthday ode, was gone. Her death was a deadly blow to her adoring father.

The fifteen-year-old Alice had already suffered several long and painful illnesses, and she was now growing rapidly weaker. Aberdeen gave up public life almost entirely in order to spend every moment with her that he could. He spent the next three winters with her at Nice, consciously looking his last on her. In the winter of 1824–5 Aberdeen cosseted Alice unceasingly, travelling in easy stages, and writing home to Harriet in agitation about her getting a cold and the swelling of her legs and feet. He arranged to take a house at Nice for six months for 150 louis, including plate, linen and crockery, the equivalent of under five guineas a week. He engaged a drawing master for Alice, and planned to get her a music master when her stepmother arrived, as she did in due course.[23]

The following winter presented direr problems. The diary Alice kept in November and December of 1825 is a moving record of her father's tenderness, and his success in keeping the delicate girl as well and happy as could be. She seemed as bubbling, as observant, and as delighted in his company as her mother had been, as she wrote of walking with him among the chrysanthemums in the Tuileries, of noticing that the royal initials effaced during the revolution had been reinstated, with the Ns replaced by Ls, and of how very ugly she found the sheep in the south of France.[24]

By mid-December, however, Harriet was writing to complain about 'agitation of mind, stomach, and nerves', and Aberdeen was begging her to 'endeavour to tranquillize' herself, and either prepare for joining him in a reasonable time, or, if she did not feel able to do so, make it clear whether she wanted him back in England with her.[25] Alice was far from well, suffering from a cold, a severe cough, fever, swellings, and pain, as well as from the new symptom of expectoration, and some lameness.[26] By January 29 Aberdeen had realized that he would have to go home to his jealous wife, but was desperately playing for time, saying that he would stay on to see Alice's cough abated for a few days, then start for home. No pleas of how unpleasant it was to leave her in that 'unsatisfactory and uncertain state', and 'in a strange country, with no person the least connected with her, or caring about her', with only servants in whom he felt no great confidence about her, and yet in such a condition that it was better not to move her, availed.[27] Nor did his assurances to Harriet that it was only such fears which worried him, 'and not the mere pain of parting from her: for most certainly the pain of separation which I experienced in leaving you was a hundred times greater than I shall feel in leaving her. I cannot conceal from myself that she is in a helpless situation . . . I felt it to be my duty to bring her here, and I now feel it my duty without any hesitation to leave her; and most certainly the effect which you say that the prospect of my coming has produced on you, amply repays me'.[28]

Two days later, after receiving a letter from Harriet, the harassed husband was again seeking to justify himself to her: 'It is true I may have lamented the impossibility of uniting two things perfectly incompatible, viz. the power of being in two places at once. I may also have said that the state of your health, and especially of your spirits, made it quite imperative on me to go to England, unless in a case of imminent danger here. And you will do me the justice to admit that I have never for a moment appeared to hesitate about it'. There was, he noted, 'a sort of dryness' in her letter, 'as if you thought it possible I could be in any degree to blame'.[29]

Harriet had her way, and on February 10 Aberdeen left Nice, fretting all the way to Paris because of the lack of news of the sick girl, and the danger of leaving her for two or three months 'with no friend or relative in a strange country, without many resources'. He never stopped to dine, in order to lose no time on the journey back, eating a cold fowl in the carriage when he was hungry.[30]

From Paris, on February 21, writing from the Meurice, Aberdeen was still trying to assuage Harriet's jealousy: 'I do not at all regret leaving Nice in the way you seem to imagine. It is not the least that I care about the separation from Alice, as I do from you. I only care about the possible contingencies which may happen in a strange place without friends, connections, or even very good advice of any kind. It is this interest only that I feel, and not the *personal pain* of separation, as I do from you. Therefore my sweetest Love, be satisfied'. And he bought her some white dinner plates, as she did not like his blue Staffordshire ones. Harriet had succeeded in reducing him to a pitiable state, and, domestically at least, almost depriving him of dignity. He had only one comfort as he made his way home. Captain John, his difficult brother, might be able to travel out and fetch the sick girl home.[31]

So, terribly torn, Aberdeen watched the last of his three daughters slipping away from him. With her would go his last blood tie with their mother.

While Aberdeen's eyes were turned inwards on his family life, time sped by. Fourteen years would have passed before he again went about the nation's business. He hardly spoke in Parliament. He was obliged to attend the scabrous and degrading 'trial' in the Lords in 1820 of the new King George IV's Queen Caroline. All summer Aberdeen sweltered in London while the 250 peers who had been unable to excuse themselves as aged, infirm, abroad or Catholic[32] considered the Bill of Pains and Penalties, since to absent himself would have cost him a hundred pounds for each of the first three days and fifty pounds for every successive one. His attitude seems to have been one of mournful neutrality. By October 18 he was writing to his wife from Argyll House, 'The business in the House of Lords seems to be as bad as possible'.[33] Two days later he tells her of the possibility of a 'sudden termination of the Queen's business', adding, 'It is difficult to say what is the best way, or rather the least bad, for it to end'.[34] His name does not appear in the *Hansard* lists of contents or non-contents, or in the three lists of dissentients, so he evidently abstained from voting. After coming near to destroying the government the Bill was withdrawn in November.

In 1821 Queen Caroline was turned away from the Coronation. At the ensuing banquet in Westminster Hall George IV all but fainted, and was revived by the vinaigrette of Aberdeen's sister, now by royal courtesy permitted to be addressed as Lady Alicia. Less than a month later Queen Caroline, to everyone's shamed relief, died. The conclusion of her 'trial' had left the way open for a renewal of the Roman Catholic controversy, and the House of Commons for the first time gave its approval to a measure of emancipation. The bill was defeated in the Lords.

In that year Aberdeen showed signs of again taking an active interest in foreign politics. Castlereagh, in an effort to heal the 1814 breach, tried to prevail on him to go to Vienna as one of the plenipotentiaries at the Congress, but in vain. Castlereagh continued to consult him privately about major decisions, and sent despatches for his comments, frankly acknowledging that Aberdeen had been more right in the past than he about Russia. So when in 1821 Castlereagh proposed sending a despatch to St Petersburg, deprecating Russian hostilities against the Porte and pressing the Czar to take no part in the Greek insurrection, he sent it to Aberdeen. Aberdeen's reply, in the light of his actions in 1829 and in 1833, makes interesting reading. To him war was inevitable, the Czar must intervene, and the Greek rebellion would sanctify the cause because of the atrocious sufferings of the Sultan's Christian subjects. He chafed at Castlereagh's cautiousness, but failed to inspire him with any crusading spirit. He even attended a meeting to whip up support for the Greeks, and shocked the government into vehement protest at his lending his name to such activities. Aberdeen subsided. Alice was now very ill. When he was not nursing his sick child he worked on an essay, *Enquiry into the Principles of Beauty in Greek Architecture*, which had appeared anonymously in 1812 as a preface to a translation of *Vitruvius* by William Wilkins. This essay would be published as a separate, highly regarded work in 1822. He had abandoned modern for ancient Greece.

So Aberdeen's sad and largely detached days passed while the nation's economic distress grew so general that cabinet ministers took a ten per cent cut in salary. Alice was growing iller, and he gave less and less thought to anything outside her sick-room. He was sufficiently interested to attend the Lords in mid-May 1825 for the heated debate on Burdett's Relief Bill for the Catholics, to sit up all night, and vote with the minority of contents, before the House adjourned at half past five in the morning. The Bill was thrown out by a majority of forty-eight.[35] The previous year he had found time and energy to introduce a bill on Scottish entails, by which a life tenant might break the entail in order to make provision for his dependants.[36]

While distress continued with the smashing of power-looms, and after a general election in a famine year to the cries of 'No Popery!' and 'Corn!', the Government 'opened the ports' to allow in cheap foreign corn. In February 1827 Liverpool was paralysed by a stroke, and the Tory party, lost and rudderless without his wise and skilful leadership, split into the 'ultras' or die-hards, intransigent against reform, and the more accommodating Canningites. When the King was pushed into appointing Canning Prime Minister, Peel, Wellington and many other Tories resigned rather than serve under him. Canning asked Aberdeen to join his cabinet; and Aberdeen refused.

On the face of it this was a surprising decision. Aberdeen's views approximated closely to those of the Canningites, since he believed in removing the Catholic disabilities and in a moderate amount of parliamentary reform, and was in sympathy with Canning's view of the Graeco-Turkish troubles. He may have refused office partly because of personal mistrust of Canning, and partly because of his intimate friendship with Wellington,* now totally inimical to Canning. At any rate, Aberdeen's decision not to join Canning proved a fortunate one for him.

When Canning died in August after his 'hundred days' the King kept the Canningites in power under Goderich, and Aberdeen watched from the sick-room while he made his 'transient and embarrassed' flight across the forefront of the stage of history. Doubtless he drew a breath of relief when in October Codrington sent the fleet of Britain's Turkish ally to the bottom of Navarino Bay and saved the Greeks. In January 1828 King George IV dismissed Goderich, and, forgiving Wellington for his desertion, invited him to form a government. Wellington offered Aberdeen the Foreign Office, and this time he did not refuse. Even Alice's health did not hold him back, for she seemed much better.

Things did not go smoothly, however. Against all likelihood the Canningites, so recently castigated by the Tories for joining a coalition with Whigs, now (to the rage of Canning's widow) struck a bargain with Wellington as to the terms on which they would leave Canning's Whiggish friends and rejoin the Tories. Palmerston would stay on as Secretary at War, and the question of Catholic Emancipation would be left open, with members of the Government free to speak on either side as in Liverpool's day. Dudley

* 'Le duc de Wellington, son intime ami.' (*Révue des Deux Mondes*, Vol. XXXIV, p. 447.)

was to stay at the Foreign Office, overwhelmed though he was by the work, and rapidly approaching mental breakdown, so as to ensure a Canningite foreign policy. Wellington asked Aberdeen to support him until he was ready to go, meanwhile accepting the nominal office of Chancellor of the Duchy of Lancaster, but in effect bearing the brunt at the Foreign Office. Dudley welcomed Aberdeen amiably enough, calling him his *coadjutor jure successionis*.[37]

The ultras who had gone out with Wellington in April 1827 had been expecting to come back with him in January 1828, and there were many offended Tory paladins forced out by the Canningites. Perhaps the compliment of the offer of a place in this cabinet was greatest to Aberdeen, the newcomer with fourteen years of almost complete inactivity behind him, and a Presbyterian dissenter who had a casting vote as a 'Catholic' in a cabinet of 13 dividing 7 to 6 in favour of Catholic Emancipation.[38]

That year Alice grew worse, and it was clear that the end was not far off. Aberdeen spent every moment he could with her. As soon as he came through the door of his home he hurried straight to the side of the dying girl. Everything that doctors and nursing could do was done.

The coalition with the Canningites could not last. Twice within three months the Cabinet nearly split up. In February Lord John Russell moved the repeal of the symbolic, if ineffective, old Test and Corporation Acts, by which all members of corporations had to pass a 'sacramental test', that is, receive communion in the Church of England. Wellington, against the inclination of the 'Catholic' Canningites, opposed repeal on the grounds that in fact dissenters were already able to join corporations without taking the test because of existing legal indemnities, and also because abolition would in his view weaken the Church of England. However, in the Commons Russell's motion was carried by 237 votes to 193 – a significant move towards Catholic Emancipation. The Government then itself repealed the Test and Corporation Acts.

Then in March there was a four-day-long wrangle in the Cabinet between Wellington, supported by Aberdeen, and the Canningite Huskisson as to the extent by which the duty on corn should be relaxed, ending in an unhappy compromise. The details of the Corn Bill were finally agreed.[39]

It was the question as to whether the representation of the vacant seat of the disfranchised rotten borough of East Retford should be transferred to a large industrial town to please the reformers, or to one of the adjacent hundreds to please the ultras, which brought about the final break in May. At 2 a.m. on May 20, after Huskisson and Palmerston had abstained on the East Retford (Absorption) Bill, Huskisson wrote a letter to Wellington apparently offering his resignation, and Wellington accepted it. Under pressure from Dudley and Palmerston, Huskisson then claimed that he had not intended to resign, but Wellington replaced him, and the Canningites, including Dudley, departed *en masse*.[40] (It is at least interesting, however, that John Cam Hobhouse wrote in his diary on 1 June 1828: 'Lord Aberdeen told my friend David Baillie that the real cause of difference between Huskisson and the Duke was anything but the East Retford question. They had long been wrangling in the Cabinet, and Lord Aberdeen added that Huskisson had no right to complain that he had not been treated with great deference, for he always had been'.[41])

Now at last Aberdeen was able to assume the title as well as the work of Foreign Secretary. For him, however, that triumph could not have come at a worse time. On 29 April 1829, at the age of twenty, Alice had drawn her last breath. Her anguished father had held her clasped to his breast for hours, and she had died in his arms. His grief was terrible. For days afterwards he had shut himself up in the Foreign Office, absolutely alone. Nearly eighty years later there would be an echo of this terrible mourning when Lloyd George, newly created President of the Board of Trade, would shut himself up in his office, refusing to return to his Wandsworth home, and rage against the heavens for the death of his adolescent daughter Mair Eilund. Harriet's harsh attitude towards her stepdaughter had long been softened, but her husband did not allow her to share his grief. Now all his Catherine's children were dead, her infant son and her three daughters. Nothing remained to him of that marriage but his memories, and he clung fiercely to those, alone in his inconsolable sorrow.

Chapter 10

Foreign Secretary

Aberdeen was forty-four when he became Foreign Secretary for the first time. His close friend and great admirer Sir Robert Peel had a picture of him with his seals of office painted by Lawrence, and gave it pride of place, hanging it above his desk in his library at Whitehall Gardens, so that he could always see it as he worked. It was 'certainly the finest portrait in the world', Peel told his wife Julia in 1830.[1] Lawrence painted a loving portrait of an outstandingly handsome man, amazingly young for his age, with curling dark hair, eyes alive with intelligence, and lips about to break into a smile. His clothes are rich, if sombre, the cravat almost a dandy's. Gone is the romantic Byronic boy of the earlier Lawrence, with swirling cloak and bared throat, his place taken by a spare man hardened by experience and full of confidence. Lawrence said of his portrait of Aberdeen's dead Catherine, 'The picture of Lady Aberdeen is like music in my mind all the time'.[2] Here the gently-smiling Aberdeen seems to be thinking of his lost love; and probably was. He was still wearing mourning for her sixteen years after her death.

The two years Aberdeen spent at the Foreign Office, seventeen months of them as Foreign Secretary, were ones of great tension because of momentous events in Europe, with France involved wherever there was trouble. Greatest of the crises with which he had to deal were war between Russia and Turkey, the 1830 revolution in France, and rebellion in the Netherlands. In each Britain played a major rôle.

First came the inherited war between Russia and Turkey.

On 20 October 1827 an English, Russian and French combined fleet, still manoeuvring in Greek waters as a result of Canning's policy and the Treaty of London of 6 July 1827, though Britain was not at war with Turkey, had had an unlooked-for confrontation with the Turkish and Egyptian fleets. The British Admiral and Commander-in-Chief, Codrington, had sent the two navies to the bottom of the Bay of Navarino, a decisive factor in the battle for Greek independence. Despite the British public's delight in the breezy affair the King's speech at the beginning of the new Wellington Government, on 29 January 1828, had referred to it as 'this untoward event'. The opposition had promptly moved a resolution congratulating the admiral on his brilliant victory, and on behalf of the Government Palmerston, the Secretary at War, had lamely explained that 'untoward' meant 'unexpected'.

Wellington's Government was deeply divided about policy towards Greece, and the ministers, as Princess Lieven wrote caustically to her brother, blackguarded each other 'like draymen'.[3] The Greeks turned to Russia, and on 18 December 1827 the Sultan, astonishingly, weak as he was, declared war on Russia. On 26 April 1828 Russia at length declared war on Turkey. The Greeks' brave struggle for freedom from the cruel Turk had commanded great sympathy in Britain, and Byron was only the most famous and articulate of the British volunteers who had responded heroically to the call. Canning's policy had been to offer mediation and associate Britain with France and Russia, in the hope of helping the Greeks without going to war. For Wellington, much less enthusiastic about the Greeks, the important thing was to keep Turkey strong enough to hold Russia at bay. Palmerston, even more pro-Greek than Canning, did not hesitate to set himself against his chief, and the two differed frequently in cabinet. The Greek rebels were in occupation of the Morea peninsula, and Wellington's objects were to reduce and limit the new Greek state to that parcel of land and push up Greece's compensation to Turkey for property confiscated by her. Palmerston opposed him on both, even supporting the Russians in their pro-Greek negotiations, and urging Wellington to make Capodistrias – leader of the Greek national revolt, and a Russian who had actually been Foreign Secretary at St Petersburg – the first head of a provisional government. He incited his brother William in St Petersburg to make Russia aware of the quarrels in the cabinet about policy.

With his long-standing sympathy for the Christian Greeks, and strong distaste for the barbarous Turks, Aberdeen was as certain as ever that it was in Europe's interest that England should help the Greeks to independence rather than that Russia should be allowed to increase her influence by doing so. At one with Wellington in his dread of Russian expansion and his desire to protect the Mediterranean and Britain's communications with the Near and Middle East, he supported him in his meticulous adherence to the letter of the law, if not in his Turkish sympathies. Turkey, he believed, should be sustained until the Balkan Christians could provide a substitute more acceptable to Western Europe. Aberdeen's fate was to be always unpopular, no matter in what direc-

tion the volatile public swung in the Eastern Question. In his
1828–30 tenure of office, when popular sympathy was with the
Greeks, he was regarded as being hardly better than a Turk himself
because he did not come out warmly for Russia, and was accused
of wanting to bleed the struggling Greeks of their scanty resources
and limit the size of the new Greece. A quarter of a century later,
when the mob would be hot for the Turks, he would be hounded
for not having been pro-Turkish enough against the Russian foe in
1828, and execrated as having sold the Turks down the river in
order to aid their rebellious Greek subjects.

When Navarino had thrown the Sultan into such a rage that he
had torn up the treaty he had just made with Russia and had
declared war, Russia had retaliated by sending troops marching
to Constantinople. Wellington and Aberdeen, prepared to stand by
the Treaty of London by which Britain, France and Russia were
bound to a policy of Greek autonomy under Turkish suzerainty,
had shipped the Egyptian garrison out of the Morea. Yet, averse
to undertaking military operations against the Turks, they had had
to sit back and watch Russia doing so, enduring the sneers of
Palmerston and Russell with what fortitude they could command.

The Czar's declaration of war was distressing to Aberdeen. His
first act as Foreign Secretary had been to send Lord Heytesbury
as ambassador to St Petersburg to discover Russia's intentions,
reminding his ambassador that Britain's main object in Europe
was to keep the peace which, with few and minor exceptions, had
lasted since 1815. Now suddenly, and without warning from Heytesbury, the Czar had broken it and put an end to Aberdeen's hopes.
The Czar continued to assert that he was determined to uphold
the Turkish Empire while he advanced relentlessly towards
Constantinople, and Aberdeen looked with dread to the almost
inevitable Russian victory. He saw little prospect of bringing France
to his side, still less of weaning Prussia from her Russian sympathies; and his strenuous efforts to bring Metternich in as an
active ally were fruitless.

Despite the threat of being starved into submission by the
blockading of the Dardanelles the Turks had refused to treat with
the Czar, and in September he had ordered the blockade. Aberdeen did not wait to call the Cabinet together, but sent a strong
protest. The French made no objection to a blockade which, as a
belligerent, Russia was in fact entitled to initiate; but Wellington
and Aberdeen took the view that the Czar had given his word not
to take action in the Mediterranean without consulting his allies,
and by breaking it had severely embarrassed England. Heytesbury

was instructed to demand the exemption from the blockade of all British ships which had left port on the authority of the King's speech, and to threaten force in the event of reprisal. The Russians yielded and withdrew their orders; but hope of obtaining the co-operation of their fleet in fulfilling the obligations of the Treaty of London was now lost.

At the end of October Aberdeen was able to report the surrender of the Turks after the fall of Varna. Wellington thought the Turks might be glad of the mediation of strong powers, and by the end of December, with the time for negotiation running out, Aberdeen's efforts to obtain Metternich's help had become almost desperate. The Russians, though victorious, were in a poor way, their campaign had been appallingly mismanaged, and five weeks before the surrender they might easily have stormed Varna. They had suffered disastrous losses, 15,000 men having died before Varna from sickness, accident and enemy action. Yet it was on the cards that they might recover, and take Constantinople in the spring. There was no such hope for the Turks. Turkey had no money, her troops were a rabble, and her Government in a state of anarchy. Aberdeen wanted Metternich to influence the Porte to as reasonable a settlement of the Greek affair as could be made compatible with the provisions of the Treaty of London. The allies had provisionally guaranteed Greece's possession of the Morea and the neighbouring islands, which might be considered to satisfy the treaty terms. By the spring of 1829 Aberdeen was trying to get Metternich to persuade the Turks to set up a Greek state, after which a successful intervention on their behalf might be organized; but Metternich still asserted that Austria should not interfere.

The Russian troops won victory after victory on their way to Constantinople. Foreseeing punitive indemnities and territorial rearrangements, Aberdeen increased his efforts to bring Russia to settle. The Sultan was determined to resist unto death; and the Russians offered terms so harsh they were rejected out of hand. Constantinople was being fortified. Aberdeen's efforts to enlist the French were also vain. Britain was obviously going to be left to rescue Turkey single-handed, although her welfare was of more immediate benefit to others. She faced the fact that if the Russians occupied Constantinople war was inevitable. Soon Aberdeen was reporting to Wellington that the Russians were only eight or ten easy marches away.

Sir Stratford Canning had resigned in February 1829, and had been succeeded at Constantinople by Aberdeen's diplomat brother Sir Robert Gordon. Sir Robert, whom Melbourne described as 'a man of integrity', but 'tiresome, long and pompous',[4] was a warm friend of the Turks, and extremely anti-Russian and anti-Greek. When the Russians arrived before Constantinople he ordered the fleet to Tenedos with instructions to pass the Dardanelles at short notice. If the Russians set foot beyond Adrianople the fleet was to sail into the Sea of Marmora and defend the Bosphorus. The brave fronts of both armies were only bravado. The Russians were shaken by internal quarrels, and the Turks so broken that Sir Robert maintained that only an immediate cease-fire could save their empire. On 14 September 1829 Russia and Turkey signed the Treaty of Adrianople. By it the Danubian principalities of Moldavia and Wallachia (the modern Rumania) were made virtually independent states, the treaty rights of Russia in the navigation of the Bosphorus and Dardanelles were confirmed, and Greek affairs were settled by incorporating in the Treaty both the Treaty of London of 6 July 1827 and the rather grudging protocol of 22 March 1829, which called for the withdrawal of Greek troops from the newly conquered areas and for the first time introduced the idea of a hereditary monarch for Greece.[5]

The Treaty was a blow to Aberdeen, and he bitterly resented the accusation of later years that he had been its author. The Emperor of Austria and the King of France both congratulated the Czar on his success and his moderation. The King of England was silent; and Aberdeen wrote sharply to Heytesbury of the terms.[6]

Now the menacing shadow of the Great Bear affected all Aberdeen's reasoning. If Greece were to be both enlarged and strengthened – Capodistrias's determined objects – the control of the southern provinces of European Turkey would be effectively handed over to Russia. Aberdeen sought to resolve this difficulty by ensuring that the Sultan of Turkey retained nominal suzerainty over Greece, which would mean that the new state could not go to war against Turkey as Russia's ally. Until the terms of the Treaty of London were fulfilled, Great Britain could not interfere effectively, either to ensure a general peace, or merely to preserve the Sultan's throne. So he was anxious for Greece to ask only such moderate terms as Turkey would be sure to consider.

Violently attacked in the Lords, Aberdeen defended himself vigorously. He did indeed regret the weakness of Turkey, he replied to Lord Holland, but not for any love of the Turks – 'God forbid! I have seen and known the effect of the barbarous rule existing there, and nobody can be more alive to the horror with which it abounds. But give me leave to say that the improvement of even Turkey may be purchased at too dear a rate, and I still think that the conquest of that country by Russia would be paying dear indeed for the amelioration of its condition'.[7] However, after the disappointment of the Treaty of Adrianople, Aberdeen gave up hope of the Turks being able to keep Russia effectively at bay, and looked elsewhere for aid. To his brother, Sir Robert, he wrote: 'The events of the war have clearly shown to the most incredulous . . . that, trusting to its own resources and without foreign aid, the existence of the Turkish Empire may be said at this moment to depend upon the absolute will and pleasure of the Emperor Nicholas . . . We may still attempt to avert the period of its final dissolution, and may possibly for a time succeed, but whenever this feeble and precarious dominion shall cease, we ought not to occupy ourselves in vain efforts to restore its existence'.[8]

Now he hoped for an arrangement which would keep the Levant peaceful as long as Turkey survived, and which, when she went, would offer a substitute in the Greek state which was so much more sympathetic to Britain. Privately he broke it to his brother that he had had a change of mind and plan. Greece should become an independent state, free of the Turkish sovereignty under which she still smarted, and her frontiers expanded far beyond the proposed limits.[9] Aberdeen found scant support among his colleagues. Peel backed him, but Wellington would not budge. After a good deal of argument Aberdeen had his way as far as the creation of an independent sovereignty was concerned, but the Cabinet would not hear of extending the limits. Wellington poured scorn on the idea of Greece as an alternative to Turkish power in Europe. Ironically Palmerston, now dismissed from the Government, attacked Aberdeen in the Commons for not having included Livadia and Attica in the new Greece.

Loyal as always to his chief and his colleagues, Aberdeen strove to make the best of a bad bargain. Since there was no longer any possibility of creating a considerable kingdom, he sought to make up for lack of size in the quality of the ruler, and addressed himself wholeheartedly to finding a man of outstanding calibre, fit to rule, not only over Greece, but possibly also over the Sultan's dominions. Prince Leopold of Saxe-Coburg, formerly the husband of Princess Charlotte, and later to make an admirable King of the Belgians, had long coveted the throne and was actually chosen. Unfortunately he played his cards badly, making his acceptance conditional on the inclusion in the kingdom of Crete and other territory, a substantial guaranteed loan, and the Greeks being given a voice in his election. Aberdeen insisted on unconditional acceptance, and the Protocol was signed on 3 February 1830. Capodistrias – deliberately, it was widely suggested, playing a double game in order to scare him off and perpetuate his own presidency – alarmed Leopold by blood-curdling reports from Greece, and he withdrew on May 21, to his own long-lasting regret. Ironically he blamed Aberdeen for his disappointment. Capodistrias himself was assassinated the next year.

With no substitute for Prince Leopold yet chosen Aberdeen left the Foreign Office. Not for the last time he had to look on as Palmerston finished a task he had begun. Palmerston wanted a constitutional monarch with considerable powers. In January 1833 the young Otho of Bavaria landed in Greece from a British frigate as an absolute monarch, with a council of regency mainly composed of Germans who as trained administrators would effectively rule in his name over the Greeks. It turned out to be a deplorable choice, leading to a nightmare reign of anarchy, banditry and misgovernment, which was to give rise to many a headache in Britain's Foreign Office in the years to come. 'I am obliged to own that one of the worst things I ever did was to consent to Otto's [sic] election,' Palmerston was to confess. To him, however, must be given full credit for the enlargement of Greece.

Bartlett, in his invaluable *Great Britain and Sea Power: 1815–1853*, blamed Canning's successors for a 'paralysis' which 'robbed Navarino of its opportunity to solve the Greek Question almost unaided, and sent thousands of Russian and Turkish troops to their deaths when British policy – or want of one – helped to precipitate the Russo-Turkish War of March 1828'. More, he continued: 'Had the unity of the three powers, Britain, France and Russia, been maintained; had the unity been demonstrated by a joint blockade of the Dardanelles to follow up Navarino, the Turks might have submitted, and Europe been spared a wait of more than three years for a British politician to resume the Greek policy of Canning'. Certainly Wellington had, while theoretically backing France in her efforts to get Mehemet Ali to withdraw his Egyptian troops, left her alone to arrange the evacuation and temporary occupation of the Morea, and had allowed Russia a free rein until the Turkish resistance collapsed in the autumn of 1829. 'All I wish is,' he wrote to Aberdeen on 4 October 1829, 'to get out of the Greek affair without loss of honour, and without imminent risk for the safety of the Ionian islands.'[10]

In the event, however, though Russia did make considerable gains, Greece had not been swallowed up; and the Turkish Empire had at least survived.

The last year of Aberdeen's period of office was marked by the revolution in France, when Charles X was thrust from his throne and Louis Philippe took his place. There had been no warning from the British ambassador in Paris, and, taken completely by surprise, Aberdeen had the difficult problem of deciding quickly whether or not to recognize the new monarchy. Was this July Revolution a direct challenge to those powers who had signed the Treaty of Paris in 1815, and with whose goodwill Charles had mounted the throne? Was it incumbent on each of them to support that monarch and suppress any revolution directed against him? Certainly the protocols and declarations of Aix-la-Chapelle in 1818 seemed to imply that. Should revolution rear its head, again to 'convulse' France and endanger the repose of other states, the contracting parties had bound themselves to unite to ensure the safety of their own states and the general peace of Europe. Revolution had arisen, beyond dispute; and France, some might maintain, was 'convulsed'.[11] The question was, whether the repose of other states was thereby endangered, requiring England to intervene.

Wellington was inclined to act. It was Aberdeen who, with commendable speed and decisiveness, advised a policy of strict neutrality. England should be watchful, ready to strike should need arise; but she would be well advised not to interfere with the *fait accompli*. In France's nervous state, such meddling could be inflammatory. It was important to afford no pretext for taking offence. If war must come France should be clearly the aggressor. Failure to recognize the new king would be bound to annoy her. After all, the system of monarchical government had been preserved, and that was the object which the signatories had sought to achieve in 1815 and 1818. The recognition should be made, Aberdeen persuaded Peel, and promptly.[12]

The decision was a wise one. Wellington too was brought to acknowledge Louis Philippe at once, and he did so philosophically, if not without a struggle. 'There are some bitter pills to swallow . . .' he complained. 'However, the best chance of peace is to swallow them all.'[13] The other powers followed Britain's lead, and Louis Philippe, already well-disposed towards an England in which he had spent long years of exile, began his reign in the glow of her approval. His gratitude was such that his own countrymen would scornfully nickname him 'the Englishman'. One who had done much to put him on his throne, François Guizot, would bring an unprecedented bonus of collaboration to Aberdeen in his struggles for friendship between their countries.

Yet it was a troubled hour, with anxious moments as to how and where the July Revolution might not spread. Austria, Italy and Prussia sat watching, prepared to take advantage of France's troubles for their own ends. Was the European peace, not yet fifteen years old, to be shattered? To prevent this, Aberdeen believed, there must be a meeting of minds between the two great powers of Western Europe, France and England. Louis Philippe was agreeable, and sent Talleyrand to cement solidarity. Aberdeen arranged for the reception and accommodation of the 'Count de Pouthieu' and his family. The fallen monarch, almost certainly at the suggestion of the Scotsman, was lodged at Holyrood Palace, that pile which had once sheltered the young Mary Queen of Scots, when she too returned from a sojourn at the French Court.

As a young man on his first diplomatic mission Aberdeen had left England with instructions to see that the British pledge to set Holland free was honoured. The Congress of Vienna had forced Belgium and Holland into the unhappy union of the kingdom of the Netherlands, and in 1830 Belgium was still resentfully clamped in it. Only a few weeks after the July Revolution the Belgians in Brussels rose in a revolt which quickly spread into a national revolution. The King of the Netherlands suspected France of whipping it up, and sought a promise of military help from England.

The King's request set a difficult problem for Britain and her allies. The Treaties of 1814 and 1815 had bound them to maintain the integrity of the kingdom of the Netherlands, and at first sight it seemed that it would be impossible to avoid intervention. Wellington and Aberdeen were, however, determined not to set foot on a road which would inevitably lead to war with a France already poised to send troops to support Belgium in her sister-revolution. They preferred to keep France inactive by initiating negotiations. 'At the same time,' Aberdeen wrote stoutly to his ambassador, 'our Treaties are sacred, and the Netherlands Government may naturally rely on the performance of our engagements. We have guaranteed the Union of Holland and Belgium, and if the King has faithfully performed his part, we must perform ours.' He emphasized, however, that England no longer commanded the physical means to defend most of Belgium against France.[14]

On September 28 the Lower Chamber of the States General decided for a dissolution of the union between Belgium and Holland. Aberdeen wrote to his brother Robert that the condition of the Netherlands was 'most critical', and that the French nation was eager to regain what they held to be their own provinces: 'I think no party in this country would agree to the separation of the Belgian provinces from Holland, and still less would tolerate their union with France. Here, then, with all our desire of peace, is a cause of war not very distant'.[15]

In the same letter Aberdeen added, 'You will be astonished to hear that old Talleyrand is on his road as ambassador'.[16] The old sinner, who was approaching eighty, would not reach London until the end of September, and Aberdeen and he would have only six weeks in which to bend their minds to the problem before Wellington's Government fell. However, the ill-assorted pair, with their common ideal of Anglo-French friendship, had by then succeeded in laying the foundations of a settlement.

Before he went Aberdeen had, at Talleyrand's inspiration, brought the great powers of Europe round the conference table in London. Since with conferences, unlike congresses, at that time, only the country in which the conference was held was represented by its Foreign Secretary, and he presided, all other powers being represented by their resident ambassadors, the meeting-place was a matter of moment, and gave Aberdeen an influential position. The conference quickly agreed to the freeing of Belgium from the Dutch yoke, with the successes of the Belgian rebels giving an added incentive for speed. Aberdeen arranged an armistice, with Belgium and Holland each retaining the territorial *status quo* of pre-Congress of Vienna days. But within forty-eight hours of his taking office Palmerston was presiding at Aberdeen's conference, and to him was left the bestowal of Leopold of Saxe-Coburg as King of the Belgians, the signing of the treaty, the nine-years-long diplomatic wrangles about the bases of separation against a background of threatening war, and the eventual achievement of a settlement.

On 2 November 1830 Aberdeen, the moderate, was taken completely by surprise by Wellington's intemperate outburst in the Lords against any measures of parliamentary reform. He often said he could have prevented it had the Duke forewarned him. Wellington, having not only eulogized the unreformed parliament but asserted, 'I will at once declare that . . . I shall always feel it my duty to resist such measures when proposed by others', sat down and turned to Aberdeen. 'I have not said too much, have I?' he asked. Aberdeen thrust forward his chin in a characteristic gesture, and replied grimly, '*You'll hear of it!*' As he left the House he was asked what the Duke had said. 'He said we were going out,' he replied tersely. A fortnight later the Government fell – a technical defeat on the Civil List, on 16 November 1830.[17]

There were some who saw Wellington's defeat in that vote as the ultras' revenge for 10 April 1829, on the issue of Catholic

Lord Aberdeen. Engraved by C. Turner
from the portrait by Sir Thomas Lawrence

Catherine, Countess of Aberdeen

Harriet, Countess of Aberdeen in 1833.
After the portrait by Sir Thomas Lawrence

Above: Argyll House, Argyll Street
Below: Haddo House

Emancipation.[18] The repeal of the Test and Corporation Acts had caused Aberdeen no pangs, and he had followed Peel and Wellington with a clear conscience, though he had predicted dire results. A month before the Government's fall he had written to his brother Robert, 'The Catholic Question has utterly destroyed all party attachment, and having separated the Duke and Peel from their natural followers, has thrown them on the mercy of the candid and impartial, who, I fear, will never give the necessary strength to any government. For myself, I assure you that I am at single anchor; there are many things in leaving office which I should undoubtedly regret, but the motives which induce me to wish to retire are becoming stronger every day'.[19] Among those motives the stress of frequent speaking in the Lords could not have figured. The General Index to *Hansard* reveals that between 1807 and 1830 he had spoken only 75 times.

Aberdeen was out. Palmerston was in. After the general election which followed the death of George IV in June 1830 he had twice been offered a seat in the cabinet, despite Peel's opinion that he was 'too discreditable and unsafe'.[20] After the death of Huskisson in a railway accident Palmerston had demanded that Grey and Lansdowne, as well as all the Canningites, should also come in. That was too much for Wellington, though his Government clearly could not last much longer. So Palmerston joined the Whigs, voting on November 15 for Brougham's resolution for a general measure of parliamentary reform, which was carried. Wellington resigned. Grey became Prime Minister on 22 November 1830 and Palmerston became Secretary of State for Foreign Affairs for the first time at the age of forty-six.

Now the man who was almost the complete antithesis of Aberdeen, both in character and in his attitude to foreign politics, his 'twin' Palmerston, sat in his place. Seen through Aberdeen's eyes, Palmerston was not an attractive figure. He had acquired the reputation of a hardened rake, and the lover of promiscuous women, among them three notorious Lady Patronesses of Almack's – Lord Melbourne's sister, Lady Cowper; the Russian Ambassador's wife, Princess Lieven; and Lady Jersey. Emily Cowper, the wife of Earl Cowper, was certainly his *maîtresse en titre*, at least, and he was thought to have fathered some of her children. Though devoted to her, he never lost his interest in other women, and nine years hence, when on the point of marrying her, he was to cause a scandal at Windsor Castle by, according to Prince Albert, committing 'a brutal attack' upon one of the ladies-in-waiting, having 'at night, by stealth, introduced himself into her apartment, barri-

caded the door, and would have consummated his fiendish scheme
by violence had not the miraculous efforts of his victim and such
assistance attracted by her screams, saved her'. (More, Lord John
Russell would later tell the Prince that it was not an isolated
incident.) No excuses about wandering into the bedroom where
another obliging lady-in-waiting usually awaited him, and finding
new temptation installed there, if they reached his ears, altered the
Prince's opinion of the incident, and there is little doubt that to
Aberdeen, totally faithful and idealistic in love, Palmerston's
notorious way of life would present an unappealing picture. He
would agree with Prince Albert's estimate of 'Lord Palmerston's
worthless private character'.[21]

Then Aberdeen, the reverse of a bigot in matters of religion, was
yet a religious man, and Palmerston's jaunty attitude of paying lip-
service to religion without belief would be repellent to him. To one
who had paid his father's debts when he came into his inheritance,
though there was no obligation on him to do so,[22] Palmerston
would seem a dishonourable debtor, for he had already been sued
by his creditors some dozen times, and would yet tot up a score
of nineteen. Only three years before, too, his name had been
tarnished by a financial scandal which had involved a debate in
the House of Commons. Palmerston's strengths of pragmatism,
flexibility, flair and verve, a philosophic and fighting courage, a
robust sense of humour, and the will and ability to survive and
retaliate in the most adverse circumstances, would not entirely
counterbalance for Aberdeen characteristics for which he would
feel a lack of sympathy, if not positive scorn.

Far worse in his eyes, however (since he had long learned to
live in the world as it was, and not as he would have liked it to be,
with equanimity), than Palmerston's personal character was his
foreign policy. It was, as Palmerston himself had said in the
Commons only the year before, one of 'intermeddling, and intermeddling in every way and to every extent short of actual military
force', in the affairs of other countries. This principle Aberdeen
believed to be, in his son's words, 'a vicious one', and 'inexpedient'.[23] To his mind the influence of Britain was not, as
Palmerston believed, increased, but diminished, by it. In fact, such
interference, he was convinced, was sure to make England hated,
and when challenged, and proved to be mere bluster, despised.
To Aberdeen it was immoral to intervene where one was not
prepared to face out the results; and the only excuse for interference was for the defence or furtherance of Britain's interests, in
which case it became a duty. Besides, as he said to Princess Lieven,

'The fact is that England never can have any real and serious cause of quarrel with any country, except with France; at least none which the efforts of men of sense, and lovers of peace, may not easily remove'.[24] He was not the only man in England to interpret Palmerston's attitude as one of unprincipled opportunism, of bullying the weak and knuckling under to the strong, of cheerful inconsistency in the making and unmaking of alliances, and of the frequent and shameless volte-face, and on those grounds was totally opposed to it.

For twenty-two years these two men, Aberdeen the Peelite and Palmerston the Canningite, each completely opposed to the other's most strongly-rooted beliefs, and entertaining a scarcely-veiled personal hostility, alternately guided Britain's foreign policy.

Chapter 11

The Years the Locust Hath Eaten

Aberdeen retired to Haddo, building farmhouses, planting on towards his fourteen million trees, fishing for trout in the lake, and for sea-trout in the Ythan, shooting grouse on his moor, chasing the wild deer, hunting otters with his famous pack of otter-hounds, and hawking the herons which stole his fish.[1] He consulted James Giles, the talented young local artist, who three years before had become a member of the Aberdeen Artists' Society formed under his patronage, about the planning of his policies and of a spacious deer park at the end of his mile-long avenue – and persuaded his brother Robert to employ him to make sketches of his home, old Balmoral Castle, the forfeited Jacobite estate he had leased, and to advise him on the redesigning of its grounds.

Aberdeen stayed at Haddo for half the year, sometimes longer, again scarcely so much as attending the Lords. There was proxy voting there, after all. He corresponded regularly with the clever, treacherous intriguer, Princess Lieven, whom he had known since her arrival in London with her husband, the Russian Ambassador, in 1812, and of whom he seemed genuinely fond, though he resisted her attempts to visit him with a determination bordering on panic. The Princess, who had become Metternich's mistress at twenty-three at the Congress of Aix-la-Chapelle, and would become Guizot's at fifty-two, was no beauty, with her long nose and long neck, but was clearly sexually attractive. Politically at one in their distaste for revolutionary change in general, they came to share a particular mistrust of Lord Palmerston.

If it occurs to one to question the ethics of a former Foreign Secretary corresponding with the wife of a foreign ambassador in this way, one's doubts are answered by the fact that Peel himself, at least as sensitive as Aberdeen as to such matters of propriety, had no inhibitions either on that score. While actually Prime Minister he would be corresponding with Princess Lieven on the subject of the Emperor of Russia's fiscal policy. Of course, too, Princess Lieven, as she said to Peel, had been '*très intime*'[2] with Canning. Thus, with no sense of guilt, Aberdeen wrote to her, 'Whether in office, or out of office, you may depend on my being a regular and frequent correspondent if you continue to encourage me'.[3] Her devoted correspondence with him is all the more interesting, as she had been a close friend of Lady Cowper's since her arrival in London in 1812, as well as, very likely, Palmerston's mistress. She had indeed begun by despising Aberdeen, in 1828, as Foreign Secretary, calling him 'an honourable man, and nothing more',[4] and even attacking him to his face. Almost from that moment, however, her attitude had changed, growing rapidly into admiration and the warmest friendship – a pattern not infrequent with Aberdeen's denigrators. It was he who drew back from a too-great intimacy, deciding that, as he said, it was 'impossible to confide in all she says'.[5] Of course there was bound to be a certain residue of reserve and even cynicism in such a relationship between the two patriots, for it was probably taken for granted that (as was indeed often the case) grist which came to the Princess's mill would go straight to the Czar; and Aberdeen doubtless fed her information with that end in view.

In the autumn of 1831 Aberdeen was active in the Lords, to the displeasure of Lord Holland, noting his offence at his 'great bitterness and sarcasm' and his 'violent and unfair speech which was an invective against the French nation and breathed war in every syllable', and his joy when 'we beat him by a majority of 37' on his 'motion on Belgium'. On the surface they were cordial, once even exchanging a bet for a sovereign.[6]

In October of the year of the passing of the Reform Bill Harriet's eldest son, the second Marquess of Abercorn, at the age of 21 married Lady Louisa Russell, daughter of the Duke of Bedford and half-sister of Lord John Russell – a Whig marriage which his Abercorn grandfather would never have sanctioned, but which his stepfather, perhaps remembering the frustration of his own hopes of marrying a Cavendish, did nothing to hinder.

Aberdeen's attitude to Reform was that of a disapproving spectator. It was 'mischievous',[7] for he stood four-square for an aristocratic constitution, and, like Peel, believed that a governing class was essential for the welfare of the nation. Convinced that the influence of the House of Lords would be decreased, if its very existence were not threatened,[8] Aberdeen would have been in favour of throwing sops to Cerberus after the 1830 French revolution by some moderate reforms and compromise with the middle classes. Then the large measures being urged by Grey, Russell and their friends might have been avoided. In default, his attitude had been that the Lords should reject Lord John's bill at the outset, but accept it when and if it was brought back. To others this seemed at best tortuous, and at worst feeble, and it brought down on his head the anger or ridicule or scorn of Tories, Radicals and Whigs. The Tories were angry at what they considered his cowardice in abandoning the fight for the Lords' right to reject any Commons measure out of hand. The Radicals were appalled at the apparent inconsistency of first opposing and then accepting a measure. As for the Whigs, Grey himself sneered to Princess Lieven about Aberdeen's strange behaviour.[9] Yet Aberdeen was a generation ahead of his time. As Bagehot said in 1867, 'Since the Reform Act the House of Lords has become a revising and suspending House . . . Their veto is a sort of hypothetical veto. They say, We reject your Bill for this once or these twice, or even these thrice; but if you keep on sending it up, at last we won't reject it. The House has ceased to be one of latent directors, and has become one of temporary rejectors and palpable alterers.'[10] Aberdeen was merely anticipating this change of function.

Circumstances altered in 1832 when Grey resigned and Wellington tried to form a government which accepted the Reform Bill. Aberdeen agreed to be his Foreign Secretary. The attempt failed, but, having compromised his anyway somewhat ambiguous former position, Aberdeen no longer vocally opposed the Bill, and confined himself to voting against it.

It was only foreign affairs which spurred him to activity, though he felt keenly the weakened and painful situation in which his party found itself in the first reformed Parliament, with Peel in the Commons deprived of support, and the Lords for other reasons in not much better case. 'In the House of Lords,' he wrote on 25 January 1833 to Peel, 'it is true that we possess numbers, but we stand self-degraded, and scarcely dare to exercise authority, after the public confession of our own impotence.'[11] He was afraid, too, as he said, that 'questions of domestic policy will press so heavily on the attention of Parliament, that I suppose we shall be able to attend but little to foreign matters . . . The state of Ireland, the church, the colonies, the charters of the Bank and the East India Company, are all so important and so urgent as to engross immediate attention. Yet it will be a pity if any cause, however strong, should withdraw all notice from the present most extraordinary nature of our foreign relations'. He pressed Peel to 'continue to find time and inclination occasionally to attend to questions of this nature, and to force them with the same effect on the attention of the House'. (Perhaps there may have been a slight element in Aberdeen's lack of interest in home affairs of the attitude noted by Bagehot as endemic in the great peers of the day, who disliked attending to 'business' such as Free Trade, and 'appointed' non-aristocrats like Peel to the task; and who regarded diplomacy as a more gentlemanly occupation. Certainly Aberdeen often refrerred to his ignorance about Free Trade in a way which could only have been affectation and conscious exaggeration.[12]) To Princess Lieven he fretted about the situation in Belgium, Portugal and Spain, and especially about 'this quasi-war of our government against Holland, and our union with France for this purpose', calling it 'the most stupidly impolitick as well as one of the most wicked acts of which any state was ever guilty'.[13]

Private sorrow continued to haunt him. In 1829, the year of Alice's death, his youngest son Arthur, a sickly child, had been born. Four years later, in August 1833, Harriet died, leaving the orphaned boy to his care. His long struggle to achieve a second happy marriage was over. He had always been willing to love Harriet, even passionately. Eleven years before, when she had been at her most difficult, he had written, 'Dearest, in your last letter you talk of loving me for some expressions of mine; but I must again intreat you not to measure love by words. When I say, with all the concentrated energy of which human nature is capable, that *I love*, I know not how to say more, for everything else is comparatively weak', and had implored her to express her own love for him. 'Be sure,' he had written, 'that I do not lose a single syllable of endearment and love: whatever I may say, they are like water to the parched traveller in the desert – I drink, and am happy.'[14]

As the years had gone by, however, perhaps realizing that Harriet was indeed, as he had once decided, 'certainly one of the most stupid persons I ever met with',[15] and not to be handled by kindness and reason alone, or perhaps only because even his patience was not inexhaustible, he had taken a somewhat firmer line with her. In 1825 he had been capable of writing to her from Nice, as she prepared to join him and Alice, 'The absurdity of taking a housemaid is beyond belief', and, in effect, ordering her to send the maid back from Paris, as she would not be 'of the slightest use'.[16] Again, describing her journey towards him as 'rather bad at all times', he had added, 'but with your single man, and your stupid additional useless maid, it must be much worse', and had repeated his wish that she should send the maid back to England in the diligence.[17] We do not know whether Harriet obeyed in this instance; but somehow he had managed to achieve a viable marriage with the strange, intransigent woman. Somehow, too, she had learned to accept his unshakable determination never to put away the living memory of his first wife, or to allow her more than a

127

poor second place. He had loved her, in his way, on those terms, and he wept for her sincerely.

When Harriet had lain dangerously ill Aberdeen had sent for Haddo at her request from the University, writing, 'Her situation is one of great danger. I fear that we must endeavour to prepare ourselves for the worst; which, God knows, will be difficult for us all . . . If we are destined to lose this pattern of all that is good, and if this dreadful separation must take place, may the mercy of God enable us to profit by his dispensation'.[18]

Not until two months after Harriet's death did Aberdeen bring himself to go to Haddo. From there he wrote to his eldest son that though 'the gloom and desolation of the place, under present circumstances, can scarcely be endured, I will endeavour to make the best of it'.[19] Eleven days later he wrote again, 'It is indeed wretchedly gloomy here; and it will be long before I can even think of it otherwise. No sunshine or fine weather, either in winter or summer, can ever make amends for the loss of that perpetual sunshine within. I take my solitary walk every morning before breakfast; and I shall go on with all the projected improvements and alterations, for your sake at least; as any pleasure which I can now receive from what is done will be but small'.[20] His sorrow was genuine, but his language was philosophical and his attitude resigned. It was a far cry from the lifelong agony of his mourning for his Catherine.

Eight months later, in April 1834, his only daughter by Harriet, Lady Frances, died at the age of sixteen. The man who loved daughters was never to rear one of his own. Three years before he had had to nerve himself to losing her, and had written to Haddo, 'In all human probability we shall soon lose poor Frances. Her weakness increases every day, and the appearances become more and more alarming. Her suffering, although great, she bears patiently . . . My dear Boy, this trial is a severe one'.[21] As Frances's mother, Harriet, so passionately devoted to her own children, watched her dying child, she may have recalled Aberdeen's stern words to her of nine years before concerning Alice's narrow escape from death: 'I have lost one, under circumstances which I shall not easily forget, and if ever you are placed in a similar situation you will perhaps learn how to feel for me'.[22]

Miraculously, Frances had recovered, only to die on 20 April 1834. Next day he wrote to Haddo, 'Yesterday morning it pleased God to take her to himself,' and told him that she had died of influenza developed from a cold 'caught by going out in the coach one day when I was at the Priory, for she felt ill at the time. It seems strange that she should have gone through the winter so well, and so much exposed in open carriages, to fall at last under circumstances of great precaution'. He comforted himself, 'that her mother was spared the pain of witnessing the event', and 'that in case of my death, however soon it may happen, I shall not leave her in a state of helplessness, requiring care and attention which it is not to be expected she could have received from anyone but me'.[23] He could not bring himself to be present at her funeral.[24] To Princess Lieven, refusing to let her come to Bentley Priory to comfort him, he wrote, 'There are some misfortunes which are too great for speech'.[25]

In 1835 his brother Charles died at Geneva at the early age of forty-five. The first of Aberdeen's original flock had gone.

Aberdeen never remarried, though he lost his wife when he was only forty-nine, and said of himself that he still felt young – 'too much so, I fear, a great deal'.[26] After his wife's death he did not go out much in public life, and from that time his deep reserve deepened into an outward austerity chilling to all but his very few intimates.[27] By the time he was fifty-one his reputation for coldness and hauteur was such that the young Gladstone went 'in fear and trembling' to his first meeting with him, to be surprised by his kindness and gentleness, and astonished that he could be so misunderstood by the world.[28] Even at this period Aberdeen was not always stiff and cheerless. We have a glimpse of him in boisterous mood at a great dinner given to foreign ambassadors at the Mansion House. John Cam Hobhouse recorded, 'Melbourne soon rose and spoke well, and was much cheered, though I saw Lord Aberdeen, who was opposite, smile. The Speaker, who had risen to return thanks for some health, on sitting down again, fell back on the ground, and then Aberdeen and Haddington burst into a loud laugh. I picked up Mr Speaker, who behaved decorously. He was in full Court-dress'.[29]

A month after his daughter's death Aberdeen was appealed to as the only man who could heal the two-years-long coolness between Wellington and Peel, which was threatening any Tory government likely to be formed when the Whigs collapsed. The rift had developed from the wide divergence between them in 1832, when Peel had refused to join in bringing in a Reform Bill based on principles to which the King was pledged but which the Tory party had strongly opposed, so forcing the Whigs to resign. Peel had been grievously offended by the language used by the Duke in the Lords – 'For myself, my Lords, I cannot help feeling that if I had been capable of refusing my assistance to His Majesty, if I had been capable of saying to His Majesty, "I cannot assist you in this affair," I do not think, my Lords, that I could have shown my face in the streets for shame of having done it, for shame of having abandoned my Sovereign under such distressing circumstances.'[30] Peel had refrained from responding in kind in the Commons, as he felt he was entitled to do. His resentment was increased in 1834, when Wellington – though reluctantly enough – accepted the Chancellorship of the University of Oxford, for which he knew that Peel was also proposed, without a word to Peel on the subject. Peel remembered, with some bitterness, that in 1829, when he had wanted to resign rather than take the lead in passing a measure for Catholic Emancipation, of which he had long been the chief opponent, and had actually offered his resignation, the Duke had entreated him to withdraw it, claiming that he could not get the Bill through without him, and he had done so. Not the least of the sacrifices this had involved for Peel was that he had felt it incumbent on him also to offer to resign his seat at the University of Oxford, and had been defeated in the subsequent election. In all the circumstances Peel believed Wellington's behaviour to be incomprehensible and intolerable.

Now, in May 1834, friends and colleagues of the two leaders of the party were gravely concerned, and Arbuthnot, the husband of Wellington's closest woman confidante, wrote to Aberdeen to beg him to use his influence to mend matters. 'Should the King be left without a Government, he can only look to the Duke of Wellington and to Peel,' he wrote. 'Unless these two can act together with cordiality, there could be no hope of safety,' and told him how on the Duke's birthday they had both dined at his table and not a single word had passed between them. He added, 'I know not which of the two is at fault. Perhaps there is no fault on either side, merely misconception. If so, you, and you I believe alone, could set it right, and you feel, as I well know, that on every ground, public and private, the restoration of cordiality between them is most devoutly to be wished'.[31]

Thereupon Aberdeen, on 5 May 1834, wrote to his friend Peel, enclosing Arbuthnot's letter, hoping 'that the motive might excuse a still greater indiscretion', and saying that he had always denied that there could be any foundation for similar fears expressed by his friends, or, where that was out of the question, had tried 'to clear up all misconceptions', and had declared that if any coldness or estrangement were to take place between Peel and the Duke 'it would be the greatest misfortune which could ever befall the country'. If he could be of any use, as Arbuthnot supposed, 'it must only be because you and the Duke both know and are convinced that in my regard for you there is an entire absence of everything like the shadow of an underhand, selfish or interested object'. Then, he said roundly, 'I should be the most ungrateful of mankind if I could ever forget the confidence and kindness with which the Duke has always treated me. But I am not blind to his imperfections, and so far as I have been able to judge, he certainly appears to me, in a great measure, to have created that state of things which our friends so much lament. At the same time it would be converting the warmest friendship into mere flattery, if I were to say that I thought you were entirely blameless'. He asked for a meeting within the week.[32]

There followed what was clearly a most difficult interview with Peel, judging merely by the note which Peel afterwards wrote, partly on the back of Aberdeen's letter, five days later. Peel frankly expressed his feelings, and seemed determined to stand his ground without concessions. Yet when Aberdeen left him the way was open for the breach to be healed. Aberdeen had managed a most delicate situation with great tact. At risk had been his friendship with his two closest friends, who were also the two most important men in his political life. Perhaps to him alone was due the fact that Peel and Wellington were able to work together thereafter and that the following winter Peel came back to power for his 'hundred days'. After all (in a passage excised from the letter as published) Arbuthnot had himself posed a vital question: 'In what state would our Party be, if the king had to seek us out while the duke and Peel were hardly on speaking terms? (This is too strongly expressed.)'[33]

It was in mid-November that Wellington, as Prime Minister, summoned Aberdeen to help him 'keep things very cool and quiet'[34] until Peel got back from Italy, the Duke holding all the non-legal 'Cabinet' offices until Peel's return. When Peel arrived he formed his Cabinet. Wellington was anxious that Aberdeen, and not he, should be Foreign Secretary, because he himself was so deaf. But, Aberdeen wrote to Princess Lieven, 'The Duke is at the Foreign Office, having been urged by me certainly more strongly than by any one, to go there. His own wish was that I should have resumed the situation; but I could not be blind to the superior weight of his name and influence'.[35] Aberdeen had been offered the office of President of the Council, which would have left him free to concentrate on foreign affairs. First, however, he was persuaded, very reluctantly, to take on the Admiralty. Then, even more against his inclination, he volunteered for the office of Secretary of State for War and the Colonies so that Lord de Grey, who had refused the Colonies, might have the Admiralty. There he was most unhappy because of the number of grievances abroad and, according to his son, the amount of patronage at home.[36] The interlude was brief. After five months away from the Foreign Office Palmerston moved back for another six years.

A spectator again, Aberdeen watched a government helpless 'under the iron domination of Mr O'Connell',[37] and grew angry at the suspension of the Foreign Enlistment Act, enabling 10,000 British mercenaries to enlist for service for Queen Isabella of Spain against her uncle Don Carlos – 'a disgraceful and a barbarous thing'.[38] On a personal level, grief and pride for his brother Alex were renewed in 1837, when the monument on the field of Waterloo was repaired at public expense.[39]

Towards the end of 1838 Aberdeen was going through a good deal of heart-searching about his attitude towards ever again taking office. Effectively eight years out of the saddle, and still desolated by his bereavements, he rebelled at the thought. In December he was writing, 'I hate London, and do not love politics, at least I have had enough of them'.[40] But, as three years before, he was undoubtedly swayed by the wishes of Wellington and Peel, who kept closely in touch with him. 'There are certainly two men for whom I would make almost any sacrifice,' he had written then. 'One, the greatest of our time, to whom I have a thousand reasons for being grateful. The other, whose friendship is a source of happiness, and of which any man may feel proud.'[41]

In 1838 the worrying state of affairs in Canada, about which he spoke in the Lords, was brought close to home when his 21-year-old second son Alexander sailed there before Easter with his battalion of Guards. 'I have felt this separation very much,' he wrote to Princess Lieven, 'and shall do so for some time.' He cancelled a long-deferred visit to Paris to see her, and busied himself about nursing 'my little boy', the sickly eight-year-old Arthur, sending him to the 'uninhabited' Priory, where he could be with him often, and where he had 'better air than in London'.[42]

The death of William IV and the accession of Queen Victoria had saved the Melbourne Government from disaster, and it had staggered on through 1838; but in April 1839 the Whigs had a majority of only five in a house of 583 on a bill to suspend the Jamaica constitution, and the Government resigned. The Queen sent for a far-from-sanguine Peel. Arthur Gordon maintained that if Peel had succeeded in forming a government Aberdeen would have returned to the Foreign Office.[43] The Queen's journal and her private letters suggest otherwise. On May 14 she wrote to her Uncle

Leopold, 'I insisted upon the Duke in the Foreign Office instead of Lord Aberdeen'.[44] The strong personal prejudice which Victoria felt at this time towards that 'cold, odd man',[45] Peel, and his friend Aberdeen, would be signally changed upon closer contact into the warmest devotion. Some of her hostility was perhaps inspired by Leopold's continuing resentment about the 1830 negotiations for the crown of Greece.

Soon the Bedchamber Crisis had aborted a Peel government, and Melbourne was Prime Minister once more, with a shaky ministry reeling from division to division, and troubles abroad in the Peninsula, China and the Levant. Aberdeen only reluctantly remained in London, to see out the session. Once, indeed, Wellington lashed out at him for abandoning him: 'It may be best to let the country go to the devil its own way, or according to the guidance of the Government, the Political Unions, the Chartists! With all my heart! Be it so! I will not desire anybody to stay! I have before stood, and I can now stand, alone'.[46]

In 1838, much against Aberdeen's will, Wellington had persuaded him to become head of the Scottish Conservatives, writing, 'You went to the Colonial Office disliking its business, and everything connected with it. You see how well you succeeded in it, and that you are now the standard of our colonial policy, as you were before of our foreign policy. This was done in a few months. The conclusion which I wish you to draw is this, that you have only to give your attention to any subject or any business, however irksome or disagreeable to you, to do it better than others, and you will master it as easily as you did the affairs of the Colonial Department'. Aberdeen was not likely to be left in peace by such friends.[47] Aberdeen was, of course, perhaps next only to Buccleuch, the most influential man in Scotland, where the Tories needed all the influence they could command, and his weight among the Scottish peers alone made him invaluable to his party.[48]

In 1840 some measure of personal happiness came to him again in the form of a beloved young woman. Nine months after Queen Victoria married Prince Albert, Aberdeen's eldest son, Lord Haddo, married Mary, the 25-year-old second daughter of George Baillie of Jerviswoode and Mellerstain. Mary was the sister of the 'wretchedly delicate'[49] Lady Breadalbane, recently appointed lady-in-waiting to the Queen. From her magnificent home in Perthshire, Taymouth Castle, Mary was married in November. This was, incidentally, yet another marriage into a Whig family. Political passions had begun to cool after the Reform Bill, and only two years before the late Lady Aberdeen's niece, Lady Frances Douglas, had married Earl Fitzwilliam's son, Lord Milton. Soon after Aberdeen wrote to Princess Lieven that the Fitzwilliams had gone up to stay at Haddo, and that he had never thought that he would entertain the Earl as a visitor. 'Party violence is softened,' he commented, 'and personal animosity is entirely subdued.'[50] Now, with the Bedchamber Crisis of 1839 still fresh in men's minds, Whigs and Tories united in celebrating a marriage. Mary's brother George would become heir-presumptive to the ninth Earl of Haddington the following year. Between Aberdeen and this late-arriving daughter, as he liked to call her, there sprang up a deep tenderness, pure but unusually close.

Aberdeen had been somewhat testy to Haddo. 'You do things in a manner so unlike other people,' he wrote to him in answer to his letter announcing his engagement, 'that I am rather at a loss to know whether your letter, which I have just received, is meant for wit; or whether it is serious. As a joke, however, it is so bad, that I shall take it as a matter of fact.' After telling his son that he had 'fully expected to be consulted' by him before he had taken such a step, and rebuking him for not making it clear either whether he had in fact proposed or merely intended to do so, or which of the two Miss Baillies he hoped to marry, he added resignedly, 'In short, if the thing is done, I have only to ensure [sic] you of my most affectionate desire to contribute to your happiness by every means in my power; and when I know *which* of the sisters is to be my daughter, I shall be quite prepared to regard her with all the love and interest of a father'.[51]

It was an unpropitious beginning; but Aberdeen lost his heart to Mary at once. 'She is quite charming,' he wrote to an unknown friend. 'There is an honesty, a candour about her, that is absolutely irresistible . . . To tell you the truth, I never expected to like anyone so well again; and from my connection with her, and the charm of her society, I look forward to more happiness than I ever hoped to enjoy. I trust my son will prove himself worthy of her, and that he is fully sensible of his great good fortune. You know well, that if ever any man had a right to be fastidious in his estimate of female character, I am that person. Such praise from me therefore is no light matter.'[52] Though she was not the most beautiful in a family of beautiful women, he wrote to Princess Lieven, 'in any other family she would be much admired'.[53]

The fact is that Aberdeen became extremely possessive about Mary and, in due course, her children. Not only did the young couple return from their honeymoon to Haddo House for the rest of that year, but for the next two years they lived with Aberdeen either there or at Argyll House, and their first child was born at Haddo in 1841. Not until May 1842 did they move to a house of their own at Windsor; and at the first opportunity Aberdeen insisted on their moving closer to him in London. His surviving letters to Mary read rather more like a husband's than a father-in-law's, and he writes to her in a different style from the stiff, if affectionate, one he adopts to his son, her husband – 'I think that I will not go to Haddo without you; but if you should be there, and it should be in my power to leave London, I do not much care what the season may be'[54]; 'She puts me a little, and but a little, in mind of you; but little as it is, perhaps it is that which has constituted her charm in my eyes'[55]; 'Notwithstanding our separation you will not be forgotten today. I am able to transport myself to you in imagination, and see you as clearly and as vividly as if really in your presence. I can hear your sweet voice.'[56] He signs emotionally, 'Dearest, Dearest Mary, Ever your most affectionate Aberdeen'.[57] It is all perfectly proper, but one feels a little sorry for Haddo, a man of much piety but poor health and unremarkable attainments. He had little beside youth on his side, and the contrast between him and the grave, handsome, passionate man of great distinction, wealth and power, who had always known how to please beautiful women, must have been painfully evident. In the very year of their marriage Aberdeen built a lodge on Buchan Ness, a promontory which is the most eastern point of Scotland. Over its door is inscribed *Procul Negotiis Beatus*, and the date, and there indeed he was happy, far from the cares of state, when he could escape to it for a few days, gazing over the grey North Sea or creating a terraced marine garden among the granite cliffs in a sheltered ravine falling to the sea – alone, or, better, with Mary by his side. It was there that James Giles painted him in oils, walking with her.

With the years Aberdeen and Mary would grow only closer. Aberdeen's tender letters rained on her whenever they were apart, making little jokes about such trifles as his visit to Smithfield cattle-show or his efforts at dancing at the Queen's Ball, detailing his headaches, asking her to read his speeches in the newspapers, sharing her worries about her children's ailments,[58] bidding her 'take care of your own most precious health',[59] and opening his heart to her on matters small and great. He pampered her. She had a good allowance from him, and must not travel without maid or man-servant, which was 'positively disreputable and improper' – let George 'clean his own boots' if he wanted to.[60] He gave her money whenever she asked for it, even when he could ill afford it. ('To say the truth I am myself rather hampered . . . But I can manage to obtain supplies, and whatever I have shall with pleasure be yours also.'[61]) When the day came that she asked him, as Prime

Minister, for a benefice for her clergyman brother, though it was an embarrassing request, he did all he could to organize it, considering involved contrivances 'to avoid the attack for appointing a relative'.[62] (And, he said, 'If anything should become vacant which I can *decently* give him, I will do so'.[63]) Once he declined two invitations to meet the King of the Belgians rather than break a dinner engagement with her.[64] He provided her with two piano-fortes, one from Blackwood's, so that she could play and sing to him both at her home and at Haddo.[65] He gave her jewellery. Arthur Gordon, at least, found her chilly, and complained of the haughty way in which she merely 'thrust the tips of her fingers' into the palm of his hand in greeting.[66] But between his father and Mary the relationship was extremely warm.

Aberdeen's relationship with his son was complicated, a mixture of affection and domination which seems to have oppressed Lord Haddo, always prone to irritability and guilt. Aberdeen had rebuked his heir for foolish extravagance at Cambridge (where he worked hard enough to get a first class in classics and mathematics in his first year's annual examination at Trinity College) for buying a silver teapot[67]; and, at eighteen, for clumsy manners to women. 'I beg that you will be on your guard,' he wrote, 'and endeavour to feel that it is always indispensable to be civil and attentive to a woman, be she old or young, ugly or pretty. A savage and morose manner to anyone is a real misfortune, to a woman it is barbarous.'[68] In 1835, at the age of nineteen, Haddo incurred displeasure by managing to get himself toasted as a Radical at a Whig meeting in Aberdeenshire, of all places, and having written to the newspapers to disclaim being a member of, of all things, a Pitt Club.[69] Aberdeen was, perhaps unconsciously, trying to remake him in his own image, and even sent him at twenty-one, and again at twenty-two, to follow his footsteps on a tour to Constantinople, Smyrna and Greece, with the journals of his own tour in his luggage.

His more serious ambitions for him were continually frustrated. Harriet's son, Lord Claud Hamilton, was Member for County Tyrone. As soon as Haddo was twenty-one, in 1838, Aberdeen attempted to buy him a seat through the Conservative party agent, Bonham, Haddo apparently agreeing to stand as a Tory despite his previous Radical lapses. By November he was set up as a candidate for the two-member borough of Penryn. When, at one stage, it seemed as if there would not be a vacancy after all, Haddo went off abroad again. By the autumn his father was again bargaining with Bonham, this time for the notoriously expensive Honiton seat, and writing that he would 'much prefer the *certain seat*, at an expense not exceeding two thousand five hundred pounds, to the chance of a contest on more reasonable terms'. Perhaps he doubted his son's abilities at the hustings. However, at the suggestion of a preliminary payment of £1000, to be laid out before the election, Aberdeen dug his heels in. 'This in fact renders nothing certain but a payment,' he wrote. 'Now it is clear that even for £1000 I might have a *chance of success* in twenty places; and it is only in consequence of what may be considered a certainty that I readily acquiesce in paying the larger sum. I think such a stipulation as that proposed is calculated to invite defeat . . . At all events it is quite different from that which I had contemplated; in which payment was to be contingent on success.'[70]

The bargain must have been struck, for by February 1841 Haddo was ready to put up for Honiton whenever called on. By then, however, his reluctance was so evident that Aberdeen lost heart and decided to withdraw from the engagement.[71] He was clearly disappointed by Haddo's lack of spirit, even with a Mary to back him.

Aberdeen had no qualms about buying a seat and bribing electors six to nine years after the passing of the 1832 Reform Act, and was sharp enough to avoid the danger of paying up without first securing the Honiton seat. He was prepared to bribe with the best to help his family. We should remember, however, that, as Professor Norman Gash points out, apropos of the experiences of Lord Aberdeen himself among others, the Reform Act had not worked an overnight miracle. 'It was the whole system that needed reforming,' he writes, 'because bribery was almost universal. All politicians were aware of its existence; most came to terms with it; a few exploited it. But it was not within the power of individual politicians any more than it was within the compass of the legislature to eradicate corruption in one grand reform of the political constitution . . . Where the law failed, a private individual could scarcely hope to succeed . . . Almost invariably, where a parliamentary candidate refused to become connected with illegal expenses, he automatically excluded himself from the House of Commons.'[72] Aberdeen knew exactly what he was doing. Yet, later, complaining bitterly of 'a vexatious opposition' to his brother Captain William Gordon (who had been re-elected, perhaps surprisingly, after Reform, by a large majority for Aberdeenshire), he wrote to Princess Lieven, 'The expense is enormous, and two contests in three years is enough to ruin a man of moderate fortune. I may be able to bear it; but it would be out of the power of many to do so. I need not tell you that there was no question of bribery or corruption of any kind; yet, that it should cost several thousand pounds to return a man to Parliament is no great proof of the advantages of popular representation'.[73] Aberdeen's astonishing claim that there was no bribery or corruption can only be explained by a desire to keep such matters 'in the family'. Many years later, perhaps in a franker mood, he would write to Gladstone from Buchan Ness, 'Influence, intimidation and corruption are inseparable from any representative system, and, with all our professions, the English are as venal as any people in Europe'.[74]

During 1840 and 1841 Aberdeen was heavily involved in Scottish church affairs. Indeed, he was induced to try to bring in a bill which would heal the schism being caused by differences about the system of private patronage in the established kirk, and whether the congregation should exercise a veto or not, and the position of the civil and ecclesiastical courts with relation to each other. As a result he landed in a hornets' nest of deceit, vituperation and conflict, and found himself being accused, among other things, of 'endeavouring to depose the Redeemer from his throne'.[75] The complicated business was to drag on until 1843, when the Aberdeen Act became law, Disruption of the Old Kirk finally came to Scotland, and the Free Church was founded. Long before then Aberdeen, as tolerant in religion as in all else, had been heartily sickened of human nature as it manifested itself in that sphere. So important was this matter in contemporary eyes that *The Times*, two decades later, in its obituary of Aberdeen, would rate the 'catastrophe' of the Disruption of the Established Church of Scotland as almost comparable in importance to the Crimean War, and would lay the blame for both on failings it considered characteristic of Aberdeen – a 'constitutional apathy' and irresolution.[76] Those who would like to look in greater detail into the history of this vexed question will find a resumé in an appendix.

During his retirement Aberdeen watched with nervous interest Palmerston's handling of affairs in the Middle East, characteristically involving the sending of a fleet to the Dardanelles and a great deal of brinkmanship about war in Europe. Mehemet Ali, Pasha of Egypt, nominally the Sultan's Viceroy, had seized Syria from him. The Sultan (after the Cabinet, to Palmerston's annoyance, had refused British help) succeeded in getting Russian aid. Russo-Turkish hostilities had ended with the Treaty of Unkiar Skelessi on 8 July 1833, granting Mehemet Ali Syria as well as Egypt, and leaving Turkey 'protected' by Russia – most alarming for a Britain anxious for a powerful Turkish empire as a bulwark against

Russian expansion. Worse, by a secret clause the treaty provided that in peacetime no foreign warships except Russian ones should enter the Dardanelles. After Unkiar Skelessi Britain, and the British public, backed Turkey because of their fear of Russia, and this hostility, in combination with anti-Russian policy, notably by Palmerston, was a strong current in the 'drift' to the Crimean War.

Six years later trouble broke out again when the dying Sultan sought British help in a last attempt to regain Syria from Mehemet Ali, and, met by Palmerston's refusal, began hostilities, with a friendly Russia looking on. Palmerston eventually achieved an effective diplomatic coup in the Treaty of London of 15 July 1840, by which Britain, Austria, Russia, Prussia and Turkey agreed to require Mehemet Ali to withdraw. France, whose special protégé Mehemet Ali had always been, was excluded. Thiers immediately declared that the Anglo-French alliance was dead, and war with France seemed imminent. It all ended with Mehemet Ali's being granted the hereditary pashalik of Egypt in return for accepting the requirement of the Treaty of London. Finally in July 1841, France, Austria, Prussia and Russia signed a convention with Britain by which the powers agreed that no foreign warships should enter the Dardanelles when Turkey was not at war. Russia had abandoned the advantages she had gained under the Treaty of Unkiar Skelessi, probably in the hope of establishing friendly relations with Britain. Twelve years hence Aberdeen would be heavily involved in events in which the terms of that convention were a potent factor.

Nor was the Near East all that concerned him. He wrote to Princess Lieven on 24 April 1840, 'In foreign affairs we have enough on our hands: a war in China; a quasi war in Persia; a state of affairs in the Levant which does not promise a continuance of peace; an absurd squabble at Naples, undertaken by us in the true Bonaparte fashion . . . In addition to all this, our relations with the United States are worse than ever'.[77]

The Melbourne Government was clearly too weak to last. When, in the Budget of 1841, it proposed to lower the tariff on Brazilian slave-grown sugar, Peel opposed the motion, and the Government was beaten by a decisive majority of 36.[78] Melbourne did not resign, deciding to dissolve instead. On May 27 Peel gave notice that he would move a resolution of no confidence in the ministry, and at 3 a.m. on June 5 it was carried, after a debate lasting for five nights, by one vote. Russell then announced the Government's intention to dissolve parliament as soon as possible. The result of the ensuing General Election was a great Conservative victory.

When Parliament met for the new session Peel moved an amendment to the address and the Government was defeated by a majority of 91. On Monday, August 30, the resignation of the Government was announced in both houses. Peel was Prime Minister, and sent for Aberdeen as Foreign Secretary.

His Cabinet included three former prime ministers – Peel himself, Wellington and Ripon – and two future ones, Stanley and Aberdeen. Gladstone, a third future prime minister, soon succeeded Ripon as Vice-President of the Board of Trade. (Disraeli, who might have made a fourth, was, to his dismay, left out, and wrote an extraordinary letter to Peel begging him, in his words, 'to save me from an intolerable humiliation'.[79]) Mary's cousin, the Earl of Haddington, was the first Lord of the Admiralty. The Government was strong. As Aberdeen observed prophetically to Princess Lieven, 'We have more to fear from a bad harvest than from all the thunders of the most formidable opposition'.[80] He himself found that the work in the Foreign Office had 'increased beyond measure' since he had last been Foreign Secretary.[81]

Within a fortnight Aberdeen had appointed his brother Sir Robert the new Ambassador to Vienna. 'Sir Robert Gordon is an honest man, slow but not illiberal,' Melbourne commented to the Queen in a letter suggesting that she express to Aberdeen her disapproval of the practice of playing musical chairs with diplomatic appointments on every change of government.[82] A more questionable appointment, possibly, was that of his brother William, who found himself by September 8 a Lord of the Admiralty. In the navy at twelve, a lieutenant at nineteen, in command of a sloop at twenty-two, a post captain at twenty-five, and Captain of the *Magicienne* at twenty-seven, William had been present at the fall of St Sebastian, and had captured an American privateer called the *Thrasher*. He had been paid off at the age of forty-five in 1830. Since 1820 he had been provided with, and regularly re-elected for, the county seat of Aberdeenshire. Now, eleven years after retirement, he was a person of some importance.

William was to do well out of his brother's public service. When in June 1846 the fourth Earl departed from office, William had already, the previous February, been appointed a Commissioner for executing the office of High Admiral. On November 9 his promotion to Rear-Admiral came through. Nothing more was to be heard of him until 1854, when his brother was Prime Minister. In February of that year he would be promoted Vice-Admiral, and appointed Commander-in-Chief at the Nore, in which capacity he served, apparently without mishap, until 1857.

Chapter 12

L'Entente Peu Amicale

So, on 3 September 1841, eleven years after he had had so abruptly to lay down the office of Foreign Secretary on the fall of the Wellington Government, Aberdeen took it up once more.

The lapse of more than a decade had changed many things. Now he was a man of fifty-seven (though Everett the new American ambassador guessed him to be four years younger) and slightly lame, beginning at last to feel the advancing years.[1] Wellington the colossus was no longer Prime Minister, and his autocratic finger would not be poked into every foreign affairs pie with quite the same devastating effect. Aberdeen, his son said, 'resumed the seals of that department [the Foreign Office] with very different authority from that which belonged to him when he first received them thirteen years before. Not only did he possess, in a far higher degree than he had then done, general confidence and respect, but his relation towards the chief of the Government was wholly different from what it had been in 1828. He had regarded the Duke of Wellington as his superior, and shown to him a deference which he never accorded to Sir Robert Peel, with whom he had grown up from boyhood on an intimate footing of perfect equality. A still more important difference resulted from the fact that while the Duke of Wellington, when Prime Minister, occupied himself largely with foreign affairs, which he liked and understood, Sir Robert Peel, who did not so well understand them, was content to leave their control and management as entirely in the hands of Lord Aberdeen, as in the Melbourne Cabinet they had been in those of Lord Palmerston'.[2]

Professor Gash takes a strongly divergent view, in a passage which is most apropos. 'Certainly,' he says, 'there was no question of [Peel's] allowing the Foreign Secretary the same undisturbed and almost private conduct of foreign affairs that Palmerston appeared to enjoy under the placid rule of Lord Melbourne. Between Peel and Aberdeen there was an incessant correspondence. The prime minister not only discussed general matters of policy but scrutinized all levels of diplomatic activity. He read, criticized, and amended draft despatches and instructions, suggested new points for

141

consideration, and proffered his views on diplomatic appointments . . .'[3]

Perhaps the truth, as so often, lies midway between the two views, and Professor Jones may have struck it happily when he pointed out that 'In minor matters Peel allowed his subordinates to run their departments, but on issues of importance he was always consulted,' but that he was not omniscient, and 'in foreign affairs . . . was considerably less informed than Aberdeen, or, for that matter, the Duke of Wellington'.[4] Professor Gash himself concedes that Peel 'rarely sought to over-ride the Foreign Secretary', though 'he frequently sought to influence him', and adds that 'with all their differences of style and temperament, and occasional disagreements over policy, nothing ever happened to shake the essential personal confidence between the two men'.[5] In short they worked excellently together. Aberdeen himself was never in doubt as to which of the two was in command, and that he could put into practice his own ideas about foreign policy.

Yet Aberdeen, it seems, was reluctant to return to office. Protestations to that effect are usually insincere; but were less so, at the least, with him. In 1838 he had written to Princess Lieven of his distaste for politics. 'This is not from a tendency to become gloomy and morose,' he declared, 'for the contrary is the fact; but I have had enough of the world, and without any extravagance, would willingly have as little to do with it as is decent.'[6] Now, when, on September 7, the Government had finally departed and the new ministers were installed in their respective offices, he could only bring himself to write to her, 'There is no use in further complaining; and I must be resigned to my fate and submit'. He had one consolation: 'I hope not to be personally unacceptable to the governments of Europe; and to be able to contribute in some small degree to the preservation of peace, and to the increase of a good understanding in all quarters'.[7] Above all he looked to improving relations with France. With Wellington, he was certain that there would soon be a war in Europe unless something happened to change the outlook. His ambition was to make a friend of France, though not to establish an alliance with her, which would annoy other nations.[8]

Aberdeen was setting himself a formidable task. The situation with France was explosive. In 1841 England and France were glaring balefully across the Channel at each other, their hackles rising every time their interests crossed in the Levant, Greece, Spain, Belgium, North Africa or the Pacific. Aberdeen had a powerful ally in *The Times* for his policy.[9] The 23-year-old Delane had just succeeded to the editorial chair. The new Foreign Secretary soon became his close friend and mentor, whose regular flow of information and advice provided the substance of many leading articles.

Real trust between the nations would not be established overnight, but in the five years in which he was able to exercise power and influence Aberdeen succeeded in creating an atmosphere very different from that which existed when he assumed office. In the end even Palmerston, despite unbridled attacks throughout his tenure of office, was almost reduced to silence by the success of his Anglo-French policy.

Louis Philippe was ready to meet England half-way. However, it was the friendship between Aberdeen and his opposite number Guizot which did most to bring about the unlikely event for which he hoped and worked. Aberdeen had only known François Guizot personally since 1840, when he became French ambassador in London, but had long considered him 'the most honest publick man in France'.[10] Guizot was three years younger than he. Like him he had suffered the loss of a parent in the vulnerable years of early childhood, for his father had been executed when he was seven, exactly the same age as that at which Aberdeen had lost his own father. His mother too had left her home with her son to take refuge in a strange city. Like Aberdeen's she had been pious, strictly moral, sensitive and loving. Similar backgrounds had bred men of similar natures. Like Aberdeen Guizot was a devout Protestant, and like him he was almost arrogant in his determination to uphold the highest standards in public life of which he was capable, though humanly fallible and living in an imperfect world. Outwardly reserved, and inwardly emotional, he had been so fine a scholar that the new chair in Modern History at the University of Paris had been created for him when he was only twenty-five. A convinced monarchist, again like Aberdeen, he had set himself against Napoleon, but had worked for the July Revolution of 1830 which had tumbled Charles X from his throne. Now he had been recalled from London to become Prime Minister and Foreign Minister of France. Only perhaps in their amorous attitudes were the two men dissimilar. When Gladstone said that of the many prime ministers he had known all but two were adulterers, he was undoubtedly including Aberdeen among the faithful. Guizot was of another stamp.

Though it is difficult to remember it, Aberdeen was in fact no lover of France or Frenchmen, and said so plainly and often.[11] He was, besides, extremely fastidious about those whom he admitted to intimacy. But this man he regarded as a brother. There were many to criticize the association in his day on both sides of the Channel.

Without sentimentality, then, and with no illusions about the French, Aberdeen was coolly determined to inspire trust abroad in the honour and probity of England and her representatives. He threw himself into the task with energy and hope. 'I am sanguine in the prospect of our foreign relations being improved, rather than otherwise, with all the world,' he wrote to Princess Lieven. 'Our course will be so plain and straightforward, so cordial and friendly with each, and so entirely without petty jealousies, or the influence of personal prejudices and passions, that it will be hard if we do not make ourselves respected by all.'[12]

Not only was the new policy initiated by Aberdeen and Guizot unpopular at home and unwelcome in France, but it was met with widespread insubordination from English and French agents overseas. The consuls were the worst offenders, disobeying orders and conducting feuds everywhere. Ridiculous as it seems, the most potentially dangerous situation which occurred between France and England during Lord Aberdeen's tenure of office arose from a Gilbert-and-Sullivan affair in Tahiti.

George Pritchard was a Congregationalist missionary in Tahiti, where French Catholic and British Protestant missionaries waged perpetual war on each other. He had come out in 1825, at the age of twenty-nine, to join the London Missionary Society, and had later become British consul.[13] Pritchard exercised great influence over Pomare, Queen of the Society Islands, of which Tahiti was the capital.[14] Pomare was an ardent Christian and great admirer of Britain, who in 1826 had begged George IV to make Tahiti a protectorate.[15] Canning had refused, promising merely a distant benevolence.[16] Ten years later, Pomare, supporting Pritchard, had expelled two French priests who wanted to set up rival missionary headquarters.[17] France had protested; but in the following year the Queen had repeated her offence.[18] On 30 August 1838, the Commodore of the French Pacific Squadron, Admiral Du Petit Thouars, had arrived off the island in the frigate *Venus*, wrested an apology and an indemnity of two thousand Spanish dollars from the Queen, and bullied her into signing a Treaty of Friendship with France.[19] Afterwards Pomare had written asking once again for British protection. 'Let your flag cover us,' she pleaded; but Palmerston would not agree.[20]

Then, in February 1841, with Pritchard away on leave in Australia and Pomare on a tour of her islands, the French consul induced four of her Tahitian chiefs to sign a petition to Louis Philippe asking for the island to be placed under French protection.[21] By September 1842 Du Petit Thouars was back, in the *Reine Blanche*. Demanding compensation and threatening to bombard her island, he bullied the Queen into asking for French protection.[22] In February 1843 George Pritchard returned from leave to find his world in ruins.[23] When the news reached England in March there were public meetings of violent protest, and angry deputations to Aberdeen.[24] The French public was also in flames, and an excited Chamber of Deputies informed Guizot that the French flag was in Tahiti to stay.

Early in November 1843, annoyed by Pritchard's insolence, Du Petit Thouars again appeared off Tahiti, and formally annexed it to France. Pritchard then committed a blunder by declaring that, since he had not been accredited to a French colony, he could no longer be a consul.[25] With nearly twenty years of influence over the natives behind him, he did not fail to make things difficult for the new French bureaucrats, and eventually, on 3 March 1844, the deputy governor of Papeete, Captain D'Aubigny, arrested him and shut him up in a blockhouse. This was *his* blunder. A British subject, a Protestant man of God, and a consul (or former consul), had been imprisoned on political and religious grounds, mistreated and humiliated by the French Government. By March 7 the governor himself had deported him.[26] On the last day of July Pritchard and the news arrived together in Britain.[27]

Suddenly the farce had turned into tragedy. The melodrama and the posturings of self-important individuals were all at once overshadowed by the menacing confrontation of two mighty nations. Sir Robert Peel flew off the handle, and made matters worse with an unwise speech in Parliament speaking of a gross outrage, of an indignity committed on a British consul, and of reparation from the French.[28] Later he expressed regret at the truculent speech; but his heart was not in it. In August the nation grew yet more indignant when, a few days after Aberdeen's formal demand for redress for Pritchard, the French fleet bombarded Tangier, where the Sultan of Morocco had not jumped smartly to heel at a French ultimatum. Guizot's specific assurance to Aberdeen that there would be no bombardment had been broken.

Aberdeen was in great difficulty. Peel had gravely embarrassed him, and most of the English cabinet were determined on measures which would have precipitated war. Pritchard himself had made him look rather foolish by his ill-judged gesture of divesting himself of his consulship. Aberdeen's health was not good, and he was troubled periodically by severe pains in the head which his doctors could not diagnose.* [29] As early as February 1844 he had written to Princess Lieven, 'I must say that although I do not particularly wish my friend Palmerston to succeed me, it seems scarcely possible for me to remain much longer, with increasing labour and failing health'.[30] At this period he more than once asked Peel to allow him to resign.[31] Guizot, Aberdeen's opposite number, too, was being harassed by his colleagues in the French Chamber. The annexation of Tahiti had been none of his doing, and he condemned the high-handed treatment meted out to Pritchard. However, the excited French deputies would not hear of apologies, retractions or even regrets. They were ready to go to war against their old enemy, England.[32]

At this most dangerous juncture the true value of the friendship and understanding between Aberdeen and Guizot became clear. It is generally regarded as indisputable that had Palmerston and Thiers stood in their respective shoes war would almost certainly have been the result. (Even if Palmerston had been Foreign Secretary in England and Guizot Foreign Minister in France, Guizot would certainly not have worked closely with him.) As it was, Aberdeen and Guizot made up their minds to resign simultaneously rather than be responsible for a war.[33] Guizot courageously repelled the attacks of the deputies, while he and Aberdeen kept in the closest touch, always acting in concert through weeks of anxious negotiations. Aberdeen's tactics were an artistic mixture of flexibility and firmness, conciliation, bluster, and, exceptionally, trickery and guile. He conveyed that he would be overborne by his truculent colleagues if the French did not meet him half-way, and even wrote, and revealed, despatches which, in the event, he did not send.[34] These tactics succeeded to admiration.

At the end of August Guizot wrote regretting the seizure of

---

* Aberdeen complained, too, over the years of 'the sound of thunder' pealing in his ears, of giddiness, of feeling 'like a gentleman walking about with his head under water' or 'submerged', or under 'Niagara', as well as of 'noise, confusion and distressing sensations in the head'. Doctors and neurologists today are also at a loss to diagnose, and though migraine, Menières syndrome, and arterio-sclerosis have been considered, none of them seem to meet the case at all points. On the whole, impossible as it is to diagnose satisfactorily from the scrappy evidence available, an educated guess might be made that Aberdeen was psycho-neurotic. Certainly he seems to have had the psycho-neurotic personality – introverted, shy and reserved, anxious, depressive, perfectionist and, if his visions and lifelong mourning of his first wife are evidence, obsessional.

George Pritchard. Even this miserable and grudging apology had not been extracted until Aberdeen had actually sent a gunboat to Tahiti. Palmerston was not satisfied even by so Palmerstonian an act, and berated him in the House for not having sent two gunboats, and for not having adopted a more hectoring tone, and obtained a more crawling apology.[35] On September 2 Guizot agreed to pay an indemnity. In a transport of fury the French Chamber refused to vote the money for it. Louis Philippe offered to pay £1000 out of the Civil List but Guizot refused to let him do so. Negotiations were still going on between the two admirals, British and French, in the Pacific, appointed as arbitrators to determine the amount, when Peel's government fell. The indemnity was never paid, though Pritchard received £1000 from the British Foreign Office in January 1845, and again in August 1845, 'on account'.[36]

To Aberdeen it was a small price to pay for peace. He had been prepared to go even further, agreeing by January 1845 to the mutual suppression of documents, and the substitution of others by Guizot, in order to help him convince the Chamber that there had been no pressure from Britain – which was not strictly true. He removed the originals from the files at the Foreign Office, and substituted edited versions. Being Aberdeen, however, he left the full story revealed in his meticulously-kept private papers for those who came after to read.[37]

It was all over by 6 September 1844, when Aberdeen wrote to Princess Lieven that 'it was impossible to deny that persons of all ranks and classes had made up their minds to war'.[38] On September 10 the French concluded a peace treaty with the Sultan and withdrew their troops from Morocco. On September 15 Victoria wrote to her uncle, the King of the Belgians, 'The good ending of our differences with France is an immense blessing, but it is really and truly necessary that you and those at Paris should know that the danger was *imminent*, and that poor Aberdeen stood almost alone in trying to keep matters peaceable'.[39] Aberdeen always blamed the press for whipping up the war-fever. Writing on 15 June 1845, to Delane, he said, 'Had it not been for the ferment created by the press in both countries, but especially in Paris, it would have been settled much earlier'.[40]

So the French were left with their protectorate and their dignity, Pritchard got his compensation, and Queen Pomare was allowed to return from banishment on the island of Raiatea within two years. Britain had lost little or nothing, commercially or strategically, and had been saved from a ruinous war. Aberdeen's reputation was deservedly high for his masterly handling of a very ugly situation.

The Greek Revolution of 1843 provided another opportunity for French and English agents to bedevil the work of their superiors. Fortunately the mischief done was not as explosive as in the Tahiti affair.

In 1843 there was a popular revolution, which secured a democratic constitution from the deplorable King Otho. Highly sympathetic to it, as a purely internal and spontaneous revolt, Aberdeen accepted, and even hailed it. Peel begged him to tone down the official expressions of his delight, but, though he did so, he insisted that England should support the revolution without delay, declaring, 'I have never known a change more imperatively called for, more fully justified, or more wisely carried out'.[41]

Unhappily for Aberdeen, the hopes of the revolutionaries were to be sadly disappointed, to some extent because of the unsavoury activities of the English and French ministers in Athens, Admiral Sir Edmund Lyons and Monsieur Piscatory. The two diplomats conducted a war of intrigue against each other, each backing a politician and blackening the candidate of the other. In 1844 Aberdeen remonstrated with Lyons for behaving in a very undignified and improper manner when Piscatory attempted the overthrow of the Ministry. In the end the benefits of a Parliament and elections proved illusory, and Aberdeen pleaded for more dignity and reserve from his agents on the internal policies of the country. He would, he said, have nothing to do with English influence which was gained at the cost of low intriguing. To him, 'the superior probity, enterprise and wealth of British merchants will always ensure the preservation of British influence. I desire no other than that which arises from this source, and from our upright and disinterested conduct in our relations with the Government'.[42]

He went so far as to complain to Guizot about Piscatory, expressing his concern lest the constitutional Government of Greece should actually founder on the rocks of these English and French agents who were betraying the great objects desired by them both. No good would come of all their mutual trust, their hopes or their endeavours, 'unless our agents shall really act in the spirit of the instructions they may receive' – a heart-cry from a Gulliver faced by an international distrust so strong that he failed to overcome it in even his Lilliputian subordinates.[43]

Nor was this the end of suspicions between Britain and France. Not only was there another large-scale rebellion in Algeria in 1845, and difficulties on the River Plate, with an Anglo-French mediation ending in mutual recriminations, but there was trouble threatening in the Far East.

When Aberdeen became Foreign Secretary Palmerston's naval and military preparations were in hand to deal with a dangerous situation which had arisen affecting British traders in Canton, and to settle for the future the peculiarly unsatisfactory relations between Britain and the Son of Heaven. Palmerston had sent out a new plenipotentiary, Sir Henry Pottinger, and important islands, including Chusan, and mainland towns had been captured. It was Aberdeen's intention to 'prosecute the war with vigour and effect', in the interests of the vast and mutually beneficial trade with China, mainly in British hands, but he extended Pottinger's discretionary power to come to an appropriate settlement with the imperial Chinese authorities at an opportune moment. The object was to gain access to four or five ports for a 'secure and well-regulated trade' to be carried on by British subjects and those of 'all other states'. Pottinger was positively instructed not to seek 'permanent retention of possessions under the dominion of the British Crown'.[44]

However, after a successful campaign in 1842, Pottinger concluded the Treaty of Nanking, by which not only were the treaty ports opened for trade and the establishment of consular offices, but Hong Kong was ceded to the Crown. Pottinger, convinced that such a settlement was necessary and desirable 'as an Emporium for our trade and a place from which Her Majesty's subjects in China may be alike protected and controlled', had frankly exceeded Aberdeen's instructions.[45] Peel wrote to Stanley that the treaty was a proper occasion for 'a feu de joie'.[46]

Pottinger's successor, Sir John Davis, was to write to Aberdeen when Peel's government fell:

'I may still turn to account those lessons of moderation and justice which were conveyed in your despatches – principles which during your too short administration have maintained a universal peace more glorious than any war . . . I am persuaded that the Chinese think better of us than ever, and if I may judge from the unbounded and reiterated terms of acknowledgment in which Keying [the Chinese Imperial Commissioner] expresses himself, their astonishment at the strict observance of all the terms of the treaty in the restoration [of Chusan] is equal to their expressed admiration of our mild and just rule of the island (infinitely superior to their own) during its occupation. Our troops were hardly removed before the Chinese soldiers began their usual trade of squeezing the inhabitants.'[47]

Regardless of the merits of the Chinese episode and its outcome, however, it had an unfortunate accidental side-effect in further disturbing the *entente*. Rumours spread that when Chusan, occupied

Chapter 13

The Spanish Marriages

The Spanish Marriages question was complicated, if fascinating, involving the conflicting interests of four nations – Spain, Portugal, France and England.

In 1833 there was civil war in both Spain and Portugal. In both countries a child queen was fighting for her throne against a usurping uncle. In Britain the Wellington Government had long since fallen, and the constitutional parties, backing the child queens, had gained the sympathy, if not the more active support, of the Whig Government in which Palmerston was Foreign Secretary.

The Portuguese trouble was settled first. In the twenties the French Government had been strongly opposed to British influence being exerted in Portugal, and Canning as Foreign Secretary had been made aware of this. After the 1830 Revolution in France, however, King Louis Philippe's Government had been favourably disposed towards Queen Maria, and Palmerston had been so much the less inhibited in exercising British influence. In fact, despite the existence of the Foreign Enlistment Act, British volunteers provided valuable help to the Liberator Army led by Queen Maria's father, Dom Pedro. Dom Pedro's army occupied Lisbon, and Queen Maria ascended her throne.

Palmerston then offered an alliance to the governments of Queen Maria of Portugal and Queen Isabella of Spain, and a Triple Alliance was concluded. Great Britain, Spain and Portugal were satisfied – especially Portugal, since it put an end to Queen Maria's troubles. France was less pleased. Talleyrand, French ambassador in London, complained that he had been kept in ignorance of the negotiations, and demanded that France should be included in the alliance. Palmerston agreed, and the Triple Alliance became the Quadruple Alliance of 22 April 1834. This uncharacteristically prompt acquiescence in Anglo-French union was due not to any change of heart but to a suspicion that Louis Philippe's Government had a mind to intervene independently, and the recognition that the Quadruple Alliance might provide a means of forestalling this.

By the Quadruple Alliance the two regents of Spain and Portugal agreed to join forces to compel the Pretenders Don Carlos and Dom

Miguel to abandon their claims. Spanish troops, at Spanish expense, were to be sent into Portuguese territory. Great Britain was to provide a naval force to co-operate with the Spanish and Portuguese armies. France was to play only a very minor rôle, perhaps because Louis Philippe was really rather lukewarm about Queen Isabella of Spain, and preferred the Pretender, Don Carlos.

By a supplementary treaty made on 18 August 1834, Palmerston further frustrated any French moves towards supporting Don Carlos against his niece. By it the King of France undertook to prevent aid reaching the rebels across the French border, and Great Britain agreed to provide Queen Cristina, mother of Queen Isabella of Spain, on her daughter's behalf with arms and war material and, if need be, a naval force against Carlos.

Faced by the Quadruple Alliance, and beaten back on sea and on land, Dom Miguel surrendered, undertaking to leave the Peninsula for ever. On 9 April 1836 the seventeen-year-old Queen Maria da Gloria of Portugal married Prince Ferdinand of Saxe-Coburg, nephew of Leopold, King of the Belgians.

In the development of this complicated Portuguese affair Aberdeen had taken only a small part – the recalling during his first foreign secretaryship of the troops sent by Canning in 1826. Unfortunately, in the subsequent negotiations Palmerston's attitude to France intensified instead of dissipating (as Aberdeen's might have done) the mistrust between the two countries, making it the more difficult to deal with the Spanish problem.

The Quadruple Alliance notwithstanding, the Spanish troubles were neither swiftly nor easily resolved. Don Carlos's support was more formidable than that of Dom Miguel. So the civil war dragged on, hardly alleviated by the 1835 Convention negotiated by the British Special Envoy between the Government of the Regent, Cristina, and the Carlists. Britain still clung to her policy of non-intervention, though, to Aberdeen's fury, Palmerston departed from it far enough to suspend the Foreign Enlistment Act and allow Queen Cristina's Government to form a British Legion in Spain – in fact, British mercenaries, and a band of undesirables whom Aberdeen denounced as the lowest dregs of society.[1] In 1839 the end came at last. When the Carlist General Maroto defected to Queen Isabella, Don Carlos escaped to France, to be interned at Bourges. Queen Isabella was really Queen of Spain at last.

The Spanish troubles, far from bringing Britain and France together, had worsened relations. Palmerston had gone so far as to attempt to include France in the business of restoring peace, but

France had been unco-operative, and in 1836 had withdrawn the legion she had stationed in Spain and sent it to Algiers. This had angered Lord Melbourne so much that no mention of France was made in the King's Speech of 31 January 1837. France had hotly resented that omission. But if the Carlist War had damaged Anglo-French relations, the question of the Spanish Marriages was to prove almost catastrophic.

In 1840 Queen Isabella was still only ten years old; but with each year the efforts to settle the question of who should be her future husband grew more feverish. The Spanish Government, still hardly recovered from the civil war, dreaded more unrest; and Louis Philippe himself sent to London in March 1842 to sound out Great Britain as to her attitude. Lord Melbourne's Government had fallen in August 1841, Peel was Prime Minister, and Aberdeen Foreign Secretary once more.

In order to appreciate the reasons for the strained interest with which both Britain and France watched the varying fortunes of the Spanish crown, one must be cognizant of the vicissitudes of the past. At the end of the Spanish War of Succession, which had lasted from 1700 to 1713, King Philip of Spain, who was a grandson of Louis XIV of France, on mounting the throne had renounced all hereditary rights of succession to that of France, both for himself and for his heirs in perpetuity. At the same time the Dukes of Berry and Orleans had renounced for themselves and for their heirs all rights of succession to the throne of Spain. These renunciations were recognized in the Treaty of Utrecht of 11 April 1713.

The fact that an unmarried Queen now sat on the throne of Spain raised nightmarish fears in the monarchs and statesmen of France and Britain. If Queen Isabella married a Bourbon prince, the line of Bourbons which had sat on that throne for nearly a century and a half would continue to rule over Spain. If she were to marry into another house results prejudicial to French interests might follow.

In these circumstances the French did everything they could to influence the choice of a Bourbon, either from their own reigning House of Orleans, or from one of the lesser branches which ruled in Parma or in Naples. (The Queen Mother and Regent of Spain herself had come of the Neapolitan branch.) To Louis Philippe it was a matter of vital importance that Queen Isabella should marry one of her close Bourbon relations. Britain's view was equally clear-cut. Squeamish or not about interfering in the internal dynastic affairs of another nation, she would not, as Aberdeen made clear to Louis Philippe, tolerate a marriage between the Queen of Spain and any son of the French King. Louis Philippe had brought himself to refuse the proffered betrothal of the Queen to his son, the Duc d'Aumâle; but he had made the refusal conditional on her marrying some other Bourbon prince,[2] and Britain was extremely nervous at the prospect. If, despite the Treaty of Utrecht, the Queen of Spain were to marry a French prince, then at some future date the kingdoms of France and Spain might yet unite, and the nightmare of centuries become reality. This situation would be insupportable. Thus France and England were at daggers drawn as to their objectives, and a long and stubborn battle of wills ensued.

Things did not go Britain's way. Before Peel came to power the Queen Mother had thrown in her lot, and that of her daughter, with the immoderate Moderados party favoured by the French. At first the unprogressive Progressistas party, which Britain supported, had prospered. Queen Cristina had had to flee to Paris, leaving the Progressistas in power. By the summer of 1843, however, the Progressistas had given way to the Moderados, and once again it began to look as if a marriage between Queen Isabella and one of the sons of Louis Philippe might be arranged.

In the face of the altered situation, Aberdeen had to re-think his position, and take a more flexible attitude. In September 1843 Queen Victoria made the first state visit to France by a British monarch since Henry VIII.[3] Aberdeen accompanied her to the Château d'Eu – both Albert and he suffering much on the water* – and discussed the Spanish question with Guizot.[4] He still emphasized the desirability of leaving the Spanish to make their own dynastic choice; but now he met the French Government half-way. He agreed to convey to the Spanish Government that England was now agreeable to Isabella's consort being chosen from among the descendants of Philip V, that is, from the Spanish or Neapolitan branches of the House of Bourbon. Two favourites of Queen Cristina were removed from the list of candidates – the Duc de Montpensier, to satisfy the British, since he was a son of Louis Philippe; and Prince Leopold of Saxe-Coburg, to satisfy the French, since he was not a Bourbon prince.[5] This was a great success for the French, though the arrangement was a loose one. Aberdeen was

---

* 'PA looked much more wretched [than the Queen], Lds Aberdeen and Liverpool too,' recorded Charlotte Canning on August 29; and, on September 13, 'She laughed heartily at the sight, first of PA dreadfully overcome, then Ld Liverpool, and then Ld Aberdeen, all vanishing in haste'. (*Charlotte Canning*, by Virginia Surtees, pp. 88, 109.)

not enthusiastic about it, but he was prepared to accept any other Bourbon in order to exclude the sons of Louis Philippe, and he was convinced by the King's apparently genuine wish to exclude his sons and by Guizot's seeming honesty. All Aberdeen really wanted was a prince who could fend off the intervention of foreign influence in Spain.

It was after that first conference on Spanish affairs at Eu that the famous phrase crystallizing all that Aberdeen hoped for between England and France was born. After Aberdeen's death Jarnac, the French chargé d'affaires, recorded for posterity the story of its *naissance à Haddo-House*. One morning Aberdeen had shown him a long confidential letter to Sir Robert Gordon, defining the relations he hoped to establish with France. His English words, 'a cordial, good understanding', were at once taken up by Guizot and translated into the conveniently apposite French expression *entente cordiale*.[5] Louis Philippe used it in his speech from the Throne in December after seeing it in a letter from Aberdeen to Jarnac.[6] Both countries adopted it and still use it to express the policy which Aberdeen fathered.

Things were not as good as they seemed, and as Aberdeen hoped, however. Guizot, in collaboration with Cristina, at once began to map out a plan for marrying a Neapolitan prince to the Queen of Spain. Quite undeterred by the thought of breaking his agreement with the British Government, and with his friend Aberdeen, while continuing to pay lip-service to the principles of Spanish independence and the Queen's freedom of choice, he deliberately and secretly promoted the candidature of a prince whom he knew would be most unpopular in Spain. Knowing Aberdeen's hatred of intervention in the affairs of other states, he relied on him to do nothing himself. In fact there was nothing Aberdeen could do about it, in any case. Furthermore, it transpired seven months later that Guizot was hatching a plan to marry the Duc de Montpensier, Louis Philippe's younger son, to the Queen's sister, the Infanta. This was particularly in breach of his undertaking with Aberdeen, since it seemed possible that the Queen would be barren, her puberty being abnormally delayed, and that the ultimate heir to the Spanish throne might therefore well prove to be the issue of a French prince.

The following year Louis Philippe returned the Queen's visit, though Franco-British relations had been recently soured by the Tahiti incident and the bombardment of Tangier.[7] Guizot accompanied him to Windsor, where Aberdeen stayed to receive them. Queen Victoria paid a second visit to France in September 1845, remaining for one night at the Château d'Eu. Lord Aberdeen again accompanied her, and once again Guizot was in attendance on Louis Philippe. Once again, too, the Spanish question was discussed; this time more urgently, since Queen Isabella was fifteen years old and rapidly approaching marriageable age. She was not an attractive creature, being corpulent and careless of her appearance, and suffering from the disfiguring disease ichthyosis, which meant that her body, and especially her head and limbs, was covered with dry fish-like scaly skin. She was, despite all this, and her tender years, and her delayed puberty, uninhibitedly and notoriously lecherous. The choice of a husband had to be made soon.

There were not many eligible bachelors among Queen Isabella's Bourbon cousins, even if 'eligibility' was established without reference to personal acceptability. Only four could be put forward. Among these were two Spaniards, the sons of the Duke of Cadiz (his heir Francisco, and Enrico, Duke of Seville), and the Count Trapani, brother of the King of Naples and of her mother Queen Cristina. The British Government preferred Enrico to his elder brother Francisco, not because Francisco was a loathsome creature of degenerate habits and subnormal intelligence, rumoured to be impotent as well, but because Enrico's politics were liberal.[8] Queen Cristina objected to him for the same reason. Both Louis Philippe and Guizot appeared to the English statesman to be agreeable to Enrico's candidature. However, by the time of Victoria's second visit to France Louis Philippe and Guizot and Queen Cristina, as we know, had put their heads together and agreed that Count Trapani – as repulsive a being as Don Francisco, and mentally retarded, as well as being Isabella's uncle – should become the Queen's husband, and had arranged an unofficial betrothal between Louis Philippe's youngest son, the Duc de Montpensier, and the Infanta. If for no other reason, the Infanta was rich enough in her own right to arouse the greed of the French King, and he was eager for the marriage.

However, at Eu it was agreed that the Duc de Montpensier should not marry the Infanta until after the Queen her sister had herself been married and had had children. Guizot and Louis Philippe had probably become anxious about British, and notably Peel's, reaction to the Montpensier plot, and fearful of a counter move by Britain to promote the Coburg candidature. In July, even before Queen Victoria and Aberdeen had sailed for France, Guizot had seen to it that a message of reassurance had reached Aberdeen. There was no suggestion, it conveyed to him, that Montpensier and the Infanta were to be married at once, and in fact no marriage was planned until after the Queen and her husband had had children. At Eu this assurance was confirmed, but verbally, and later on much was to turn on what King Louis Philippe and Guizot had then said, or were supposed to have said.

It was Aberdeen who had insisted that not one child, but children, should be born before the Montpensier marriage took place, so as to ensure the succession. The long wait might bear hard on the affianced pair, if they approached their marriage with anything but distaste, but even so gentle and romantic a lover as Aberdeen could not afford to take such matters into consideration. Whatever his personal feeling, too, he must press for the marriage of the Queen of Spain to either the doltish Trapani or the degenerate heir to the Dukedom of Cadiz in preference to a son of the French King, no matter how charming and personally desirable he might be.

On the evening after the discussion at the Château d'Eu Aberdeen wrote to Peel, reporting in clear and simple terms the unequivocal undertaking by the King and Guizot. 'With respect to the Infanta,' he noted, 'they both declared in the most positive and explicit manner that, until the Queen was married and *had children*, they should consider the Infanta precisely as her sister, and that any marriage with a French Prince previously would be out of the question.'[9]

Only one condition seems to have been made, if condition it was, with regard to this agreement between the British and French governments. During Aberdeen's audience with him, Louis Philippe had asked him to promise that his Government would not support a Coburg candidate, and Aberdeen had given his precise undertaking to that effect. According to Louis Philippe, writing to his daughter the Queen of the Belgians, he had said, 'As to the candidature of Leopold of Saxe-Coburg, you can be tranquil on this point. I answer that it will not be either avowed or supported by England'.[10]

A good deal of argument was later to arise about whether or not the exclusion of Prince Leopold was actually a condition of the French promise. All such sophisticated arguments were for the future, however, when things had gone awry. At Eu in 1845 everything seemed arranged to everyone's satisfaction, even Queen Cristina's, and Aberdeen could congratulate himself on the good feeling that existed on all sides, and feel that Montpensier's marriage to the Infanta 'would never be thought of . . . for three or four years'.

However, Aberdeen was fighting an uphill battle at home. At the time that the Queen was paying her second visit to France it appeared to be a losing one. Public opinion in England not only remained hostile to France, but grew increasingly so, and the Opposition bayed its outrage at this attempted neighbourliness (or meek submissiveness, as they preferred to believe it) towards a foreign nation. That was bad enough, but not unexpected or intolerable. It was the difficulties put in his way by Lord Aberdeen's own colleagues which came near to nullifying his efforts to maintain the *entente* with France.

They were without exception full of mistrust. Wellington was foremost among them, rejecting from the first friendship with France as dangerous, distasteful and positively unnatural; but Peel was not far behind him.[11] It was no light matter for Aberdeen. It is always difficult for a foreign secretary to advocate a conciliatory foreign policy against colleagues who express genuine fears for the safety of the realm in the face of possibly hostile foreign powers. After all, Louis Philippe and Guizot were neither immortal nor invulnerable, as time would show. Wellington was eager to prepare England for war because of the unquestionable acceleration of French naval expansion, and of the Anglophobia manifested in the French Chambers and press with alarming ferocity. Aberdeen, on the other hand, took his conciliatory policy to such lengths as to maintain two fewer ships of the line in the Mediterranean than did the French. So seriously did Aberdeen take the lonely position in which he found himself, and the prospect of the disappointment of all his hopes, that he took the momentous step of offering to resign.

On 18 September 1845 he wrote to Peel, saying that he seemed to have hardened against France – 'A policy of friendship and confidence has been converted into a policy of hostility and distrust' – and declared, 'It is my deliberate and firm conviction that there is less reason to distrust the French Government, and to doubt the continuance of peace at the present moment, than there was four years ago, when your administration was first formed'. He rejected the insinuation that he was making England vulnerable in thus carelessly exposing her to the mercies of a wolf in sheep's clothing: 'For my own part, I would never for an instant forget the possibility of war, and would make all reasonable provision accordingly; but I would continue to live under the conviction of the greater probability of peace'. Time was to prove him right.

He warned Peel against the danger of panic, which might itself cause war. He quoted with scorn the incident whereby the Prince de Joinville could not come across the Channel and have a look at the new floating breakwater at Brighton without being taken for a political spy. He referred openly to Wellington's 'strong opinions', and pointed out that his position was growing increasingly lonely and difficult because of them. 'He must necessarily consider me as the only obstacle to the adoption of measures which he sincerely believes to be indispensable to the safety and welfare of the country,' he said; and he concluded, 'Under all the circumstances . . . it is my belief that it will be the safest course for you to allow me now to retire from the Government. No difference as yet has taken place, and none whatever is expected. It is well known to my friends and connections that office is not only irksome to me, but that considerations of health have more than once pretty urgently called for this proceeding. No other motive will be assigned, and it will be the more easy to sanction this, as I have no wish ever to enter the House of Lords again'.[12] As usual Aberdeen was doing his utmost not to embarrass his friends, however much they embarrassed him.

There is no doubt that Aberdeen had certainly been suffering from his distressing medical symptoms all through his foreign secretaryship, but in reply Peel insisted that whatever motive he gave for resigning, the real political one must be revealed to the Queen and his colleagues and that in itself would have the most disastrous results. He could not agree to be a party to using the excuse of ill-health as a way out of the difficulty. 'I will say nothing as to the effect of your retirement with reference to my own personal feelings and position,' he wrote. 'Independently of the evil consequences of the retirement on the particular ground above alluded to. I should consider your loss *irreparable*'.[13] Wellington warmly agreed as to the personal loss and the public mischief which would result from Aberdeen's resignation,[14] and Graham wrote that his loss would be 'fatal and irreparable'.[15]

The crisis, as far as Peel was concerned, was over. Lord Aberdeen did not resign.[16] Yet he was aware that real feelings had altered not a whit, and he worried about what that might bring forth. That October he forwarded to Peel a letter of Guizot's which emphasized that to prepare for war in order to preserve peace was a policy unsafe for the great powers, for modern political systems, and for the present state of society, and attempted to convince him that France was not a threat by saying that all that he feared from her had in fact been present in the situation four years before, at the outset of the ministry. There had been a French army of 350,000, Paris was being fortified, and revolutionary changes had already taken place. 'Nevertheless we thought it possible not only to remain at peace with France but to live and act with her in the spirit of peace and friendship,' Aberdeen argued. 'Our policy is now changed, and every newspaper is filled with the account of our hostile preparations. We still talk of peace, having war in our hearts.'[17]

Meanwhile in Madrid the British and French ambassadors, Bulwer and Bresson, had been undoing Aberdeen's work, and seeking to outwit each other in diplomatic intrigue. Guizot had worked hard to persuade the King of Naples to allow his brother, the Count Trapani, to be a candidate for the hand of his niece, but had failed. Queen Cristina appeared to have transferred her support from her brother to Prince Leopold of Saxe-Coburg though this may have been a trap laid for Britain. The clever and upscrupulous Sir Henry Bulwer had long been meddling in the various intrigues, though frequently instructed by Aberdeen not to do so. From the autumn of 1845 he had opposed Trapani's candidature, and had even tried to convert Aberdeen to giving support to Prince Leopold. In the spring of 1846 he had actually written to him, 'I may add that *I could make the marriage* if you instructed me to do so, and that your instructions to me were kept secret'.[18] Aberdeen had replied on May 7: 'Whatever we may feel towards an amiable and deserving young prince, nearly connected with our own Queen, we have really no political interest whatever in his success. On the contrary, I can easily conceive that it might lead to much inconvenience, notwithstanding his personal merits; for it is probable that he may be regarded by the Spanish Government as likely to receive the countenance and active support of England, if placed in the situation of the Queen's husband. Now, I have no belief whatever that such would be the case; and, even if it were, it could only lead us into the most impolitic and embarrassing engagements. As we have no English candidate, I should be sorry to see you actively engaged in the support of any other, be he who he may'.[19]

That was clear enough. However, before he had had the reply Bulwer was already up to his ears in a palace intrigue which ended in Queen Cristina's addressing a letter to the Duke of Saxe-Coburg, who was conveniently in Lisbon, offering her daughter in marriage to his son. Bulwer had certainly had a hand in its writing, and preened himself on it; but he had been at Queen Cristina's mercy as soon as he had allowed himself to be drawn into an operation which dishonoured the undertakings made at Eu, and he had profoundly embarrassed his Government. He had triumphantly dispatched a copy of the letter to Aberdeen, together with an outline of a devious conspiracy which had been set up, and which was to involve in its various stages a change of ministry, the summoning of the Cortes, the proposal of the Queen's marriage to Trapani, its rejection, and finally the proposal, approval and celebration of her marriage to Prince Leopold. Then, and only then, was the French Government to have been informed that it had taken place. With a somewhat naïve cunning, Bulwer had proposed a bribe which was at that stage to set everything right with the French. The marriage, he suggested, of the Infanta and the Duc de Montpensier might be allowed to take place immediately.[20] Aberdeen acted at once, sending Bulwer a sharp reprimand for his insubordination in departing from his instructions as well as for his dishonourable plotting. He was deeply distressed to be attacked where he least welcomed it – the honour and integrity of England which it was his prime aim to uphold in the eyes of the world, and chiefly before France.

He had at once informed St Aulaire of the letter to the Duke of Saxe-Coburg, he told Bulwer, and had told him that Bulwer knew of it. 'I added, too,' he wrote, 'that you had acted in the matter without my instructions, and entirely without my knowledge, but that our own views and opinions had undergone no change.' Peel too sent his strong condemnation of Bulwer's behaviour.[21]

Unhappily, soon after this incident Aberdeen had had to lay down his seals, and all hope of a tactful settlement went with him. It was on 9 June 1846, only nine months after his threatened resignation, that Peel had carried his Bill on the repeal of the Corn Laws and destroyed the Conservative Party. On June 27 the Government fell, and Lord John Russell came in, with Palmerston as his Foreign Secretary. Aberdeen had not yet removed Bulwer from Madrid, probably only because the French demanded it, and Palmerston retained him. Things went from bad to worse, and ended disastrously.

Neither Louis Philippe nor Guizot liked working with Palmerston at the best of times. In the existing situation the revelation of Bulwer's discreditable behaviour reawakened French fears. Bresson henceforth clearly considered himself free to use any means, however dubious, to outwit his disingenuous diplomatic colleague. Alert for every piece of intelligence, he outdid himself in a despatch to his Government announcing that Queen Isabella, at sixteen, had just become a woman – '*La reine est nubile depuis deux heures*'.[22] Less amusingly, in direct contradiction to the compact struck at Eu, he suggested to the Queen Mother that the Queen and her sister the Infanta should now be married simultaneously.

On July 19 Palmerston sent a despatch to Bulwer, in which he reduced the roster of candidates for the Queen's hand to three, naming as first among them Prince Leopold of Saxe-Coburg. In it he also abused the Spanish Government, and criticized its handling of internal affairs.[23] Not only was Bulwer instructed to pass on the gist of this despatch in Madrid, but Palmerston showed it to Jarnac and offered him a copy for Guizot's eyes.[24] This incredible document set in train a series of events which destroyed the labours of long years, poisoned relations with both France and Spain, and united all the Bourbon monarchies against England.

In the despatch Palmerston had resuscitated the discarded candidature of Don Enrico, the liberal Duke of Seville. The despatch went via Jarnac to Guizot and Louis Philippe, and thence to Bresson in Madrid, who showed it to the Queen Mother. This was enough to unite the Queen Mother and Louis Philippe, both of whom detested Don Enrico; and the King and Guizot persuaded Queen Cristina to marry the Queen to the Duke of Cadiz, and the Infanta to his son the Duc de Montpensier – at once and simultaneously. The marriages were celebrated at Madrid on 10 October 1846, on the Queen's sixteenth birthday. Louis Philippe and Guizot had had their revenge for 1840. All Aberdeen's work had gone for nothing; and the *entente cordiale*, or what was left of it, was in ruins.

By 14 September 1846 the Queen was lamenting, 'If our dear Aberdeen was still at his post, the whole thing would not have happened,'[25] and a private letter from Aberdeen to Delane gives his own succinct view. Dated 30 October 1846, it reads, 'Perhaps there is no person who has more reason to complain of the marriage of the Infanta and the manner in which it was accomplished than myself. I think that you were informed at the time of the engagement entered into with me at the Château d'Eu by the King and Guizot, and the conditions under which the project was to be entertained. Had I remained in office it is probable that this engagement would have been observed, for although it might have been irksome and onerous, they could not, to me, have made use of the only argument which has been adduced to justify its violation. They had received from me undoubted proofs of a determination not to encourage the notion of a marriage with Prince Leopold of Saxe-Coburg; but they profess to believe that Ld. Palmerston has not acted with the same good faith . . . The *entente cordiale* is undoubtedly at an end as it formerly existed; but that was really the case when I left office'.[26] He was right. Examination of Palmerston's letters makes it clear that he had abandoned Aberdeen's policy of friendship with France. To him France was

162

a potential enemy, working against British policy, and so Britain must work against French interests.

All those who had been so busy for so long about the matter might have spared themselves their pains. The Queen had many lovers, and children, though Don Francisco was almost certainly not their father; and there was never any question of the children of the Infanta and the son of Louis Philippe succeeding to the throne of Spain.

More immediately, the annexation of independent Cracow by Austria, in breach of the Treaty of Vienna, has long been put down to the failure of the *entente* at this time, separate protests by England and France being ineffective as compared with a joint one. This can be a matter only for speculation, of course; and it may well be that no protests, joint or otherwise, unbacked by the threat of force, would have been a deterrent, while the geographical remoteness of Cracow made any such threat implausible.[27]

To Princess Lieven Aberdeen gave his last word on the affair: 'The Spanish marriages were an ugly business, but it is now well over, and I have no wish whatever to refer to it, except as an example that notwithstanding M. Guizot's personal opinion and views, we cannot be certain of the conduct of the [French] government'.[28] It was a kind comment, as far as Guizot was concerned, but a judicious one, as written to his mistress.

What judgement is to be made of Aberdeen's handling of the Spanish marriages question? As is usual where he is concerned, verdicts tend to polarize to contempt and, less often, to admiration. Perhaps the most valuable, coming from certainly one of the most informed and objective sources, is that with which Jones Parry, that respected authority, has chosen to sum up his detailed and precisely authenticated account of the whole history of the affair.[29]

Aberdeen, he says, reluctant though he was to become the instrument of Coburg ambitions, but anxious not to alienate his sovereign, had played with the idea of a Coburg marriage in the spring of 1846 in such a way as to encourage Bulwer to believe that he attached less value than before to the engagements made at Eu; and had issued instructions often so self-contradictory as to mislead the ambassador. But he points out that the mainspring of Aberdeen's actions was his 'belief that British honesty and fair dealing provided the safest guarantee against a breach of faith by France', and reminds us: 'Aberdeen's loyalty to his engagements had proved the greatest stumbling-block to the development of Guizot's designs. "There is something about you," wrote Jarnac to him on his retirement, "which inspires and begets confidence, which calls forth every noble impulse of the mind and of the heart, and renders it as impossible to resort to deceit with you as to apprehend it from you."[30] In practice, it is true, Aberdeen's integrity had not met with such a generous response from Guizot; but however dexterously he had profited in the past from the trust imposed in him by the other, it is as certain as any such speculation can be that had Aberdeen remained in office, Guizot would have found it extremely difficult, if not impossible, to break the pledges which he had given him in 1845. Certainly Aberdeen, having engaged his own Court to do nothing detrimental to his policy, would have afforded him no pretext for doing so'.

And, Jones Parry goes on, 'By frankness, scrupulous good-faith, and by the very force of his own character he had bound Guizot to his engagements. Therein lay the strength of his policy; therein, too, lay its weakness. "No system which depends on the personal connections of a particular individual can hope to survive for long."[31] By relying too exclusively upon his own peculiar qualities, Aberdeen, like Castlereagh, had made it almost impossible for a successor to continue his policy'.

Guizot, Jones Parry says, let Aberdeen down, and it was a pity that Aberdeen did not realize that in dealing with Guizot and Louis Philippe he was risking too much by his determination 'to explore every avenue of argument and persuasion' before going to extremes. 'Conciliatory methods which lack the appearance if not the reality of firmness are apt to be construed as a sign of weakness and to be exploited by an adversary to his own ends.' It is that point which Aberdeen's critics seize upon – the delicate balance between conciliation and 'firmness'. It is a fortunate foreign secretary who is not confronted by this dilemma, with much at stake. Palmerston perhaps leaned too far towards 'firmness', Aberdeen too far towards conciliation; but luck as well as judgement can operate towards success or failure in either. Jones Parry in his concluding sentences pronounces his own judgement.

'Nevertheless, Aberdeen must be judged by his achievements, and not by the unfortunate consequences which followed his fall. He had kept Guizot to his engagements, and had he remained in power, it is difficult to conceive of any circumstances in which the French Foreign Minister would have dared to break them at the cost of Aberdeen's friendship and of his own good name. "Few have ever made the virtues of private life so eminently useful in public affairs. One cannot wish for a reputation more enviable than that of having brought diplomacy in all cases to a successful issue by straightforwardness and sincerity." '32

On that final verdict, quoting, of all men, Bulwer, who might have considered himself to have suffered from those virtues, and written, as it was, two days after Aberdeen's departure from the Foreign Office, so that self-interest could have played a minimal rôle in its conception, one might leave the sad and sordid history of the Spanish marriages.

Chapter 14

American Problems

In the tactics employed in the settlement of the Maine and Oregon boundary disputes, as well as other inherited difficulties, Lord Aberdeen was determined to attain his objective of peace without sacrificing Britain's interests. To this end he was prepared to go to the limit of patience, reason and compromise, extending to concessions and even to ambiguous apologies, now giving his agents wide discretion, and now insisting on his own way. Among other devices to which he resorted were guile, judicious bribery, bluff, and, in the last resort, threats of force – all weapons he detested, but would employ if he considered them to be necessary. In a most complex situation affected by the explosive state of Anglo-American hostility, by deepening depression at home and the need to cut military expenditure, by stagnating mutual trade, by political pressures on both sides of the Atlantic, by an easily combustible Prime Minister, and above all by his own delicate self-appointed task of conciliating both France and America while destroying the collaboration between the two which had operated against Britain in two wars, Aberdeen achieved success against disheartening odds.

When Aberdeen became Foreign Secretary in 1841 the new American President, Tyler, and his Secretary of State, Daniel Webster, were disposed to improve relations with Britain. Palmerston's departure from the Foreign Office gave some hope of success despite the violent crisis over the indictment of one Alexander McLeod in connection with the so-called *Caroline* incident, which under Palmerston's handling had been escalating to war. The Americans' long-standing hostility was rooted in memories of their war of independence; resentment of a British colonial presence across the still partly undefined border with the Canadian provinces; fear of British territorial aggandizement; anti-British prejudice from Irish immigrants; and Britain's obstinate insistence on the right of search of ships suspected of carrying Africans into slavery. An additional cause of friction was the thrusting of the American population southward and westward into Mexico's Texas and California and beyond the Rocky Mountains into the Anglo-American joint territory of Oregon. Despite these pressures, Tyler and Webster approached Peel and Aberdeen in order to try to settle outstanding issues. Peel was receptive, and Aberdeen appointed Lord Ashburton to head a mission to deal with Webster and negotiate settlements. Problems left outstanding by Palmerston were the comparatively trivial *Creole* incident (in which an American ship engaged in the domestic slave trade, manned by mutineers and murderers, had put in to Nassau in the Bahamas, whereupon the murderers had been detained pending trial, but the other slaves set free, by the British authorities)[1]; the *Caroline* case; the signing of an extradition treaty to discourage the flight of criminals across the Canadian border; the fulfilment of America's obligation assumed in the Treaty of Ghent to suppress slave traffic; and, above all, the troublesome boundary problems in Oregon and, especially, Maine. These two boundary issues were of supreme interest in the United States whereas in Britain they were of secondary importance – a perennial source of misunderstanding.

Aberdeen had been careful to select an envoy who would be acceptable to the United States. No professional diplomat, Ashburton had close business connections with the States as head of the banking house of Baring, and an American wife. 'The great necessity for Ashburton's mission,' Aberdeen later recalled, 'was in consequence of our having a Minister [Fox] at Washington, who although not without ability, did nothing. He passed his time in bed, and was so detested by every member of the US Government that they had no communication with him, except as it was absolutely indispensable.'[2]

Aberdeen and Ashburton worked well together, and the mission was a success, particularly as to the Maine boundary, where territory larger than Belgium was in dispute. In 1828 the two governments had agreed to the arbitration of the King of Holland, and Britain had accepted the award, but the disappointed Americans had rejected it, leaving the quarrel to be settled by negotiation.[3] There were many obstacles to be overcome before the end, and some of them were raised by Aberdeen's colleagues.

Wellington, as Prime Minister, unlike Peel, as we know, had been keenly interested in foreign affairs. Though merely a member of the Cabinet without office, he continued to intervene with very strong opinions – opinions which Aberdeen treated with the greatest respect, even when they were most at odds with his own. Now he created a major difficulty which Aberdeen overcame with panache. The difficulty arose from Wellington's determination, with security the dominating factor in his mind, that not an inch should be ceded on the Maine frontier, and the story is best to be read in three despatches from Aberdeen to Ashburton, dated in February, March and May.[4] Aberdeen had in fact challenged Wellington by ensuring that Ashburton was armed with very wide powers, and given instructions to settle the dispute as best he could, provided only that at least a third of the disputed area remained in British hands at the end of it. Of the 12,000 square miles in question he was to secure as a minimum about 4000 square miles, which was the area which had been awarded by the King of Holland as arbitrator. With these instructions Lord Ashburton sailed in HMS *Warspite* in February.[5] However, Wellington was exceedingly wrathful when he received his copy of the instructions, and at once demanded of Aberdeen that Britain should stick out for the whole claim.[6]

Aberdeen was in a quandary. He sent on the protest to Ashburton, perhaps hoping that it was too late for him to receive it.[7] However, bad weather had forced the *Warspite* to put back to Yarmouth; and Ashburton had it at once. He was extremely put out, and made his feelings plain in his reply.[8] The clash between Aberdeen and Wellington is embodied in the despatch of March 31, which contained two inconsistent sets of instructions. In the earlier part was set forth once again the 4000-square-miles-minimum as the object to be achieved. But the document then went on to outline Wellington's demands for the minimum to be increased to cover the whole area north of the St John river, which would free the road between Quebec and Halifax for future military movements.[9] When this despatch reached Ashburton he asked in strong terms for the inconsistency to be resolved, and for definite instructions.[10]

In May Aberdeen blandly explained that the minimum intended had always been the 4000 square miles of the arbitration award, and he admitted to having difficulty with Wellington, whose 'tenacity', he said, Ashburton well knew.[11] This apparently tipped the wink to Ashburton, for the negotiations went on apace, and it was agreed that the time had come for compromise. At home, at the suggestion of his Cabinet colleagues, Aberdeen called in military expert opinion to assess the strategic importance of the disputed territory. Faced with the opinions of Sir James Kempt (Governor-General of Canada, 1828–30), Sir Howard Douglas (Governor of New Brunswick, 1823–31), Lord Seaton (Lieutenant-Governor of Upper Canada, 1828–38), and Sir George Murray (Master General of the Ordnance), which differed enough to leave Aberdeen freedom to manœuvre, the Duke gave way.[12] Ashburton secured a thousand square miles more than the minimum agreed, just over half the disputed area on the Canadian frontier, and a good bargain for Britain. Fighting his often lonely battle against his Prime Minister, Wellington, the rest of the Cabinet, the Opposition, private business interests, and the press, Aberdeen moved on to the next problem. Never too much swayed by economic considerations, his motives were always long-term and international.

Next on Ashburton's list was the *Caroline* question. Among the painful Anglo-American difficulties of the past had been the 1837 Canadian Rebellion, which had been crushed by the British Government. The rebels had been driven across the border into America, but, finding a good deal of support there, had continued to make raids into Canada. Just after Christmas 1837, in the process of repelling one of these, the Canadian militia had crossed the Niagara river to the New York side and had fired the *Caroline*, a small rebel steamer lying at anchor, which had been ferrying men and arms and supplies into Canada. Unfortunately, in the process they had killed an American, Amos Durfee. An outcry for threats of war against Britain because of the incident followed, but President Van Buren remained commendably firm and cool, merely protesting mildly to Britain, and ordering the Canadian border to be patrolled, so as to prevent his countrymen continuing their raids from the American side.

Three years after it had occurred, however, trouble flared up once more, when Alexander McLeod, a member of the Canadian militia, boasted in his cups during a visit to New York of having taken part in the burning of the *Caroline*, and went into lurid details about the events of that famous night. He was lying, having been far away at the time, but he was arrested, charged with Durfee's murder, and gaoled.[13] A vital and complicating factor was that by the terms of the American constitution the federal authorities had no right to intervene in the court proceedings of the state of New York. This was widely regarded in Britain as mere evasion on a technicality.

This unfortunate business put discussion of the north-eastern boundary dispute almost out of the question. The British had been as enraged as the Americans, Palmerston had adopted an extremely hard-line attitude, and had sent a Note demanding McLeod's release. Palmerston was so bellicose, and his language so violent, that war would almost certainly have resulted if McLeod had been executed. He wrote to Fox, 'McLeod's execution would produce war, war immediate and frightful in its character, because it would be a war of retaliation and vengeance'.[14]

McLeod was taken to court, and all but lynched. Strenuous efforts made to quash the proceedings were unavailing[15]; and McLeod's trial for murder went on, watched by the two nations in a high state of tension. In Britain feeling grew to almost the same pitch as it had reached in America, and Tory Members of Parliament called for strong measures to save McLeod. Almost too late, with collision imminent, Palmerston tried to alter course, adopted a more moderate tone, and decided to await the result of the trial before further action. He had left the Foreign Office before McLeod came to trial.

This was the dangerous situation which Aberdeen found when he came in 1841 to the Foreign Office, and about which he could do little or nothing. In the end things worked out better than might have been expected. McLeod came to trial in the autumn, the US Government paid for his defence, and he pleaded an alibi for the night of the raid on *Caroline*. The jury disagreed, McLeod was acquitted and smuggled out of prison to safety across the border, and Aberdeen drew a breath of relief.[16] He could now implement his own policies.

Ashburton was home again by the end of September 1842, the Ashburton Treaty having been signed in Washington in August. As well as having settled the north-eastern boundary dispute he had cleared up the aftermath of both the *Creole* and the *Caroline* incidents. (He told Aberdeen that the *Creole* incident gave him 'more trouble than all the other questions taken together',[17] but in the end the Americans conceded that escaped slaves could not be reclaimed, and the British that American ships in British waters were not 'within the exclusive jurisdiction of England'.[18]) He had succeeded in getting the extradition treaty signed. Nothing had been given away except a cunningly worded apology that was not, diplomatically speaking, an apology, over the *Caroline*. Then, too, Ashburton had agreed to relinquish the demand for a mutual right of search in exchange for an undertaking that the Americans would send eight ships for joint patrolling of the West Coast of Africa on the lookout for slavers. In none of the issues, even that of suppressing the slave trade, were the details of compromise and concession vitally important to Aberdeen because they were not vitally important to the national interest, and what he wanted seemed to have been achieved with Ashburton's Treaty. 'The good temper in which you left them all,' he wrote to him, 'and the prospect of continued peace, with, I trust, improved friendly relations, far outweigh in my mind the value of any additional extent of Pine Swamp.'[19]

Aberdeen's denigrators have not failed to find scope for blame in his handling of the North-East boundary question, accusing him of over-hasty and inadequate preparation of his case, chopping and changing his instructions to Ashburton, ineptitude in leaking information, and lack of alertness as regards commercial interests. Even one of his most hostile critics admits, however, that the final settlement was within Ashburton's discretionary powers, and that it gave Aberdeen what he had sought from the start – a general settlement with the United States to remove the continual threat of war – and that he was indifferent to its details. That critic acknowledges, too, that Aberdeen showed himself on occasion as having steadier nerves than Peel, and being more realistic than Peel or Palmerston, and admits that not only did the British Government probably get a better bargain than it knew, but that in fact the boundary settlement was 'not a bad one'.[20]

On the other hand, a no less informed, but perhaps more objective, historian, praises Aberdeen for that very flexibility which allowed frequent modification of Ashburton's instructions, giving him freedom to manœuvre when faced with emotional and obstinate opponents, and for his willingness to engage in a 'disorderly' – or informal – negotiation, thus making it possible to achieve 'that success in America which he believed was absolutely vital to the success of his French policy'.[21]

It cannot be denied that within a year of Aberdeen's taking office disputes which had gone on for fifty-eight years, and which had brought England to the brink of war, had been settled. Palmerston was not content with the Treaty, but exceeded himself in abuse, blackguarding the negotiator and his wife in private letters, writing hostile articles in the press, and offending against the proprieties by references to Lady Ashburton on the floor of the House.[22] This gave wide offence, angering Whigs as well as Tories, even in that robust age.[23] To the fastidious Aberdeen such behaviour was unpardonable. Neither in public speeches nor in private letters did he ever descend to personal abuse. A little languid and waspish sarcasm, under extreme provocation, was the most he ever permitted himself. While this may seem almost too good to be true, research into his papers confirms his son's claim that 'after reading . . . many thousands of his public and private letters . . . they never contain any ill-natured remark about others or any story told to another's prejudice'.[24] The researcher, too, will probably decide, as Arthur Gordon did, that this 'peculiarity' was 'the natural result of his habit and tone of mind', and not of 'any formed and conscious resolution'.[25] The incident did nothing to lessen Aberdeen's distaste for the extrovert and uninhibited Lord Palmerston.

*   *   *

Ashburton, however, had left the question as to the occupancy of the Oregon Territory unsettled.

In 1783, in the Treaty of Versailles which had ended the American War of Independence, there had been no definite agreement about distinguishing what territory belonged to Britain and what to the States; and since then only an unsatisfactory joint occupation had been achieved by an 1818 Convention, with the 49th parallel of latitude recognized as the boundary between United States territory and British North America as far west as the Rocky Mountains. Until about 1840 the Americans had not shown much interest in the Pacific coast territory, and it had been left to the Hudson's Bay Company's agents and the Indian and half-caste trappers who supplied them with skins in exchange for stores. In the 1820s Canning had tried to secure the Columbia River line with only an American enclave north of it, but the United States held out for the whole area south of the 49th parallel. A new convention in 1827 extended the provisions of the 1818 agreement indefinitely subject to abrogation upon one-year notice. That was how matters stood when Aberdeen took office in 1841. Things were changing, however. American immigration into Oregon was beginning and would grow into a torrent.[26] The pressure of the American settlers brought matters to a head. In 1842 Aberdeen had instructed Ashburton to try for a settlement on the lines of Canning's proposals of the 1820s. At first Daniel Webster had been favourably disposed, but a combination of circumstances operated for postponement. Such differing factors as the difficulties about the Maine dispute and Ashburton's queasiness at sea and consequent desire to sail for England before the autumn gales probably acted with equal weight.[27]

Daniel Webster retired in 1843, and the negotiations of the next three years were not made any easier by the fact that Aberdeen had to deal with two different presidents and three different secretaries of state in rapid succession. Further, the British representative in Washington during the critical last two years was Sir Richard Pakenham, who caused many difficulties.

In 1842 the American colonists in the south of the Oregon territory sent a delegate to Washington to press their claims to exclusive possession; and when he returned in the spring he brought with him a large number of Americans from the middle west, who set to work to farm the valley of the Columbia river, and sought to push out the Hudson Bay settlers. Both sides clamoured for public support, and Congress decided to look into the matter. It was the presidential election of 1844 which raised

172

Polk to power, and let loose a spate of hysterical war-talk. The country took up the cry of 'Fifty-four forty or fight!'[28] Yet behind the scenes the American diplomats were prepared to settle for the 49th parallel, and though Britain responded with an official claim for the territory to the Columbia river she too was prepared to accept the same boundary.

In America the problem was complicated by sectional difficulties about Texas. In 1845, after nine years of independence, the former Mexican territory of Texas was anxious to become a part of the Union; but all was not plain sailing. The pro-slavery party in the United States was fervid for annexation, the anti-slavery one against it, for if Texas were to become the 28th state, she would lend strength in Congress to the slavery party. The gain of the 'free' Oregon territory, however, would provide a way out of this impasse; for the two acquisitions would cancel each other's votes in the Senate. This gave additional impetus to the move for claiming the territory, and 'Oregon Fever' became an epidemic.

By 1845 the situation was deteriorating rapidly, the American settlers coming up the Oregon trail in such numbers that the British were swamped and could not hold the Columbia valley against them. The fur trade, too, was a diminishing asset. It was clear that the time had come to settle matters once and for all. In January 1845 Pakenham had suggested arbitration, but President Tyler (for Polk, though elected, would not assume office until March) would not agree. Moreover, in his inaugural address, Polk – who had been elected on the 'Fifty-four forty or fight!' slogan, and was a belligerent exponent of the 'Manifest Destiny' school of thought – warned off all other powers from meddling in the affair by helping Mexico's efforts to retain sovereignty over Texas, and asserted that the American title to the Oregon territory was 'clear and unquestionable', and would be maintained at all costs.[29] All the claims which had been acknowledged over the years as rightly possessed by Britain were now being denied.

On 4 April 1845 Polk's inaugural address, with its threat to terminate the Convention of Joint Occupancy, was brought before Parliament. Peel expressed regret at the means which had been used by the new President to air his views, and at his tone and temper, in a resolute speech envisaging war.[30]

Aberdeen's statement in the Lords ran hand in hand with Peel's. 'My Lords, I consider war to be the greatest folly, if not the greatest crime, of which a country could be guilty, if lightly entered into; and I agree entirely with a moral writer who has said that if a proof were wanted of the deep and thorough corruption of human nature, we should find it in the fact that war itself was sometimes justifiable.' But if peace should not be possible, he went on, 'I can only say that we possess rights which, in our opinion, are clear and unquestionable, and by the blessing of God and your support, those rights we are fully prepared to maintain'. He sat down amidst 'loud and general applause'.[31] Never since 1812 had war looked so close between the two nations, and Britain took a number of military precautions in preparation for it.

As soon as he received the American notice to terminate the joint occupancy of the Oregon territory Aberdeen forwarded a new draft Convention to Washington. By it the 49th parallel became the boundary to the sea, Vancouver Island was Britain's, and British fur traders held navigation rights down the Columbia river.

In July came the next stage in the struggle, when the American Secretary Buchanan forwarded a Note as equivocal as had been Aberdeen's instructions to Ashburton. The United States claimed the whole territory right to the Russian border, then offered to compromise on the 49th parallel.[32] Unfortunately Pakenham refused the offer without referring it to London[33]; and in December, announcing it to Congress, Polk used intemperate language.[34] Pakenham's later request for the renewal of the offer, on Aberdeen's instructions, was refused and a reference to arbitration declined. By March Polk was urging the Senate to consent to an increase of land and sea forces.

However, Polk's military commitments to the American Texans in their struggle with Mexico were such that he could ill afford to undertake any others, and his need for more forces was really directed to the approaching Mexican War, not a British one. The resolution for the abrogation of the 1827 Convention for Joint Occupation of the Territory passed by Congress was phrased as an open invitation to Britain to treat again. Peel and Aberdeen were ready, and the President received a draft Treaty dividing the territory from the Rocky Mountains to the sea by the 49th parallel, and giving Britain Vancouver Island and the navigation rights on the Columbia. The President passed it to the Senate and the Senate approved it. The draft, verbatim as drawn up by Aberdeen, became the Convention which was signed on 15 June 1846.[35] Polk's diary entry, of 4 January 1846, 'The only way to treat John Bull is to look him in the eye', had been empty bombast.[36] If Britain had been pushed into making greater concessions than in the Ashburton Treaty of 1842, they were once again of importance neither to her nor to Aberdeen. He achieved all that he had expected to get for the past two years. What is interesting is that rather than give way, and for the sake of British honour and prestige alone, Aberdeen had been prepared to embark on a war, a single month of which, as Peel soberly told the Commons, would have been 'more costly than the value of the whole territory'.[37]

The long-drawn-out wrangles and squabbles about the Canadian frontier were at an end. Aberdeen had been fortunate in that the United States was at the time trembling on the brink of war with Mexico, and that horror at Palmerston's imminent return to the Foreign Office had forced the hands of her statesmen. Peel's government was drawing to its close, and it was obvious to all. As soon as he repealed the Corn Laws the return of the Whigs was inevitable, and Palmerston would as surely succeed Aberdeen. As Aberdeen did not fail to point out, this would be fatal to Anglo-American friendship.

Even Palmerston, conscious that Aberdeen's problems would soon be his, was silent before the sensible compromise. There was none of the blood and thunder with which he had greeted the settlement of the Maine border dispute in the Ashburton Treaty in 1843. He welcomed the Oregon settlement as reasonable, and even said that he looked forward to improved relations with the United States.[38]

Not the least satisfactory element in the situation was that France had given staunch co-operation to Britain throughout the crisis. The British Government had been extremely nervous of her reaction, and Croker had written to Aberdeen, 'For God's sake end it; for if anything were to happen to Louis Philippe we shall have an American war immediately, and a French one just after, a rebellion in Ireland, real starvation in the manufacturing districts, and a twenty per cent complication in the shape of Income Tax'.[39] Guizot, however, had worked well in harness with Aberdeen. If there had been no other fruit of it, the value of the *entente* was proved beyond question at this time.

There remained the matter of the Mexican war. In March American forces had invaded Mexican territory. Aberdeen offered to mediate and the Mexicans welcomed the offer, but the Americans rejected it. Hopeless of being able to hold California, which was a seething cauldron of new American settlers, Mexico offered it to Britain in May 1846, in the expectation that she would join her and protect it from attack by America. Aberdeen was intrigued by the magnificent offer and played with the idea of accepting it, especially in view of Britain's interests in California. However, Peel was not interested, and the French would not risk war with the

States to guarantee Californian integrity. So Aberdeen abandoned the idea. In the end the peace treaty would leave America in possession of both Texas and California.[40]

By the time a revolution of American settlers against the Mexican government broke out Aberdeen had gone. On June 29 Peel had resigned; and Russell had become Prime Minister. It fell to Palmerston to conclude matters. Here Palmerston played the rôle of peace-lover as strongly as Aberdeen, and, little though he liked the thought of the United States seizing California and divers other pieces of Mexico, was not prepared to go to war to prevent it.[41]

The sorry business of the Argentinian troubles was also left to Palmerston to conclude.

Aberdeen had inherited from Palmerston a dilemma posed by civil war between the Blanco and the Colorado factions in Uruguay. Abhorrence of involvement in the internal affairs of foreign nations conflicted with the interests of commerce in the River Plate, which were a potent influence on Peel's government, especially as Britain climbed painfully out of economic depression. Uruguay's internal stability was essential to enable British traders to take advantage of the potentially rich resources of pampas-bred cattle and the splendid harbour of Montevideo, so it was tempting to intervene in order to secure decisive victory for one or the other faction. However, to back the Blancos meant rupture with France, deeply committed to the Colorados, and to back the Colorados meant war with Argentina, damaging the vast British commercial interest in Buenos Aires, opposite Montevideo on the Plate, for Argentina's dictator-president General Rosas was not only passionately committed to the Blancos but subject to long-standing claims by France for damages allegedly due to French merchants.

When Aberdeen assumed his responsibilities Palmerston had already unsuccessfully proposed terms for a peaceful settlement of the civil war to Rosas and the Colorados. Aberdeen's policy, pursued through successive British envoys in Buenos Aires, as revealed in his instructions and their despatches, show him willing the end – that is, to disengage Rosas from his support for the Blancos and establish a Colorado president in Uruguay, thus maintaining the cherished *entente* with France – while shrinking from ordering in so many words what appeared to be the only means of achieving that end – the abandonment of mediation or negotiation from a neutral position in favour of intervention jointly with France by naval and military force against Rosas. During Aberdeen's term of office the end was not achieved, but the means were certainly employed, and fruitlessly. Indeed the British envoy, exceeding the letter of Aberdeen's regrettably indecisive instructions, and acting with the French envoy, took drastic and bloody naval and military action against Argentina. This was the 'gunboat diplomacy' to which it must be acknowledged Aberdeen was surprisingly, and surprisingly often, prone in his dealings outside Europe – as evidenced also in his relations with China in 1844 – and for which he was denounced in the Commons by, of all people, Palmerston. Aberdeen himself, with his usual self-condemnatory frankness, wrote shortly before leaving the Foreign Office in 1846 that 'after shedding much blood' Britain had given Rosas 'just grounds for complaint against us'.[42]

By the peculiar irony which destiny so often reserved for Aberdeen, the end he desired was eventually to be achieved in the treaty with Argentina in 1848, by negotiation, and by Palmerston. By then the long-standing blockade of Buenos Aires by Britain and France would have been abandoned, and the economic depression, and with it commercial pressures on the Government, would be lifting, and trade with Uruguay would have in any case become of negligible importance in comparison with the benefits of good relations with Argentina.

Some historians have been harsh in their judgements on Aberdeen, notably H. S. Ferns, in his monolithic work, *Britain and Argentina in the Nineteenth Century*. 'The fact is,' he writes, 'that under the Earl of Aberdeen a split developed in British policy in the River Plate: one part of the official mind caused instructions to be drawn up about which General Rosas could scarcely have complained; the other part stimulated actions which Aberdeen admitted were wrong and injurious to Argentina.' And, with the routine underestimation of Aberdeen's intelligence, he adds, 'In the presence of an international-cum-civil war involving Argentina and Uruguay Aberdeen appears to have believed that he could act as a mediator bringing peace to the contending parties *and* as a supporter of one of the parties. The incompatibility of these two rôles seems never to have occurred to him. This contradiction serves to explain in some measure why it always happened that Aberdeen's determination to bring peace ended up in the use of force against General Rosas'.[43]

Six years after he left the Foreign Office Aberdeen would declare in the Lords, speaking as Prime Minister, that for the past thirty years the principles of the foreign policy of the country had never varied, though there might have been differences in their execution, 'according to the different hands intrusted with the direction of that policy'. 'It has,' he would say, 'been marked by a respect due to all independent States, a desire to abstain *as much as possible* from the internal affairs of other countries, an assertion of our own honour and interests, and, above all, an earnest desire to secure the general peace of Europe *by all such means as were practicable* and at our disposal.' Perhaps the reservations, italicized here, stemmed not least from his memory of the problems of the River Plate.[44]

Britain's commitment to the abolition of the Brazilian slave trade had been a preoccupation of British foreign secretaries since Canning had imposed upon a resentful Brazil, as a condition of recognizing her independence from Portugal, the anti-slave-trade treaty of 1826.

The treaty was enforced by the Royal Navy mainly on the West African coast where African chiefs brought slaves for embarkation. The slavers could sail with impunity under the Portuguese flag because Britain's anti-slave-trade treaty with Portugal did not apply below the Equator. Palmerston failed to negotiate a treaty to remedy this, and eventually his Government passed an Act, of highly dubious validity in international law, conferring upon the Royal Navy the right to search Portuguese ships anywhere and seize slavers. The slavers then took to using the Brazilian flag, under which, by the terms of the 1826 treaty, they were at least protected as long as no slaves were actually aboard.

However, in 1845 part of the 1826 treaty was due to expire – that vital part which had given the Navy the right of search and established joint Anglo-Brazilian courts to deal with captured slavers. The Brazilian government refused to negotiate a replacement. Aberdeen was thus faced with national impotence, in this important area, in Britain's international crusade.

Less cavalier in his attitude to strict legality than his swash-buckling predecessor had been, Aberdeen was none the less determined to arm the Navy with legal powers. To the outrage of Brazil, the Law Officers devised an ingenious legislative scheme. This famous and much criticized 'Aberdeen Act'* was founded upon the barely tenable proposition that, by virtue of the unexpired part of the 1826 treaty, slave trading could be equated with piracy. Thus the Navy could, in international law, carry on as before, since its prey would thenceforward be pirates. More, these pirates would no longer be subject to the Anglo-Brazilian courts under the expired part of the 1826 treaty. Thanks to the 'Aberdeen Act',

* The Slave Trade (Brazil) Act of 1845.

178

they would be subject to the jurisdiction of the British Vice-Admiralty courts, less prone to partiality to slavers.

At the same time Aberdeen succeeded in negotiating an anti-slave-trade treaty with Portugal to achieve the purpose of Palmerston's frankly dubious Act, which it was then possible to repeal.

Ultimately, it may be argued, the slave trade ceased because the slave-importing countries abolished slavery. Be that as it may, Britain's relentless pressures on the trade in the first half of the nineteenth century kept it down to the minimum possible, and in that process Aberdeen played a by no means insignificant part.

The news of the conclusion of Aberdeen's good work in the States reached London on the morning of the day on which Peel announced the resignation of his government to the House of Commons.[45] The Queen wrote to Aberdeen expressing her 'great delight at the news of the settlement of the Oregon question', and went on, 'This is an immense thing for the peace of the world, reflects such credit on Lord Aberdeen; and it is such a very great satisfaction to us, that Lord Aberdeen should have settled this question, which he alone she fully believes could have done'.[46] The Prince Consort, too, wrote his congratulations on Lord Aberdeen's having been allowed to complete this work 'triumphantly'.[47]

Aberdeen wrote a farewell from the Foreign Office to Everett, the former American ambassador in London. After the ministerial crisis of the year before, he said, it had been obvious to him that the Government must fall. 'I told Sir Robert Peel I had no other desire than that our Government should last long enough for him to carry the Corn Bill and for me to settle Oregon,' he said. 'It is delightful to think that there is now no question of difference remaining between our governments, and that free scope may be given to the development of the immense commercial resources of both countries.'[48]

He had been sad at the prospect of coming to office; now he was sad at having to leave it. The record of his five years, crowned on the day of departure with another success, must have had more than a little to do with this feeling of regret, so unusual for him, at departure from public life. To Princess Lieven, at any rate, writing on June 25 that the ministers would be offering the Queen their resignations next day, he said, 'It happens singularly enough that the day of our great triumph is also the day of our overthrow; for the Corn Bill passed the House of Lords last night . . . I do not deny that I leave with regret the management of great affairs, and the transaction of business with those I personally like and esteem;

but above all I regret the interruption of that policy founded upon mutual confidence and regard, and upon which I have so cordially acted with M. Guizot for several years past'.[49] Whether that cordiality, by which he put so much store, would have continued, is doubtful, for the Orleans régime was growing ever more unpopular, and Guizot would henceforth frequently be forced into an anti-British rôle with the object of making it less so.

When Aberdeen left office the three changes he had hoped would come to pass had done so. Explosive American hostility towards Britain had at least subsided, and there was, as he claimed, little left for the two nations to quarrel over.[50] Then he and Guizot had gone far to overcome the historic enmity between France and Britain, and had created an atmosphere in which, intervening difficulties notwithstanding, it would be possible for France to be Britain's ally in the Crimean War and in the 1858–60 war with China.

He had, too, concluded the signing of the slave trade treaty with France.[51] The credit should have gone to Palmerston, who had negotiated for years to get the Five Power treaty, which was in 1841 only awaiting formal signature, concluded. However, during the General Election of 1841 Palmerston had summoned press representatives to Tiverton, his constituency, and had delivered a violent attack on French policy in Algeria. That speech had led to great resentment in France, a protest from Guizot, a distraught communication from Bulwer at Paris complaining about the damage it had done to Anglo-French relations, and Guizot's decision to withhold his signature until Palmerston had gone from the Foreign Office. Despite Palmerston's protest to Bulwer, on 10 August 1841, that it was 'very shabby of Guizot' to delay 'in order to sign with Aberdeen a treaty which I have been hammering at these four years',[52] Guizot had not only waited until Palmerston's departure, but had made sure that Bulwer knew that the Tiverton speech was the reason.[53] On 20 December 1841 Aberdeen had been able to lay the treaty, signed by him that day, before the Queen, rejoicing that there was now little left for her to do, 'by means of negociation [sic] with Foreign Powers, in order to extirpate this traffic altogether'.[54] He frankly acknowledged that the delay had been caused only by an 'objection . . . chiefly of a personal nature' and that 'the only share therefore, which Lord Aberdeen can properly be said to have had in this transaction, is that of having been enabled to afford Your Majesty the great satisfaction of completing this blessed work at an earlier period than would otherwise have been the case'.[55]

Rejoicings were premature. Aberdeen had to write again to the Queen on the same day to inform her that the Chamber of Deputies had caused the ratification to be deferred[56]; and things dragged on through 1842, 1843 and 1844, with the French obstinately objecting to the Mutual Right of Search, and Aberdeen as obstinately insisting on retaining it as 'the only efficient measure hitherto adopted for the abolition of the Slave Trade'.[57] Not until 29 May 1845 was the treaty at last ratified.

Thirdly, in those five years the relations between France and America had distinctly worsened. He had, in short, achieved what he had set out to achieve in order to preserve his country's safety in a community of hostile nations.

The distinguished American historian Professor Wilbur Devereux Jones, professor of history at the University of Georgia, who has specialized in the study of Anglo-American relationships in the nineteenth century, and of the Peelites, and whose books, *The American Problem in British Diplomacy, 1841–1851, Lord Aberdeen and the Americas,* and (in collaboration) *The Peelites, 1846–1857,* have gone far to correct the long-prevailing denigration of Aberdeen by Whig-orientated historians, has summarized his views on Aberdeen as a foreign secretary as follows.

'The traditional view that he was a timid, even inept, foreign secretary, who was fearful both of American bluster abroad and Palmerstonian bluster at home, is quite wrong. The bases of his 1841–1846 foreign policy were to end the traditional Anglo-French hostility, to settle all outstanding issues with the United States, and to sever the tenuous Franco-American tie by acting with France in projects likely to disturb the United States. While his settlement of the Maine and Oregon boundary disputes, as well as his adjustment of other issues, drew criticism from both British and American nationalists in his day, they have stood the test of time, and I do not think anyone in Britain, the United States or Canada today can view his solutions other than as a blessing for all three countries. His collaboration with France in Texas and Argentina were the main developments in the third area of his policy.

'These were enormous accomplishments. Could Palmerston have brought them about? I do not think that he could have done so, and he might, indeed, have embroiled his country in another useless Anglo-American war. Because his public image was so strongly nationalist, he always found it difficult to make concessions to other nations, even when the dispute involved only the most minor of British interests.

'It seems to me that Aberdeen's diplomacy was intensely personal, and supremely rational. He operated on the assumption that war was a terrible folly brought on by the defects inherent in human nature, but that it was never inevitable – rational men could avoid it. In world affairs, man had a freedom of choice. Conflict was not written in the stars. While I cannot speak for France, I believe that Americans trusted Lord Aberdeen more completely than any foreign statesman of the century.

'The reason that history has been so kind to Palmerston, and so neglectful of Aberdeen, lies in the essential irrationality of man. Historians think in strongly nationalistic terms, and love to record incidents that glorify the strength and power of their own country, while reducing unpleasant compromises to a footnote. American historians, for example, love to turn the Maine and Oregon boundary settlements into triumphs, which they were not.

'It seems to me that Aberdeen's skill as a diplomatic tactician was demonstrated in every one of his settlements. Probably the most sensational of them in this area was the Oregon Boundary settlement, in which he used the threat of force to bring some American politicians to their senses.'[58]

On that assessment, from a source both authoritative and disinterested, one might well leave the controversial subject of Lord Aberdeen as Foreign Secretary.

Peel and Aberdeen parted from the Queen with great emotion on what Victoria described to her uncle Leopold as 'a very hard day for me'. 'They were both so much overcome that it quite overset me,' she wrote, 'and we have in them two devoted friends. We felt so safe with them. Never during the five years that they were with me did they *ever* recommend a *person* or a thing which was not for my or the country's best, and never for the party's advantage only: and the contrast *now* is very striking.' Again, on a more personal note, she mourned, 'But I can't tell you how sad I am to lose Aberdeen; you can't think what a delightful companion he was'.[59]

'We had ill luck,' Aberdeen said succinctly to her, 'if it had not been for this famine in Ireland, which rendered immediate measures necessary, Sir Robert would have prepared them gradually for the change.'[60] It was ill luck for which Aberdeen had been long prepared. On taking office in 1841 he had written to Princess Lieven, we remember, 'We have more to fear from a bad harvest than from all the thunders of the most formidable opposition'.[61] On 1 November 1845, faced with the failure of the potato crop, and the need to open the ports to other supplies of food, Peel had tried to persuade the Cabinet to suspend the existing Corn Laws by

182

Order-in-Council, and summon parliament to ratify it, while warning his colleagues that there would be no returning to the situation as before. Met by stony disapproval, Peel had appealed to Aberdeen, who had created something of a sensation by declaring that he had always considered the Corn Laws logically indefensible, but had hitherto regarded their abolition as out of the question. Sir James Graham and Sidney Herbert had also supported Peel; but Aberdeen had led the way.[62] The rest of the Cabinet was solidly against repeal, and despite Herbert's strenuous pleadings for immediate abolition a decision was deferred until the end of the month, in the hope that in the light of fuller information the crisis would then seem less grave.[63]

Before the Cabinet met again on November 24, however, the situation had been revolutionized by the publication in the *Morning Chronicle* of Lord John Russell's 'Edinburgh Letter' of the 22nd – a letter, written from Edinburgh, addressed to his constituents in the City of London, blaming the Government for apathy in the crisis, announcing his conviction that it was 'no longer worth while to contend for a fixed duty', and demanding 'the extinction within a short period' of any duty imposed. More, he exhorted the electors to present petitions in order to push the Government into ending 'a system which has proved to be the blight of commerce, the bane of agriculture, the source of bitter divisions among classes, the cause of penury, fever, mortality, and crime among the people'. Lord John had put Peel into a most embarrassing position, in which the steps he had meant to take would now look, not like the 'voluntary and spontaneous action' urged by Herbert, but like capitulation to Lord John.[64]

By November 24 the crisis was all too clearly seen to be of the utmost gravity, but Stanley and Buccleuch would not shift, and though others wavered they still played for time. At a final Cabinet on December 4 it was decided that abolition followed by resignation was the only proper course; and by December 3 Aberdeen had been confident enough of the outcome – he was probably anxious to impress the Americans with news of Britain's conversion to free trade – to have sent for Delane and given him information which prompted a premature leader announcing abolition.[65] Peel resigned on December 5, and on December 8 Lord John Russell received the Queen's summons.

However, the new Lord Grey – for Howick had recently succeeded his father – expressed his concern about Palmerston as Foreign Secretary in a talk with Sidney Herbert in the library of the Travellers' Club on December 17. 'I wish we could keep Lord

183

Aberdeen,' he said. 'I prefer him to Lord Palmerston. He is a much safer and better Foreign Minister.'[66] In fact, Russell's attempt to form a government foundered on Grey's refusal to serve with Palmerston, on the grounds that he would wreck the good relations which Aberdeen had built up with France, and Palmerston's adamant insistence on serving in that office and no other.[67] At the time Aberdeen had behaved with exemplary generosity. As he wrote to Guizot: 'I have never desired to injure Lord Palmerston; on the contrary, at the time of our ministerial crisis in December, I endeavoured by every means in my power to smooth his advent to office. Party men, or mere politicians, will not understand this conduct, and I doubt if Lord Palmerston comprehends it himself, but you will have no such difficulty'.[68]

Peel had come back from his hundred days and a Queen's speech recommending immediate consideration of the Corn Laws preparatory to their total repeal. Palmerston had gone off to Paris for a visit designed to create the impression of his personal goodwill to France. He was well received, to Aberdeen's perhaps understandable irritation, and that made him popular at home.[69] In July 1846 he again took up the seals which Aberdeen had been forced to lay down in the moment of triumph. Before two years had gone by Victoria and Albert would be demanding that Russell remove Palmerston from the Foreign Office. It would need only three months for him to realize that no visit to Paris could undo the harm he had done to Franco-British relations. The French had still not forgotten the Treaty of London of 1840, and their exclusion from it, which had led to the immediate declaration by Thiers that the Anglo-French alliance was dead. Nor had they forgotten the Tiverton speech of 1841. Civilities in Paris notwithstanding, Louis Philippe and Guizot were thirsting for revenge.

Chapter 15

Cincinnatus Recalled

At the age of sixty-two Aberdeen was out of office again. He went home to Haddo immediately for the seven months before Parliament reassembled in February, and wrote joyously to Princess Lieven of his occupations, 'each more delightful than the other', and how he found 'no day long enough'.[1] That was on August 27, but he did not mention that that month Captain John had been tried by court-martial on board the *Victory* for sailing for England from Valparaiso on April 26 in disobedience of the orders of his Commander-in-Chief, and that the court had found 'that in sailing from Valparaiso in the *America* with treasure on board' Captain Gordon was 'not actuated by his pecuniary advantage', but had adjudged that he 'should be severely reprimanded'.[2] He was distressed by the incident, however, writing frequently to Captain Baillie-Hamilton, the husband of his stepdaughter Harriet, and Second Secretary to the Admiralty, about it. On September 8 he mourned, 'I hope we are getting to the end of this disagreeable business. It has been scarcely possible to write or think about anything else'.[3] Two days later he wrote that his brother was fighting hard to keep his command of his ship for a bit, and leave later, so that it would appear as if 'the Admiralty did not attach any vital importance to the sentence of the Court Martial'.[4] On the 28th he wrote, 'I had an amazing sort of letter from Captain John the other day, about the Court Martial. I shall endeavour to silence him; for the less he says about it the better. I have told him to follow your advice in the matter of retirement'.[5] (Perhaps Captain Baillie-Hamilton's advice was that Captain John should not retire, for he retired only in 1863 as a Rear-Admiral.) Finally, on November 3, writing from his chilly retreat at Buchan Ness, Aberdeen wrote that he was trying to have the *America* ordered home, so as not to have Captain John relieved in a foreign station, which would mean his 'having to find his way home as he can'. The Admiralty, he said, was kindly disposed, and wanted to have him 'superseded graciously'.[6]

That year Aberdeen resigned from the Society of Antiquaries, of which he had been President for 34 years, since members were apt to consider him to be deserting his post when he put the nation's business and the question of peace or war above what he called 'the moderate folly of their pursuits'.[7] It is true that between 1841 and 1846 he had not presided at any meetings at all. Aberdeen himself would have been neither surprised nor sorrowful at his enforced retirement. As long ago as 1835 he had written to Hudson Gurney, his Vice-President, 'I am still President of the Society of Antiquaries in London; but I am quite aware that from my neglect of that worshipful body, I deserve to be dismissed', and had said that 'the rubbish of ancient times' had ceased to interest him.[8]

His attitude to the British Museum, of which he had been a trustee for the same length of time, was quite different. He had regularly attended its meetings, had worked on a sub-committee on Egyptian antiquities, and had even begun a series of bequests, which was to be sporadic but lifelong, with a presentation in May 1818 of 'two bas reliefs from the ruins of Persepolis, and an inscription in the Persepolitan character from the same place'.[9] Now, he wrote to Princess Lieven, he could 'look forward to occupations more congenial to my taste' than 'the torments of office'.[10] As a trustee of the National Gallery since 1824, too, according to his son, he was acknowledged by his fellow-trustees as 'one of the first of connoisseurs'.[11]

Now Aberdeen was able, in his quiet, unobtrusive way, once more to enjoy himself as he preferred, though he suffered greatly from very bad headaches, involving pain and 'noise and confusion'.[12] Always reticent, and often abrupt when he sought to avoid what seemed to him, in Arthur Gordon's charming phrase, 'unprofitable intercourse',[13] he never volunteered either his opinion or any information, but freely gave them to the many who, aware of his exceptional and exceptionally wide knowledge, sought his help. Samuel Rogers the poet consulted him about his verses; and that September he was corresponding authoritatively with Croker, who was in difficulties about Thucydides,[14] and setting him right on the minutiae of Greek scholarship. He was able to resolve 'the most puzzling questions of ancient Greek currency or geography, or explain differences in the nomenclature of the inhabitants of the Demes of Attica. It was the same with the annals of European states, the genealogy of illustrious houses, the growth of schools of painting, or of typography; with every topic, in short, connected with art or history. His memory was a storehouse of the most varied and accurate information in all branches of literature'.[15] 'He was one of the most distinguished men in Europe, a trusted friend of all the Continental Sovereigns in the great contest with Napoleon, and had a wide reputation for culture of all kinds,' wrote Argyll in his memoirs.[16]

Aberdeen's knowledge was as impressive in the by-ways as in the highways. Not only was his acquaintance with the Italian poets deep and thorough, not only was he familiar with, in the words of his friend, Monsieur de Barante, 'every French author who wrote before the Revolution', but he surprised even his son when, for instance, he was able to 'quote, and discuss with Dean Milman, the later classical and Byzantine authors, with the same intimate familiarity as if they had belonged to the highest age of classical literature'.[17] Indeed, those about him were frequently surprised by some new revelation of his encyclopædic knowledge. When a friend interested in botany visited Haddo House, Aberdeen, who had never betrayed any sign of interest in that subject, or mentioned it to his family, gathered for his visitor as they walked about the estate together rare and curious plants from hidden or inconspicuous corners, and was able to indicate exactly where every scarce moss, fern or flower was likely to be found. Intercourse with his 'wholly unbotanical' family circle on that subject he had clearly judged 'unprofitable'.

For the next six years Aberdeen would leave London for Scotland at the end of one session and return only when the next one began. At Haddo he settled into his chosen way of life, an eccentric *mélange* of feudal grandeur and personal austerity. His peaceful, ordered existence was in strange contrast with that of the previous autumn, when he had had to forgo his annual homecoming because of his September visit to the Château d'Eu, and when there had been conflict with Peel and Wellington about rearmament, war threatening between Mexico and the United States, untoward events in the La Plata region, and the Corn Law crisis of November which had ended by destroying the Conservative party. He had been tired and low-spirited that autumn, so much so that he had written to Mary, 'I am about to leave England with a presentiment that I may never see you again. At all events, you will not receive this letter until I am no more . . . The great care which oppresses me is the fate of Arthur. I intreat you by every motive which can have weight with you to take him under your own special care and protection . . . George [Haddo] will do what you think right in this, and in everything else . . . I send my love and blessing to George and to all my dear children. But my poor Arthur: the last words of his mother are still sounding in my ears!'[18]

Despite his presentiment Aberdeen soon recovered, and relaxed into the life he loved. Rising early to walk with one of his sons, he returned to what Jarnac called a solid Scotch breakfast where (as at luncheon) no servants waited on him or his guests, wrote letters to catch the morning post, gave his bailiff the day's orders, and, as twelve o'clock struck, descended the broad flight of steps from the drawing-room to the terrace, to go the rounds with his head gardener and head forester. At noon on Saturdays he descended the flight on the other side of Haddo House to receive all his people who had business with him. Lord Aberdeen and the Countess of Sutherland were the last to practise this form of 'sitting in the gate', which had been common among the great Scottish landlords of the eighteenth century, accepting the burdens and cost of building roads and bridges, schools and churches, and of poor relief, and acting as referees and arbiters in many matters which in England would have been settled by the Petty Sessions. This practice, rapidly disappearing elsewhere, as the poorer classes learned to write, survived at Haddo, doubtless because of Aberdeen's personal standing with his people.

In the afternoons Aberdeen drove his fast-trotting ponies to inspect work in progress beyond walking distance, or strolled in his favourite valley of Formartine. At dinner, as Jarnac found, '*La table était excellente, les vins très recherchés, car Lord Aberdeen tenait à recevoir somptueusement ses amis, et en matière de bonne chère, comme en toute choses, son goût était fin et délicat.*' On Sundays a long procession of vehicles set forth from Haddo bearing the whole household to church, with Aberdeen bringing up the rear in a huge, lumbering old coach holding six passengers. The minister in gown and bands and the whole congregation gathered, whatever the weather, to greet him outside the church; and not until the Earl and his family had climbed the steep flight of stone steps, curiously placed on the exterior of the building and leading to their pew in the 'loft', was the congregation free to enter and the minister to ascend to his pulpit, passing with difficulty the old women in red or clay-coloured cloaks and high stiff white 'mutches', who sat, because of their deafness, on the pulpit stairs. At the end of the service the minister turned towards Lord Aberdeen and made a low obeisance, which was returned by an equally deep bow from His Lordship, standing. On Sunday afternoons Lord Aberdeen took a solemn walk with the whole family and guests to the top of the hill in the deer-park, going round the lakes and passing the rock where his gloomy friend, the actor John Kemble, had once loved to sit, and concluding with the kitchen garden. Finally, after dinner, the entire household assembled in the library for family prayers written and read by Lord Aberdeen himself.[19]

This life was somewhat oppressive for the young. Even Mary found its rigid etiquette tiresome, and described how the two admirals read their papers in an anteroom in silence while the younger people spoke in lowered voices in a corner, and she dared not speak to Aberdeen till spoken to.[20] Aberdeen never tolerated what he called 'a deficiency of deference towards myself'.[21] To everyone, including his family, he was, formally, His Lordship. With certain friends, of course, Aberdeen was easier. He unbent sufficiently with Jarnac to refer to Nelson as 'the inspired booby' (le nais inspiré), lèse-majesté of a notable kind in that era, especially to a Frenchman. On the other hand he was growing careless, and a trifle seedy, in his sombre dress. His complexion too, always sallow and now pitted (presumably from smallpox, though I have found no record of an attack), was such that he was sometimes disrespectfully referred to behind his back as Old Brown Bread. Ribaldry and deference notwithstanding, everyone understood that his somewhat awkward and rather touching stateliness was natural to him, and that the determined avoidance of ostentation, so much in contrast to life in other great houses, was because of his great humility and instinctive good manners.

Even strangers, if perceptive, recognized the real man behind the unpretentious façade. Towards the end of this period of retirement an American visitor who met him at a Scottish country house wrote, 'Lord Aberdeen has the name of being the proudest and coldest aristocrat of England [sic]. It is amusing to see the person who bears such a character. He is of the middle height and rather clumsily made, with an address more of sober dignity than of pride or reserve. With a black coat much worn, and always too large for him, a pair of coarse check trousers very ill made, a cravat of the most primitive négligé, his aristocracy is certainly not in his dress. His manners are of absolute simplicity, amounting almost to want of style. He crosses his hands behind him and balances on his heels; in conversation his voice is low and cold, and he seldom smiles. Yet there is a certain benignity in his countenance and an indefinable superiority in his simple address'.[22]

Mary at least had no cause to find her father-in-law cold. In 1845 the Queen had made him Ranger of Greenwich Park, with the use of the Ranger's House at Blackheath. Aberdeen had promptly insisted on Haddo's moving his family into it. Most reluctantly Haddo left his home at Windsor, and his second son James was born that year under Aberdeen's roof.

Haddo himself had become rather eccentric. Painfully shy and unworldly, but impulsive, conscious of his irritable nature and lack of drive, he lived austerely despite an allowance of £3000 a year, in order to devote his money to (often ill-judged) good works. In January 1848 he underwent (to Mary's initial horror) what he called a 'more decided spiritual conversion' and, oppressed by a sense of inadequacy and guilt at lost opportunities, longed to abandon his inheritance and responsibilities, fly to a distant land, and live there with his family under an assumed name. He gave up the idea only because of the effect it would have on his 'aged father' – who, at sixty-four, was still four years from undertaking the most demanding task in the kingdom. 'Had he died at this time,' Haddo recorded almost wistfully in his diary, 'I believe I should have sought a settlement in Australia; there to lead a life of piety, which I seemed to want courage to do here.'[23] He did his best, however. By 22 May 1850 he had built a Church of England church at the cost of £10,700 in Cable Street, Stepney, and called it St Mary's after his wife. Masochistically, he had sold his treasured and discerning collection of pictures at Christie's, at a sacrificial price, to help pay for it. (No mean artist himself, he had been hung twice at the Royal Academy.[24])

Haddo was still a source of annoyance to Aberdeen because of his attitude to going into Parliament. On 28 March 1847 Aberdeen wrote to Mary, 'George has taken a fancy for Parliament at rather an inconvenient time. I have now no interest to procure a seat, and no money to fight a Contest'.[25] As Admiral William, he explained, had given up his office of High Admiral to please his constituents – who presumably wanted to see more of him – they would insist on returning him at the next election, although Aberdeen had brought him into Parliament twenty-five years before, and had paid all his election expenses, on the 'express understanding' that he was to keep the county seat warm for George. 'It was unfortunate,' he said, 'that George was so indifferent about being called up to the House of Lords in my lifetime; as with Sir Rbt. Peel as Minister, I might possibly have accomplished this. It is true that he may probably not have very long to wait . . .' If, however, George still wanted to go into the Commons, he promised to talk the Admiral into retiring during the next year, thus allowing Haddo to be returned at the by-election. But it must be, he said, kept *perfectly secret*. And again, 'The only essential thing is not to mention a word about it; so that there should be no suspicion of any arrangement of the kind. A notion of this might defeat the whole affair'.[26] Mary and Aberdeen were arranging matters between them; but something went wrong, and their plans were not carried out in 1848.

In June 1849, Haddo had been given another opportunity to become a Member of Parliament elsewhere*; and, despite his reluctance to leave Mary and his comfortable domestic life, and, as he believed, expose himself to ridicule when 'supporting the religious questions', had accepted it, largely because refusal 'might be taken amiss by my father and others who heard of it'. To his relief, it turned out to be too expensive, and he withdrew.[27]

As a Peelite Aberdeen supported Russell's government, maintaining the Whigs in office and keeping out Stanley and his Protectionists; but it was with anguish that he watched Palmerston, as he believed, undo all his work with the Spanish Marriages. By 17 November 1847 he could write, 'I see ground for apprehension everywhere – Spain, Italy, Switzerland, and Greece, each presents a picture, for some of the worst features of which I fear that we are not free from blame . . . We are gradually becoming estranged from all our allies, as well as from France; and I do not see that we have any friends in Europe, except the *Pope* and the *Sultan*; in addition to the Radicals of all countries'.[28] In the same letter he wrote of the sudden death of Sir Robert Gordon from choking on a bone at Balmoral Castle, which he, an extravagant man,[29] had built for use as a shooting lodge.[30] 'His loss to me is great indeed,' Aberdeen wrote, 'for thirty years of confidence on my part, and of attachment and devotion on his, had established a kind of relation which can never again exist in any other quarter . . . His loss would have been still greater, if I had entertained any project of now actively engaging in political or official life; but as this is not the case, it is only as a private personal calamity that I feel the blow.'[31] (Actually, Aberdeen, while assiduously helping his brother up the diplomatic ladder, had often been infuriated by his ineptitude and unreliability as an ambassador – notably at Vienna, during the Spanish Marriages affair – and had castigated him mercilessly.) As a childless widower Sir Robert had made a will leaving everything he possessed to Aberdeen, including Balmoral. The Queen later took over the lease from him.[32]

In that year, too, his only sister, Lady Alicia, died, with Aberdeen at her bedside,[33] and it may have been as a memorial to this brother and sister that Aberdeen in the same year erected a huge urn at the end of his mile-long avenue. It bore only the inscription:

---

* The name of the constituency in question is left blank in Haddo's diary as published.

Georgius Comes Abredonensis
MDCCCXLVII
Haud Immemor

His own name alone appears on it, and it might have been a private memorial, not only to them, and to Alexander, the hero of Waterloo, but also to his two wives and four daughters – or perhaps it was only for Catherine. He never revealed the secret, and when one of his employees had the temerity to ask him what 'Haud immemor' meant, he replied brusquely, 'That's for the learned'.[34]

He was not pleased when in 1848 his stepson Lord Abercorn leased Bentley Priory to the Queen Dowager, Adelaide, widow of William IV, and expressed himself as 'heartily glad' that he had not been there for her preliminary visit. 'It is more than forty years since I first was taught to consider the Priory as a home, and for many years I occupied it as its master. I never go there without going to seek the dead as well as the living. But I have not the least reason to complain. Every man has the right to do what he likes with his own; and all this is a matter of little consequence. It will soon be of still less.'[35]

In fact his passions were almost as deeply engaged with the Priory as with Haddo; in some ways perhaps more so. In its magnificent rooms, many of them added to the original house by the first Marquess, in its Italian garden and along its terraced walks, in its deer-park, and by its ornamental lake – both of which he had imitated for his own Scottish estate – he had walked and talked with Pitt, Addington, Canning, Liverpool, Wellington, with Sir William Hamilton and his wife, Nelson's Emma,* with Sir Walter Scott, and with Samuel Rogers. There in 1807 Scott had corrected the proofs of his *Marmion*, and added complimentary lines on Fox, at Abercorn's instigation. There the Prince Regent had come with the King of Prussia to meet Louis XVIII when he left Hartwell to return to France. There Aberdeen himself, while Abercorn had been a schoolboy at Harrow, only visiting his inheritance in the holidays, had been able to entertain a stream of the fashionable, the talented and the celebrated, continuing the tradition established

---

* In September 1854 Aberdeen as Prime Minister would be faced with the problem of the children of Nelson's 'adopted daughter', Horatia, by Lady Hamilton, recommended by him to the care of the country before Trafalgar. Aberdeen would add her three daughters to the Pensions List, to avoid the 'much scandal and disagreeable debate' in Parliament which a special vote would entail. (R.A. A3 23/145, Sept. 1 1854)

by his father-in-law, that grandee of grandees.[36] And there he had laid both his wives and all four of his daughters.

The advent of Queen Adelaide was only a warning of worse to come. In 1850 Aberdeen had the great shock of learning that Abercorn was in dire trouble. 'The information I have now received of the state of your affairs,' Aberdeen wrote to him on April 20, 'has fallen upon me like a thunderbolt . . . The truth is that you are on the very brink of ruin; and nothing but the most vigorous measures, and the greatest sacrifices, will prevent this ruin from being irretrievable . . . I perceive that at Coutts's your present obligations, including simple contract debts, the amount of which is not accurately known, are estimated at not much less than £400,000.'[37] Queen Adelaide had died in the previous December, and Abercorn was determined to sell, not only Barons Court – the style adopted by Lord Aberdeen; an alternative is Baronscourt – his County Tyrone estate, but Bentley Priory. The blow to Aberdeen was devastating, yet he directed his energies to stopping Abercorn from disposing of Barons Court.

'I really care nothing at all about Barons Court,' he wrote; 'and I express these opinions entirely from a conviction of what is due to yourself and your family. This you may readily believe, from the course I have followed with respect to the Priory; for although in your situation I would rather have lived on bread and water for the rest of my days than have sold it, I could not honestly say that it was a place for a man on the brink of ruin to keep, who had fortunately contrived to get rid of all the feelings which would naturally have attached him to it . . . I have nothing further to say. You must do as you like best.'[38]

Abercorn did not sell Barons Court. He succeeded in selling Bentley Priory in 1852 to a rich railway engineer.

On the political front the year 1848 brought revolutions in virtually every continental capital outside Russia. Louis Philippe and Guizot barely escaped with their lives and sought refuge in England. Aberdeen offered Guizot the permanent hospitality of Argyll House, but Guizot, and Princess Lieven, preferred to settle initially in Pelham Crescent. The two old friends saw each other almost every day when Aberdeen was in London. Metternich, too, became a feature of London society.

By that year Aberdeen was once again a regular attender in the Lords. The young Duke of Argyll, on taking his seat 'on the "Duke's bench", next the Woolsack, on the left of the throne', found Aberdeen 'an invariable occupant of it'. Once again a man with a great prejudice against him, regarding him as 'a "dour" man – obstinate and narrow-minded' (largely because his father and Aberdeen had been at opposite poles on the question of the Scottish church schism), found that 'this impression melted away like snow in a thaw' when he came to know him personally. 'He was, indeed,' he wrote, 'silent and reserved, but his voice, when he did speak, was unmistakably the voice of sincerity and truth. With an immense knowledge of men and of affairs, he possessed penetrating observation, with the calmest and most measured judgment. There was an indefinable charm in him which stole upon me, gradually at first, but which took entire possession of me at last. Absolute sincerity and truthfulness of character was the fundamental note in a perfect harmony. I became strongly attached to him, and I was gratified to find that he liked me.' His friendship with Aberdeen, which lasted until Aberdeen's death, he described as 'one of the happinesses of my life'.[39] Argyll was 25 to Aberdeen's 64 when they thus met in 1848. Even making allowances for the fact that Argyll was to be made a member of Aberdeen's Cabinet at the age of only 30 four years later, the sincerity of this tribute is evident; and by the time Argyll wrote his memoirs, published in 1907, four years after his death, he had nothing to gain from a man dead for forty years.

At that time Aberdeen was less than always calm on one subject, at least – Palmerston. By August he was writing to Princess Lieven (to whom he usually referred to Palmerston as 'your friend' or 'our friend at Downing Street'), with some annoyance about him. '*Your friend*, not having enough on his hands, has lately attacked me in some scurrilous articles in the "Globe" newspaper. They all have relation to the Spanish Marriages, and are equally remarkable for their impudence and falsehood, as well as their absurdity. This last beats all – imagine *my loyalty* being in doubt, because I have seen the King and M. Guizot!'[40] Perhaps he felt a fleeting sympathy with Anstey in his unsuccessful attempts to impeach Palmerston for having betrayed his country on twenty-three occasions. A year later he was angrily accusing him of being 'entirely without principle',[41] and following whatever course seemed likely to make him popular. He continued to protest vigorously against Palmerston's policy.

Peel kept in close touch with Aberdeen by letter during these years, and they exchanged frequent visits, Peel sometimes visiting Haddo, or Aberdeen travelling to Drayton Manor. Aberdeen considered this important, in order, as he implied, to keep Peel on the rails about foreign policy. 'It is always useful,' he wrote that year, 'to discuss foreign affairs with him from time to time; as, if left to himself, he is apt occasionally to entertain some strange notions'.[42] On the face of it, at least, Aberdeen still saw himself as being the dominant partner when it came to foreign affairs. Aberdeen sometimes showed him Princess Lieven's letters too, though he would find himself in trouble about that with her. That year he visited her in Paris – his first visit in the twenty-five years since his journeys with Alice to Nice – and enjoyed himself by her fireside.

He was not very well. In the spring he had suffered from a nervous facial tic, which he found 'rather alarming'.[43] In the winter, too, he worried himself into such a state about Mary's expected confinement in December, that he refused to leave London, or even stay for more than a minimum few hours at Drayton, where Peel had summoned him, until she was delivered. 'She has suffered so much, and her constitution is already so much broken, that the result must be doubtful,' he wrote. 'At all events I could not leave her until I see her in safety.'[44] In the event Mary came through without mishap, and was to live to a ripe old age.

By the spring of 1850 Aberdeen was so irritated by Palmerston's continuing cocksure, unsigned, articles in the *Globe* that he tried to push Peel into censuring him in the House.[45] Afraid that if Palmerston fell the Government would do so too, bringing in the protectionist Stanley and a new Corn Law, Peel refused.[46] Then Palmerston bullied Greece into paying an exaggerated claim for damages in an attack by a mob on the house of one Don Pacifico, a Spanish Jew born in Gibraltar but later naturalized Portuguese, who had in the past been discovered forging a document and dismissed from his post as Portuguese Consul in Athens. When Palmerston seized Greek gunboats and merchant vessels in the Piraeus, in order to coerce Greece while France was actually trying to negotiate a peaceful settlement, even Russell admitted to Prince Albert that Palmerston's personal quarrels with the governments of foreign countries were doing serious damage, saying that he felt 'very strongly that the Queen ought not to be exposed to the enmity of Austria, France and Russia on account of her Minister'.[47] Aberdeen teamed up with Stanley, Gladstone and Disraeli in what Russell called an 'unprincipled coalition'.[48] Aberdeen and Stanley led the attack in the Lords. Stanley moved the motion, and Aberdeen, who had put in weeks of work on it, and had been well briefed by Princess Lieven, delivered a strong, closely argued, and often caustic speech, condemning the blockade by a fleet 'equal to that with which Nelson won the victory of the Nile'. The Government's proceedings in Greek waters had, he said, called forth 'a cry of indignation' from one end of Europe to the other, and had

appeared to the world in general 'utterly unintelligible'. 'Unfortunately,' he continued, 'we who know [a] little more of the reckless
mode in which our foreign affairs are conducted, will have less
difficulty, perhaps, in believing the motives assigned, and in seeing
in it no policy more profound than the exercise of certain feelings
of hostility and the display of overwhelming force.' He went
further, referring to 'animus' and 'that double dealing which, I am
sorry to say, has prevailed of late in the foreign policy and conduct
of this country', and at one stage accused the Foreign Secretary,
in parliamentary language, of lying – 'Now, I say that is a deception,
that is the thing which is not.'[49]

Aberdeen's climax was a slashing attack on the Government's
whole foreign policy. 'When I look back but four short years,'
he declaimed, 'and recollect that this country was then honoured,
loved and respected by every state in Europe, with an intimate,
cordial good understanding with France, and without the slightest
diminution of our intimacy and friendship with all other powers,
I confess I do not look with any great satisfaction even at this new
species of friendship which the noble Lord has discovered to exist
between us and other countries.'[50]

The motion of censure was carried by a majority of 37 in a very
full house, on June 17. It remained only for the performance to be
repeated in the Commons. The Government arranged for a vote
of confidence to be moved there. Peel, in a speech full of eulogies
of both Aberdeen and Guizot, was forced to condemn the reckless-
ness with which Palmerston had alienated two friendly and powerful nations, France and Russia, Britain's co-guarantors of the Greek
state, by his unilateral action.[51] Then, on the second night of the
four-day debate, Palmerston, who had never lost his reputation for
being a bad speaker, rose to make his four-and-three-quarter-hours
long *Civis Romanus sum* speech, speaking for once brilliantly, and
besting all his enemies, including the Queen and her Consort, most
of the Cabinet, all foreign nations, and *The Times*. The effect was
all the greater, as Jasper Ridley points out, because this oratorical
tour de force was so unlooked for.[52] Palmerston made much of
the persecution, not only of Pacifico, but of the Scottish historian
of Greece, Finlay, who had had his garden seized from him by the
Greek Government in 1830, while Aberdeen had been Foreign
Secretary, without compensation, and had put in a claim for £15,000
for land for which he had paid a mere ten or twenty pounds.
Palmerston's climax, when he asked the House to decide 'whether,
as the Roman, in days of old, held himself free from indignity when
he could say *Civis Romanus sum*; so also a British subject, in

whatever land he may be, shall feel confident that the watchful eye and the strong arm of England will protect him against injustice and wrong', roused the Chamber to a fever pitch of British patriotism, and he sat down to seemingly unending cheers.[53]

Aberdeen was obviously disappointed, but not much surprised. He had expected Stanley's motion to be successful in the Lords (though he had feared the influence of Lady Palmerston's soirées on the votes there); but he had had his doubts about the Commons. 'No doubt,' he had written six weeks before, 'this would infallibly ruin any other minister, but luck and impudence may do wonders.'[54] As soon as he heard of Palmerston's triumph, he resigned himself to the fact that his 'most able and very effective speech' would probably influence the vote.[55] In due course he was wryly amused at hearing that Don Pacifico was awarded only about £130 of the £27,000 originally demanded for the loss of documents. (In fact he apparently received £150.)[56]

It was on the day after the debate that Sir Robert Peel was thrown from his horse in a fatal accident. The shock to Aberdeen of the death of this close friend of more than fifty years was comparable only to that caused by Pitt's. Typically he tried to conceal it under his usual mask of reserve. But those who knew him best were able to penetrate it. At Blackheath the day before Peel died his grandchildren asked, 'Why does Grandpapa stand so very still today?'[57] Their mother, Mary, so close to him, understood, and was not surprised to hear that the effort to suppress all outward emotion had meant that at night he had suffered from the physical reaction of violent spasms. 'A great Light has gone out of the Land,' Aberdeen wrote to Mary; 'and we must endure the loss as we best can. But what shall we say for that poor heartbroken woman that remains!'[58]

Not until August did Julia Peel feel able to write to her friends, and she turned for comfort to the kindest man she knew, and one who had suffered as direly thirty-eight years before.

'My dear Lord Aberdeen,' she wrote on 2 August 1850, 'I feel sure you will forgive my writing to you. I can hardly say why I do. But, in truth, I am so unhappy. I turn at last to you, fancying I may find some little comfort if I write to one who was so kind, so true, so valued a friend. My beloved one always talked of you as *the friend* whom he most valued, for whom he had the sincerest affection, whom he estimated higher than any. Dear Lord Aberdeen, he was the light of my life, my brightest joy and pride. Religion points the way to peace, and with kind ministers of religion I have devoted all this dreary season of intense grief to the consolations and the hopes she offers; but I turn to the awful realities of the bereavement I deplore, and I can do nothing but grieve.'[59]

She wrote to one who had never been reconciled to the loss of his Catherine, and who was too honest to offer facile words to another stricken creature. His reply, especially when one remembers that he was sincerely religious, shows how different a man he was from the stuffy and canting creature he is so often held to be.

'It is not from me that you can expect consolation,' he wrote; 'for I know too well how vain would be the attempt. I believe there is nothing but time, and a gradually confirmed submission to the will of God, which can ever regulate and render endurable those feelings which at present are beyond your control . . . His ways, it is true, are past finding out; for they are not as our ways, or His thoughts as our thoughts. Here then is our great trial and difficulty . . . Most truly do I pray that this comparative calm may in time be vouchsafed to your endeavours.'[60]

On Peel's death Aberdeen, whom he had placed, according to Julia Peel, unequivocally first among the giants by whom he was surrounded, was recognized as leader of the Peelites – a dwindling band, indeed, but one still representing much of the talent of his administration. Aberdeen refused, however, according to his son, 'to assume a public position of formal leadership', maintaining that the Peelites were not a party in the strict sense of the term, but a collection of individuals only bound together by their regard for Peel and their anxiety to safeguard one particular enactment, the repeal of the Corn Laws, and all ultimately certain to join one or other of the two great existing parties. Elaborate machinery for organizing what he put at about twenty peers and forty Members of Parliament seemed to him 'slightly ridiculous'. Besides, Peel himself had always discouraged the organization of the Peelites into a party. Then, again, the Peelites were very unpopular, which to him rendered the step 'particularly inopportune'.[61]

However Gladstone took a different view, and by the autumn of 1851 was pressing that either Aberdeen or the much younger and less experienced Duke of Newcastle, a close friend who had got him his first seat, should be actually elected to the leadership. Newcastle had his doubts about Aberdeen's suitability, which he expressed to Gladstone. 'The objections to Lord Aberdeen are, to speak frankly to a friend for whom I have the most sincere regard, his age and consequent unfitness for the wear and tear of body and mind, his being little known (I really believe even by name) to the great bulk of the community in consequence of his exclusive devotion to Foreign Affairs, his want of manner or knowledge of how to deal with mankind, his leaning to despotism on the Continent, his utter ignorance of Finance, and, I *fear*, his lack of courage. Nevertheless, I say to you now, as I said more than once to Sir Robert Peel, Lord Aberdeen is the only Public Man (now that *he* is gone) whom I would willingly serve under. I see his unfitness, I fear the consequences of his being our recognized Leader in Opposition; but if others concur, and *he himself will* (for this I doubt), he shall have no more faithful and zealous follower (for in his integrity I have the firmest reliance) than myself . . .'[62]

Aberdeen's own son was later to be critical of his father's suitability for his task, though his judgement was, not unnaturally, expressed less harshly. 'Slow to act, distrustful of his own judgment, and totally devoid of party spirit or personal ambition, he was not the man to lead vigorous and impassioned attacks upon political opponents, or to defend, for party reasons, measures felt by him to be in themselves indefensible. But as a mediator and conciliator he stood unrivalled, and in the position then occupied by the Peelites, mid-way between the two great conflicting political parties, he well represented those with whom he acted. He was respected by all as a man wholly incapable of intrigue or insincerity, and, by those who knew him, for the sagacity of his judgment; while he was not only respected but loved by those admitted to his closer intimacy.'[63]

In the end Aberdeen consented, in Newcastle's words, to 'leave his easy-chair and summon his friends',[64] and was unanimously elected leader of the Peelites. Newcastle was as good as his word, serving loyally under him, perhaps unfortunately for Aberdeen, as things were to turn out.

The troubles of the year 1850 did not end with Peel's death. In September came a Papal bull converting Roman Catholic vicars apostolic in England into diocesan bishops with local titles derived from their sees – a fiat violently resented throughout the country,[65] and by Russell above all, as the establishment of a Romish hierarchy in England with territorial titles, and an assault on the supremacy of the Crown. Just at a time when it seemed that the Whigs and the Peelites might coalesce, Russell proposed to bring forward an Ecclesiastical Titles Bill, waging war on the Pope, which alienated the sympathies of men like Aberdeen and Graham. Having been all his life the friend of toleration and of religious liberty, Aberdeen said in disgust, he could not now 'act the part of a bigot and persecutor', and 'join him in such a course of

199

proceeding'.[66] He was particularly opposed to the penal element in the Bill.

It was becoming clear that the Government could not long survive, and early in 1851 Russell resigned. The Queen sent for Stanley, who declined the commission, frankly explaining that there were no men in his party 'who combined great ability with experience in public business' – not even Disraeli, who had never held office – and 'that he should have great difficulties in presenting to the Queen a Government fit to be accepted unless he could join with some of the late Sir R. Peel's followers; that he considered, for instance, the appointment of a good person for Foreign Affairs indispensable, and there was scarcely anyone fit for it except Lord Palmerston and Lord Aberdeen'.[67] He declined the task, but agreed to try again if the efforts of others to form a government failed.[68]

The Queen then sent for Lord John Russell, who tried to form, with the Peelites, an extended government, 'in which,' according to Arthur Gordon, 'Lord Palmerston was not to be included'.[69] The Queen herself stipulated that Palmerston should not be Foreign Secretary.[70] Russell made his first offers to Aberdeen and Graham, and the Queen and the Prince Consort met the three principals at Buckingham Palace to discuss matters.[71] Aberdeen, elegantly deprecating his grasp of the complexities of Free Trade, said that since Peel's death it was a matter of piety not to abandon it. Then, too, he considered a dissolution which might lead to a corn-tax highly dangerous, and on this Stanley, despite the opposition of Disraeli, continued to insist. Above all Aberdeen disapproved of Russell's proposed Ecclesiastical Titles Bill. The question of electoral reform, Russell's hobby-horse, was no obstacle to him, 'for though he was called a *despot*, he felt a good deal of the Radical in him sometimes'.[72] The meeting broke up with the Queen's demanding that one of the three gentlemen '*must*' form a government, and Aberdeen's laughingly parrying her autocratic injunction by comparing her with the French President.[73] Privately Russell revealed to the Queen and her consort that he did not want Aberdeen at the Foreign Office,[74] and would not serve under him or Graham.[75] There was no question, in any case, of such a coalition, for Aberdeen and Graham formally declared their undying hostility to the Ecclesiastical Titles Bill, and their refusal to enter into any negotiation unless Russell withdrew it.[76] Lord John then agreed to abandon all its clauses except the first, but Aberdeen refused to agree to the penal clause, and Russell would not – for he could not, at that stage, after all his pledges – withdraw it. Russell later acknowledged that Aberdeen had been right, writing in his *Recollections and*

Suggestions, 'The course suggested by Lord Aberdeen would have been as effectual, and less offensive, than that which I adopted'.[77]

The Queen then decided that she must send for Aberdeen, but first asked whether he and Graham together would undertake the task. In the words of Prince Albert's memorandum of 25 February 1851, 'The Queen put it to them whether *they* could form a government, to which they replied that they had turned it in their heads a hundred times, that there was nothing they would not do to show their readiness to serve the Queen, but that they did not see a possibility of forming an Administration which could stand a day. They were most likely at the moment the two most un-popular men in England, having declared that nothing should be done in Parliament against the Papal Aggression, which the whole country clamoured for; the Whigs would be very angry with them for their having broken up the new combination; they might find favour with the Radicals, but that was a support upon which no reliance could be placed'.[78]

Aberdeen was then asked whether he alone would try to form a government, and declined.[79] Like Peel, he was more ambitious than he affected to be, and it was rather wistfully that he wrote to Arthur Gordon, 'I might have been Prime Minister at this moment had it not been for my resistance to the Ecclesiastical Titles Bill'.[80] In the Lords he was leading opposition to it, and, as Russell observed to the Queen and her Consort, if he had joined the Whigs he would have 'lost his influence' there.[81] Aberdeen knew, as he said in the Lords, that his opinion of the Bill was not shared by a majority in either House.[82] His motion for rejection of the Bill there in a speech breathing wisdom and toleration was defeated by the overwhelming majority of 227.[83] His son claimed that at the end of the session he left London convinced that he had excluded himself from office for the rest of his life. As usual he bore unpopularity philosophically, shrugging his shoulders at 'rancour, bigotry and intolerance'.[84]

Next the Queen sent for Stanley, to his dismay. 'On his question,' Prince Albert recorded, 'whether there was any hope of Lord Aber-deen joining him and taking the Foreign Office, we had to tell him that he must quite dismiss that idea. He replied, with a sigh, that he would still try and see him; he had thought of the Duke of Wellington taking the Foreign Office *ad interim*, but felt that he could hardly propose that, considering the Duke's age and infirmity.'[85]

Stanley had to abandon his attempt; and Russell agreed to carry on. 'He would prefer,' wrote Prince Albert, 'not to make any

201

arrangements for the Coalition now, but merely to engage to resign again after having carried the Papal Bill, when the Queen could try the Coalition, and that failing, could entrust Lord Aberdeen and Sir J. Graham with the carrying on of the Government, whose chief difficulty would then be removed.'[86] Russell agreed that it would 'strengthen his hands' if the Queen made it a condition that he should resign after carrying 'the Papal Bill'.[87] Russell's colleagues, however, refused to act as what they called '*warming-pans*' for a coalition government, and threatened immediate resignation.[88] On Wellington's advice to the Queen, Russell decided to carry on as before, knowing that his Government would be very weak, and likely to fall quickly.[89] 'Lord John promised,' wrote Prince Albert, 'to move Lord Palmerston in the Easter recess, or to resign then himself if he should meet with difficulties . . .'[90]

By 1850 the Queen's patience with Palmerston's high-handed ways had snapped. Infuriated by his obstinacy about sending off despatches without having submitted them to her, she had delivered a swingeing snub to him in the form of a memorandum commanding him not to repeat the offence. Now he blundered. On 2 December 1851 came Louis Napoleon's *coup d'état*, at which Palmerston rejoiced in unguarded terms both to the French ambassador in London and to the British ambassador in Paris. Then, the Cabinet deciding on a policy of strict neutrality, he had to pick up the pieces as best he could – and once again was caught by the Queen sending off a despatch without showing it to her. Russell had to demand his resignation from the Foreign Office. With Palmerston gone in disgrace – 'a beaten fox',[91] as Disraeli called him – there was little to prevent Aberdeen's joining Russell; and he regretted the refusal of Graham, Newcastle and other prominent Peelites individually approached by Lord John, to do so at the beginning of 1852.[92]

In February, however, came Palmerston's famous 'tit-for-tat', supposedly, according to Russell, the result of a plot between Palmerston, the Peelites and the Protectionists to defeat the Government on the Militia Bill.[93] Palmerston carried his motion, and Russell was forced to resign. Disraeli, transported with delight at the prospect of coming into office, said he 'felt like a young girl going to her first ball'.[94] Palmerston refused to join Derby. In Jasper Ridley's words, 'The only real obstacle to his [Palmerston's] joining the Conservatives was free trade. Palmerston's political doctrines were flexible, and he had always been opportunistic in his attitude to political parties; but he had his principles, and there were none which he held more sincerely than his devotion to free trade'.[95] Derby formed his Government without him. There were no men of experience and few of talent in this Cabinet, dubbed the 'Who? Who? Ministry' because the deaf Duke of Wellington, sitting beside Derby in the Lords, and enquiring about its composition, was heard throughout the chamber loudly demanding, 'Who? who?' as Derby shouted each unfamiliar name into his ear.[96] In such a government, with Derby in the Lords, Disraeli had his own way in the lower House. He had strong motives for preventing any combination of parties in it, for, as Argyll observed, the union of the Peelites with his own party 'would have destroyed his own solitary reign in a cabinet of mediocrities'.[97] Both Government and Opposition were bargaining hard for the support of Aberdeen and his Peelites. Aberdeen offered it to Derby if he renounced Protection and No Popery, but the price was too high. So now Aberdeen found himself in the anomalous position of agreeing rather more with the opponents of his whole political lifetime, Lord John Russell and his party, than with Derby and his Protectionists.[98] Yet he could not expect to command the support of the mass of the Whig party, however cordial a relationship were to exist between its leaders and himself. Besides, Gladstone, Sidney Herbert, Graham and Newcastle, his principal Peelite supporters, held strong and often irreconcilable views about coalition with one or other side – anti-Whig, anti-Protection, anti-reform, or, simply, anti-Derby or anti-Russell.[99] He devoted himself to trying to bring his supporters, individually, to a more co-operative attitude, so that the Peelites might adhere to either party, and help provide a stable government for the Queen.

Derby's Government could not last; and everyone knew it. An early general election was regarded as inevitable, and on July 1 Derby went to the country. He gained over a hundred seats, but he still did not have a working majority. Russell led the opposition, but could not unite it. The Queen was already considering whom she should send for in anticipation of a Government defeat.

Before December the Conservatives abandoned Protection, and were saved, but only for a short time. When Disraeli, as Chancellor of the Exchequer, introduced his house-tax proposals in his Budget, the Peelites joined with the Whigs and Radicals and the 'Irish Brigade' and brought about Derby's defeat by a majority of 19. At 4 a.m. on December 17 Derby resigned. The Queen sent Prince Albert's secretary, Colonel Phipps, to Woburn to seek the advice of the Duke of Bedford, who had been holding a conference with Aberdeen, Lansdowne and Lord John Russell to determine what advice to give. Bedford advised the Queen to send for Lansdowne and Aberdeen.[100]

On December 18 the Queen saw Derby. According to Prince Albert, Derby declared himself ready to support any government 'sincerely anxious to check the progress of democracy' – that is, reform.[101] He had heard that the Whigs and Peelites had come to an agreement and were ready to form a government on Conservative principles to exclude the Radicals under Aberdeen's lead, believing that with all the talent at their disposal they could command confidence in the country, and hold the balance between the two extreme parties in the House. Derby advised the Queen to send for Lansdowne, the Whig, and not Aberdeen, the Peelite, to begin with. Prince Albert then said that the Queen thought of sending for both Lansdowne and Aberdeen, and Derby acquiesced.[102] Derby was obviously suffering from resentment against the Peelites. He severely attacked Aberdeen in the Lords in his resignation speech, in his absence, for factious opposition by the Peelites, and had to apologize to the Queen.[103]

Argyll later posed the question as to why Aberdeen and Lansdowne were the two men to be approached at this time, and answered it. There were, he said, at least three kinds of prime minister in our country. First, there were a few men of commanding genius, like Pitt, who succeeded as of right; and, secondly, there were the 'all-round men', like Peel, who began at the bottom, served in many offices, and distinguished themselves. 'But there is another class of Prime Minister,' he wrote, 'consisting of men who have lived a long life outside the leading currents of political contention, but with a native strength and probity of character, which has received universal recognition, and has secured universal respect and honour. These are the men round whom rival politicians will sometimes cluster when they will refuse to serve under each other.' In 1852, there were two men of this class; one, Henry Petty, Marquess of Lansdowne, once Grenville's Chancellor of the Exchequer. 'The other of the two men,' Argyll said, 'who occupied a somewhat similar position was the Earl of Aberdeen; his name, however, was not much brought forward until, at the very close of the year, it was found to be the only one possible round which the jarring elements could be made to crystallise.' He added that, in the midst of the doubts and difficulties, Aberdeen became more and more a centre of correspondence and consultation, 'because all sections confided in his incorruptible integrity and simplicity of character, in the moderation of his opinions, and in the complete absence in him of any personal ambition'.[104] In this context it is of interest that Professor Conacher has written, 'There is of course no question of [Peel's] superiority to Aberdeen as a prime minister, but I doubt whether he would have been as successful in getting along with the Whigs. Indeed, he might not have succeeded in inducing them to serve under him as the respected and amiable Scottish aristocrat was able to do. (Even the Peelites showed greater affection for Aberdeen than for Peel.)'[105]

On December 18 the Queen summoned both Lord Lansdowne and Lord Aberdeen to Osborne. The seventy-two-year-old Lansdowne was suffering from one of his attacks of gout, and declared that he was unable to leave London. Aberdeen, preferring not to give himself any advantage by going to Osborne alone, notified the Queen that he would await further orders, and called on Lansdowne.[106] Gratified by Aberdeen's 'considerate delicacy', Lansdowne told him that he did not want to be Prime Minister, though 'much pressed' by Palmerston and others; that he was opposed to further measures of reform, and aware of the probable reluctance of some Peelites to serve under him; and that on the whole he considered Aberdeen the man best fitted for the task at that juncture. He was anticipating a request to Aberdeen and Russell to form a coalition government, and had already written to the Queen suggesting that she should summon them both. Now he asked Aberdeen to go to Osborne alone, if summoned, and promised his help in reaching a settlement with the Whigs. However, Graham, whom Aberdeen consulted next, 'strongly urged on Lord Aberdeen the impolicy of accepting any such joint commission', mainly on the grounds that Lord John would regard any offer from him in such circumstances as proof not of personal regard but of royal favour, and see himself as a rival. Aberdeen was persuaded, and assured Graham that 'he would only accept undivided authority'.[107]

Returning home on foot from Graham's house in Grosvenor Place across Hyde Park, Aberdeen met Lord John Russell. According to Graham, who heard the details from Sidney Herbert, and later had them confirmed *in toto* by Aberdeen, and noted them in his diary, Russell volunteered to lead in the Commons and to accept the seals of the Foreign Office. Lord Aberdeen, he recorded, 'jumped at the offer, commended its generosity, and closed with it on the spot'.[108] Uncertainty as to what actually took place was to lead to endless trouble. Sir Spencer Walpole, drawing on Lady John's diary, wrote that Russell had only told Lord Aberdeen that 'he thought he should accept office under him'.[109] But Aberdeen, only a month later, wrote to Lord John that it had been his intention to refuse the Queen's commission 'without the certainty of your accepting the Foreign Office and the lead in the House of Commons'; and that he had been 'relieved from all doubt' when Russell had 'voluntarily expressed such an intention' before he had gone to Osborne; and that he had found him 'precisely in the same frame of mind' when he had returned from Osborne on Sunday night.[110] Not only was Aberdeen a scrupulously truthful man, but the assertions he made in this letter were apparently never denied by Lord John.[111]

The fact is, that Aberdeen was faced with a very difficult situation, where, as the Duke of Argyll pointed out, 'the leadership of Lord John Russell had become invincibly distasteful to everybody except a small personal and family clique', but Lord John 'could not be got to see this', and was convinced that he had a prescriptive right to the premiership because of his 'great, and, indeed, immortal services to the Liberal party'.[112] Aberdeen, therefore, properly regarded Russell's support in his Government as a *sine qua non* to his accepting the office of prime minister. At the same time he feared that Palmerston might set himself at the head of an opposition party, and regarded his co-operation, too, as essential. Aberdeen's offer to Russell of the leadership in the Commons (which, as he said to Prince Albert, 'made him virtually as much Prime Minister as he pleased')[113] and of the Foreign Office, were, he was convinced, accepted, and on the strength of that he kissed hands as Prime Minister on December 19. He emphasized to the Queen on doing so that 'it was of the greatest importance that only one person should be charged with the task and be responsible for it, and that the new Government should not be a revival of the old Whig Cabinet with an addition of some Peelites, but should be a liberal Conservative Government in the sense of that of Sir Robert Peel'.[114] He said nothing of the wide divergences which had developed since Peel's death between the leading Peelites in their degree of antipathy towards the Tories. Graham, the most hostile, had stood in 1852 effectively as a Liberal, while Gladstone had looked with sympathy to the possibility of a junction, except in his personal inimicality towards Disraeli.

Next day, December 20, however, at breakfast, Aberdeen found a letter from Lord John saying that his health forbade his taking on both the Foreign Office and the lead in the Commons – a disastrous blow to Aberdeen. The letter was followed by Lord John himself, announcing that he would rather stay out of the Government altogether and give it his independent support – an assurance which from such a source would give Aberdeen scant comfort. (By the 20th, too, Graham had heard from Sidney Herbert that he had

had information that Palmerston, if not included in the Government 'would place himself at the head of the Opposition in the Commons'. 'He thus,' commented Graham, 'shows us the point of his sword, and hopes by threats to prevail.'[115]) Aberdeen remonstrated with Lord John, telling him that he would have acted differently in such circumstances, and reported to the Queen.[116] The Queen at once wrote to Russell, calling on him to be patriotic and to co-operate with Aberdeen.[117] After Lansdowne, Macaulay and Clarendon had all brought their influence to bear on him, Russell offered to lead in the Commons and sit in the Cabinet without portfolio[118] – therefore without having to fight a by-election, which would have been expensive and, possibly, even in the City of London, dangerous for Lord John, with his long record of losing safe seats. Aberdeen 'objected to so great an innovation',[119] and decided, on Graham's advice, to make Russell's acceptance of some office an essential condition. At this critical juncture, Russell always claimed, Aberdeen intimated that, as soon as the temporary obstacles to Russell's becoming Prime Minister had been overcome, he would retire in his favour. Forty-three years later Lady John referred to the arrangements in her excited way: 'No oath was taken, no pen and ink used, but the agreement as between gentleman and gentleman was . . . as binding as if there had been twenty oaths. *On this agreement alone* John consented to take office'.[120] The arrangement seems to have been known to the Court and the Cabinet, and to have been strongly disapproved of by both.[121] In the end, on December 23, after much vacillation, Lord John once again agreed to be Foreign Secretary, provided it was only for a short period, and that as soon as it proved too much for him he would be free to give it up to Clarendon. So, by this extraordinary arrangement, Aberdeen was at last enabled to form his Government. He had had his first taste of being at the mercy of the thoroughly unreliable Russell.

On the other hand, Aberdeen had something to answer for. His giving an undertaking to go was unwise, and almost certain to lead to embarrassment. Then, he had greatly offended Russell earlier in the year, when they had been corresponding at length about a possible collaboration, by sending him a letter written by the Peelite Duke of Newcastle for Russell's eyes, which proposed the abolition of the title 'Whig' – 'rather a strong proceeding', as Aberdeen admitted, while himself suggesting the substitution of 'Conservative Progress'.[122] Besides, Aberdeen had written to Graham: 'You may fall back upon Whiggism, in which you were bred, but I was bred at the feet of Gamaliel, and must always regard Mr Pitt as the first of Statesmen'.[123] These tactlessnesses were certain to rouse the ire of the all-too-touchy Russell and his cohorts.

A dreadful week followed, while Aberdeen, Graham and Russell tried to agree on appointments. 'The power exclusively confined to Lord Aberdeen', as Graham noted, had 'fluttered the dove-côte', and Russell was prodded not only by 'home influences' but by Whigs resentful at 'an act of submission' to a diehard Tory.[124] What ensued has been described as 'one of the most unabashed place-hunting rat-races since the eighteenth century'.[125] The Whigs not unfairly expected the number of places allotted to them to reflect the support they brought, while the Peelites maintained that ability was the key consideration, and behaved as if they had a monopoly of it. Aberdeen, indeed, as he had forewarned the Queen, set about forming a government dominated by Peelites. At one stage Russell complained, 'Of 330 Members of the House of Commons 270 are whig and radical . . . thirty are Peelites. To this party of thirty you propose to give seven seats in the cabinet . . . to the whigs and radicals five, to Lord Palmerston one'.[126] Every time agreement seemed to have been reached Russell arrived with more demands, fighting pertinaciously for his men, and on Christmas Eve, the Queen noted, he 'sent in such a list of persons whom he required in the Cabinet . . . that having been very yielding hitherto, Lord Aberdeen was obliged to be peremptory in his refusal'.[127] On Christmas Day Aberdeen was able to present his final list of major offices to the Queen; but after Christmas, as Graham wrote, 'the Whigs returned to the charge, and claimed in a most menacing manner a larger share of the minor offices . . . It was one o'clock – the House of Commons was to meet at two by special adjournment, and the writs were to be moved punctually at that hour. Sir Charles Wood intimated that unless some further concessions were made the arrangement was at an end, and that the moving of the writs must be postponed. I said that I should go down to the House and make then and there a full statement of the case, and recall by telegraph my address to the electors of Carlisle which declared my acceptance of office. This firmness coupled with my rising to leave the room brought the gentlemen to reason. Hayter was sent to the House of Commons, and moved the writs'.[128] None the less, the battle for minor offices was resumed next day. 'I have never passed a week so unpleasantly,' Graham wrote. 'It was a battle for places from hostile camps, and the Whigs disregarded fitness for the public service altogether. They fought for their men as partisans and all other considerations, as well as consequences, were disregarded. Lord Aberdeen's patience and justice are exemplary. He is firm and yet conciliatory, and has ended by making an arrangement which is on the whole impartial, and quite as satisfactory as circumstances would admit. Disraeli's observation is true that "the cake is too small for us".'[129]

Unfortunately for future relations, however, the Peelites had offended the Whigs beyond forgiveness by their exclusion from office of men both able and influential. 'A very tiny party,' as Brougham commented, 'had entirely swallowed up the great Whig party.'[130]

The Cabinet was formed, for good or ill, and in Gladstone's opinion, at any rate, probably no man but Aberdeen could have led the negotiations to a successful issue.[131] Palmerston was in. Aberdeen had offered him the post of First Lord of the Admiralty, and Palmerston had refused it.[132] ('Lord Aberdeen said,' noted Prince Albert, 'that when he saw Lord Palmerston, who then declined office, nothing could have exceeded the expressions of his cordiality; he had even reminded him that in fact they were great friends (!!!) of sixty years' standing, having been at school together. We could not help laughing heartily at the *Harrow Boys* and their friendship.'[133]) Lady Palmerston, however, disapproved of her husband's refusal, and was most anxious to have him back in office,[134] though, as Prince Albert noted, 'Lord Palmerston looked excessively ill, and had to walk with two sticks from the gout'.[135] Hearing this, Aberdeen offered Palmerston his pick of all the departments except the Foreign Office, and Palmerston settled for the Home Office.

The Cabinet of thirteen consisted of six Peelites, six Whigs and one Radical. Looking round the table at the dinner he gave to his Cabinet colleagues on December 29 at Argyll House, Aberdeen would feel confidence in the backing of his friend and great admirer, Sir James Graham (First Lord of the Admiralty), the tall, handsome, balding landowner, with the powerful frame and weak voice, who could produce when required in debate what Aberdeen called 'Graham's sledgehammer'[136]; in Gladstone (Chancellor of the Exchequer), who, despite the trouble he had given him the year before by his precipitate and headstrong actions over political prisoners at Naples, was one of his strongest supporters; in Newcastle (Secretary for War and the Colonies), a staunch Peelite, and a loyal, industrious and conscientious worker, if without brilliance or initiative; in Sidney Herbert (Secretary at War), an excellent and ready speaker; and in the young Argyll (Privy Seal), on whom he relied to help him in debates in the Lords. He could not but be disturbed at what might eventuate from relations between Palmerston and Russell, whose swords had so recently clashed, as well as between himself and Russell. The other Whigs, Cranworth (Lord Chancellor), Granville (President of the Council), Lansdowne (without office), Wood (Board of Control) and Molesworth, the one Radical (Woods and Forests), were an unknown quantity as far as support for their new leader was concerned.

It was an imposing, even a brilliant, Cabinet, called at the time a second Ministry of All the Talents,[137] but one not without weaknesses. In a celebrated entry in his diary Sir James Graham wrote, 'It is a powerful team, but it will require good driving. There are some odd tempers and queer ways among them; but on the whole they are gentlemen, and they have a perfect gentleman at their head, who is honest and direct, and who will not brook insincerity in others'.[138]

Aberdeen's old opponent of the field of Leipzig, Charles Stewart, now Lord Londonderry, a high Tory, was less hopeful. Calling the coalition 'this English *coup d'état*', he demanded of Lord Clarendon, the Whig Foreign Secretary designate, 'Do you mean to assert that Sir R. Peel would ever have acted in couples with Lord John? And yet Aberdeen, who lived only, as he swore, in the spirit of the departed, has not only harnessed himself to the car of the Whig party, but at the head of only some 30 or 40 tail has plunged into a whirlpool of difficulties, doubts and incalculable results . . . So utterly meretricious (forgive the word) and apparently indelicate and inexplicable an alliance was never before contemplated, much less seen. It is not in human nature to lay aside personal incongruities, injuries and squabbles, so as to embrace, forget and forgive, in a few months, as if unblemished individuals on these heads came together'.[139]

The Queen, at any rate, was pleased and confident. Only three months before, when the Duke of Wellington had died, she had written to her Uncle Leopold: 'He was to us a true, kind friend and a most valuable adviser. To think that all this is gone . . . We shall soon stand sadly alone; Aberdeen is almost the only personal friend of that kind we have left. Melbourne, Peel, Liverpool – and now the Duke – *all* gone!'[140] Now she wrote again to him, speaking of the formation of so brilliant and strong a Cabinet as 'the realisation of the country's and our most ardent wishes', and saying, 'it deserves success, and will, I think, command great support'.[141]

On Christmas Day *The Times* contemptuously dismissed Russell – 'Lord John Russell has so little of the accomplishments required for his new office that we can only suppose he is keeping it for a successor, most probably Lord Clarendon, who otherwise will not have a seat in the Cabinet'.[142] Lord John was very angry. 'I have *never* seen him so mortified and annoyed,' wrote Lord Clarendon, protesting to the paper's leader writer, 'because the friendship between Lord A. and Delane is, as he said, well known, and nobody will suppose that attacks on him would find their way into *The Times* unless they were agreeable to Lord A.'[143] In less than a week trouble was brewing.

Chapter 16

'Chained to the Oar'

When Aberdeen became Prime Minister he found France and Russia snarling over the 'sick man',* Turkey, impatient to kill him off and divide the spoils. Aberdeen himself was still anxious to keep Turkey inviolate for the sake of the balance of power, yet horrified by her barbarities to the Christians.

Since the Crusades France had had custody of the profitable Holy Places of the Holy Land, and had been protector of the 'Latin' or Roman Catholic Church in the Ottoman Empire – a rôle which brought her in conflict with the Czar, Defender of the Greek Orthodox Church, and acknowledged protector of its fourteen million members in the Ottoman Empire. In 1850 France had reacted to a claim by the Greek Orthodox priests to the key of the Church of the Nativity by sending to Constantinople to demand full reinstatement of the Latin Church in its custody of the Holy Places. The Czar had determined to exploit this 'churchwardens' quarrel' as a pretext for reasserting Russian power over the Sultan, carving up his dominions, establishing more principalities under Russian domination, and reducing France to the status of mere onlooker. The quarrel had continued for two years, and in December 1852 the French had sent a warship, the *Charlemagne*, to Constantinople in violation of the Straits Convention and brought the Sultan to heel.

Aberdeen found the Turks harassed by the threats of both France and Russia and the Ottoman army locked in a life-and-death struggle with the Montenegrin Christians, who had revolted against the Sultan and been supported by the Czar in their bid for independence. The British ambassador in St Petersburg, Sir Hamilton Seymour, was taken by surprise when, in early January 1853, the Czar ordered his troops to concentrate on the frontiers of the

---

* 'We have on our hands a sick man, a very sick man; it will be, I tell you frankly, a great misfortune if one of these days he should slip away from us, especially before all necessary arrangements are made.' (The Czar to Sir George Seymour, Jan. 1853. Martin, *The Triumph of Lord Palmerston*, pp. 34–5.)

212

Danubian Principalities, and summoned him to invite Britain's co-operation.

The Czar was counting on his 1844 talk with Aberdeen, and the memorandum* recording his plan that in the event of Turkey's integrity being threatened, Russia and Britain would consent on joint action. Aberdeen had not replied to it, but to Nicholas that silence implied consent. Britain's approval would render him invulnerable. Everything looked promising; for his old enemy Lord Stratford de Redcliffe, who had been so long a power in Constantinople, had resigned that January.

By February the Czar's proposals had been submitted for Britain's consideration. All the European provinces of the Ottoman Empire were to become independent principalities under Russian protection, and Great Britain could have Egypt and Crete. Lord John Russell at once rebuffed the proposals. The Czar returned with more specific offers. By then Lord John had gone from the Foreign Office, but Clarendon's reply was in tune with his, since he could hardly reverse so recently enunciated and unequivocal a view from the Foreign Office. Even more dubious was Lord John's sending back to Constantinople as ambassador the imperious Stratford de Redcliffe, though it is only fair to add that Stratford's popularity in England as the 'Great Elchi' who knew how to deal with Russia, and the fact that not sending him back at such a juncture would have looked like knuckling under to his old enemy the Czar, were potent pressures for doing so. In fact, the worst aspect of the decision, as J. L. Herkless has effectively established in his article, *Stratford, the Cabinet and the Outbreak of the Crimean War*,** was the Cabinet's distrust of its ambassador, leading to mutual suspicions and misunderstandings, and not his own attitude. The Cabinet indeed consented reluctantly enough to the appointment, and later efforts to be rid of Stratford proved abortive. Thus in the mere two months in which Lord John remained at the Foreign Office he set a course which was to run the nation on the rocks of the Crimean War – and perhaps not by

---

* Copies of Nesselrode's Memorandum in English and French are to be read in the British Museum, Add. Mss. 43144, fos. 106–484b, with a covering note from Brunnon to the French one, undated. The official English translation is to be found in Parliamentary Papers (1737), 1854, LXXI, 866–8; the MSS office copy is in P.R.O. F.O. 65/307; and the whole memorandum is reprinted in English in Bourne's *The Foreign Policy of Victorian England*, Selected Document No. 32, pp. 258–60.

** H.J. XVIII, 3 (1975), pp. 497–523.

accident, since, on his accepting the office of Foreign Secretary, his mentor, 'Lady John', had written to her father, Lord Minto, that, in view of Lord Aberdeen's 'old despotic tendencies', John must do what he could 'in one little month to set foreign affairs on a proper footing'.[1]

Austria had sent a special ambassador to the Porte about the Montenegrin troubles, urging the Sultan to withdraw his troops, and the Sultan had promptly obliged. Both had behaved wisely, and at the end of February 1853 the Czar found that he could no longer use the excuse of the troubles of the Montenegrin Christians as a pretext for invading the Sultan's territory. He was left with two other excuses – the quarrel about the Holy Places, and his newly-inflated claim to be protector of all the Greek Orthodox Christians in the Ottoman Empire. Deciding on a show of strength, he sent the overbearing Prince Menschikoff on a special mission to the Porte. Menschikoff terrorized the Sultan, insisted that the Greek Orthodox rights over the Holy Places should be restored at once, demanded a secret defence alliance between Russia and Turkey, and asked for an insertion in the Treaty of Kainardji, acknowledging that the Greek Orthodox Church was under permanent Russian political as well as religious protection, and giving the Czar the right to interfere in Turkey's internal affairs to enforce the protectorate.

Badly upset, the Turks laid the demands before the British Chargé d'Affaires acting in Lord Stratford's absence. Colonel Rose sent an urgent summons to the British fleet at Malta to sail for the entrance to the Dardanelles, having agreed with the French Chargé d'Affaires that his Government would take similar action. As there was no telegraph service to Constantinople, he asked without consulting his Government. Admiral Dundas refused to obey his orders, and the English Government at once countermanded them, but the foolish action had caused irreparable damage. The French Cabinet had already decided to dispatch their Toulon fleet to Salamis. Clarendon did his best to cool French passions through our ambassador, Cowley, in Paris; but the Czar was offended, and would neither withdraw nor modify his demands. So Great Britain was first brought into the quarrel between France and Turkey and Russia by Rose's precipitate action.

Lord Stratford arrived on April 5, five weeks after Rose had sent off his despatch – weeks full of demands and refusals. Determined that the Czar should not have his protectorate over the Sultan's Christian subjects, though preferring to stop short of war, he was pleased to find that the Turks had rejected the protectorate

214

demand while being prepared to look into the question of the Holy Places, and not displeased to find Great Britain already somewhat committed to the Turks because of Rose's hasty action. He persuaded the Turks to guarantee the spiritual privileges of the Christians, and on April 22 the 'churchwardens' quarrel' was settled. Now Menschikoff had to come out into the open about his real purpose or go home.

On May 5 Menschikoff issued an ultimatum and a draft Convention drawn up as between the Sultan and the Czar. This purported to secure for ever to the Greek Orthodox Church and clergy 'all the rights and immunities which they had already enjoyed and those of which they were possessed from ancient times', making the rights of Ottoman subjects dependent on a Convention with a foreign power. The ambassadors of the four great powers, Britain, France, Austria and Prussia, unanimously advised the Porte to refuse to sign the Convention. Taken by surprise Menschikoff offered on May 20 to accept a mere diplomatic Note instead of a Treaty to the same effect. The ambassadors decided that Turkey should reject this too. On May 21 Menschikoff sailed for St Petersburg, and the whole staff of the Russian embassy at Constantinople was withdrawn. The price of his loss of temper was that there was no longer any possibility of direct negotiation between the governments of Russia and Turkey.

The curtain had come down on the first act of the drama.

The situation was clearly serious. Palmerston was calling for the English and French fleets to be sent to the Dardanelles. He had been whipping up anti-Russian feeling in the country through his influence with the *Morning Post*. Lord John Russell was as hot for action. Aberdeen considered such a move would be futile since it could not help the Turks. The Cabinet should wait to see whether the Czar violated his treaty engagements to England, and move with weight or not at all. Yet his most trusted friends were eager to dispatch the fleet, on almost any excuse – even that of the popular appeal of a war.* He succeeded only in willing their reluctant agreement to support him if he decided to keep the fleet in Malta.

The second act of the drama was about to begin.

---

* For the influence of public opinion, see *The Triumph of Lord Palmerston, A Study of Public Opinion before the Crimean War*, by Kingsley Martin. (Revised edition, London, 1963.)

Back in Russia Menschikoff was greeted by an outburst of wrath from the Czar, who exclaimed that he felt the smart of the Sultan's fingers on his cheek. It was only with difficulty that his Foreign Secretary Nesselrode was able to prevent him declaring war at once. On May 31 he sent a despatch to Constantinople threatening that unless Menschikoff's Note was accepted within eight days without alteration his troops would cross the Pruth and occupy the Danubian Principalities without declaring war. (This ambiguous statement and action were possible because of Russia's rights and interests in the Principalities, which allowed her to enter them so as, technically, to restore order.) This was, in effect, an ultimatum, since the Russians would remain in the occupied territory until they got what they wanted.

On May 29 the Cabinet was split into two parties. Aberdeen was firmly against sending the fleet to Constantinople, and with Gladstone's backing determined to resist all suggestions from Palmerston and Russell that Russia was bent on attacking Constantinople. (That afternoon Palmerston met Malmesbury, who had been Derby's Foreign Secretary, in Pall Mall, stopped to speak to him, and walked his horse by him to Waterloo Place, where they talked for a quarter of an hour about Prince Menschikoff's departure. 'Lord Palmerston,' Malmesbury wrote in his diary, 'spoke very openly on the subject . . . He is for decided measures against Russia, so that between him and Lord Aberdeen there is a complete difference of opinion.'[2] To anxious enquiries from the French and Russian ambassadors as to the probable outcome of this difference Malmesbury replied that 'the strongest character of the two, which, undoubtedly, is Palmerston's, will prevail'.[3]) A divided Cabinet and hysterical fears of Russia were problems enough. Mutual suspicions between France and England spread their poison everywhere.

By May 31, just when the Czar was sending his ultimatum, Aberdeen's hand was forced by Palmerston, Russell, Lansdowne and his Foreign Secretary. Clarendon's defection to the war party was a bitter pill. From then on he would be an unreliable ally in the struggle for peace. Before the end he would leave Aberdeen to fight almost alone, and, in the end, alone.

The unsatisfactory compromise eventually agreed upon was that Clarendon should send Stratford a despatch which approved Turkey's rejection of Menschikoff's Note, commended Stratford's handling of affairs, ordered the fleet to the Aegean, and authorized Stratford to summon it to Constantinople if need arose. By this despatch the Straits Convention of 1841, which closed the Dardanelles to foreign warships, was, effectively, broken. All Aberdeen could do was to try to camouflage the fleet movement as an ordinary manœuvre and hope that it would not be taken as a threat. He still sought to convince his colleagues that a union of the four powers in 'firm but friendly representations at St Petersburg' was the best hope for peace; but they were impervious to his arguments.[4]

Above all Aberdeen regretted the power given to Lord Stratford. 'The authority given to Lord Stratford to call up the fleet to Constantinople is a fearful power to place in the hands of any minister, involving as it does the question of peace or war,' he declared. 'The passage of the Dardanelles, being a direct violation of treaty, would make us the aggressors, and give Russia a just cause for war.'[5]

The rift between Aberdeen and Palmerston was now complete, and Aberdeen was so tried by his efforts for peace against the Laocoön of press, public opinion and war-mongers in his Cabinet that (as Clarendon reported to Greville) he lapsed into 'some of that sneering tone in discussion which so seriously affects his popularity in the House of Lords'.[6] Typical of his sarcasm was the remark, when at odds with Palmerston about the danger of yielding to public opinion, 'On some occasion, when the Athenian Assembly vehemently applauded Alcibiades, the latter asked if he had said anything particularly foolish!'[7] The question has always been asked (when the answer has not been taken for granted) whether war would have been averted if at this stage Palmerston's policies had been adopted. Palmerston, Russell and Lansdowne wanted, simply, to frighten the Czar into submission. They would have had to convince him that Britain was prepared to go to war for Turkey. But Nicholas, harking back to his 1844 talk with Aberdeen, was absolutely convinced to the contrary. Then, too, Princess Lieven, while forwarding to Aberdeen copies and summaries of letters from the Russian ambassador in Vienna, may well have reported back to him Aberdeen's strong bias towards peace. Lord Strangford wrote to Croker in December: 'Madame de Lieven says openly that Nicolas [sic] has been drawn into a snare by the pacific assurances of Aberdeen, who wrote to him [sic, her] just at the time of the passage of the Pruth (and when all the world thought that it must lead to war), that he, Aberdeen, "had once seen forty thousand men, dead or dying on the field of battle", and that he had solemnly vowed never to be connected with a government engaged in war! This, of course, she communicated to Nicolas [sic], and hence he was encouraged to go on, step by step, in the conviction that, do what he might, pen and ink would have been the extent of our opposition'.[8]

The Czar, moreover, was an extremely arrogant man, as well as constitutionally all-powerful. Argyll, at least, meeting him during his visit in June 1844, had been impressed by this. 'Nobody who was ever in his presence,' he wrote, 'could fail to see that he was a man who might be influenced by argument and persuasion, but who would not only never yield to menace, but would be hardened by it into more defiant determination.'[9] The war party opted for what was probably no more than a gamble. Threats to Russia would very likely have only hastened disaster. Professor Conacher has said, 'The policy of Aberdeen . . . had it not been compromised, was the only one that would have guaranteed peace, and at this distance the price seems reasonable weighed against the heavy cost in blood and treasure the Crimean War was to exact'.[10] Now Clarendon's defection had reduced even the small support that policy had commanded in the Cabinet.

By June 28 Palmerston was demanding that the occupation of the Principalities be considered an abrogation of the Treaty of 1841, and that England and France should feel entitled to enter the Straits. A few days later he was urging Aberdeen to send the British fleet to the Black Sea as soon as news arrived of the Russian occupation. Aberdeen resisted him strongly. 'At present,' he declared, 'we are drifting hopelessly towards war, without raising a hand to prevent it.' Once again he held the Cabinet in check and defeated Palmerston. He was adamant above all against increasing Stratford's powers, believing them to be 'already too great'.[11]

In fact the Russian occupation of the Principalities had begun on July 2. The Turks were burning to repel it, but the western powers could not accept it as an act of war since Russia was technically acting within her rights. Brilliantly, now, Stratford held back the Turks from actual war. Taken completely by surprise the crestfallen Russian armies had to remain frozen on the Danube without a foe with whom to engage, without a battle, and without a triumph.

Then, act of war or no, the four powers decided to protest unanimously against the invasion. No one at that stage wanted war. Suddenly even the British Cabinet was united for peace, and anxious that Turkey should be advised not to declare a retaliatory war, and that France, Prussia and Austria should explore terms which Russia and Turkey could both accept. Everywhere schemes for achieving a peaceful settlement were being thought out and put on paper. The facts that there had been an open rupture between

Russia and Turkey, and that the allied fleets were actually in the Aegean, seemed to bring men to their senses. Knowing that the Czar still believed her to be a potential friend, Britain and France urged Austria to summon a conference at Vienna. She agreed to mediate, and Britain and France each drew up a draft convention.

Aberdeen continually hammered it home to his Cabinet that the fleet had been sent to the Dardanelles not to insult Russia but to protect Constantinople if necessary, and that Constantinople was not yet even threatened. He was in favour of leaving on one side for future discussion the vital questions as to how far Britain would go if Russia and Turkey went to war, and under what circumstances she would feel justified in taking up arms against Russia. Britain was, he emphasized, under no treaty obligations to do so, and was 'free to adopt such a course as may appear most consistent with our real interests and honour'.[12] The Cabinet as a whole set its face against him, and he lost the battle for adding to the English draft convention a declaration to the effect that England would not go to war even if war was declared. In fact it nearly broke up the Cabinet, with Palmerston and Lord John, more in tune with the overweening confidence, based on long peace and prosperity, of the public at large, determined to resist it to the end. Perhaps it was at this moment that the battle for peace was finally lost, though war was not to be declared for several months. Arthur Gordon was always to regret that his father did not press for the adoption of this declaration, believing that, even if Lord John had resigned and brought about the Government's collapse, Aberdeen would have been personally absolved from responsibility for the war. Going out, his son concluded, in such circumstances, he might well have soon returned with increased strength as a minister for peace.[13]

This would certainly have been an easy way out for a man who had never wanted to shoulder the burdens of his office. Once it is accepted that he was convinced that it was the more cowardly part to abandon the ship to men who he was sure would run her on the rocks, the concessions which one by one he was forced to make in order to keep his Government together can be seen in their true light. They went against the grain and were excruciatingly hard to decide on, for it was a matter of the nicest judgement as to how far it was safe to go. More, it was largely a matter of luck whether those concessions achieved their objectives. From then on, Aberdeen would be like a man who chops off his limbs to feed the pursuing wolves and ends by dying of his wounds.

The Turks did not approve the English draft convention. They preferred the one drafted in Paris; so it was that document which went forward to Vienna and St Petersburg.

Meanwhile Austria's Foreign Secretary, Count Buol, had invited the Porte to propose a Note of its own for his ambassadorial conference in Vienna to forward to St Petersburg as from the four powers. The Note was produced, but only after a most unlucky week's delay caused by a Turkish governmental crisis. Had it been possible for this Note – damagingly misnamed 'the Turkish ultimatum' – to have been sent by telegraph war might have been averted. The Czar had had time to calm down and was ready to receive approaches from the four powers. Things were far from hopeless.

However, on July 24 Count Buol assembled the council of ambassadors at Vienna, and began to draft a Note based on the French draft convention, which had been well received at St Petersburg. 'The Turkish ultimatum' reached him a day too late, when the Conference was formally committed to the French Convention. It threw out the Turkish Note. It was the Vienna Note which was despatched to Constantinople and St Petersburg.

The curtain rose on the third act of the drama.

If there had been delay about despatching the Turkish Note to Vienna there was none about sending on the Vienna Note to the powers concerned. Clarendon had it by wireless by August 2, accepted it at once, and sent instructions to Stratford. On August 5 the Czar accepted it. If the Turks did the same the crisis would be over.

However, the Vienna Note was a disastrous piece of work. The Czar had preferred Austria to Britain and France as mediator, so the Note went to St Petersburg as from Count Buol and his Vienna Conference, underwritten by all four powers. However it had been drafted in Paris in a pro-Russian spirit, sent privately to the Czar, and then amended to suit him. When the Sultan received the draft he saw that it was little different from the original Menschikoff Note, though the four powers who had unanimously rejected that Note were pressing him to accept it. The Sultan recoiled, scenting danger, since it left Russia free to claim the protectorate which had caused all the trouble, and which he had sincerely believed the four powers were resisting on his behalf.

In England Parliament was prorogued on August 20 before the decision of the Turks was known. As far as home affairs went there had seldom been a more successful session than that of 1853, or one which closed more triumphantly for the government of the day. Gladstone's first Budget, and the Government of India Bill, introducing competitive examinations into the Civil Service, had gone swimmingly.

Inside the Cabinet things had not been so happy on the home front. The Peelites and Whigs had worked well together on all domestic questions except electoral reform. There the rifts had been wide and dangerous. Russell had again raised a plan he had first proposed as Prime Minister in 1849, and again in 1851, for introducing a reform measure which would give the vote to a small section of the working class in the towns. Palmerston had been the most adamant of those of his colleagues who were opposed to it. As to Aberdeen, in 1851 he had felt, and said, that in the present state of the world it looked 'like madness to raise such a question, without necessity'.[14] Now, however, Argyll, visiting him at Haddo, found him to be 'although well known as a Tory in foreign politics . . . so "Liberal" as to be almost a Radical in home politics', and 'ready to entertain very large proposals of departure from the settlement of 1832'. He remarked on Aberdeen's 'curious confidence in the fundamental loyalty of the British people to the constitutional system under which they live', and noted that, as far as Aberdeen was himself concerned, 'there was no obstacle to his acting with Lord John Russell in any combination'.[15] So Aberdeen had appointed a sub-committee of his Cabinet, including Palmerston, to consider Reform; and Russell and Graham had persuaded Aberdeen himself to agree to introduce a bill in the next session of Parliament along the lines proposed by Russell, despite Palmerston's vigorous objections.

That was a shadow which hung over the future. Meanwhile the new Prime Minister, all agreed, had begun splendidly, and the foreign policy which had served his nation so well in the past looked like once again averting threatened war. Russia's acceptance of the Vienna proposals had been a cheerful note on which to close the session. The Lord President of the Council, Granville, told Greville that the expected success on the Eastern Question would 'be principally owing to Aberdeen, who has been very staunch and bold in defying public clamour, abuse, and taunts, and in resisting the wishes and advice of Palmerston, who would have adopted a more stringent and uncompromising course'.[16] Gladstone, too, congratulated Aberdeen on the situation, writing, 'There is clearly no other man in the Cabinet who combined calmness, solidity of judgment, knowledge of the question, and moderation of views, in a manner or degree (even independent of your personal and official authority) sufficient to have held the country'.[17] Aberdeen himself summed up his position with justifiable satisfaction in a letter to Princess Lieven. 'We have brought the session of Parliament to a triumphant close,' he wrote; 'we have carried many useful and important measures; our majorities were numerous; and although a coalition of very different materials, we have adhered well together. For my part, I think I have done quite enough, but when *chained to the oar* it is difficult to escape.'[18]

Aberdeen felt that he could now keep his promise to hand over to Lord John Russell. Indeed Russell had informed him that if he did not do so he would not remain a member of the Government, and Aberdeen had gone so far as to mention the situation to the Queen. 'The Queen,' according to her husband, 'taxed Lord Aberdeen with imprudence in talking to Lord John of his readiness to leave office, which he acknowledged, but called *very natural* in a man of seventy.'[19] Gladstone was stonily against Aberdeen's going, greatly concerned at what he called the 'embarrassments and dangers'[20] which were sure to follow. Perturbed, Aberdeen made up his mind to invite Gladstone to Haddo and try to influence him in favour, for fear that he might refuse to serve under Russell and break up the Government. In the event Gladstone fell seriously ill, and continued so all during September, and Aberdeen himself had to abandon his plan for a visit to Haddo. The meeting never took place.[21] Aberdeen kept Graham fully informed about his intentions to hand over to Russell, but postponed a decision until matters should have settled down.[22]

On August 19, the day before Parliament's prorogation, the Sultan's Grand Vizier had announced that the Turks had refused to sign the Note except with modifications of their own. Cruelly disappointed, and calling their conduct suicidal, Aberdeen maintained that the Turks had no right to ask the Czar to accept modifications at that stage. Clarendon blamed Stratford for not being prepared to back any scheme but one of his own, and never forgave him.

By the beginning of September things looked so bad that Aberdeen recalled Lord John to London for talks with Clarendon and Palmerston. The three were eager to enter the Dardanelles, but Aberdeen pleaded that the plan was premature and in any case needed full Cabinet consent. Russell, defeated, went back to Scotland, leaving Aberdeen and Clarendon alone in London waiting for news from St Petersburg. Even if Russia should reject the Turkish amendments, Aberdeen believed, all was not lost. On September 7 the Czar refused to accept any amendments to the Vienna Note. He would evacuate the Principalities only if the Turks signed it as originally drafted. Even Palmerston could not dispute his right to reject modifications to a Note which the powers had prepared on Turkey's behalf. Aberdeen, Palmerston and Clarendon now decided that they must be abandoned. Lord John disagreed, and was overruled. At Vienna Count Buol told the Conference that he was pressing the Turkish Government to sign the original Note.

Unhappily, on September 17, news came of the leak to a German newspaper of a confidential Memo from Nesselrode to the Russian minister at Berlin. This gave the Russian Foreign Secretary's reasons for rejecting the Turkish amendments, and put it beyond dispute that Nesselrode interpreted the Vienna Note differently from the powers and fully vindicated Turkish fears – a sad blow in the struggle for peace. Britain could no longer, in Clarendon's view, honourably ask the Turks to sign the Note.

On September 22 Aberdeen wrote to Graham that nothing could be more alarming than the present prospect: 'Although at our wits' end, Clarendon and I are still labouring in the cause of peace, but really, to contend with the pride of the Emperor, the fanaticism of the Turks, and the dishonesty of Stratford, is almost a hopeless attempt'.[23]

Had Aberdeen been able to prevail at this stage he would have insisted that the Turks accept the Vienna Note willy-nilly, ignoring the Nesselrode Memorandum. He had already attempted, though in vain, to disengage the nation totally from any future war on Turkey's behalf, and obviously considered himself fully justified in doing so. The purpose of supporting Turkey was to maintain her integrity, and thus the balance of power. War, he clearly considered, was too high a price to pay even for that, and certainly too high for taking a gamble with the Czar's temper. As he wrote to the Queen, 'No doubt it may be very agreeable to humiliate the Emperor of Russia; but Lord Aberdeen thinks that it is paying a little too dear for this pleasure, to check the progress and prosperity of this happy country, and to cover Europe with confusion, misery and blood'.[24] He was convinced that Russia would 'regard the entrance of line of battle ships into the Black Sea as a virtual declaration of war against herself'.[25] Was it in fact feasible, in view of the Turks having been so ill-used, to insist now on their accepting the Vienna Note? To this Professor Conacher has answered, 'To say that this was impossible was to deny the Western allies any freedom of action. Turkey might still have gone to war and been defeated, as she had been in 1829 and was again in 1877, but the powers could still have placed limits on Russia's pretensions as they did in 1878'.[26] Now Aberdeen watched the Turks with horror, as he said, getting their way step by step, drawing Britain into a position in which she was committed to their support.[27]

Lord John was threatening resignation, but Aberdeen was beginning to realize that it was too late to hand over to him. Developments abroad meant that he could no longer retire on a tide of success. If he went it would look as if he were 'running away from an unfinished question',[28] as he put it. His popularity and prestige, at one time very high, had slumped to nothing. Even Greville, with his strong stomach for scandal, stood aghast before 'the violence and scurrility of the press' at this time, finding that it exceeded 'all belief'. Every day, he recorded, Radical and Tory papers alike poured forth 'the most violent abuse of the Emperor of Russia, of Austria, and of this Government, especially of Aberdeen'.[29] The attacks had been very bad all through July and early August; then there had been a short lull; but in September even the Peelite paper, the *Morning Chronicle*, had, to Aberdeen's distress, joined the baying hounds. War frenzy in England was nearly as bad as in Turkey.

That month Russell told his brother, the Duke of Bedford, that 'matters could go on no longer as they were, and that very soon he could no longer act without being primarily responsible for the policy of the Government'. Greville had it direct from the Duke that Lady John and her clique were pushing Lord John to bring about the change from Aberdeen to him.[30] As things grew rapidly worse Aberdeen became increasingly averse to leaving the helm in the midst of a crisis. He found too that Gladstone's determination not to serve in a Russell government had hardened into obstinacy.

Riots and demonstrations broke out in Constantinople on September 11 and 12. The British and French ambassadors were disturbed enough to call up four allied steamships – Lacour had asked for the whole fleet, but Stratford had refused. On September 14 the ships sailed towards Constantinople. In England the riots aroused such alarm that Aberdeen and Clarendon, forgoing Cabinet approval, decided on September 24 on their own initiative to instruct Stratford to call up the fleet to Constantinople, in cooperation with the French, in order to protect the lives of the British and the Sultan.

There were many strange aspects to this move, not least that Aberdeen and Clarendon did not wait for the Czar's reaction before taking exactly the kind of warlike initiative which they continually and vocally deprecated in prospect from Stratford. They did not even wait for Stratford's despatches to reach them. The normally equable, when not positively cheerful, Clarendon was certainly tired, nervy, and cracking under the strain. So depressed was he at this time that he wrote that he would prefer death to his present responsibilities if it were not for his children.[31] Unlike Clarendon, Russell was growing increasingly cock-a-hoop, impatient for the Porte to declare war and force Russia to evacuate the Principalities. On September 27, with a braggadocio more in Palmerston's style, he wrote, 'I know something of the English people, and I feel sure that they would fight to the stumps for the honour of England'.[32] He was eagerly looking forward to taking over as Prime Minister. Aberdeen told him plainly that if he pushed things too far he would probably break up the Government and have to pay the price of 'the odium'[33] of having done so. Russell eventually declared grudgingly that he had given up the idea, but Aberdeen was not deceived. He accused him openly of wanting to 'sit in the chair which I now occupy', and Russell did not deny the charge.[34] On September 30 Aberdeen actually wrote to Mary that Arthur had 'better look sharp' about coming back from abroad, 'as it is *just possible* that he may not find me still a minister. Perhaps I am a little too expeditious, but I look forward to it, not with impatience, but with satisfaction. *This to yourself*'.[35]

With October came increasing difficulties in the Cabinet at home, and an astonishing series of events abroad. The battle began between the Turks' open desire for war and the Russians' apparently sincere desire for peace. In fact the fourth act of the drama was about to unfold.

In the course of a session that lasted from September 26 to October 4 the Turkish Grand Council determined on a policy of declaring war. Meanwhile the Czar and Nesselrode went to Olmütz to discuss possible peace terms with Austria and the allied ambassadors there. The Czar seemed to be disembarrassing himself of the Nesselrode interpretation of the Vienna Note, and offered to recall his troops from the Principalities as soon as it was signed – in its original form, but with a strong declaration of the purity of his intentions towards Turkey.

Aberdeen was delighted. But in the same letter of October 3 in which he told the Queen of the ultimatum and the proposal-cum-declaration he added a sombre postscript: 'P.S. – 3 o'clock – a telegraphic message from Constantinople, just arrived, announces that the Turkish Divan has declared war'.[36] He asked the Queen to speed her return to the capital in anticipation of a state of war involving grave decisions and the possible downfall of his Government.

On October 5 the French rejected the Olmütz proposals. On October 7 and 8 the British Cabinet confirmed the French rejection and authorized the fleet to enter the Black Sea. Aberdeen had been extended to the full in trying to stop such dangerous action. Palmerston had proposed that Russian ships cruising there should be detained, and that Britain should offer naval assistance to Turkey. The Cabinet was in no mood even to consider the Olmütz proposals reasonably, regarding the Czar as discredited by the Nesselrode Memorandum. After a struggle Aberdeen achieved an unhappy compromise. The Black Sea should be entered, but only strictly in defence of some point on Turkish territory which had been attacked. Since he did not expect any attack to be made, peace might continue.

The rejection of the Olmütz proposals was an error with tragic results. There seems little doubt from this distance that the Russians were sincere in seeking a way out of the impending war, and were ready to evacuate the Principalities if they could do so without being shamed before Turkey. Aberdeen was right, and had been right all along. Had he but had the support he deserved all would have been well. But the divisions within and the outcry without would have been too much for any man in his position. The proposals were coldly rejected, with no accompanying overtures for fresh negotiations.

Aberdeen never ceased to regret that he had not been able to take advantage of this opportunity unexpectedly given by the Russians. He wrote to the Queen that he 'was not satisfied with the tone or substance of the answer to the Olmütz proposal',[37] and deplored the dispatch which had been sent to Vienna. It was Russell, Palmerston and Lansdowne who as usual had pushed for bellicose action, and Clarendon had backed them. The more level-headed Sidney Herbert and Argyll were aghast at the way things were going, but they were too young and without sufficient weight to carry the day against the war party. Graham was absent. Gladstone had just returned after his prolonged illness and was of no help.

Aberdeen still battled on. Only days before he had written to Palmerston that he looked upon war with Russia 'with the utmost incredulity'[38] and that Brunnow, the Russian ambassador, was frightened out of his wits at the prospect. He had warned Graham that if they did not take care they might have war in a week. He had recognized that the fleets could now go up to Constantinople as of right, since the Turkish declaration of war had opened up the Dardanelles; but he had also seen that an entrance into the

Black Sea would mean war with Russia. More and more he had felt his growing isolation: 'Indeed, I feel that, very possibly, I may stand alone. I am almost inclined to hope so'.[39] Gladstone was the only friend he had found, and that strange man was never to be wholly relied on. On October 14 Palmerston wrote to Graham that he was 'perfectly willing to incur the responsibility of war with Russia if Turkey can be saved by no other means', and that 'that war . . . is not so near as some of the Cabinet anticipate, and if near it is not so dreadful a calamity as they imagine'.[40]

Clarendon blamed the decisions on public opinion: 'With reference to public feeling in England, we could not well do less . . . I see little chance of averting war, which, even in the most sacred cause, is a horrible calamity; but for such a cause as two sets of barbarians quarrelling over a form of words, it is not only shocking but incredible'.[41] His eyes were open; yet he and his colleagues denied Aberdeen their support.

At Windsor the Queen was deeply troubled, and Prince Albert in a memorandum recorded his view that Aberdeen was 'against his better judgment consenting to a course of policy which he inwardly condemned'. He believed that 'his desire to maintain unanimity in the Cabinet led to concessions which by degrees altered the whole character of the policy, while he held out no hope of being able permanently to secure agreement'. They were convinced that the only hope was for him to remain Prime Minister, and that that could only be if he kept his Government together.[42]

It was, if not too late, the eleventh hour.

Chapter 17

'Odd Tempers and Queer Ways'

While Aberdeen played for time Stratford produced a proposal to modify the Vienna Note so as to meet the demands of both Turks and Russians. The Turks were almost out of control, but he succeeded not only in reining them back from active war but in persuading them to accept his scheme – effectively, a truce. Clarendon prepared a draft Note based on it, which the Cabinet considered on October 10 and 12. Struggling hard to enable England to regain her freedom of action, Aberdeen felt it imperative to convince the Turks that if they refused to sign they could not count on British support. If this could be established, he wrote to Clarendon, Britain would no longer be 'dragged in the wake of a barbarous power whose movements we are not able to regulate or control'.[1]

For once Palmerston raised no objection, but as time went on he and Russell chipped away at the proposed Note, so that it became more and more satisfactory for the Turks and less and less so for the Russians. When at last it was settled, still without Cabinet discussion, by agreement between Aberdeen, Russell and Palmerston, its form was very far from what the Prime Minister had originally intended. The following extract gives the paragraph which Aberdeen had asked to be inserted into Lord Stratford's instructions, and which would have allowed Britain to escape from the trap closing about her, and between square brackets indicates in italics the modifications Lord John succeeded in having inserted into it.

'Considering the assurances of support already given to the measures actually adopted by Great Britain for the protection of the Turkish territory, it is indispensable that all further progress of hostilities should be suspended by the Porte [*for a reasonable time*] during the course of the negotiation in which Her Majesty's Government are engaged for the re-establishment of friendly relations between the Porte and Russia [*upon the understanding that no hostile movement is made upon the part of Russia*].'[2]

The Turks would take advantage of the imprecision of that phrase 'for a reasonable time', since the interpretation was left to them, and limit the duration of the truce to a mere fortnight, with fatal results. Again, they would construe the last phrase not merely, as intended, to mean any attempt by the Russians to cross the Danube, but, literally, as meaning any resistance which their armies in the Principalities offered when attacked there by the enthusiastic Omar Pasha, the Sultan's commander-in-chief.

By October 20 the French and English ambassadors had summoned the fleets to Constantinople, almost a month after Aberdeen and Clarendon had authorized them to do so. Two days later the allied fleets entered the Dardanelles. Next day the Turks, having interpreted 'a reasonable time' as a fortnight, began hostilities. By October 25, in Vienna, Count Buol had announced to the British, French and Prussian ambassadors that Russia had offered to negotiate through him for peace with Turkey. Here was a fair wind for peace, unexpected, and much to Russia's credit.

On the same day Count Buol had thrown out Stratford's newly-arrived truce plan on the grounds that it was no longer relevant since the Turks had begun hostilities. The time for Notes was past, he explained. Only a treaty could now settle matters between the two warring powers, Russia and Turkey. Thus, thanks to Lord John's insertion, all the advantages of Stratford's peace plan, so opportunely ready to hand in Vienna when Russia made her welcome offer to treat with Turkey through the ambassadors there, was lost.

On October 30 the Czar suddenly wrote a friendly personal letter to Queen Victoria. Clarendon, full of mistrust, refused to accept it as a sincere plea for peace and friendly relations, and so the Queen rebuffed him with a formal expression of her Government's views.[3]

On November 5 Clarendon's Note based on Stratford's *original* proposals arrived in Constantinople. The Turks rejected it. They had accepted Stratford's Note, now defunct thanks to Count Buol; but try as he might Stratford could not now persuade them to receive Clarendon's Note which was actually based on it. Had hostilities not been begun they might have done so, but Omar Pasha was proving far too successful against their old enemy for the Turks to feel inclined to lay down their arms. It was, in short, too late.

Peace proposals or no peace proposals, the Cabinet was at war within itself. Palmerston and Russell grew more and more peremptory for warlike action, Aberdeen more and more horrified at the thought of going to war to defend such people. Besides, Clarendon was now deserting him.

Aberdeen's own position had never shifted. Now he recapitulated it for Palmerston's benefit. From the beginning he had tried to preserve England's freedom of action. Menschikoff's demands had been unreasonable and the invasion of the Principalities unjustifiable. On the other hand England was not bound by any treaty with the Porte, and was perfectly free to take any course she wished consistent with her own interests and the justice of the case. The 1841 Straits Convention had imposed no obligation other than that the straits of the Dardanelles and the Bosphorus should be closed to foreign warships when the Porte herself was at peace. When Menschikoff had broken off diplomatic relations with Turkey Britain's object had been to preserve peace by advising Turkey to make reasonable and timely concessions. That had always been, and still was, his policy. It had been clearly agreed that sending the fleet to the Porte and promising to defend her against naval attack were no bar to negotiation. The Turks should help England's efforts for peace; but Omar Pasha had crossed the Danube after the Sultan had decided on a truce, and war had been declared in defiance of Stratford's protests. The preservation of Turkey was a European necessity, but one that should be accomplished by peaceful means. War would be full of danger to the Ottoman Empire. It might well spread; and then the Empire would disappear for ever. Let none imagine that he, Aberdeen, was not prepared to go to war, however, if war were justified and desirable: 'I should be perfectly prepared to oppose, even to the extremity of war, the possession by Russia of Constantinople and the Dardanelles, with the approaches to the Mediterranean, and I think that this decision would be justified by English and by European interests'.[4]

Aberdeen told Palmerston too that he had no doubt that the Czar desired peace, and would prove reasonable when faced with the difficulties his position presented, though he must not be humiliated. Nothing that came to pass in the future proved him wrong; much indicated that he had been right in all his attitudes and opinions. But the point of no return was dangerously close.

So while the British public cried out angrily for war, a seemingly endless series of Notes went to and fro in persistent efforts to achieve the armistice that Aberdeen considered the only way out. At one moment Aberdeen's armistice looked possible. Two days later the Turks made it impossible by rejecting Buol's draft. That day the allied fleets arrived at Constantinople, to the joy of the Turks and the outrage of the Russians.

All this was complicated and disturbing enough; and behind the events was a great deal of stress in personal relations. There had been many Cabinet meetings throughout that November, with much friction. Aberdeen had found himself particularly at odds with

Palmerston about proposals that new treaties should be drafted at a conference to be held in London as opposed to Vienna. Both the Prime Minister and his Foreign Secretary were showing signs of strain, and on November 22 Aberdeen had called on Clarendon and had a show-down about their lack of unity on foreign policy – none too soon, one might think.

Significantly, Arthur Gordon thought, Aberdeen had taken his stand on the point that there could be no hope for peace unless it was accepted that the Czar was sincere in his protestations. Aberdeen had said that, even if he was not, they must seem to believe him. His son had had the impression from his father that all had gone off well, but Clarendon told Greville there had been a scene, and he had rebuked Aberdeen for letting things pass in the Cabinet and raising objections to them afterwards. Clarendon was now openly one of the war party, and patently put out by Aberdeen's efforts to undo, like some Penelope, the work which he could not prevent being done in Cabinet. The unhappy Prime Minister, faced with intransigent opposition from his most influential colleagues, had obviously been reduced to desperate straits.[5]

The tortuous processes of diplomacy continued.

When an Anglo-French Collective Note suggesting that Turkey should accept Russia's proposals with modifications had on November 29 been at last forwarded to Vienna, it was initialled there on December 3, then sent by one mistrusted minister, Lord Westmorland, to another, Lord Stratford. Another sin of omission had been committed. It had been left to Stratford to decide how to present this important document to the Sultan. With yet another stroke of ill-fortune the Note itself arrived in Constantinople too late. Before its arrival the battle of Sinope had taken place, and by the time it reached them the Turks were in a state of insensate fury at the Russians.

That was not all. Before the arrival of Buol's Note Stratford had succeeded in persuading his ambassadorial colleagues to adopt other proposals of his own. He was now trying to achieve an armistice by the renewal of existing treaties and the dispatch of a Turkish representative to deal direct with the Russians. So when he received the Collective Note and realized that it had been left to him to put it forward to the Sultan he set it aside in favour of his own proposals. That was on December 16. The Turks accepted them by the end of the month; and they went forward to Vienna. The result was an explosion from a Buol offended by Stratford's arrogance, and his effort to get his own Note delivered to the Turkish ambassador in Vienna. The British Government blocked this. Less intransigent than Stratford, Buol would agree to Stratford's armistice proposals when they eventually reached him, and transmit them to St Petersburg by January 13. Much would have happened before then, however.

The fact that Lord John's phrase 'for a reasonable time' had allowed the Sultan to open hostilities without contravening the agreed truce had started a chain of events which ended in catastrophe.

The Turks had driven the Russians before them, and the Czar had retaliated by deciding to invade Turkey itself. He had ordered his Black Sea fleet to operate on Turkey's coast, cocking a snook at Britain and France. He had insulted and upset Austria by military movements which frightened her into mobilizing heavily on her vulnerable frontier. By the time Stratford's armistice terms were agreed by the Turks the Czar was in no mood to discuss them, since talk of peace would then have looked like success for the Turks. Things had greatly changed in the few weeks since he had voluntarily offered to negotiate. If only Lord John had not inserted his troublesome phrase hostilities would not have broken out, and the Czar would have been able to continue negotiations which he had himself initiated.

As we know, the Russians had also been displeased, and the Turks excited, by the arrival of the allied fleets at Constantinople on November 24. Stratford had succeeded in stopping Admiral Dundas from sending six allied ships into the Black Sea, and had with difficulty restrained the Turkish navy from patrolling in strength there. He had not, however, opposed the sending of six of their warships into the Turkish harbour of Sinope. Thus on November 30, with the battle of Sinope, the fifth and final act of this drama of suspicion, aggression, misunderstanding and misfortune unrolled.

While all this had been going on there had been continuing trouble in the Cabinet about Russell's proposed Reform Bill, which was being prepared for the next session. Early in December Palmerston wrote to Lansdowne expressing his strong objections to the Bill, saying that he did not 'chuse [sic] to be dragged through the dirt by John Russell',[6] and threatening resignation if modifications were not made to it. Then he sent Aberdeen a copy, with Lansdowne's reply, asking for its return, and including in his covering letter a lengthy criticism of the Government's policy in the Eastern Question.[7]

Aberdeen at once showed the correspondence to Russell and

Graham, writing to Graham, 'This is a very dexterous move. P. has stolen a march, by combining the Eastern Question with Reform. I am at a loss what to do . . . Truly he is a great artist'.[8] However, in the knowledge that he had the full backing of the Queen and his chief ministers, Aberdeen called Palmerston's bluff, brusquely refusing any modifications and emphasizing (on Graham's advice as to how best to deal with this 'crafty foe'[9]) that he had had his letter copied before returning it.[10] Palmerston would not be able to maintain that his resignation, if it came, was about anything but Reform.[11] Then came the devastating news of Sinope.

On November 30 a large Russian naval force had entered the open bay of Sinope and sunk all the Turkish ships at anchor there, with the loss of about 4000 Turkish seamen's lives. This was a perfectly proper act of war, since the Turks had declared war and opened hostilities over a month before – indeed one that would have won a hero's acclaim for a Drake or a Nelson successfully attacking an enemy's fleet in one of his own ports. Yet when, a fortnight later, the news was published in the British press, there was a great outburst of righteous indignation, and the deed was called a 'massacre'.[12] It came most opportunely for Palmerston, who, despite his wife's pleas to wait, at once resigned.[13] Aberdeen had indeed called his bluff, but to no purpose, for the British public was convinced that the resignation was because of Palmerston's disapproval of the Government's foreign policy, and his own paper, the *Morning Post*, went out of its way to say that it was because of Sinope. Palmerston was making a transparent bid for the leadership. Now he stood in opposition to the Prime Minister on two major questions, and awaited events.

Even so early Aberdeen was questioning his own actions, and doing so to opponents. In this he was unusual among prime ministers. The day before Palmerston resigned Aberdeen had written to Lord John, 'I cannot say my conscience is perfectly at ease in consequence of sacrifices I have made to the opinions of others'.[14] By this time Clarendon had gone over almost completely, not only to the war party, but to the extreme Russell wing of it, and had pushed Aberdeen into agreeing to intercept Russian ships in the Black Sea if the Czar's troops crossed the Danube. According to Sir James Graham, Aberdeen was prepared to go to war if the Russians crossed the Balkans, but he was baulking at the Danube, and still trying to persuade his colleagues to act by agreement between the four powers and not separately, with only France for ally.[15] The Coalition was falling apart.

When the Cabinet met on December 20 Aberdeen was filled with foreboding. By then the British and French had ordered their fleets into the Black Sea to protect the Turks. That day Aberdeen wrote to Lord John, saying that he was now so deeply committed in the unhappy business that there was nothing left to hesitate about except the actual declaration of war: 'For myself, I confess that I feel a little like King David, when he said, "I labour for peace, but when I speak unto them thereof they make them ready to battle" '.[16]

Then a hectic dispatch arrived from Paris.[17] The vengeful French public, it declared, was demanding the seizure of Russian ships and munitions found in the Black Sea; and on December 22 the Cabinet gave way to the pressure to accede. Aberdeen saw that this might well drive Russia to declare war, but gave as his reason for acceptance the need to keep the French as allies. Sinope had incited France to adopt an 'exacting and peremptory' tone, and he admitted that unfortunately public opinion in England would not allow of taking the risk of dissolving the Anglo-French alliance merely for the sake of 'such a small act of independence'.[18]

On Christmas Eve, too, Palmerston was to be found again in the Cabinet. He had made it clear that he had not wished to resign, and Aberdeen had made it possible for him to withdraw his resignation.[19] He had won the battle against Russell's Reform Bill, for the Government agreed not to introduce it in the 1854 session, but to defer it for a year, while Russell and Palmerston tried to agree on a compromise. He had been absent during the making of some very important decisions, but had no fault to find with those which had been taken concerning the Eastern Question.

Two days after Christmas Clarendon notified Russia that the British fleets would be occupying the Black Sea. Aberdeen was disgusted by the public outcry. 'In a case of this kind,' he observed bitterly, 'I dread popular support.'[20] Now he was riding two wild horses, his Cabinet and the public, and, much as he longed to be rid of both, he still saw himself as possibly the only man in the kingdom who truly desired peace. He steeled himself to carry on, in order at least to limit the war and bring it to an end at the earliest possible moment.

Since October 8 Stratford had been empowered to send ships to the Black Sea. Arthur Gordon maintained that, having mistakenly given him that 'fearful power', ministers at home were fatalistically convinced that he would use it,[21] and that when a false report arrived in England by telegraph that he had done so they and their French colleagues gave what they believed was merely formal sanction to a *fait accompli*. This, and only this, he believed, was the reason for ordering the fleets to Constantinople – an extra-ordinary enough explanation for an extraordinary enough action, but perhaps only one more poisonous flower of the prevailing suspicions of individuals and nations. Stratford had refrained from using his power for more than two months, and did not do so until long after Sinope. By that time Clarendon's despatch of December 20 ordering him to summon the fleets had arrived, in any case. He sent the whole fleet into the Black Sea, and the entry was completed by 3 January 1854.

Clarendon's order of December 27, which warned the Russians of Britain's intention of ordering their ships back to port and resisting by force any act of aggression directed against the Turks, was delivered at Sebastopol by HMS *Retribution*. While this action was being taken negotiations were still going on, and now the Russians showed every sign of genuine surprise, regret and mortification, Nesselrode expressed his sorrow to Seymour that the British Government should have taken such drastic action just when strenuous efforts were being made in Vienna to arrange a peaceful solution.

Even so late all was not lost. The last effort to settle the quarrel by diplomatic means was reaching its climax. On January 13 the second Vienna Note, proposing peace terms between Russia and Turkey, approved by all the powers and accepted by Turkey, was sent from Vienna to St Petersburg. Louis Napoleon believed that if the Czar accepted its terms all danger of war would be over. On the other hand some believe that long before he received the peace terms the Czar had been taunted beyond possibility of accommodation. In any case neither Louis Napoleon nor the British Government awaited the Czar's answer before taking action. He had had, for six months, to watch the British and French fleets moving, under pressure from Louis Napoleon, abetted by Palmerston, up to their new hostile position. On October 22 they had passed the Dardanelles, on January 3 they had entered the Black Sea. On January 12 the Czar was informed of the orders that Russian ships must return to Sebastopol, and on January 13 he received the Second Vienna Note. He rejected it outright and sent it back with unacceptable counterproposals.

On January 20 Stratford's proposals reached St Petersburg via Vienna. The Russian Government did not answer. On January 28 Orloff arrived in Vienna with his unacceptable counterproposals. On February 2 the Conference rejected them.

The British Cabinet was set on war, and the British public had taken the bit between its teeth. Even Members of the House of

Commons gave way to the madness in the air, which now took a peculiarly virulent form. It was widely believed, and suggested in the press, that the Prince Consort was treasonably involved with Russia, and Aberdeen's name was associated with his in the slanders passed from lip to lip. It was between Orloff's arrival in Vienna and the rejection of his counterproposals, on January 31, the day before the reassembly of Parliament, that huge crowds gathered on Tower Hill expecting to see the Prince Consort and Lord Aberdeen committed to the Tower. Both were burnt in effigy.[22]

On February 4 and 5 the Russian ambassadors were recalled from Paris and London and on February 8 Orloff left Vienna.

Now one last attempt was being made, this time, strangely, by Louis Napoleon. On January 29, with the approval of the French and British Governments, he had written a letter in his own hand to his 'good friend and brother the Czar',[23] suggesting the suspension of hostilities, the withdrawal of Russian forces from the Principalities, and the recall of French and British forces from the Black Sea, so that fresh negotiations could begin between Russia and Turkey, dealing direct with each other. Nicholas had returned an insult which could not fail to infuriate a Bonaparte, boasting that Russia 'would prove herself in 1854 what she had been in 1812'.[24] That was on February 9.

In vain now did Austria, backed by Prussia, make her own pleas for delay and offer to support the allies in fresh diplomatic efforts. Neither Louis Napoleon nor the British public were interested. On February 27 the Franco-British ultimatum, supported by Austria, was presented to the Czar from London and Paris simultaneously, and received no answer. On February 28 the first British army detachments sailed for the East. On March 27 France declared war on Russia, and next day Britain followed suit.

Aberdeen's old friend, the Russian Princess Lieven, had fled Paris, not knowing where she would go. She sent him a farewell:

'Vagabond!-à mon age! Adieu mon cher Lord Aberdeen, mon cher ami, mon cher ennemi.'[25]

It seemed to encapsulate the tragedy of the war, that war which Disraeli called 'a just but unnecessary war',[26] the war which, as some at least believed, 'was undertaken to resist an attack which was never threatened and probably never contemplated'.[27] Aberdeen's long rearguard action against the wilful madness of a nation and its statesmen was over.

Aberdeen sought no excuses for himself, and scorned self-justification. Gladstone, Argyll and Granville, all so strong for peace at the outset, all defended the declaration of war. Clarendon went into print to do so. Not so Aberdeen. From early on in the moves towards war his conscience had pricked him. On February 22 he had asked Gladstone whether he might not retire if war came. He had all along, he said, been 'acting against his feelings, but still defensively'.[28] Now that it was a question of taking the offensive he felt he must withdraw. Gladstone had insisted that the war would be a defensive one, only a matter of 'warning Russia off forbidden ground',[29] and had persuaded Aberdeen that he must remain. Now, however, Aberdeen castigated himself, rehearsing over and over how war might have been prevented if he had acted differently. If only he had won the battles against sending the fleet to the Dardanelles, and for advising the Turks to accept the Russian demands! Russell had shrugged off the implicit criticism. 'The only course,' he wrote on March 3, 'which would have prevented war would have been to have counselled acquiescence to the Turks and not to have allowed our fleet to leave Malta. But that was a course to which Lansdowne, Palmerston, Clarendon, Newcastle and I would not have consented, so that you would only have broken up your Government if you had insisted upon it. My belief is that the Czar, after acquiescence and submission, would only have given the Sultan six months' respite.'[30]

Aberdeen would not be consoled. Miserably he replied the same day that he had no wish to continue a correspondence, the result of which, if he won the argument, would be that he would be condemning himself; but that he did not agree. 'On the contrary,' he maintained, 'I believe that there were in the course of the negotiations two occasions when, if I had been supported, peace might have been honourably and advantageously secured . . . But I repeat that the want of support, though it may palliate, cannot altogether justify to my own conscience the course which I pursued.'[31]

Before the outbreak of war, also, he had written to Russell bewailing a decision which might prove to have been impolitic and unwise: 'My conscience upbraids me the more because seeing as I did from the first all that was to be apprehended it is possible by a little more energy and vigour, not on the Danube, but in Downing Street, it might have been prevented'.[32] Another man might have laid the blame squarely on his colleagues. Certainly none of them shared his sense of guilt and compunction.[33] Even Gladstone, Argyll and Granville, originally strong for peace, were totally persuaded of the justice of the war when it finally came about. Indeed Gladstone always maintained that Aberdeen had been wrong to take on himself blame for the war, claiming that it had come about from the natural evolution of the concert of Europe operating to restrain a transgressor member offending against the law of nations, and not properly supported by Prussia and Austria.

As so often, Aberdeen had personal as well as public worries oppressing him at the same time. From early March he had been concerned for 'dear little Harriet', one of his three granddaughters by Mary, who was ill. In the midst of his massive distresses he now wrote anxiously to enquire after her. On March 22 he wrote to her mother, 'I could not get to you on Sunday, although my carriage was at the door for nearly three hours in the hope of my being able to do so'. Astonishingly, he was capable of saying in the same letter, 'I very much hope before the end of Easter to be able to go to you for a day or two. You know how much more I care for all that belongs to you than for the wrangling of Turks and Russians, and I may say for anything else!'[34]

It is possible that Aberdeen had some form of breakdown at this time, though his resolution and self-control were such that it appears to have gone unnoticed. He never recovered from the conviction that his hands were bloodstained. On the day he wrote to Mary he had told John Bright that his grief was such that at times he felt as if every drop of blood that would be shed would rest upon his head.[35] He would obstinately carry this sense of guilt to his grave. But now, in what he regarded as defeat, he rallied and took upon himself a harder task even than those which he had already fulfilled. Totally unsympathetic to the blood-and-glory element in warfare, utterly contemptuous of all the demagogic tricks inseparable from it, he set himself doggedly to waging the war like his mentor, Pitt, and finishing it as speedily as possible.

Chapter 18

A Russell at Home
and a Russell Abroad

The war must not be allowed to spread; and Aberdeen must strike hard and quickly and with everything the nation could produce.

The trouble was, the nation could not produce much in a hurry, not even an army capable of winning such a war. By the time of Waterloo England had added £1000 million to her national debt. The army had been rapidly run down, and in four years had been reduced to half its original strength – a mere 120,000 men. Yet Aberdeen might comfort himself that this army had proved its effectiveness in Ceylon, Burma, Northern India, China, Afghanistan, New Zealand and South Africa, and the first Sikh war. He could count on it to see him through the short, sharp campaign he, like everyone else, envisaged.

No time was lost. Ten regiments had been recalled from service overseas a full month before war was declared, and ten thousand men and a fleet awaited its outbreak in Malta. After the declaration the Cabinet increased the strength of the army and the militia by another 30,000 men, and the navy by an additional 5000. Enlistment was expedited, so as to release seasoned soldiers for active service. Graham produced 32 ships for the Black Sea and 44 for the Baltic. The troops at Malta re-embarked immediately to join the French contingents already at Gallipoli. The rest of the British expeditionary force arrived under Raglan at the beginning of May. In all one cavalry and five infantry divisions set out, though all were under strength. The French had four divisions, each of 10,000 men, twice as many as a British division. The British force totalled 26,000 men. The French would nearly double that figure.

Unfortunately the outbreak of war caught Aberdeen at the height of a wretched crisis created by Lord John Russell. He had chosen this inopportune moment to threaten resignation and demand a dissolution, though it meant sacrificing his Reform Bill, because he was not prepared to announce its inevitable postponement. Aberdeen did his best to meet him half-way, offering a temporary postponement of the bill, with a pledge to go on with it in the next session, but Lord John was impossible to satisfy. Letters flew between the Queen, Aberdeen and Russell, and by April 4 – a week after the declaration of war – Aberdeen was reduced to suggesting to Prince Albert that he might put royal pressure on Russell through his brother the Duke of Bedford.[1] Two days later Russell was still obstinately calling for a dissolution.

That day questions were asked in the Lords about the landings at Gallipoli and the conditions the troops had found there. That day, too, Aberdeen's second son, Colonel Alexander Gordon, joined his regiment, taking with him a charger as a parting present from the Prince Consort. Next day the storm grew worse, with Earl Grey making a formidable attack on the whole system of administration of the war, and calling for the splitting of the War and Colonial Offices. Within days of the outbreak of war two elements had been introduced into the conduct of affairs which were to acquire for Aberdeen and his loyal supporters a grim and sickening familiarity – criticism of the system of administration which the coalition Government had inherited, and the capacity for mischief of its Leader in the House of Commons.

Lord John was whipping himself into a condition bordering on hysteria. According to Greville, by April 8 he was in a state of 'vexation and perplexity', had made himself quite ill, and was unable to sleep.[2] He asked Aberdeen to put his resignation before the Queen. A Cabinet meeting was called for the same day. At one stage both Palmerston and Lord John were offering to resign. Even the determinedly co-operative Aberdeen must have thought of them at such moments, like Victoria, as 'those two terrible old men'. Their colleagues managed to dissuade them both; and it was agreed that Lord John would announce the postponement of his bill, and that it should be brought forward at a more suitable time than at the outset of a war. Everything seemed to be settled, and Lord John was warmly congratulated by everyone, including the Queen,[3] for his great self-sacrifice, and the service he had done to his country by avoiding a dissolution in the first days of a war.

By Sunday Lord John wanted to withdraw from his agreement and press on with his bill after all. He wrote to the Queen of 'the deep feelings of mortification'[4] which were oppressing him, and said he wanted to think things over before coming to a final decision. This time the Queen was chilly, if not caustic. Russell persisted in his histrionics, insisting that the Cabinet preferred to follow Palmerston, rather than him, and that therefore he must resign. Palmerston himself urged him to think again, and went so far as to write: 'It really seems to me that there can be no reason why

240

Two Colleagues should separate because they think that at some future Time they might not agree as to such matters of Detail'. He said bluntly that Russell's resignation must upset the Government, which would not be in the public interest, and he actually offered to resign himself if Russell refused to remain in the same Cabinet, on the grounds that most of their colleagues in fact leaned to Russell's views and not his, and he was not indispensable. He could not have done more.[5]

Nothing would shift Lord John. On the next day, Monday, he told Aberdeen and Graham that he did not after all feel able to make the necessary statement to the House, and so must go. Aberdeen replied that this was 'really too monstrous'[6] in the face of all the assurances which had been given to him by the Queen, the Prime Minister, and all his colleagues except Palmerston. Lord John continued to object 'with the greatest bitterness'.[7] The three had been at loggerheads when Palmerston's letter had arrived, and Aberdeen had then asked Russell whether he would be satisfied if Palmerston resigned. Russell did not consider that it 'would mend matters'.[8] 'Lord Aberdeen's opinion, however,' wrote Prince Albert, 'is that it is what Lord John, and still more what Lady John, wants.'[9]

Lord John had driven Aberdeen into a very awkward corner. If he were out of the Cabinet Palmerston would expect to lead the House, which, to Aberdeen, was 'perfectly ludicrous'. (He frankly admitted this to be for 'personal . . . as well as public reasons', and that their having been lifelong 'political antagonists' weighed with him as well as the fact that Palmerston was 'the only anti-reformer' in a reform government.[10]) The result would probably be the formation of a new government, possibly under Newcastle and Gladstone. So likely did Aberdeen believe this to be that he arranged to see Newcastle and Gladstone that evening with Sir James Graham, and made plans to see Palmerston and Russell next morning. 'This is all really very bad!' Prince Albert concluded his memorandum that night.[11]

It really was. Lord John had thrown a spanner in the works, and was doing the Government great damage at a dangerous time. 'Curiosity and excitement,' according to Greville, were 'very great', since Russell had not made the expected statement that day.[12] The Cabinet devoted the whole morning on Monday, and again on Tuesday, to the problem. The Duke of Bedford was now definitely said to be trying to influence his brother. Then Sidney Herbert made a valiant effort to break the deadlock with a letter to Lord John composed of almost unanswerable arguments.

'The whole Cabinet are agreed that the Reform Bill must be postponed,' he wrote. 'To bring the measure forward wd be to incur certain defeat, & . . . a defeat wh could not be repaired or avenged. In the interests of Reform, therefore, postponement is inevitable. So far we are unanimous. One man in the Government [Palmerston] dislikes the bill, & thinks the measure a bad one. One is perhaps luke-warm, but still assenting [Aberdeen], and being a man of honour beyond suspicion his assent is sincere. All the rest of the Govt are hearty supporters of the bill wh embodies the policy of which by your previous services you are the recognized champion!'

Postponing the measure, he said, implied adherence to the principle of Reform, and an understanding that they were in honour bound to carry on with it. It was Palmerston and not Russell who would have to go if the bill were proceeded with. Was the prospect of Palmerston's being obliged to retire under certain circumstances next year any justification for Russell's resigning then? Herbert begged Lord John not to evade 'great difficulties and great responsibilities', and to be prepared to help his country.[13]

Aberdeen was convinced that Lord John meant to carry out his threat to resign. At the meeting with Newcastle, Gladstone and Graham it was decided that it was out of the question for Palmerston to lead a Reform government in the Commons; and they nerved themselves to ask him whether he would serve under Gladstone. Next morning Lord John unexpectedly gave way, and that afternoon, actually in tears, made a highly dramatic speech to a sentimental House of Commons. Greville was contemptuous of both speaker and audience.[14]

A good deal of time and trouble had been wasted, and much strain added to the Prime Minister's heavy burdens, which included some stressful family ones. In the opening days of a war to which he was determined to devote all his energies, he had had to expend every thought, every effort, and almost every hour, on strenuous and almost undignified attempts to woo from his tantrums the unpredictable Lord John. Even his never-failing patience must have been sorely tried to hear that Lord John had been acclaimed for his sincerity and high principles in the House of Commons at the end of this cruel farce.

That crisis was over for the time being. If Aberdeen thought that Lord John would subside, however, he was rapidly disillusioned. Having been deprived of his bill, he at once turned his attention to the conduct of the war. In a matter of days he produced a long memorandum on the command structure of the army and the organization of the Ministry of War, raising the question of withdrawing responsibility for the Colonies from the War Department, and, by implication, attacking the Duke of Newcastle as Colonial Secretary, and, in effect, War Minister.

Until then the war itself had not taken up much of Parliament's time; nor was it to do so to any great extent for some time to come. Serious fighting would not begin before the early autumn, when Parliament would no longer be sitting. Already, however, there had been worrying repercussions from the front, and awkward questions asked and rebuffed in the Lords. To Aberdeen the fates would not be kind. He was to be beset by a Russell abroad as well as by a Russell at home. Both would do him unparalleled damage.

William Howard Russell was the war correspondent of *The Times*. He was almost the first of his kind, and certainly the first to do more than rehash diplomatic handouts for publication. The fighting Dubliner, ex-schoolmaster, ex-Parliamentary reporter, and ex-Conservative candidate for Chelsea, was emotional about the welfare of the soldier in the field, and his lurid accounts from the front were to light a great conflagration at home.

When he had set off with the expeditionary force both Russell and his editor, Delane, had expected the war to be over by Easter. From Valetta Russell had written to his wife that it was generally believed that the troops would never see a shot fired. Nothing seemed to go right with this war, however. Chaos on the quayside had been followed by shortages of coal, candles, food, tents and forage at Malta. At Gallipoli the troops had landed to find the French already comfortably installed in the best places, and had had to camp eight and a half miles away in wretched conditions, without even beds for the sick.

At once the Government was blamed for miserliness. Yet the estimates had been generous – ten million pounds for the army and nine million pounds for the navy – and passed almost without debate. Even the Chancellor of the Exchequer had not tried to skimp, and Gladstone had confined himself to a grumble about the Almighty's punishing mankind for going to war by making it expensive.[15] (In fact that passionate and deeply repressed man had responded to the excitement of war as Aberdeen never did, confessing: 'There is pomp and circumstance, there is glory and excitement about war, which, notwithstanding the miseries it entails, invests it with charms in the eyes of the community'.[16]) Later he would double the income tax, first for six months, and then for a year, resolute and challenging steps to take.

The real cause of the trouble lay in the forty-years-long peace and its results. A system which had served Marlborough well, and which the genius of Wellington had been able to manipulate to victory, was now dreadfully out of date. Not only was the army a shadow of what it had been, but it was commanded by officers who had bought their commissions and then been promoted by seniority instead of merit; the artillery was antiquated and inadequate; and the soldiers had no experience of major war. Vitally important units which had come into being in the Napoleonic Wars had been abolished. Had the Waggon Train (which conveyed supplies, and formed an ambulance corps after battles) and the Staff Corps (for studying current problems and keeping military thinking up to date) still been in existence the history of the Crimean War would have been different.

Worst of all, the military departments had become vast creaking machines for churning out paper-work. Their duties overlapped; and their chiefs were bureaucrats to whom form-filling was the over-riding priority. This system had been challenged, but Wellington, in the way of old men, had preferred to leave things as they were. He had died only in 1852 at the age of 82; and now his ancient veterans were being automatically appointed to take command of a mighty modern war between great powers – even being encouraged against their wills to come out of retirement to wage this all-demanding campaign overseas. Had Wellington still been alive, old, deaf and subject to paralytic attacks, doubtless he too would have been pulled out of retirement to lend the glory of his name and take the chief command. As it was, at the head of the expeditionary force went his one-time Military Secretary, Fitzroy Somerset, Lord Raglan, 65 years old, reluctantly torn from the desk where he had spent 25 years after Waterloo in one capacity or another before becoming Master General of the Ordnance in the coalition Government. In charge of the navy was Admiral Dundas, nearly 70, in whom the First Lord had so little confidence that he sent out with him, as second-in-command and spy, Rear-Admiral Sir Edmund Lyons. Only two other admirals had been available, and since one had been nearly eighty and the other in failing health the Baltic Fleet had had to be given to the only Vice-Admiral to be had, Sir Charles Napier. Other veterans of the Napoleonic Wars commanded the Light, the Second, and the Fourth Divisions, and the Chief Engineer, Sir John Burgoyne, was seventy-two. In such a world junior officers were not even considered for promotion.

There were those who were aware of the disadvantages under which England went to war in 1854. Earl Grey's massive attack in the Lords was based on first-hand experience, for he had been, first, Secretary at War for five years, and then Secretary for War and the Colonies for the six years running up to 1852. He might have chosen to remain silent, for in every man's mind as he spoke was the thought that he himself had done little to better things when in office. But he denounced the anomalies by which responsibility for vital matters was shared out among several independent departments.

The army was the responsibility of the Secretary for War and the Colonies, for it was taken for granted that the Colonies would be a perpetual source of trouble. Under him was the Secretary at War, in direct contact with the Commander-in-Chief of the army. The Commander-in-Chief commanded the troops (or nearly all of them) but could hardly lay out a shilling without having obtained consent from other departments. The Secretary at War had to answer to Parliament, not only for the misspending of money voted in the estimates, but also for any mismanagement of the services for which it was used; yet he had no say in the way in which it was laid out by the Commander-in-Chief. Then there was the Master General of the Ordnance, not necessarily a soldier but always a minister, who controlled the issue of all military equipment and the supply of food to troops at home. He was the effective C.-in-C. of the engineers and the artillery, but he also had a plethora of other duties concerning the general management of the army. The organization of the Secretary of State for War and the Colonies was not linked to that of the Master General of the Ordnance, and neither was linked to that of the Commander-in-Chief. Worst of all, and most dangerous of all, the Treasury controlled the Commissariat, that artery supplying life-blood to the troops abroad. Grey blamed the bad mortality rates in some tropical stations on this division of authority between War Office and Treasury, which led to economies, and thence to bad quarters and poor rations for the troops. The Army Medical Board was yet another organization undesirably dependent on the Treasury.

Unification of all the various authorities had been urged since 1810; and Grey could claim that in 1837, as Secretary at War and chairman of a Royal Commission, he had himself recommended changes in the organization of the army. Nothing had been done. Now, urgently, he was demanding, firstly, that responsibility for war should be withdrawn from the orbit of the Secretary of State for the Colonies, and, secondly, that the financial and military administration of the army should be consolidated in one department.

Newcastle met all these suggestions with stony opposition. The system, he declared, was satisfactory. Such shortcomings as there might have been had been put right. The various authorities worked smoothly together. There might possibly be a case for taking away the Commissariat from the Treasury, but Wellington himself had preferred to leave it there. So certain was Newcastle that all was well that he asserted: 'I should look with much less confidence than I do to the departure of that force which is about to be despatched to the East if it were not possible to send with that army, I believe, as capable, as intelligent, and as able a body of commissariat officers as ever accompanied an army into the field'. Today those words read like a knell; but Newcastle went further: 'I have a right to say that, under the circumstances, and at this time, the fact of having sent a large body of men to the East in better condition, in more admirable order, and with greater expedition than we had formerly any idea of, either in this or in any other country, does reflect the highest credit upon the efficiency of every department engaged in the undertaking . . . I believe that such careful preparations never were made before, whether I look to the food which has been provided for the men, to the arrangements for their comfort and convenience, or even to the indulgences in the shape of beverages and matters of minor importance, which have been supplied to them'.[17]

Grey was defeated, but he wound up the debate with a memorable warning. He declared himself sceptical of Newcastle's claims about the harmonious working of the system; and he reminded him 'that the time for boasting was not when the harness was put on, but when it was taken off'.[18]

It seemed as if the battle for reform of 'the system' was lost; but it found another champion. Lord John brought to this new cause his usual violent enthusiasm. In his memorandum of April 24 on the command of the army he rejected Grey's proposal for an Army Board, and came out against transferring the powers of the Secretary of State to the Secretary at War. He wanted to see a new, fourth, Secretaryship of State. That is, he wanted to give the Secretary of State for War control over all the other authorities – the Commander-in-Chief, the Board of Ordnance, the Secretary at War and the Commissariat – but to relieve him of the Colonies, which would then be handed over as a separate department to the new Secretary of State. The Secretary of State for the War Department would deal with all military requirements, and settle with the

Cabinet the disposition of the forces.

Aberdeen gave general approval to Lord John's proposals, but deferred consideration by the Cabinet. Russell refused to be fobbed off, and on May 5 wrote the Prime Minister a peppery letter. Aberdeen had suggested to him in conversation that if the division came about Russell himself might take the War Department or the Colonies. Once again Russell brandished the threat of resignation, using Aberdeen's handsome offer as a weapon against him. The indecisiveness and reluctance to adopt strong measures to force the Czar into submission evident in recent cabinet meetings had caused him to lose confidence in the Government, he said, and he could not continue in office under him. Aberdeen replied that the matter had slipped his mind at the last cabinet meeting, but that he would bring it forward at the next one. He was obviously trying to defer further attacks on the harassed Newcastle, perhaps hoping that Lord John might make another of his frequent somersaults.

A fortnight later Russell was circulating yet another memorandum on the separation of the two offices, on the grounds that the Secretary of State for War was over-burdened in time of war.[19] At the next cabinet meeting Aberdeen and his friends agreed to everything he had asked, even including a speedy changeover. Aberdeen was far from enthusiastic; and in his report to the Queen hoped that it would be possible to make the changes 'innocent if not greatly advantageous'.[20] He told Lord John that he hoped the arrangement would prevent any changes taking place, at least for the time being, in the general administration of the army. It was clear that he had given way, not from conviction, but, once again, simply to avoid breaking up the Government, and that, far from being seized of the need for further reform of the system, he was anxious to avoid it.

Aberdeen still hoped that Lord John would take the Colonies; and Lord John still demurred. He developed his ideas in yet another memorandum; and now he urged that the new Secretary of State for War should start to consolidate and simplify the military departments. Aberdeen at once became alarmed. This was what he had hoped to avoid; and he protested that the only change contemplated was the dividing up of the duties of the over-burdened Secretary of State for War and the Colonies. Certainly no immediate change in the military departments was in prospect.

In fact, Aberdeen characteristically sprang to Newcastle's defence, seeking to rally support to him. The Queen gave Newcastle the Garter to show her confidence in him. With the wisdom of hindsight we can see that Aberdeen should have grasped the

247

opportunity so fortunately presented to him on the division of the War and Colonial Offices to replace Newcastle with a more vigorous and imaginative War minister.

It was not until the beginning of June that Aberdeen authorized Lord John to announce the division of the two Offices in the Commons and appointed Sir George Grey Secretary of State for the Colonies. Lord John himself was to be Lord President of the Council. Even that did not go off well, for the Peelites rebelled at Grey's appointment, which meant another Whig in the Cabinet; and Aberdeen had to ask Lord John to agree to a less controversial reshuffle. Lord John refused, and angry passions raged behind the restrained countenances and genial protestations of colleagues tested by him almost beyond endurance. Gladstone was furious enough to write an unguarded letter to Canning, the Postmaster-General, blaming Lord John's wife for much of the nuisance from which the Cabinet was suffering, and speaking of 'the depths of a certain woman's restlessness and folly', and of the influence it might have on her husband 'in bringing him both to a pitch of wilfulness and to an abyss of vacillation and infirmity of purpose, which are in themselves a chapter in the history of human nature'.[21] To Arthur Gordon Gladstone wrote once again in almost reverent admiration of his father, 'I doubt if there is any man in England, except Lord Aberdeen, who could have borne what he has had to bear during the last seventeen months from *Lady* John'.[22]

When Parliament resumed after Whitsun Newcastle was sworn in for the War Office, Sir George Grey for the Colonial Office, and Lord John as Lord President of the Council. Discussions began about the extent of the reorganization. Newcastle was touchily aware that the public did not want him for Minister of War, but did not want to go. At least the Commissariat was being transferred from the Treasury to the War Office. But as late as July 17, when Lord John introduced the estimates for the new War Department, the Government was being criticized for not having made up its mind about the new Department's duties or settled the anomalies of divided authority within the army, and for keeping on the office of the Secretary at War.

Sidney Herbert, holder of that office, replied: 'Give us time – that is only fair – and I am satisfied that we can introduce into the military department changes which will promote the efficiency of the service, and which will enable the Government and people to look with perfect confidence, as to efficiency in every respect, upon those forces upon whom now the honour and safety of this country depend'.[23] But there was no time. Even while the negotiations for the separation of the Secretaryships of State were dragging on through May and June, with Lord John making life intolerable for everyone, war fever in England was mounting higher and higher and conditions for the army overseas were deteriorating with frightening speed.

In mid-April the troops had begun to arrive in Scutari, opposite Constantinople. The original idea of having to defend Constantinople had long given way to a more aggressive strategy, since the Turks were successfully holding the Russians some 500 miles away on the Danube. Now the army command expected the Russians to advance across the river into northern Bulgaria, and planned that an Anglo-French contingent would move up and contain them on the Ottoman side while the Turks advanced on their right flank. At Scutari the troops had been housed in barracks vacated by the Turks in an incredible state of filth. They had suffered terribly from the heat in their constricting uniforms with leather neckstocks.

At the beginning of June they had sailed for Varna, a Bulgarian town on the Black Sea coast 300 miles away, the port of disembarkation for the proposed operation; but in dire pandemonium and muddle and only to camp in the all-too-well-named Valley of Death. By June 1 the Light Brigade had arrived at Varna, and on June 13 the First Division had followed it; but without enough transport for it to go forward to help the Turks, valiantly holding the Russians at Silistria on the Danube. Ten days later the Russians raised the siege. Mid-June found them in full flight. That was the moment when an Allied offensive might have proved effective; but neither the British nor the French had been ready for it, and they were at a loss what to do next.

Since Constantinople was not in need of defence a totally new offensive strategy was called for. The Turks had long been agitating for an invasion of the Crimean peninsula and the capture of the Russian naval base at Sebastopol, from which the Russians had sailed to destroy the Turkish fleet at Sinope. Not only would the taking of the base provide vengeance, but it would destroy Russian power in the Black Sea. The French Commander-in-Chief, St Arnaud, considered that the Allied forces were in no shape for such an operation, and for once Raglan found himself in agreement with him. However, both were harassed by their governments in London and Paris, and they in turn were being harried by public opinion. So the British and French armies remained at Varna, immobile in the increasing heat, bickering about whether to launch the invasion of Russian soil their governments were demanding.

At Varna the truth about the Commissariat, of which Newcastle had been so proud, became clear. Still bound by Treasury red tape, and foolishly relying on local resources to provide the vast quantities of stores and transport needed, they were in dire straits. Soon, for lack of fresh meat, the troops were existing on salt pork and tortured by thirst in the heat. The French managed better, which did not help the British bear their trials cheerfully. Even worse, cholera had broken out.

The facts, plain and unvarnished, were bad enough. The British public was not receiving them plain and unvarnished, however, from Mr Russell at the front, and they were reacting violently. Delane, his editor, had taken up Lord John's campaign for separation of the departments, and now backed his correspondent's emotive diatribes with strong leaders and private pressures.

Even before the declaration of war Russell had reported serious shortages and deficiencies in organization, and had prophesied the horrors to come, pleading for doctors, young men in command, and an efficient army. He did not spare his public the most nauseating details – details of a kind which had always been common to war, but with which the British reading public at home had never hitherto been tormented. Largely newly literate, and ignorant of the horrors of warfare, it was subjected to a fusillade of Russell's colourful descriptions, and roused to a state of anger and guilt which cried out for action. 'In the stagnant water which ripples almost imperceptibly on the shore there float all forms of nastiness and corruption, which the prowling dogs, standing leg-deep as they wade about in search of offal, cannot destroy . . .' he wrote in a typical example. 'The smell from the shore is noisome, but a few yards out from the fringe of buoyant cats, dogs, birds, straw, sticks – in fact, of all sorts of abominable flotsam and jetsam, which bob about on the pebbles unceasingly – the water becomes exquisitely clear and pure.'[24] The horror and the drama were strengthened with surprisingly accurate statistics, such as the 110,000 lb. of fodder and the 27,000 lb. each of meat, bread, rice, tea, coffee and sugar needed every day for horses and men. Cholera spread swiftly. Russell wrote of medical orderlies sleeping in corridors after fifty-six hours on duty. The great fire which lasted ten hours and destroyed biscuit rations, sabres and nineteen thousand pairs of shoes gave him another opportunity, brilliantly taken.

Perhaps the despatch of Russell's which most anguished and alarmed the British public was the one describing the Valley of Death and the results of the ravages caused by dysentery. So completely exhausted was the Brigade of Guards that 3000 of 'the flower of England' had to make two marches in order to get over the ten-mile distance from Aladyn to Varna. 'But that is not all,' it read. 'Their packs were carried for them. Just think of this, good people of England, who are sitting anxiously in your homes, day after day, expecting every morning to gladden your eyes with the sight of the announcement, in large type, of "Fall of Sebastopol", your Guards, your *corps d'élite*, the pride of your hearts, the delight of your eyes, these Anakim, whose stature, strength, and massive bulk you exhibit to kingly visitors as no inapt symbols of your nation, have been so reduced by sickness, disease, and a depressing climate, that it was judged inexpedient to allow them to carry their own packs, or to permit them to march more than five miles a day, even though these packs were carried for them! Think of this, and then judge whether these men are fit in their present state to go to Sebastopol, or to attempt any great operation of war.'[25]

On and on they went remorselessly, those despatches which inflamed the British public and filled it with shame and fury. They had cried out for war against the Russians, and had expected a speedy victory. The Government must be to blame for these terrible things that were happening overseas. Long before that despatch of Russell's was published they were in a dangerous mood.

It was on 8 June 1854 that Parliament had resumed. Next day the division of the War and Colonial Offices had been announced. On July 24 there had been debates in the Lords and the Commons on the outbreaks of cholera abroad. By that time Russell's despatches had done their work; and in the Commons Aberdeen was bitterly attacked.

Chapter 19

To Sebastopol

It was as if the whole nation had gone mad. Here were press, public and politicians loudly expressing their alarm about the higher command, the administration, and the conditions and sickness at the front, and yet demanding more and more strongly that the seemingly impregnable fortress of Sebastopol be attacked and taken without delay.

By early April Newcastle was pressing Raglan to take the offensive. No sooner had Raglan landed at Gallipoli than he received instructions to assess the strength of the fortress and the Russians. A month afterwards Graham was writing privately to him to insist that the capture of Sebastopol and the Russian fleet would be 'the blows which would knock down and win the battle in the shortest time and with the greatest certainty'.[1] Raglan was still pessimistic, passing on a report from Admiral Dundas which compared Sebastopol to Gibraltar and estimating the Russian forces in the Crimea as not 30,000 but 120,000, a figure Newcastle refused to accept. He, too, was being pushed, and by formerly peace-loving Cabinet ministers. By June 15 *The Times*, though it regularly published its correspondents' warnings as to the state of the troops, had embarked on a great campaign for taking Sebastopol.

In fact the order to attack had already been given. After the good news of the Turkish stand at Silistria Newcastle had written to Raglan pointing out that every member of the Cabinet was in favour of besieging the fort. Then, without waiting for more information, he had drafted the fatal despatch of June 29, ordering Raglan to initiate the siege.

Kinglake vividly described the scene when Newcastle read his momentous despatch to the Cabinet at dinner on a fine midsummer day's evening at Pembroke Lodge, the house in Richmond Park which in happier days the Queen had lent to Lord John. That evening some of the Cabinet nodded while Newcastle outlined his plan (which, in fact, they had already heard) for 60,000 allied troops to be landed near Sebastopol and attack it from the north while the navy hammered it from the sea. The young Argyll was nervous, but Palmerston had suggested the idea months before and was as confident as a boy.[2]

Time was running out for Raglan. He was warned that there must be no delay, and that there was no question of a safe and honourable peace until Sebastopol was taken. The Foreign Office estimated that there were at the most 45,000 Russians in the Crimea, including their navy; and neither Raglan nor St Arnaud could supply more accurate figures. It was not till later that an agent put the number at 70,000, of whom 40,000 were in Sebastopol.

By mid-July Aberdeen had become immensely unpopular. He had made things much worse by a piece of tactless honesty. Sincerely anxious to strike the enemy hard so as to end the war quickly, he still had no intention of misrepresenting facts as he saw them to attain any object, however desirable. The war was a just one, and Russia's claims were inadmissible; but that did not mean that the Czar was a slavering monster or a threat to Western Europe who must be eliminated and have his dominions taken over. Coolly contemptuous, he refused to be unjust even to an enemy, and when on June 19 Lord Lyndhurst had launched a diatribe in the Lords against the Czar, Aberdeen snubbed him. With a withering moderation and objectivity, he impartially assessed Russia's conduct; and it was a very different picture from Lyndhurst's. The speech offended, and in his son's words, 'raised a storm of obloquy which he had some difficulty in fully understanding'.[3] The many who so frequently criticized politicians for deviousness and loudly proclaimed their desire for an honest man did not care for him when they got one.

Arthur Gordon was better able to understand the critics, who 'not unnaturally' drew the conclusion that Aberdeen would shrink from decisive and energetic measures for the war.[4] His best friends, while almost idolizing him for his honesty and forthrightness, were hard put to it to forgive such unworldliness at such a time.

Less remote than he from the public, even on a throne, the Queen wrote to him with patience, good sense, and affection to explain the feelings of outrage of his critics. 'With them the steam is fairly up, as it ought to be in going to war, and Aberdeen is a standing reproach in their eyes, because he cannot share the enthusiasm while it is his part to lead it,' she wrote. Despite her admiration, she did not mince her words about the effect of his speech, and hoped that he would 'not undertake the ungrateful and injurious task of vindicating the Emperor of Russia from any of the exaggerated charges brought against him and his policy, at a time when there is enough in it to make us fight with all our might against it'.[5] Clarendon too tried to bring Aberdeen to a sense of political reality, as he saw it, writing, 'It is not safe, and can answer no good end, to damp the excitement under which great sacrifices are being made, and more will be required'.[6]

Faced with this obstinate idealist and man of truth, realists were appalled at the damage he was doing. He could offer only excoriating contempt for their low expediency. Did they perhaps begin to wonder whether a man of such unshakably high standards could only afford them, with safety to others, outside the world of politics? Could the nation afford the luxury of a leader with such high principles when there was so much at stake?

Worse was to come. Only a week after the vexed question of dividing the two departments had been finally resolved Aberdeen was strongly attacked in the debate on the special vote of credit, and by members on his own Government benches.

On July 21 a royal message went to both Houses of Parliament requesting the authorization of three million pounds for additional expenditure for the war. Aberdeen's brief address aroused no opposition in the Lords,[7] but in the Commons Lord John stirred the pot by referring to Russian aggression and the reluctance of the allies to make peace if it meant returning to an unsatisfactory state of affairs. Sebastopol would have to be taken if the Turks were to be safe from future attack.[8]

In the debate which followed Government back-benchers censured the Government for not prosecuting the war 'with becoming vigour'. Layard criticized the administrative arrangements for the troops and the failure to send out qualified leaders or call on the advice of experienced men, going so far as to make a prolonged and intemperate attack on the adequacy of Lord Aberdeen himself as a wartime Prime Minister. He urged that Palmerston be appointed War Minister, and Lord Dudley Stuart claimed that Palmerston's name alone would be worth 'a whole army'.[9]

This terrible debate had lasted for nearly six hours, with all the criticism coming from Government members, when Disraeli rose to castigate an insipid policy, an insipid leader, and an insipid Cabinet.[10] Next day further debate took place, and Lord Dudley Stuart deplored the lack of firm leadership. To a cry of 'Hear, hear!' he added that he believed that if they had had any other Minister than Lord Aberdeen the war would not have come about; but that 'the fluctuating and pusillanimous conduct of the Premier' – unworthy as it was of a great country like this – rendered war 'inevitable'.[11] Sidney Herbert staunchly repudiated Layard's charges against the Commissariat and the medical services. He made much of the blockade of the Baltic ports being effected by Admiral

Napier, and reminded the Commons that great battles could not be won on distant fields in four months, and that Waterloo had not been won in Pitt's lifetime.[12] Lord John wound up; and he did in fact speak up for Lord Aberdeen, and took Cabinet responsibility for decisions for which the Prime Minister alone had been blamed. In the end Lord Dudley said that he was satisfied by Lord John's speech.[13] The Government had been harshly attacked, but it had been defended, and the criticisms had been withdrawn.

Lord Aberdeen, however, was angry, and took it personally, as well he might. He had endured consistent political strain, taking many different forms, for twelve months, with the life of his Government always in danger. He had blundered in the Lords. He had been rebuked by the Queen. To cap it all, he was in deep personal distress. Not only was his second son serving with his regiment at the front from which such disturbing reports were coming, but his eldest son, Lord Haddo, was now seriously ill. During the previous summer he had begun to sicken with an obscure wasting disease which the doctors called in by his alarmed family failed to diagnose. Since then, though nearly six feet tall, his weight had dropped to just over eight stone, and in June he had been sent to Malvern for a prolonged cure under the famous Dr Gully. 'When I think of his state,' Aberdeen wrote to Mary at this period, 'and of your affliction, it is hard to be compelled to attend to matters which at any time would give me little satisfaction, and are now regarded with extreme disgust.'[14]

The most loyal of men himself, Aberdeen was deeply offended by the shocking exhibition of mass disloyalty, and particularly resentful of the failure of any Peelite colleague in the Commons to defend him. On July 26, on his way to Osborne, he wrote angrily to his friend Graham: 'I shall have a great deal to say to the Queen. And it will require a little time for me to recover my equanimity, after having been made the subject of repeated attack during a long debate, without a single syllable said in defence . . . I should have no pleasure in meeting the Cabinet today at dinner'. (According to a note made by Graham's biographer, C. S. Parker, Arthur Gordon preferred not to have that letter published, and consequently objected to Graham's reply to it appearing in his biography. Graham's daughter, Mrs Baring, suppressed the reply.)[15] Arthur Gordon, soon to be returned for Beverley in a by-election, had written to Gladstone: 'If my father is personally attacked tonight he is very desirous that *you* should speak in his defence. I am very anxious about it too, for I have heard him say that you have never done so yet – not of course that he doubts your willingness'.[16] Aberdeen had gone a long way to canvass much-needed support, and was the more wounded at its lack. Graham produced a weak excuse, Gladstone an even weaker one. The latter replied only that since he was 'commonly supposed to be tarred with the same stick' – presumably, being too pacifist in his sympathies – he had feared that this weakened his ability to defend Lord Aberdeen effectively.[17]

The troublous session ended on 14 August 1854, not before another attack had been launched on the conduct of the war. Two days before Parliament rose Lord Clanricarde in the Lords had criticized Admiral Napier's ineffectual blockade of Russian ports in the Baltic, the failure to provide light-draught warships for operations there, and the sincerity of Austrian intentions, especially as regards occupying the Principalities. Too much had already been sacrificed for the mirage of this alliance, he grumbled. Still, he welcomed reports that there was to be an expedition against the Crimea. Clarendon, replying for the Government, had rebuked Clanricarde for disclosing information of value to the enemy, had strongly denied most of his charges, and had rehearsed all that had been done in the first four months of the war.[18]

So the session came to its end. There had as yet been no heavy fighting overseas. It was obvious, however, from the amount and strength of the criticism in Parliament, especially from Government benches, that things had better go right very soon in the East or there would be trouble at home.

It was obvious, too, that the people, the press, and the politicians, the Prime Minister and the Queen, expected the troops, whatever their condition, to take Sebastopol, and to take it soon. Aberdeen and his Cabinet had a strong ulterior motive for this. They realized that the fall of Sebastopol would probably be the most effective counterblast to their great and growing unpopularity. With an exciting victory to announce, Aberdeen could go to the country at once, certain of being returned with a good majority.

The rising of Parliament brought no easing of his burdens to the Prime Minister. On the contrary, his troubles seemed to take a turn for the worse.

On August 6, after six weeks at Malvern, his son Haddo had written to Mary that, when last weighed, he had failed to reach the eight-stone minimum on the doctor's scales. He had closed his letter: 'What an odd coincidence, my election just now!'[19] Just when, at long last, Aberdeen's political ambitions for his heir seemed about to bear fruit, Haddo lay gravely ill, unable even to appear at his unopposed election. Captain William had given up the Aberdeenshire county seat to his nephew after enjoying it for 34 years. That year he became Vice-Admiral and Commander-in-Chief at the Nore, a coincidence which seems remarkably like compensation for sacrifice, since he had virtually been in retirement for 24 years. On August 8 Haddo wrote, with a courage and quiet dignity unexpected in one so self-doubting: 'My dear Father – Dr Gully told me yesterday that, unless an unexpected change should occur, it is not probable that I should see another spring'.[20] On February 14, the day Parliament rose, Haddo left Malvern. The doctors held out no hope, but thought that a winter in Egypt would help to alleviate his sufferings from the English cold.

Now Aberdeen had to face a harrowing parting from his son at a time when he was hard beset. Writing to the Queen to ask to be excused from attending at Osborne so as to see his son and daughter-in-law sail from Southampton in the Viceroy's yacht on September 9, he spoke of Lord Haddo's 'very serious illness', and added, 'Humanly speaking, Lord Aberdeen can never expect to see his son again'. Although he had never slept out of London, he said, since the prorogation of Parliament, he had been going down to Blackheath to see him for two or three hours every day – a demanding journey by coach, which would have very likely consumed an hour each way in travelling time, and made a severe additional toll on his strength. 'Your Majesty may easily imagine the situation of poor Lady Haddo with her children,' he wrote. 'Lord Aberdeen can be of little use or assistance, but his love and admiration are inexpressibly increased by seeing the tenderness, devotion and fortitude which it [is] possible for a woman in such a situation to exhibit.'[21] He found time to inspect the 'Egyptian ship' at Southampton, and pronounced to his family that she was 'perfect' – immense, airy, 2400 tons, with excellent cabins, and 'no peculiar smell'.[22]

After receiving orders from London and Paris to attack Sebastopol, the allied commanders had met to confer about how to carry them out. Even so, when news came at the end of the month that the Russians were withdrawing from the Principalities, the French Commander-in-Chief had tried to get Raglan to agree to call off the operation on the grounds that now any hope of an Austrian intervention must be abandoned. Raglan had refused. The severe attack of cholera which had devastated the ranks of the allied armies, and the great fire of Varna, had done nothing to increase his ardour, and preparations were delayed; but the day came at last when the transports for invasion were assembled, and the coast near Sebastopol reconnoitred.

So this strange situation unfolded itself, in which ministers who complained that they had hardly any information of value from the front ordered Raglan to his gigantic task, and he, who knew the conditions in the Black Sea, obeyed like a mindless automaton. Despite their determination to go ahead, the ministers at home felt themselves to be working in the dark, and were highly nervous about the orders they had issued. Would Raglan carry them out, or would he not? They were worried by his failure to communicate with them. As late as September 7 Newcastle was writing anxiously to Aberdeen that Raglan's letters were 'singularly meagre as usual'.[23] By then, too, they were at last beginning to understand how serious was the outbreak of cholera. Perhaps because it had been raging at home during the summer, its incidence abroad had been treated too lightly. By the end of August, however, Aberdeen had written to Argyll, 'We have been in great alarm at the effect which the prevalence of cholera might produce on the decision of our commanders in the East'.[24]

All that August W. H. Russell's terrible despatches incensed the public and damaged the Government. Ironically enough, reading them, one is often reminded of Aberdeen's letters from the front to Lady Maria forty years before. It was with the same sick recoil that Russell wrote of the horrors of his daily life, so like those which had made Aberdeen a minister of peace.

Not only were the British and French armies in no shape for a sustained attack on an army of unknown strength in strange terrain and with winter ahead; not only were they disorganized, disillusioned, decimated, and dispirited; they were full of loathing for the Turks, for whom they were fighting. Aberdeen's own son, Alexander Gordon, described himself as 'a Russian at heart', and said that he thoroughly despised 'the filthy Turks for whom we are endeavouring to uphold the Crescent against the Cross'.[25]

Now Aberdeen was realizing that the French had never relished the expedition to Sebastopol, and that our own officers were far from optimistic; that both British and French had lost considerable numbers of men; and that 'the whole mass', as he wrote to Argyll, was 'much dispirited and broken down by disease'.[26] Raglan's silence weighed on him; but he still trusted 'that we may fairly hope the troops are at this time on the sea or landed'.[27] He was in no doubt as to the rightness of the operation: 'I am very sanguine of success; and after the execution of our guns at Bomarsund [by Admiral Napier's Baltic fleet], I fully expect the same result at Sebastopol. We shall, then, indeed make a great step towards peace'.[28]

Chapter 20

'Anxiety and Suspense'

On 24 August 1854, then, embarkation began at Varna.

The original strategy had been to engage Russian forces where the Ottoman and Russian empires touched. Later, when action on that front was obviously not likely to develop, the plan was evolved to attack Russia's naval base at Sebastopol. Discerning historians have recognized this as being the moment of fatal error. Such an operation by such a force at such a time and in such circumstances was not a prudent military undertaking.

The gigantic task of embarkation, a source of pride to ministers at home, was accomplished by September 4. Newcastle wrote to Aberdeen: 'Whilst the armies were on the sea, an attempt was made by our *gallant* allies to turn tail – they literally *funked*, and wanted by shabby pretexts to put the whole affair off to next year. Luckily, Raglan and all our officers stood firm, and they are now in for it'.[1]

This schoolboyish effusion reflected the prevailing attitude of ministers as they waited for news through August and early September. In the field misgivings had not lightened. Writing to his family, old Sir John Burgoyne, the Chief Engineer, called the operation 'the most desperate enterprise ever attempted'.[2] St Arnaud, the French Commander-in-Chief, had told him that the allies had only undertaken it because they could not resist the demands from home.[3] He believed that Raglan had been forced to it by taunts from England, and this certainly appears to have been the case.

At the beginning of September Raglan had changed the proposed landing plan to the gloomily named Calamita Bay, 35 miles north of Sebastopol. Both Raglan and St Arnaud were sure the campaign would be short, and the troops landed in September without winter equipment. Lord Aberdeen fretted continually for the expedition to begin. At last, on September 14, Clarendon was able to write, 'The expedition, thank Heaven, has sailed from Varna'.[4] In fact, the French had set foot on Russian soil at seven o'clock that morning, at Calamita Bay. Transport was short, as usual, and no tents were landed on the first day, so the British troops were soaked by a heavy storm during their first night ashore. This caused an immediate and serious increase in illness. Cholera travelled to the Crimea with the troops from Varna; and 150 dead were buried on the crossing.

The Queen and her ministers greeted the news of the landing with delight. Everyone was optimistic, Lord John already looking to the next campaign; but to the correspondent of *The Times* the army was ashore in strange and difficult enemy country, facing a huge army fighting to defend its native land, while the British and the French hardly knew why they were there. The British had little transport, practically no food, and no ambulances for the vast numbers of sick and wounded yet to come. (About 300 men were landed so sick they were unable to move.) Nor were the drenching endured by the British troops and the consequent miseries trivial matters to him. The French, with fewer ships and many of them sailing ships, had managed to land their tents.

At last the sun had come out, only to dry up the drinking water. The Russians, instead of attacking, had retreated towards Sebastopol, burning crops and villages as they went. On September 17 news came that 15,000 of them were assembled twelve miles south of the allied camp on the River Alma, which lay across their route to Sebastopol. On September 19 the allied advance towards Sebastopol began, and on September 20 battle was joined.

The allies were superior in numbers, but the Russians held a high ridge to the south of the river, which the allies had to scale in the face of fire from the heavier Russian artillery. The allied armies were poorly co-ordinated, with little battle-plan, but the valour of the British won the day, and by 4.30 p.m. the Russians were beaten, with 5709 acknowledged casualties. The allies had lost more than 3000 men – 2002 of them British, and 362 of them fatalities. The French had lost fewer, since the British had borne the brunt, and the Turks had lost none.

The first news of the battle reached England ten days later, at the end of September. On September 17 Lord Aberdeen had accepted the Prince Consort's pressing invitation to stay with the royal family at Balmoral. Prince Albert assured him that he could take decisions just as well from Scotland and that he should ignore accusations that he was abandoning his post.[5] The Queen wrote, 'The Queen must therefore almost insist on his coming speedily North,' and again, 'She urges him against most earnestly to come down here without further delay'.[6] They had finally overborne his genuine reluctance. Aberdeen had stayed only a short while at Balmoral and had gone on to Haddo where, he told the Queen, he had a good deal of private business urgently requiring his attention.[7] 'The terrace looks beautiful,' Arthur Gordon wrote on arrival, 'and the beds of scarlet geraniums about the fountain are bright enough to put one's eyes out.'[8]

He was there when news of the victory of the Alma reached him. The message was received at Perth, and sent on by special messenger to Balmoral and thence to Haddo, to be received on October 1, a day after reaching England. It was a pity that the Prime Minister was not the first to know, and much was made of the fact that he was not at his post at such a time.

'Lord Raglan reports though without date the storming yesterday of the heights of Alma,' the telegram ran. 'The position was formidable, and defended by numerous heavy guns. British loss considerable but no general wounded. Enemy supposed to have from forty-five to fifty thousand infantry. Some prisoners, including two generals and two guns, were captured by the British army. Nothing could exceed the bravery and good conduct of the troops. This news left Constantinople the 24th September.' That is, four days after the battle. It had travelled via Lord Stratford and Belgrade.[9]

Relaying this Admiralty signal to Aberdeen, the First Lord, Graham, added a personal postscript to his friend, 'Do not lose sight of your great opportunity, take the tide at its rise, and let us have a new Parliament'.[10] It seemed good advice, and Aberdeen might well have taken it, had it not been for a most unfortunate event. At the same time as the news of the victory of the Alma a rumour reached England from Bucharest that Sebastopol itself had fallen.[11] Once again, the telegraph was proving both a blessing and a curse, and on the same day.

Beside this second piece of 'news' the worthwhile victory of the Alma was discounted. The people went wild with excitement. They rang church bells and illumined their windows. No one had any idea that Raglan and St Arnaud were sitting immobile watching the Russians, and would be doing so for another three weeks. Meanwhile the Russians would be fortifying their ill-defended northern side, and by scuttling their fleet would block the harbour mouth.

It was October 5 before the false report was exploded, and by that time most people, including Aberdeen, had given way to wishful thinking.[12] From then on, instead of joy and gratitude for the great victory of the Alma, won with inspiring courage by men exhausted by heat, thirst, sunstroke, dysentery and cholera, the public felt only a sulky disappointment and irritation at having been cheated of the greater triumph to which it believed it was entitled.

There was yet another cruel twist to events. Military historians (and many of those present on the spot) have agreed that if only Raglan had ordered the cavalry to follow he might well have wiped out all traces of Russian resistance and entered Sebastopol to all intents unopposed. The troops did not pursue the retreating Russians; and they did not leave the heights of Alma for Sebastopol Harbour until the 23rd. Instead, they buried an acre of Russian dead, and Raglan argued with Burgoyne the merits of attacking Sebastopol. Only a week before cancer killed him, the gallant St Arnaud agreed that the land-locked little port of Balaclava should be used as the British supply base for the siege. The flanking march to positions south of Sebastopol began, and soon the allies had invested the Russian stronghold. The bitter wait had begun, with the Crimean winter ahead. No one guessed that it would be a year before the fort was emptied of the Russians.

Terrible despatches continued to arrive in England telling of worsening conditions, and *The Times* correspondent in Constantinople added his quota of horrors about hospital transport ships arriving from the Crimea in Scutari, where there were only tottering Chelsea pensioners for ambulance corps and not even bandages for the wounded. Delane called for action, raised money, and set up depots all over the country to collect rags for bandages and dressings. Florence Nightingale began her great work.

Even as late as October, however, Aberdeen and his Cabinet were still far from realizing the true state of affairs in the Crimea. The Cabinet was to meet in mid-October, when Aberdeen would be back from Haddo. Early in September Clarendon had been grumbling to Greville that the Prime Minister was out of humour, did not take the interest in things he should do, or press matters on, that he hardly participated in Cabinet discussions, and was not exerting himself to reconcile ministers who disagreed with each other. Clarendon admired Aberdeen. His attitude to him was that he was a good man and an honest one; but he did not think him fitted for his post. On the other hand Clarendon was openly disgusted with the behaviour of Lord John, and his disloyalty in allowing his adherents to disparage Aberdeen. He had sprung to Aberdeen's defence when Russell had written scathingly about his absence from London, and pointed out that he had not been away since December 1852, and that he had only gone to Scotland at the insistence of the Court. 'But,' he wrote, 'he was so completely upset by parting with his eldest son whom he will never see again, and his alarm about his youngest son [*sic*, Alex] who for ten days was missing, and though telegraphed for all over France and Switzerland, could not be heard of, and lastly by the unceasing attacks upon him in the Press, that his friends became seriously alarmed for the state of his mind as well as body, and at their earnest entreaties he left or was rather forced to leave London, intending only to be absent one fortnight. If he had not stirred out of Downing Street he could not have hastened the departure of a single man, because he could not have procured ships which were not to be had at any price.'[13]

So unlike himself was Aberdeen at this period that for once he came near to striking back at those who were constantly maligning him. He was due to deliver an address at Aberdeen on October 10, and considered making it a platform for defending himself. Sir James Graham advised him that such a step would be undignified. 'Facts are better than words in refuting calumnies . . . Just think what you have done!' he wrote, and went on in ecstatic mood:

'Six months have barely elapsed since it [war] was declared, and we have closed the White Sea, the Baltic, and the Black Sea against even the appearance of the Russian Flag. We have sent a larger army to a greater distance in a shorter time than ever before was transported from the shores of England . . . and the power of England . . . is exalted higher than ever; and her place among nations is secured. The extravagance of poetry is realized, it is too much for the good citizens of Aberdeen. You have rounded the pillars of Hercules. You have navigated the Aegean. You have passed the Symplegades. You have touched the Chersonese. You have swept the Crimea. And all this has been accomplished in one short summer, while the British fleet at the same time offered battle to the Russians in the harbour of their northern capital, destroyed one of their strongholds in the Baltic, and visited their fastnesses within the Arctic Sea. Here are topics for a song of triumph in which Sovereign and people, Ministers and Parliament, Provosts and Town Councils may cordially join, and in this loud and general acclaim the screeching of slanderers and the hissing of serpents will be drowned and soon forgotten.'[14]

It was on October 6 that hopes of the fall of Sebastopol were dashed for Aberdeen. At three o'clock in the morning he had a telegram telling him the truth. He confessed his disappointment to the Queen, and his hope 'that the blow may be struck forthwith'.[15] Now he looked with dread at the possibility that the Russians might receive reinforcements.

Trouble was brewing at home, too. Lord John was showing signs of being up to something. Soon he wrote to Graham complaining that important steps were being kept from him.[16] 'What can Lord John mean?' Aberdeen asked, on being shown the letter. 'I fear mischief, but of the grounds of his complaint I have no conception.'[17] On the day that brought him the disappointment about Sebastopol he was looking bleakly at the prospect of another crisis, and wondering whether Lord John and Palmerston were for once combining to create it.

Gladstone heard the news from Arthur Gordon, and put it down as usual to the machinations of his *bête noire*, Lady John. 'I must say the time has come and more than come to plant the foot firmly, and stand in that direction,' he asserted. 'We have a little woman to deal with who is of necessity as inevitable as the gates of a certain place: and it is perfectly vain for Lord A. to make concessions to her.'[18]

At this time Aberdeen was resisting pressures to remove Admiral Dundas from the command of the Black Sea fleet because of his lack of initiative. There was much criticism of his having failed to prevent the Russians from blocking the mouth of the harbour at Sebastopol by scuttling their ships, and for not successfully blockading Russian Black Sea ports. Aberdeen refused to disgrace the 70-year-old Admiral publicly, but agreed that he should give up his post in the normal course of events in two months' time. More and more criticism came the way of 'Admiral Damned Ass' – probably unjustly – because of the part he played during the week-long bombardment of Sebastopol which began on October 17.

Colonel Alexander Gordon had been newly appointed to the post of Assistant Quarter-Master General in the field, and he expressed himself as gratified that the promotion had been earned and not achieved by string-pulling at home – but perhaps that was only because Aberdeen had refused him the office of Secretary to the Master General of the Ordnance, professing his abhorrence of nepotism.[19] From 'Before Sebastopol' Colonel Gordon wrote about the naval bombardment, and his letter was not calculated to allay his father's anxiety.

'The naval attack yesterday was a complete failure,' he reported to his 'Dear Papa'. 'They could make no impression on the Russian batteries. Some lay the blame on Admiral Dundas for not getting nearer than 1500 yards. He might just as well have remained 15 miles off . . . The navy have only 70 rounds per gun – how is this? Surely Admiral Dundas should be called to account for not having enough for the service on which he is engaged.'[20]

The difficulty about Admiral Dundas illustrates very well the

Mary Haddo painted by Mrs Carpenter

The Coalition Ministry of 1854 by J. Gilbert. *From left to right:* Charles Wood, Sir James Graham, Sir William Molesworth, W. E. Gladstone *(seated)*, Duke of Argyll, Lord Clarendon, Lord Lansdowne, Lord John Russell, Lord Granville, Lord Aberdeen, Lord Cranworth, Lord Palmerston, Sir George Grey, Sydney Herbert, Duke of Newcastle

Lord Aberdeen in 1855 after a portrait by Mayall

kind of morass in which Aberdeen's administration was struggling to survive. Having found themselves at war, with a system which saddled them with an Admiral Dundas, the ministers had at least tried to mitigate the damage by sending Lyons with him. Unfortunately this arrangement had deteriorated into intrigue and counter-intrigue, and ended in tragi-comedy. Newcastle, alarmed by the growing hostility to Dundas, had interfered, advising Raglan to call on Lyons to disobey his Admiral if he thought fit.[21] Graham had refused to recall Dundas, but had carried on a correspondence with Lyons behind his back, disclosing instructions he was giving to his Admiral, and saying: 'I rely on you for the infusion of some fire and energy into these movements [of the French and British fleets]. Were it not for your presence with the Fleet I should be in despair'.[22] Lyons replied that Dundas had opened the letter, and Graham responded indignantly: 'I am bound to believe that this was done by mistake; and I cannot bring myself to harbour the suspicion that he read any part of a confidential communication which obviously from its very commencement was addressed to you. There are some things so impossible among Gentlemen that proof is necessary to ensure belief, and this is one'.[23]

Thus Aberdeen was being let down, not only by colleagues at home, and by the system he had had no hand in creating or maintaining, and by senior officers in the army, but also by the naval command. Even the imponderables of the conventional etiquette of how gentlemen should behave to one another were working in disadvantageous ways. On the whole the concept of honour, always in the forefront of men's minds, and springing quickly to their lips, was a leaven and a strength. But with the war-mongers it was a weapon too often flashed and dangerous in use since it was employed to incite men to war. Aberdeen never misused it in this way. But with him the loyalty proper to an honourable man could grow into a weakness, as the idea of the correct behaviour of 'a gentleman' could, with Graham, attain the level of farce. After all, if Graham was going to be so nice, he could be himself indicted of behaving in a thoroughly ungentlemanly and disloyal manner since he was intriguing with a subordinate behind his senior officer's back.

During the bombardment of Sebastopol much damage was, in fact, done, and it is surprising that the allies did not attack and finish off the war. On the contrary, they watched, like spectators, the Russians steadily bringing in reinforcements by land. The French refused to attack. Raglan would not act on his own. It is true that the British army had been slashed almost in half by sickness, and that even men who returned from hospital at Scutari as fit for service were too feeble to march to their camps without collapsing. Raglan had good cause for holding his hand, with an army of raw, sick soldiers, which, since cholera struck so swiftly, might disappear overnight. The wonder is that these men, so badly led at the highest level, devastated by the fear, as well as the ravages, of cholera, ill-equipped, almost untrained, and living under intolerable conditions – from the time of their arrival they were actually starving because their rations could not be transported from Balaclava to the camp over the impassable clay road – were about to win two hard-fought victories.

By October 24 a Russian force of 25,000 men had assembled, and the next morning news came that this vast army was marching on Balaclava. At the end of that day's bloodshed W. H. Russell sat down to write despatches which were to make him famous. The Charge of the Light Brigade, thanks largely to his pen, became a legend. The Battle of Balaclava was claimed by both sides as a great victory. The Russians had failed to dislodge the allies and take Balaclava, and had withdrawn their forces. On the other hand, after the battle they were in possession of three important hills on the British flank which had formerly been allied outposts, and the British had lost control of the Woronzoff road connecting Balaclava with their camps on the heights before Sebastopol. Where was now the spectacular offensive strategy which had brought them to the Crimea? They were trapped.

'The first 24 days of November,' as the Duke of Argyll was to write, 'were days of intense anxiety and suspense.'[24] On November 9, as the Foreign Secretary had gone off to the Lord Mayor's banquet, he jotted down a note to his wife, 'Do what I will, I can't help gloomy forebodings. The Emperor L.N. [Louis Napoleon] offers to send 20,000 troops to reinforce if we will convey them. Graham sends me word we have not a vessel of any kind, and that all our stores and winter clothing are going out in sailing ships.'[25] The problem of transport had been causing the Cabinet great concern. (The Queen had offered her yacht, but it had been refused on the grounds that it might look as if the British were in desperate straits.) Raglan had been instructed to send some of his large steamships to Toulon, where 8000 men were supposedly ready to embark.

That November the Queen expressed to Arthur Gordon her concern about the effect the newspapers were having on his father. In his diary Arthur Gordon wrote:

'She came up to me, with, "Why *do* you let Ld Aberdeen read all those attacks on him in the newspapers? It can do no good and I know it worries him." "It is not with my good will he reads them, ma'am." "But you should take them all away, and put them into the fire – say, I told you. It is really no use, and Ld Aberdeen has public and private anxiety enough without those scribbles. I am quite annoyed at it . . . I do so hope your brothers will come safe home. Your father has had more trouble than most men in his life already" '.[26]

It was at this nerve-racking time that Prince Albert chose to deliver a royal broadside across Lord Aberdeen's bows with a long memorandum dated November 11: 'The Government will never be forgiven, and ought never to be forgiven, if it did not strain every nerve to avert the calamity of seeing Lord Raglan succumb from lack of means'.[27] Lord Aberdeen took two days to reply, and said that in about a month the extra men and stores would reach the troops.

At last, on November 15, news came of the battle of Inkerman, which had been fought ten days before, an expensive defeat for the Russians, who lost 12,000 men, most of them in dead. The allies had had only 740 fatalities; but Raglan's despatch asked for reinforcements, and informed the Cabinet that 6000 of the 30,000 men who had gone out to the Crimea had been killed in action in seven weeks, and 8000 were wounded or sick of cholera. On the evening of November 22 Aberdeen himself went with his son Arthur to read the list of killed and wounded which had been telegraphed to England, and found that Alex was safe.[28] It was decided to call a special session of Parliament in December to vote money for the reinforcements.

After Inkerman it was clear that the allies were bound to triumph in the end. They had better communications and the command of the seas, and Sebastopol must fall sooner or later. And, sooner or later, had he remained Prime Minister, Lord Aberdeen could have taken the credit for that fall. Had he only been able to survive his present troubles, his place in history would have been a very different one. The question now was, however, when that fortress would fall; and in the meantime the allies had neither the strength nor the desire to take it. They settled down to wait out the winter.

Letters arrived in England from the front, among them Colonel Gordon's. Three days after the battle he wrote to his father to report his narrow escape, and the loss of the horse given him by the Prince Consort: 'You will have heard that we have had another terrible battle in which we were at length victorious, but with a loss which we can ill afford. Owing to the mercy of God I again escaped

267

unhurt although my horse was shot under me. The battle lasted for nine hours, and hard fighting most of the time'.[29]

This brave soldier, recommended for gallantry in the field,[30] warned his father that he need not expect to hear of the fall of Sebastopol that winter. He reckoned that there were 125,000 Russians facing them, shortly to be increased to 200,000 by reinforcements from the north and Odessa. He hoped, and it must have caused Aberdeen a pang as he read it, that his father had not been an advocate of the expedition, though he knew that of course he must have sanctioned it.[31]

Five days later he wrote again, urgently, 'Unless you send out 10 or 12,000 men, militia or anything, immediately, we shall not be able to keep our position here through the winter. You should also send out directly several shiploads of hay, for the horses are fast dying of starvation and cold. It is a great misfortune that our supplies of winter clothing were not sent out sooner. The men want them very much; having nothing but what they had during the hot summer months, and their clothes are almost worn out. Although I hope it will not be necessary, yet you need not be surprised to hear by any post that we have raised the siege and fallen back upon Balaclava'.[32]

The day after those grim and ominous words were written a hurricane broke, and flattened the headquarters camp. Half the horses broke free, and the wounded of Inkerman were exposed to the elements. Vast quantities of stores, including powder, shot and shell, beds, blankets, warm clothing and medical supplies, were lost or ruined, both ashore and in the holds of the twenty-one ships which were wrecked. That hurricane spelled a winter of disaster for the shivering troops in the dire Crimean cold. Next day a snow-and-sleet storm followed on the heels of the hurricane. Battered and battle-weary, the men had not even the strength to re-erect the tents. Conditions were indescribable.

Colonel Gordon's strictures on senior officers were hardly less severe than those of the correspondent of *The Times*, whose reports were often dismissed as exaggerated by those who did not care for their purport. 'Sir de Lacy Evans is going home, being broken down by age and inability to stand the fatigue and cold of a winter campaign,' he wrote. He added, 'His parting advice to Lord Raglan was, "My Lord, save your army and raise the siege". I believe the same advice would be given by every general and officer of experience in this army, *if his opinion were asked*'.[33]

If those words struck a chill to Lord Aberdeen's heart he gave no sign of it in the loving letter which he wrote to his adored daughter-in-law in Egypt, sending her the latest news. 'Alex has been mercifully preserved at the dreadful battle of the 5th Nov.,' he told her. 'It seems to have been the most desperate and bloody upon record. Our loss of generals and of men is frightful, but the victory was complete. Alex had the horse given him by the Prince shot under him. The situation of our army is critical, but we are sending ample reinforcements.'[34]

The Prime Minister was holding tight and hoping for the best, but the mood of the nation was growing uglier. W. H. Russell had been largely responsible for turning its pride in the victories of Balaclava and Inkerman into a surly and self-righteous anger at the waste of every kind. Admiral Napier had disappointed, and would shame them, when he returned in December to be ordered to strike his flag.[35] Never had a great people been more intoxicated with honour and glory, and the shame and humiliation which were unexpectedly becoming their daily fare was in contrast all the more bitter.

In the Crimea things grew only worse. To Aberdeen and his friends it seemed unbelievable. Britain was richer than she had been at the time of the Napoleonic wars, and had been correspondingly more generous. She had supplied better rations and more warm clothing, she had doubled the number of medical establishments and had increased comforts for the sick and wounded. For the first time women nurses had gone out to care for them. Yet things grew worse and worse.

There was mismanagement, certainly, but there was also bad luck. The mismanagement accounted for such things as medical supplies being left behind in Varna, for shipments never unloaded, for beds sent in two parts in different ships, for fresh vegetables going bad in transit, and for the arrival of boots of the wrong sizes, and poor-quality digging tools. The hurricane which sank twenty-one ships and their cargoes had been a piece of misfortune which, added to the fire at Varna and the heavy casualties of Balaclava, made things extremely critical. Colonel Gordon was not exaggerating. Here was an army of weak men, in need of clothes, blankets, fuel, horses, forage, mortars, siege guns, arms and ammunition and reinforcements. Some of the reasons for the muddle can be tracked down today. Lord Stratford failed to carry out orders for medical supplies at Scutari, and recommendations for hospital ships to evacuate the wounded were never implemented. Raglan did little to repair the appalling roads. For months the Scutari hospitals were supplied with medical comforts from Delane's fund.

The worst feature was the incidence of disease. In all wars in the past more men had died from disease than in battle; but in the Crimean War the sick were sent back to recover in infected places, so that their chances of survival were greatly reduced. Six hundred thousand men were to die in that war. By mid-January the effective British strength would be a mere 13,000 as compared with 70,000 French. Reinforcements, mostly raw recruits, came out in sad little trickles, and the newcomers quickly fell victim to the dreadful conditions.

When by November and December the worst of the news began to reach the British ministers they were aghast. At last their confidence in Raglan was seriously shaken. Still, it took Newcastle until December 22 before he demanded from him the reason for 'the complaints which thicken from all quarters of the want of system and organisation which prevails in all departments of the camp',[36] asked why the French camp was reported as being in so much better condition than the British, and probed into the incredible confusion in Balaclava harbour and the state of the roads for which he was being blamed in Parliament. On Christmas Day he was enquiring with some heat about the alleged shortage of rations for the men in the trenches. On New Year's Day he was really angry, and lashing out somewhat wildly. Now he was worried about the public's irritation at stories of the horses dying of starvation and bad conditions for the sick and wounded; and he warned Raglan that the public would take their revenge, and that 'You and I will come first, but those who are most to blame will not escape'.[37]

But who was most to blame? Newcastle did not seem any too sure. On January 26 he wrote again to Raglan: 'The present condition of the army – wet, cold, and hungry, within seven miles of warm clothing, huts, fuel, and food – must be caused by improvidence by somebody. Who is it?'[38]

Chapter 21

A Stormy Session

The brief recapitulation of events in the last chapter dealt with those matters most closely affecting the war, both at home and abroad, and omitted much that was going on at the same time.

Lord John Russell was looking for trouble again and, as usual, finding it. It was probably after Aberdeen's speech in the Lords the previous June had brought down so much unpopularity on his head that Lord John had decided to come out into the open with his campaign to oust him from the premiership. It was at that time that some of his constituents in the City had tried to organize a public meeting to censure Aberdeen and congratulate Lord John for his patriotic speeches. Far from rebuking them, Lord John had merely drawn Lord Aberdeen's attention to these activities.[1] A very successful speech of Aberdeen's in the Lords a few days later had pricked this promising balloon. However, Lord John had found backers among those left without office, and who could only hope for places at a change of government. Aberdeen could not fail to take note of Lord John's disloyalty. Whigs as well as Peelites in the Government were shocked by it; and Clarendon told him plainly that if he did succeed in getting Aberdeen out not a member of the Cabinet would serve under him.

Lord John grew more and more restless. It was generally accepted that he was tormented by the thought that even if the Government were to fall he might not automatically become the next Prime Minister, and was brooding on the length of time he had been Leader in the House, the dissatisfaction among his followers, and the possibility that the public would grow bored with him if he did not seize power, a belief borne out by his later behaviour. His evident impatience was probably increased by his realization that the Cabinet was overcoming its disagreements and working harmoniously together. By November he could wait no longer. As soon as he returned to town he wrote to Aberdeen to demand the removal of Newcastle from the War Office. Palmerston, he suggested, should take his place.

It was not quite as simply done as all that, of course. First Lord John objected to the forthcoming estimates being framed on the basis of a Secretary at War as well as the Secretary of State for War.[2] Then he proposed the abolition of the office of Secretary at War, and making it obligatory for the Secretary for War to be in the Commons to answer there for military affairs. This would neatly dispose of both Sidney Herbert and Newcastle. Next he argued that the direction of the war should be constantly and energetically undertaken by the Prime Minister himself, or by a Minister of War 'strong enough to control other departments'. The only minister he could find to meet all these requirements was his old rival, Lord Palmerston.[3] He asked Aberdeen to show the letter containing these proposals to Newcastle.[4]

Lord Aberdeen was horrified. He dreaded Palmerston's becoming War Minister, knowing that he wanted unashamedly to widen the scope and objects of the war. There was no doubt, however, that the public wanted him; and Arthur Gordon felt that if Aberdeen had given way and made Palmerston War Minister things might well have taken a happier course later on when Lord John attempted his *coup de grâce*.[5] But in Lord Aberdeen's mind there was no excuse for dismissing Newcastle, the minister under whom the army had been organized and had won the victories of Alma, Balaclava and Inkerman.[6] He thought highly of Sidney Herbert, too, believed him to be 'deservedly popular', and was convinced that at seventy Palmerston, though a few months younger than he, was too old to be asked to take on the labours of *two* ministries. He rejected Lord John's proposal out of hand, and refused to advise the Queen to accept it.[7] The arguments went to and fro, with Aberdeen defending Newcastle and Lord John continually reverting to the need for the Prime Minister to be the moving spirit at the centre of the war machine, or for the Minister of War to be able to control other departments. Neither moved the other an inch; and at the end of the correspondence Lord John threatened to bring his recommendations before the Cabinet; then did not do so.[8]

Aberdeen showed the letters to a highly indignant Graham, to Gladstone and to Herbert. He showed them to Newcastle too, and the Duke was so 'deeply mortified' that he actually offered to go, at the same time making it clear that he was anxious to stay.[9] The Queen also saw the letters, and expressed herself as 'horrified' by Lord John's 'wickedness' and 'levity'.[10]

Ministers who had been away from London returned in December to find a cabinet box full of the correspondence between Aberdeen and Lord John, in which they could not fail to read an open threat by Russell to usurp the rôle of Prime Minister.[11] When the Cabinet met Lord John touched on his views on the War

Department, but went no further. The next day Graham wrote a very candid letter to Aberdeen: 'As the question was stated yesterday in the Cabinet, your displacement would seem to be the move intended; whereas the correspondence in circulation recommends a course entirely different'.[12]

The correspondence with Lord John was discussed at a cabinet meeting at Aberdeen's house on December 6. There the Prime Minister, taking the bull by the horns, observed that Lord John's objections really pointed not to a change in the departments, but in the head of the Government. What everybody knew but had not cared to say was now out in the open. If Lord John could get the Cabinet, or any Cabinet, to join him, Aberdeen continued, he would not stand in his way. He had not wanted to remain as Prime Minister, but had found it difficult to go. He was ready and willing to depart.[13]

Lord John, in this awkward position, did not attempt to criticize Newcastle, even though he was actually demanding his removal from office. All he could find to say was that he felt uncomfortable as a leader whom nobody followed; and he repeated that he felt the War Minister should be in the Commons and that Palmerston should fill the post.[14] Palmerston gave him no help. If ministers were to be turned out for lack of support, he said, then it was he who should go, for he had not succeeded in passing a single measure of any kind through the House of Commons during the last session of Parliament. At that moment of great tension there came the blessed relief of the one piece of humour recorded in all these odious exchanges. Palmerston's failure, Aberdeen said, must have been due to want of vigour. The laughter which erupted was as much a tribute to the zestful Pam as to the quip itself.[15]

Palmerston himself said that the only criticism he had to make of the general policy of the Government was that the expedition to Sebastopol should have been undertaken sooner, but that when he had mooted this it was Lord John who had opposed him.[16] Lord John was forced to agree. With no one supporting him, he again had recourse to the trump card he always kept up his sleeve and pulled out so frequently. He would resign after the December adjournment of Parliament. Despite all attempts, including Aberdeen's, to dissuade him, he stood by his threat, no less dangerous because used so tediously often.[17]

Lord Clarendon wrote a vivid description of this extraordinary Cabinet dinner. 'John Russell was wrong in his facts, insolent in his assertions and most ill-tempered in his replies,' he said. 'No spoilt child could be more perverse or inaccessible either to kind or firm words, and his look was as if he had plied himself with wine in order to get courage for doing what he felt was wrong, for he several times compared himself to the juryman who complained of the eleven obstinate fellows in the box with him . . . Aberdeen's conduct was a most remarkable contrast, and there the matter rests.'[18]

The meeting ended, according to Gladstone, 'with his menace standing before us, and a tacit permission to him to lead [in the Commons], and defend the Government at the meeting of Parliament'.[19] Everyone in the Cabinet knew what Lord John was up to. 'Johnny is preparing another breeze,'[20] Clarendon warned his wife. He was profoundly disgusted with his selfish and unpatriotic conduct, and would not, any more than Aberdeen, be a party to an outrageous slur on the Duke of Newcastle.[21]

Still, the Cabinet hoped that Lord John would change his mind. After all, he had often done so before. If he did not, it was not from lack of persuasion, from political supporters as well as opponents. His Whig friend Sir Charles Wood remonstrated strongly, feeling that it was a remarkable achievement on Newcastle's part to have put 30,000 men in the field at such short notice, when two years before Britain was said to have had a movable army of between ten and fifteen thousand men. The Government at home had sent out plenty of stores, and were not to blame for mismanagement in the field. 'It would be treason & no less to break up the Government at present,' he said.[22]

But Lord John was pushing Aberdeen hard, and Aberdeen was reacting in violent distaste. He had told Clarendon after the cabinet meeting that there were certain things his personal honour made it impossible for him to bear, and that he could not go on with the Leader of the House of Commons telling him every day that he was incapable.[23] Yet he could not resign himself, since not one of the Cabinet would serve under Russell, and he could not tolerate the thought of Palmerston, the only alternative.

Newcastle and Aberdeen had stayed in London, working hard to meet the needs from the front and anticipate future ones with the help of the best advice available. If Aberdeen was unenthusiastic about replacing Newcastle, it was partly because he realized that no reshuffle could work miracles, and only miracles could save the army now at the mercy of the Crimean winter.

The next cabinet meeting was equally stormy. Aberdeen had left the Cabinet working on the speech from the Throne and had gone down to Windsor. He reported to the Queen that the whole Cabinet were indignant with Lord John, and that Graham and

Gladstone were urging him to accept his resignation, but said that he was averse to making him a martyr, and felt that the Government could not go on without him.[24]

Now Lord John began to show his hand even more blatantly. Talking to Palmerston, he had said that he had understood when the Cabinet was formed that Lord Aberdeen would soon 'give me up my old place'; but that the Government had lasted more than two years, and he seemed to be 'enamoured with office'. Palmerston had asked him sarcastically what he would say to the country after he had succeeded in bringing down the Government which had difficulty enough in holding its ground 'even with your assistance'. He asked, 'Will you say, "Here I am – I have triumphed and have displaced in the midst of most hazardous operations all the ablest men the country had produced, but I shall take their place with Mr Vernon Smith, Lord Seymour, Lord Minto [his father-in-law], and others whose ability the country despises"?' The royal couple and Lord Aberdeen agreed that when and if Lord John went, Lord Palmerston must succeed him as Leader in the House of Commons – an intolerable thought for Aberdeen.[25]

Lord John found another bone to pick in the hope of whipping up support on a subject he might resign on – the case of Mr Kennedy, originally appointed by him, and rather misguidedly dismissed by Gladstone from his office of Commissioner of Woods and Forests. Technically, Aberdeen, as First Lord of the Treasury, bore ultimate responsibility, and Lord John was gunning for him, and might well have succeeded in bringing him, Newcastle, Gladstone and Graham down on this mere technicality. Lord John's line was that of loyalty of the very kind he was busy denigrating in Aberdeen's support of Newcastle. Aberdeen supported Gladstone, as Gladstone had failed to support him in the debate of the previous June. It led to threats of an enquiry, a serious quarrel between Gladstone and Lord John, and Lord John's declining to submit to any Cabinet decision on questions regarding his personal honour.[26]

Lord John was determined to create a *casus belli* and it was left to his friends to persuade him that the introduction of such petty personal matters at a time of great crisis would do him no good. In the end he gave way, and by December 15 had told Lansdowne to burn a letter of his in which he had set out his demands concerning departmental changes.[27] Graham and Gladstone were all for his going, the other Peelites were outraged, and his own friends were surprised and ashamed at his behaviour. He could not fail to be aware of the atmosphere he had created. But, far from going, he turned up at the cabinet meeting on the 16th and took part in the discussions as if nothing had happened. Afterwards, when Aberdeen referred to their correspondence, he simply, and without embarrassment, said he had changed his mind, and was now convinced that the timing was wrong – a disingenuous answer, as his recognized object was the removal of Aberdeen.[28]

'It is true that there can be no security for a single week,' Aberdeen told the Queen, 'and it is impossible to escape from a sense of self-degradation by submitting to such an unprecedented state of relations among colleagues; but the scandal of a rupture would be so great, and the evils which might ensue so incalculable, that Lord Aberdeen is sincerely convinced it will be most advantageous for Your Majesty's service and for the public to endeavour, by a conciliatory and prudent course of conduct, to preserve tranquillity and union as long as possible. This does not exclude the necessity of firmness, but, in the present case, Lord Aberdeen has yielded nothing whatever, and he has received Lord John's change without resentment or displeasure.'[29]

Aberdeen recognized that his troubles were far from over. At this time he was writing to Mary, in Egypt, 'I am sorry to tell you that the state of the Government is most critical. I do not see how it is possible to escape going to pieces. We have weathered many storms but, I fear, within a very few weeks our fate is inevitable'.[30]

Quite another series of events throughout this year, which provided time-absorbing problems enough to have occupied both Premier and Cabinet to the exclusion of anything else, were those on the diplomatic front.

One had no connection with the war, though it was the war which eventually prevented it from developing into an unnecessary and destructive quarrel (or, some thought, actual war) with the United States. This was about Britain's claim to a protectorate over the Mosquito Coast in Central America and the mainland settlement at Greytown. Next, arising out of the war, was the ironical rôle forced upon Aberdeen of the military occupation, in combination with the French, of Athens, in order to subdue the Greeks (itching to exploit any embarrassment of their age-old Turkish enemies and oppressors) into neutrality. Also connected with the prosecution of the war was a protracted diplomatic flirtation with the idea of an alliance with, or subsidization of, Sweden, with the object of military operations against Russia in Finland. This eventually came to nothing, partly because Gladstone and Aberdeen were repelled by any such enlargement of the scope of the war beyond the objectives of the Eastern Question.

Finally, and interminably, the Government was maintaining its vain attempt to inveigle Austria into an active military and diplomatic commitment. Endlessly repeated efforts to tie Austria down were not made any easier by the intriguing behind Britain's back of the Emperor Louis Napoleon during the summer, or by Russia's unexpected withdrawal from the Principalities, which were on Austria's border and therefore the focus of her interest. Aberdeen, to the irritation of other cabinet colleagues, never quite abandoned hope and faith in Austria, his old friend. 'Unadulterated selfishness is the policy of Austria'[31] was the opinion of his Foreign Secretary, while to him she was 'perfectly honest'[32]. Right at the end of his administration, when the reports of Inkerman and the hurricane were reaching England, the British Cabinet was considering Austria's proposed revisions to a French draft treaty which was finally signed in Vienna on December 2. The powers were still arguing about elucidation of the Four Points embodied in it when the Coalition Government fell.

All this, distracting, time-consuming and nerve-racking, was going on while significant decisions about the war itself were being taken. There were some twenty cabinet meetings helds between November 10 and December 31 alone.

In despatch after despatch Raglan was crying out for reinforcements; and the ministers were doing their best to supply them. By withdrawing troops from garrisons overseas and reducing depots at home to skeleton strength they had provided an expeditionary force of some five divisions, but there was no reserve for a regular flow. Everyone had thought the war would be over quickly; but already many months had gone by.

By the end of August 33,586 men had gone to the East.[33] In September and October 4141, and in November another 7037, joined them.[34] On December 12 Herbert was able to announce that more than 54,000 men had been sent out, or were waiting to go.[35] If in January there were few men available in the trenches this was largely due to the sick-roll – 11,236 in August, 11,988 in October, 23,076 in January.[36]

The Prince Consort had been worried about the numbers and quality of recruits, and had suggested a foreign legion.[37] Many ideas (short of conscription, which the French had adopted) were put into action, and Sidney Herbert was stimulating recruitment by every means. The age limit and height qualification were reduced, and a bounty offered.[38] There was still surprising apathy in some quarters. When Louis Napoleon offered 7000 extra men if Britain would transport them, the Admiralty maintained that there were no ships available, but Clarendon insisted on the First Lord's going to the steamship companies, and Mr Samuel Cunard supplied the ships. Graham was abashed, and Argyll was shocked, and lost his confidence in bureaucrats for ever.[39]

The ministers were faced with a situation which could not be easily or quickly solved. Circumstances, however the blame for them may be apportioned, had meant that the action they had taken was somewhat belated, but they were working hard to compensate for that. Parliament had been hastily summoned to consider the whole case before Christmas.

On December 12 the Queen opened the special sitting of the new session.[40] The ensuing debates were historic. In the Lords Derby vituperatively attacked the Government for its slowness, lack of foresight and ineffectuality.[41] Newcastle made the worst of his case in what Greville considered a 'dull and feeble' speech.[42] *The Times*, still backing the Government, was infuriated by it. His cold statistics offered no balm to the anguish of those daily reading stories of horrible suffering in the Crimea. Newcastle admitted deficiencies in the medical services, and blamed them on peace-time parsimony. It was all most unfortunate in the mood of a press and a country looking for a scapegoat, and sure that he was the appropriate one. For Aberdeen, who had supported him against criticism, it was disastrous. The broken reed had pierced his hand.

In the Commons Sidney Herbert did better, laying the blame for the smallness of the force and reinforcements on England's system of 'improvident economy' in peace-time. He drummed it in that it was 'the fault of all parties, all Administrations and every Parliament', not failing to condemn himself as much as anyone.[43] Lord John, with deplorable lack of loyalty, tacitly agreed with insinuations that members of the Cabinet were at odds with one another.[44] Disraeli jeered at Herbert's effort to use, as he said, elaborate statistics to answer charges that had not been made, and attacked the lack of overall planning in the war.[45]

The two Houses struggled on with the Foreign Enlistment Bill and the Militia Bill, and two days before Christmas Parliament adjourned for a month. The Government had survived, but only just.

On Christmas Day Aberdeen wrote to Mary: 'Our short session has been very stormy, and bodes ill for the future. External and internal causes combine to make one think that the Government

278

cannot last; and it would not surprise me if we did not meet Parliament again; but I am accustomed to great uncertainties in these matters. I assure you that my chief cause of regret in leaving office would be the fear that your comforts in Egypt might be diminished. The children of an ex-Vizier will scarcely meet with much respect. We are all in great anxiety about Sebastopol. It is expected that the assault will take place just at this time. It will be a murderous affair, and the loss must be very great whether successful or not'.[46]

The change in attitude of *The Times* must have caused Aberdeen particular distress, coming at that time. At the opening of Parliament it had trumpeted that 'never was war prosecuted so vigorously and resolutely as this at this moment'.[47] Seven days later it came out strongly against British army organization in the Crimea, especially as compared with the French.[48]

On the day Parliament rose its tone grew more hostile. Inevitably the preparations for Christmas festivity in England were contrasted with the sad lot of the army in the Crimea, and its leader claimed 'that the noblest army England ever sent from these shores has been sacrificed to the grossest mismanagement. Incompetence, lethargy, aristocratic hauteur, official indifference, favour, routine, perverseness and stupidity reign, revel and riot in the camp before Sebastopol, in the harbour at Balaklava, in the hospitals of Scutari, and how much nearer home we do not venture to say'.[49]

On Boxing Day (the day after Aberdeen had written to Mary hoping that the attack on Sebastopol had begun), *The Times* said that it at least did not expect the early fall of Sebastopol. When the generals sought more reinforcements, it added, the disappointed public would be demanding new leadership as well. Raglan was openly criticized. 'All this time we are surpassed by everybody, and only boast a sorry superiority over the Turks, whom, accordingly, we abuse very freely,' it complained. 'The French surpass us in their roads, in their port, in their huts, in their food and clothing, in their hospitals, in everything, and are beginning to look on our helplessness much as we look on that of our barbarous allies. The Russians surpass all three – French, British and Turks – in everything except in mere physical strength and courage. *There* we come off the best. Yet how disgraceful that England, so wealthy, so mechanical, and with such infinity of resources, should after all depend upon the rawest material of war – the British soldier – and should be reduced to throw him away by wholesale in order to make up for our want of military science, not to say common sense!'[50]

That was the tone of a paper which 14 days earlier had asserted that no war had ever been prosecuted so vigorously. What had caused the change? Apparently, it was the spate of letters from officers and their families who implored *The Times* to give the truth to the country. 'Hundreds of letters,' said *The Times* on December 30, in the last issue of that terrible year, 'tell, in uniform language, the almost total disorganisation of our army in the Crimea and its awful jeopardy, not from the Russians, but from an enemy nearer home – its own utter mismanagement'.[51]

Apparently, it continued scathingly, failure was better 'than that one iota of the official system of patronage, of seniority, and of all that semblance of order, that has kept up the illusion of military strength through a profound peace of 40 years should be rudely swept away or reformed'; and better that Raglan and his staff should return with honour over the bones of 50,000 British dead than have 'a single recall, or a new appointment over the heads of those now in command'. *The Times* called for the 'throwing overboard without a day's delay, all scruples of personal friendship, of official punctilio, or aristocratic feeling and courtly subservience'. It was a damaging attack, and it finished harshly, for it said that it was 'a crime in a War Minister to permit an officer to remain for a single day in the nominal discharge of duties the neglect of which has brought a great and victorious army to the verge of ruin'.[52] It was after Raglan's head – and Newcastle's.

So ended the terrible year. 'The last day of one of the most melancholy and disastrous years I ever recollect,' Greville recorded in his diary on the 31st. 'Almost everybody is in mourning, and grief and despair overspread the land.'[53]

Chapter 22

'Treachery and Deceit'

Parliament adjourned for a month. On January 7 Lord Aberdeen wrote to Mary:

'I have not been able to leave London at all during the winter, notwithstanding the adjournment of Parliament. We shall meet again on the 23rd, when much is expected which may affect the existence of the Government. No doubt the difficulties are very great and I always felt that it would be scarcely possible for us to carry on the war; but I should not altogether despair of overcoming all these difficulties if the Cabinet were really united. But the intrigue which has existed during the whole of my administration has now become more formidable than ever, and must, in all human probability, shortly lead to our dissolution. I should care little for the loss of office, but it is hard to be the victim of treachery and deceit.'[1]

There, for the first, and almost the last, time, Lord Aberdeen gave his full and frank opinion of Lord John Russell's behaviour. Doubtless he spoke as freely to his son and secretary, and to his friend Sir James Graham, and to Gladstone. But to Mary, who supplied his need for a woman in whom to confide, he could not speak, and must write. So we know what he truly felt, his notable discretion notwithstanding.

In the Royal Archives at Windsor Castle there is a letter in very shaky handwriting from Samuel Wilberforce, then Bishop of Oxford, dated 16 May 1854, in which he informed the Prince Consort 'that, at the present moment, under the reiterated attacks made on him, it would be peculiarly gratifying to the feelings of Lord Aberdeen if as a Mark of Her esteem Her Majesty pressed on him the Vacant Garter,' and added, 'I know not that I should venture to write this to Your Royal Highness but for the terms in which you recently spoke to me of Lord Aberdeen. But from the intimate knowledge which I saw that you possessed of Lord Aberdeen's noble and sensitive Nature, I am convinced that you will know that you would never hear from him of the Existence of such a feeling and will in its fullest Sense believe my assurance that he has not the Slightest Conception of this Communication being made to you. Will Your Royal Highness allow me to add that what I am now doing is not known to any living being?'[2]

Now, on 10 January 1855, the Queen offered Aberdeen the Garter 'before Parliament meets for probably a very stormy session'.[3] Aberdeen replied at once, saying (with what seems like a trace of disingenuousness in the light of Wilberforce's letter), 'When Your Majesty mentioned the subject to Lord Aberdeen some time ago, he had not thought of any such distinction; and perhaps at his time of life, and with his present prospects, he scarcely ought to do so'.[4] At any rate, after thinking it over, he asked the Queen to give the Garter to Lord Cardigan because of his 'great gallantry and personal sacrifices', and suggested that she 'postpone' his own Garter.[5]

The Queen replied crisply that his suggestion about Cardigan did not meet with her approval, 'and would hardly be understood by the Army and the Country'. That an opponent of the Government, who could not receive even the GCB by the rules of that Order, should be given the highest order in the land, not bestowed even on Raglan or Hardinge, would never do, and, 'Moreover, Ld. Cardigan's personal character does not stand very high in the country'.[6] Aberdeen retreated from what certainly seems to have been an extraordinary suggestion, and proposed that he should receive the Garter before the reassembly of Parliament.[7]

Lord Aberdeen was preparing to fold his tents and steal away. However, he and his Cabinet were far from giving up hope, and there was an unprecedented amount of activity going on between the adjournment of Parliament on December 23 and its resumption on January 23. Sidney Herbert had seen the ominous signs of approaching storm about the military departments, and was making an enormous effort to be prepared to meet it. On January 8 he wrote to Newcastle, 'If we intend to outlive it we must make vigorous use of the fortnight between this and the meeting of Parliament.' In that fortnight he put forward various suggestions for immediate reform; gave his blessing to Lord Grey's Army Board; pressed for regular meetings with departmental heads and the circulating of minutes; and urged Newcastle to come to Cabinet meetings more often and keep Lord John more fully briefed. He warned his colleagues that they had 'a terrible arrear to make up in this fortnight'.[8]

Yet all this activity went on, it seemed, in a state of bewilderment as to why it should be necessary. Argyll expressed it well in his memoirs:

'This period of 38 days which elapsed between the end of the session and the date of the next session when the Aberdeen Ministry was overthrown was a period of pain and grief to us, such as I remember with horror, and find it impossible to describe. The splendid army of over 30,000 men which we had organised and had sent out with such brilliant success to the Crimea, was reported to us every week as dying by inches in the besieging lines. Yet we were kept in complete ignorance of the causes. What we did know was that reinforcements of great strength and whole flotillas of supplies had been poured into Balaclava. The silence of Lord Raglan was positively excruciating. Nothing came from him but the dryest [sic] facts. One of these seemed to me to be alarming in the highest degree – namely this: that our effective force in the Crimea did not exceed 16,000 men, with about 9000 in hospital. I do not know if Palmerston remembered, as I did, the conversation we had together in July, when the Sebastopol expedition had been ordered – how I had been full of anxiety, and he had been still more full of hopeful, confident expectations. I am bound to say that nobody was more vexed and angry than he was now. I recollect him one day listening to a very bad account of the army which had reached us – an account which was expressed in the sentence that we were losing a regiment a week. "But why should this be?" said Palmerston, almost starting to his feet. This was the question we were all asking, and were all equally defeated in getting any guidance in reply.'[9]

So much for the problems at home; vast problems to be solved in a fortnight. Overseas the difficulties were equally daunting. For how was it possible to restore overnight this army which was going to pieces so rapidly? The contributions from home, whether of men or materials, seemed to disappear into a bottomless pit.

Raglan and his staff had been loyally supported and defended by the ministers at home; but now those ministers began to realize with a sick horror how little their confidence had been justified. Granville, Lord President of the Council, could not believe that the Commander-in-Chief and Master of the Ordnance was so inadequate at administration, in which he should have excelled, and was appalled by his persistent refusal to make use of experienced officers on the spot. Nepotism dictated his staff, which was composed of feeble young relations, and for replacements he preferred to send home to England for doddery retired generals rather than promote merit in the field.[10] Granville saw that the time had come to hearken to the outcry for the dismissal of incompetent leaders. Like Argyll he was in a quandary as to how the Government was to establish with any accuracy exactly where the blame for that incompetence fairly lay. In the end Raglan was merely informed of the Government's qualms about the Quarter-Master-General's department, and urged to take more vigorous action.[11]

There were those in the Government who were prepared to deal out the blame more bluntly. Palmerston was one. Clarendon was another. He wrote to Lord John on January 2: 'More than enough of everything required for the army has been sent by the Govt, yet the army has been in a state of miserable and disagreeable destitution . . . Not only has the administn. been defective, but the orders of the Govt appear in several instances to have been disregarded . . . Somebody must be to blame for so much negligence, and it wd seem to rest on the Adjutant-Genl and the Qr Master Genl. Ld. Raglan shd be empowered to remove them . . . and if he does not do so he shd give his reasons for approving of their conduct'.[12] This brought the criticism painfully close to home, since Colonel Alexander Gordon was Assistant Quarter-Master-General.

Palmerston was even more forthright, writing to Newcastle that it was 'quite clear that in many essential points Raglan is unequal to the task which has fallen to his lot, but it is impossible to remove him', and demanding that Airey and Estcourt, two incompetent men under him holding key posts, should be got rid of.[13] Newcastle did not even attempt to defend them, and replied in helpless agreement: 'I have never concealed my opinion that Airey and Estcourt are not fit for the responsible offices they hold, and I am quite prepared to recommend their removal if better can be found. What, however, can I do? I should not be justified in removing Airey, whom Hardinge [the General Commander-in-Chief] recommended as the *best* man for Quarter-Master-General, and whom Raglan appointed as *second best man*, and whose unfitness neither have yet admitted, without having some substitute of marked fitness to send in his place'.[14]

One does not know whether to be sorrier for the men in the field or the men at home in this predicament.

Other ministers might not know what to do about the desperate situation. Lord John was certain that he did. At the end of December he had produced a memorandum outlining all the military problems, and had suggested ways to defeat them. The six basic causes of trouble he put down as (i) soldiers overworked in the trenches, (ii) no changes of dry clothing, (iii) transport animals dying for want of forage, (iv) shortage of rations because of lack of forage, (v) lack of huts and shortage of timber, (vi) bad medical care of the sick and slowness in moving them.[15] Angered at the lack of response to these initiatives, he had again come close to resigning – or at least to sending off a letter of resignation to Aberdeen – on New Year's Day. This time the burden of his plaint was that he was being ignored for fear of casting a slur on Newcastle, and that, since it was more important to win the war than to spare the feelings of one man, he could not continue to lead for the Government in the Commons.[16] He never finished the letter, and to Aberdeen, nervously watching him, he seemed calmer and less bellicose in Cabinet.[17]

Aberdeen was the more surprised when he did get an acid letter from Lord John, again pushing for the Prime Minister to take over the direction of the war, and asking for Newcastle, Herbert or Hardinge, the Commander-in-Chief, to go to Paris to talk things over with Louis Napoleon and his staff.[18] Aberdeen replied: 'I was a little surprised by your letter yesterday; for I thought that the recent cabinets were rather satisfactory. Certainly many deficiencies were supplied, defects remedied, and assistance offered to Lord Raglan by the appointment of competent officers'.[19]

Indeed, Herbert and he were able to claim that a great deal was being done. The French had taken over the trenches, as Lord John had wished. Plenty of clothing had gone out. Newcastle had agreed to a separate transport corps for forage. All the men's huts and half the officers' huts had been shipped out, and by January 6 Raglan had begun to erect them. The sick had already been moved from Balaclava to Scutari, and an inquiry initiated. Herbert himself was personally setting up a separate hospital corps.[20]

Lord John was still far from satisfied. He wanted more co-ordination in supplies between the army and the navy. He wanted Raglan to be given more precise information about how many troops he could expect, and to be invited to give his opinion about the use of available resources. Herbert did not turn a deaf ear. He agreed with many of Lord John's ideas, and suggested that his memorandum should form the basis for a public despatch to Raglan, strengthened by criticism about his failure to build a road, create divisional depots, or make use of the supplies of forage in Balaclava. He was willing to press Raglan to replace his senior officers with men on the spot.[21]

There is no doubt that at that stage the Cabinet were clearly admitting that much had gone wrong. In a memorandum which he himself prepared, Herbert acknowledged that the allies had been caught napping about the Russians' ability to send reinforcements in to their Sebastopol garrison. The allies, it stated, were unlikely to increase their own strength beyond 100,000 men; which meant that the Russians were almost bound to overtake them in numbers. There would even be a question as to whether Sebastopol could be held if taken.

Now Herbert also frankly faced the possibility of failure and the need to evacuate the troops. He agreed that the generals should be made aware of all the alternatives, and given full discretion. He and his colleagues would try to decide what they thought should be done; then try to get the French Government to agree; then send instructions to the allied generals; and then get Raglan to give his opinion of the position of the army, the nature of the operations which he contemplated, and his expectations of success or failure. He went so far as to say that Raglan 'should give his opinion as to the advantage or disadvantages of an armistice, should . . . negotiations at Vienna be commenced'.[22]

More and more, in those bleak January days, was the truth admitted in Cabinet.

On January 11 Newcastle read to the Cabinet a draft dispatch to Raglan dwelling on the 'want of foresight or of ability' on the part of some of Raglan's officers, admitting that it had 'led to an amount of suffering and sickness . . . which ought to have been avoided'. He acknowledged, too, that the evidence of 'neglect and inefficiency' was overwhelming, so much so that he had no alternative but to demand that Raglan should conduct an inquiry into the whole question of the organization of the camp. 'If the army grows weak by disease not attendant upon warfare,' he declared, 'and is perilled by want, exposure and distress which the departmental care of your staff should have provided against, the people of England, regarding results, and painfully sensitive to the possibility of a disastrous future, will, on behalf of the sufferers and of the national honour, call upon your Lordship to recommend such changes as may correct the evils they deplore and ward off the dangers they deprecate.' Any aid or money Raglan needed would be 'cheerfully provided'.[23]

By the time Raglan replied – stung to anger for once, but not very effective even in self-justification – Newcastle was out of office.[24]

Herbert, now as anxious for action as Lord John, unburdened himself to Graham about the lack of co-ordination between the army and the navy, and the inefficiency at home: 'While we complain of the gross mismanagement and confusion at Balaclava we have unfortunately under our own eyes the same scenes at home. The arrangements about packing our ships are a public scandal . . . Who is to blame I know not – but this I am conscious of, that the Government which cannot prevent or correct or punish such neglect will become contemptible'. He asked for a searching inquiry, and interdepartmental changes to 'prevent these disastrous failures'.[25]

Lord John had seized the opportunity of a family visit to Paris early in January to visit Lady John's sick sister, to confer with Louis Napoleon, much to the trepidation of the Queen and Aberdeen, for the negotiations with Vienna were then at a dangerous stage.[26]

On January 9 Aberdeen wrote to Mary, 'We have just received intelligence of the greatest importance in the fact that the Emperor of Russia has accepted our terms proposed as the basis of peace and agrees to negotiate accordingly. Should he really be sincere we may have peace shortly, but there will be many difficulties on our side. Of this, however, I am quite determined. If reasonable terms should be within my reach I will make peace, or someone else shall carry on the war'.[27]

If Lord John, being abroad, could not attend the cabinet meetings – he missed the important ones of January 9 and January 11 – he could still wreak havoc by means of pen and paper. When his account of his interviews with the French Emperor and his Foreign Minister, M. Drouyn de l'Huys, was read to the Cabinet they realized to their consternation that he had been misinterpreting its attitude in vital respects in those important quarters.

Lord John was back on January 16, in time for a five-hour cabinet meeting, having landed only that day from Boulogne. Now Raglan and Canrobert, the successor to St Arnaud, were at loggerheads, and there were diplomatic problems to be sorted out. Lord John's trip abroad had done nothing to quiet him down, but for once he was acting like one of a team. 'We had three cabinets on the 18th, 19th and 20th of January,' wrote Argyll. 'At all of them Lord John was not only present, but taking an active part in measures of his own, upon Education [Lord John wanted a more effective civil service entrance exam], [and] on church rates, thus giving every indication of his continued membership and fellowship with us.'[28]

All through January *The Times* continued its lambasting of the Government, growing more violent as the reassembly of Parliament on the 23rd drew near. On January 20 it was vehement: 'Affairs are left in the same incompetent hands . . . the Cabinet is engaged in endless discussions which lead to no result . . . A torpor and lethargy seem to have fallen on the spirit of our rulers; they go on mechanically sending out men and stores to the fatal harbour of Balaclava, without seeming to advert to the fact that men and stores under the present circumstances of the British army are only sent, one to perish, the other to be wasted'. Hardly two thousand men of the troops on active service, that leader sternly charged, were in good health; and the whole army was face to face with disaster.[29]

The same day a second leader dwelt on the fatuity of the pre-Christmas meeting of Parliament. Both the measures which it had passed were a dead letter, it jeered. Not a militia regiment had been sent abroad, and not one foreigner had been enlisted at home for the foreign legion.[30] On January 22 it asked rhetorically why there had recently been so many long cabinet meetings. Was this in aid of solving the Crimean problem, of finding a new general, or perhaps of handing over the British army to the French Commander-in-Chief? No, it answered itself. The ministers were dealing with the great Kennedy case; and perhaps at the end of the meeting half an hour would be left to deal with the war: 'The British public at least will learn with disgust how its rulers are trifling with its anxieties and griefs'.[31]

On the 23rd the ministers who opened their newspapers found the attack still unrelenting. *The Times* was castigating the results of the military system as 'failure, failure, failure', and complaining: 'The deadlock is absolute, final, inevitable, and desperate, from Whitehall to the camp before Sebastopol. The Minister of War, the Commander-in-Chief at home, the Commander-in-Chief in the Crimea, down to the purveyor of stores at Scutari, and the miserable lad dozing hungry, naked and frostbitten in the trench are all equally dummies'.[32]

It was very cold that January, one of the coldest spells for many years. Everyone thought of the troops suffering in the even colder Crimean winter, with no comforts to alleviate their miseries.

The 'little piddling, pottering war with Johnny', of Gladstone's contemptuous phrase,[33] was about to erupt into something he would not be able to dismiss so lightly. No one would have guessed it. Not only had Lord John behaved reasonably in the cabinets of the 16th 18th and 20th, but on the eve of resumption he had sent to Lord Aberdeen the outline of some measures for military reorganization which he said he meant to propose at the next cabinet meeting, and which were really an extension of Herbert's Army Board scheme. When the House met on the 23rd he gave notice of his intention to move to introduce the Education Bill he had prepared on an early day.[34]

It is possible that Lord John was not taken by surprise by what happened next. Arthur Gordon at any rate believed that he had anticipated a motion of censure. Lord Aberdeen himself had heard that one might be moved by Sir Robert Peel, and that Lord John had said that he was glad he would not have to face his father, the great Sir Robert, in replying as Leader of the House.[35]

If this were true, then Lord John could hardly have been taken by surprise when that day Roebuck, the obstreperous Radical MP for Sheffield, gave notice of a motion for a committee of inquiry on the conduct of the war. In fact Lord John had even discussed with the Government Whip whether there should be an amendment or not. The House adjourned early; and he walked home with a colleague. He said nothing of the step he was about to take.[36]

Strangely and interestingly, Arthur Gordon himself had sat down on the eve of Lord John's historic decision, the night of January 22, to write in his private journal in vivid terms his own assessment of the situation.

'Parliament meets again tomorrow,' he wrote. 'That the session will be a stormy one is evident; but what will be its result is not so clear. Lord John is the one source of trouble and weakness. We cannot exist with or without him. Wayward, uncertain, querulous, it is impossible to imagine what he may or may not do next . . .

'At present things look better than they have done for some time as regards his disposition on great questions. He seems wholly to have withdrawn his late plans of War Office reform, and at the Cabinet proposed a scheme for its reorganisation not very practical or practicable, but unobjectionable. He is not disinclined for peace, and agrees that an effort to secure it must be made at Vienna. His Lordship and Lord Clarendon are not without hopes that he may be induced to undertake the negotiations himself.'[37]

Gordon's judgement was that Palmerston wanted things to go on as they were: 'It suits his game far better than Lord John's decided pre-eminence would'.[38]

Lord John puzzled him, as he did everyone. 'It is curious how *alone* Lord John is. The world without think the Cabinet is divided into two distinct parties; but this is most untrue. There is not a shade of difference between Lord Clarendon, Sir Charles Wood,

Granville, Sir George Grey, Cranworth, Molesworth, and the Peelites. Lord John stands solitary, and Palmerston, Newcastle and Lansdowne are the fire-eating war party.'[39]

Reverting to his father, Gordon asked a question. 'Will the Blue Ribbon, which the Queen has pressed on His Lordship, do him good or harm? At all events it has greatly pleased him, and at that I rejoice, for he has not too much of what he likes in his daily life.'[40]

That night, alone with his diary, Arthur Gordon also wrote down a piece of information which he regarded as so indiscreet that he kept it a secret ever afterwards. Even when, years later, he wrote the biographies of his father and of Sidney Herbert, this highly significant piece of information was not revealed.

'The Duke of Newcastle – I hardly dare to write what is known, I believe, to none of his colleagues in the Cabinet – means to resign, not admitting the justice of the outcry against him, but avowing that with such unpopularity he cannot usefully discharge the duties of the office. He is right, and in the long run he will gain by it; but I am afraid His Lordship wishes to appoint Herbert in his place. This will be a mistake. It must, under existing circumstances, be Palmerston. Not that Herbert would not fill the office better, but because if a change is made, this is the only one that will give real confidence.'[41]

On January 23, then, the House met for the first time after the recess.

As Arthur Gordon recalled, there was little excitement or interest evident, and the House was not very full. Roebuck gave notice of his motion for a Committee of Inquiry, and was cheered by Radicals and Tories. Lord John, as President of the Council, gave notice of a Bill on Education. Sir Benjamin Hall brought in a Bill on the local government of the metropolis, and embarked on a long, dull speech. 'Whereupon, in the innocence of my heart, I went into the lobby to write letters,'[42] Arthur Gordon recorded. Both Houses rose early, and at eight o'clock Gordon went home to dinner at Argyll House. He reported that the session had opened quietly. He had not an inkling of the bombshell which was about to explode.

Father and son dined quietly together as usual, and at ten o'clock Arthur Gordon went into the library to look at the day's despatch boxes. In the first one he opened he found Lord John's letter of resignation.

He went to the drawing-room at once to summon his father. Lord Aberdeen was averse to coming, and did so only very reluctantly, grumbling, 'Don't bother!' and 'Can't it wait?'[43] He came at last; and was as surprised as his son. His first reaction, as often in times of shock, was one of amusement. After all, Lord John had resigned, or threatened to resign, so often. His next was, not surprisingly after all that he had been through in the past month, one of relief and determination not to plead with Lord John. His son was not so relaxed; and that night he wrote in his journal that, of course, it was 'impossible not to see that by resigning now he will probably upset the coach again as he has so often done before'. He hinted to his father that Lord John would probably think better of it. 'But on this point His Lordship's mind was firmly made up,' he wrote. 'Whatever happened, this resignation should be real. He would not voluntarily submit to a repetition of late scenes.'[44]

Aberdeen sent off his son to fetch his old friend Sir James Graham. Sir James came down to Gordon in his dressing-gown, and Gordon noted his reaction – he was 'alarmed lest His Lordship should have had another attack'. (Aberdeen had been having bouts of giddiness.) Gordon told him what had happened. As he gave him his father's message there must have been fresh in his mind another passage he had written in his diary only the previous evening: 'Sir James Graham, at once rash and timid, is a warm friend and a dangerous adviser. I wish His Lordship did not listen to him so exclusively. Every day he comes; to him alone is confidence unreservedly given; and he has more than once contributed to results which he little deserved'.[45]

Perhaps Graham's mind also ran back on this night to the paean of praise for Aberdeen's record as Prime Minister which he had written only the previous October. At any rate he hastily threw on a 'great fur coat' and went back in a cab with Aberdeen's son to Argyll House. 'I could not help wondering,' Gordon wrote in his journal, 'as we jogged along slowly, with our feet in the dirty straw, who had been the last and who would be the next fares of the sleepy driver, and what they had talked and would talk about.'

Sir James's first reaction, as Gordon's had been, was that Lord John was sure to change his mind; but, said Gordon, 'when we reached Argyll House, he very soon saw that on this point my father was quite determined'. Despite this, Sir James began to devise schemes for winning Russell back. Aberdeen would not hear of any of them.[46]

The question in everyone's mind, and one which is still unanswered, was, When had Lord John decided to resign? Even Arthur Gordon, incensed as he was at what Lord John had done to his father, could not believe that his treachery was deep enough for him to have deliberately concealed his intentions. As it was, said Arthur Gordon, after the change of mind which Lord John had claimed on December 16, after his having actually taken part in the preparation of measures for the coming session, and in the certain knowledge that a vote of censure was going to be proposed – after all that, it was incredible that he should resign on notice being given of that vote without so much as a hint to a single colleague that he had such a thing in mind.

It seems certain that if Lord John did make up his mind after reaching home that night, as Arthur Gordon tried to believe, he was not persuaded by Lady John. At least, she told her father Lord Minto that she had begged him not to write to Lord Aberdeen without first talking things over with his friends.[47]

In a retrospective memorandum on the reasons for his resignation Russell maintained that it had been made simply on the grounds that the House of Commons, following precedents of 1757, 1777 and 1810, had the right to demand such an inquiry as Roebuck was doing, and that as Leader he was in no position properly to oppose it. Aberdeen himself considered it an intolerable attempt on the part of the House of Commons to interfere with the executive Government and the royal prerogative. He was shocked that it should have been brought at all.

Had Aberdeen taken a different view he might have defused the whole crisis (and have denied Russell the pretext for his resignation which he was later to put forward) by the simple expedient of not resisting Roebuck's motion for a select committee. It is probable that the retrospective damage done to the Coalition Government by the eventual report of a select committee would have been effaced by the fall of Sebastopol in September. Then the Aberdeen Government would have been seen to have itself effected those steps which in the end secured victory, despite some dangerous and blameworthy failures on the way, and would have been given the credit to which it was entitled. On the other hand some other excuse might well have soon been found for putting down a straightforward motion of censure.

In his formal letter of resignation Lord John had baldly said that he did not see how Roebuck's motion could be resisted, and that, as it involved the censuring of the War Department led by his colleagues, the only course open to him was to tender his resignation. Even at this stage he took care to include a brief covering note avowing 'his regard' for Aberdeen's 'personal character', and his sense of the Prime Minister's 'kindness and liberality'.[49] (They were, for once, at a low ebb.) He sent a copy of his letter of resignation to the Queen – a most unusual step[50] – and wrote personal letters of explanation to Palmerston and Granville.[51]

Chapter 23

The Fall

So the morning of the 24th dawned. Thanks to the Duke of Argyll we have a racy record of its events.

'On the 24th we had another Cabinet. I walked down to it alone and rather early. On entering the room I found that Palmerston was there, and nobody else. As he was not generally more than punctual, I was surprised. The mystery was soon solved when he handed me a note, saying, "Read that". It was a note from Lord John, telling Palmerston in three lines that he would hear a letter from himself read to the Cabinet and that it was a painful and necessary step.'[1]

That morning Aberdeen had taken Lord John's letter to Newcastle. He had at once offered to resign his office to Palmerston; but he was still speaking of this as a 'sacrifice', and one made only in order to 'appease the public'.[2] Next Aberdeen had called on Palmerston himself. Palmerston had been highly critical of Lord John's behaviour, and had said that he did not believe he could administer the War Department half as well as Newcastle. If, however, it was necessary in order to avoid the Government's fall, then he 'was prepared to try it'.

Palmerston had told Lord John outright in a letter that he considered his resignation most ill-timed. Everyone had foreseen that there would be some such motion as Roebuck's; and if Lord John had not been prepared to oppose it, then he should have warned his colleagues earlier on, and have given them the chance to make up their own minds as to what they were going to do about it. 'As it is,' he went on:

'you will have the appearance of having remained in office, aiding in carrying on a system of which you disapproved, until driven out by Roebuck's announced Notice; and the Government will have the appearance of Self-Condemnation by flying from a discussion which they dare not face; while as regards the country the action of the executive will be paralyzed for a time in a

293

critical moment of a great war with an impending negotiation, and we shall exhibit to the world a melancholy spectacle of Disorganization among our political men at Home, similar to that which has prevailed among our military men abroad. My opinion is that if you had simply renewed the Proposal which you made before Christmas, such an arrangement might have been made, and there are constitutional & practical grounds on which such a motion as Roebuck's might have been resisted without violence to any opinions which you may entertain as to the past Period.'[3]

Aberdeen attended the cabinet meeting which assembled at two that afternoon. He read out Lord John's letter. According to Argyll, Newcastle again offered to resign, 'as he knew the run was against him and the Cabinet could not go on unless he left the War Department'. But, Argyll went on, 'We all felt it would be dishonourable to ourselves to make him our scapegoat for events for which we ought all to share the responsibility in our several degrees'. Lord John's act – an unparalleled one – was universally condemned by all his colleagues. He had sent his resignation without consulting one of them, and late at night, after taking part in the business of the House. 'Aberdeen told us that he received it with very great surprise,' Argyll wrote, 'as this was almost the only occasion on which he should have thought such a course impossible. To desert the friends with whom he had been acting just at the moment when they were about to be attacked would indeed seem a strange course.'[4] Palmerston indicated his attitude, then Grey and Wood declared that Roebuck's motion could not be resisted. Clarendon countered this by suggesting that Lord John might be persuaded to withdraw his resignation in view of Newcastle's 'generous offer'. Gladstone objected to this.[5]

The decision lay with Aberdeen. He rejected the proposal with a firmness which he had never before shown with Lord John. They 'might be justified in sacrificing the Duke to the wishes of the country,' he said, 'but they could not to Lord John, with any degree of honour'. So once again on the note of honour a great decision was taken.[6]

As the Whig members of the Cabinet were supporting Russell in his view that Roebuck's motion could not be resisted, it was decided that the whole Cabinet would have to resign. They agreed to meet again next day, and Aberdeen at once departed for Windsor to lay their resignations before the Queen.

After Aberdeen had gone the ministers decided that Lord John should be informed, and the task was delegated to Sir Charles

Wood. To their astonishment Lord John asked whether he should attend the Cabinet next day. Wood advised him not to do so.[7]

The Queen refused to accept the resignation of her ministers, and persuaded Aberdeen to make one more appeal to them.[8] Lord John's action in sending a copy of his letter of resignation to her had done nothing to appease her. She sent him a curt note expressing 'surprise and concern at hearing so abruptly of his intention to desert the Government on the motion of Mr Roebuck'.[9] Lord John was very upset. He replied immediately, protesting that he had 'sacrificed his position and reputation for two years', and that it was his belief that it would not be for the benefit of the country to resist the Roebuck motion. 'It is the cause of much pain to him,' he ended, 'that, after sacrificing his position in order to secure Your Majesty's service from interruption, he should not have obtained Your Majesty's approbation.'[10] The Queen replied tartly, 'If Lord John will consider, however, the moment which he has now chosen to leave her Government, and the abrupt way in which his unexpected intention of agreeing in a vote implying censure of the Government was announced to her, he cannot be surprised that she could not express her approbation'.[11]

It was beginning to dawn on Lord John that he had wrongly assessed the effect his resignation would have in various quarters. Arthur Gordon was sure that he and his friends had expected Aberdeen to resign as soon as he realized that he had lost the support of his most powerful colleague. If he did not, Gordon believed, then Lord John at least expected that the old Whigs who normally backed him would all resign with him. Then, with the Cabinet broken up, before any parliamentary censure on it, 'Lord John might be able to present himself as the head of a new, more vigorous, and purely Whig Administration'.

On the morning of Friday 25 Lord John was visited by the Whigs' Chief Whip, Hayter, who found Vernon Smith, one of the disappointed Whig office-seekers, and Colonel Romilly already with him. The three eagerly interrogated Hayter, and expressed great disappointment at hearing that so far it was only Lord John who had resigned. The day wore on. It became clear to Lord John that no one meant to join him in deserting Lord Aberdeen. 'He began to feel that he had made a mistake, and that, though he had probably ensured the defeat of the Government, he might have seriously injured himself.' So Arthur Gordon, once again.[12]

Thus, on the evening of the 25th Russell sent a mutual friend to Lord Aberdeen to bargain with him, offering to reconsider his resignation if certain guarantees were given to him about the future conduct of the war. He was willing to close at the appointment of Lord Palmerston to the War Office.[13] In fact that had already been arranged, and Newcastle had finally made up his mind to resign after the short pre-Christmas session. Unhappily Newcastle had not only deferred his resignation until after the new session had begun, but had insisted that Lord Aberdeen should not inform his colleagues of his intention.[14]

At that stage Lord Palmerston was inclined to back a reconciliation with Lord John on his own terms. 'But these overtures were at once peremptorily rejected by Lord Aberdeen,' said his son. 'Matters had in this instance gone too far for repentance, nor, come what might, was he prepared at that time to accept Lord John again as a colleague.'[15] That is not to say that Aberdeen showed these feelings of natural resentment to Lord John. In accepting his resignation he thanked him for his kind remarks and assured him that nothing could ever alter his own warm regard for him – surely more than formal courtesy required, and an astounding example of turning the other cheek. He actually saw Lord John on the 25th, and from his report Queen Victoria was able to note that he had found Russell 'personally civil' but 'very much excited and very angry' at her letter to him, which he had just received.[16]

The Cabinet met again that day, only in order to learn the arrangements for its members to relinquish their offices. Argyll said that their astonishment was great when Aberdeen arrived from Windsor and told them that they were still ministers of the Crown because the Queen had refused to accept either his resignation or theirs. She had commanded Aberdeen to tell them that their resignation under such conditions was unjust to her, harmful to their reputations, and indefensible towards the country. The ministers held differing views about the wisdom of carrying on; but 'none of them differed in recognizing that the Queen had exercised her prerogative with wisdom and with strength'.[17] Gladstone noted for posterity the remarkable effect which the Queen's wish had on all. Grey, he recorded, was the first of the Whigs to retire from his position of the day before and reverse his decision to resign, and the others followed his lead. There seemed to be some relief at not being pushed by the Whigs into fleeing before Roebuck's motion, and now all concurred with Argyll's previous stand, that they should await the verdict of the House of Commons.[18] The Queen had, in fact, in Prince Albert's words, merely 'insisted that Lord Aberdeen should make an appeal to the Cabinet to stand by her, which he promised to do to the best of his ability, but without hope of success'. Prince Albert later seemed surprised that Aberdeen had 'put the Queen's desire that the Cabinet should reconsider their former decision in the strongest terms'.[19] Argyll at least believed the Queen had sent a command within her prerogative, not an appeal.[20] It was therefore agreed that when Lord John announced his resignation Palmerston would ask for the adjournment, and the Government would accept the House's decision on the Roebuck motion.[21]

Aberdeen saw the Queen again that Friday evening. He told her that Grey, as a good and loyal Whig, had reserved his right to retire after the motion had been dealt with; but that Clarendon reported him as being 'perfectly beside himself with rage at Ld. John'.[22] Wood too was using very strong language against him, swearing he would ruin himself and his party as well. If Lord John had expected Grey, Granville and Wood to resign he was greatly mistaken, and was to show obvious disappointment when they did not, complaining to Grey that none of his old colleagues had tried to get him to withdraw his resignation.[23]

It is obvious, then, that, as Gordon maintained, Aberdeen's first intention, to retire before almost certain defeat, was overruled by the wish of the Queen and the Cabinet's reaction. Every member of that Cabinet, according to Gordon, wanted publicly to testify its disapproval of Lord John's action.[24]

The Duke of Argyll added a comment on Newcastle's position: 'Amid all the uncertainties of the situation, one thing was certain – all the world around us was in a passion. The House and the public were determined to hang somebody. The Duke of Newcastle was the obvious victim. Newcastle told his colleagues that he must resign and that he meant to do so the moment the division was announced whatever it might be'.[25]

This decision, which might have been welcomed earlier, now only put the Cabinet in an awkward predicament. If the resignation was announced to the House before the division, it might save the Government, but Newcastle's colleagues would be indicted of Lord John's crime – desertion in the face of the enemy. To them this was dishonour. There was no word of reproach for Newcastle's having let them all down by refusing to go until it was too late. The Cabinet was unanimous in its decision to face the music in the Commons as a united team. Graham had said that it was a Cabinet of gentlemen with a perfect gentleman at their head, and over forty years later, when he was the sole survivor of that historic Cabinet, Argyll wrote proudly: 'There is nothing I remember in my public life with greater satisfaction than the conduct of the Aberdeen Cabinet at this, the last moment of its existence. An overpowering sense of personal honour told us that we must stand or fall with him [Newcastle]'.[26]

So, once again, it was honour which played the tune which these men followed.

On that day, Friday, January 25, Lord John's resignation was announced in the Commons. Then Palmerston, according to plan, asked for and got the adjournment of the House for the Roebuck motion to be debated next day.[27]

Lord John, with his usual lack of judgement, was probably surprised and hurt to read *The Times* next morning. *The Times*, after all, had been slating the Government, and might have spared him. It denounced his resignation as 'a wide and painful deviation from the rules of political conduct' which were normally accepted, adding, 'He must be something worse than a bad minister who can choose such a moment of national calamity for personal resentment or party intrigue'.[28]

That day Aberdeen read Lord John's letter to the House of Lords, and announced that the Queen had accepted his resignation. Characteristically he recalled to their Lordships' memories that he would not have formed his Government at all if Lord John had not been a part of it. In the existing circumstances, however, he felt it only proper that the Government should remain in office to deal with the motion which was at that moment being moved against it in the Commons. There was no discussion.[29] Lord Aberdeen was followed by Lord Berners who, according to *The Times*, 'inflicted on the House a disquisition on Roman Catholic processions'[30] – a typical parliamentary anticlimax.

In the Commons events unrolled more dramatically. Lord John, rising to explain his resignation, said that the motion could not be resisted either on the ground that the 'evils' did not exist, or that 'sufficient means' had been taken to remedy them. Nor could he remain a member of a Government which accepted the motion, with 'the military departments . . . constantly overlooked and checked by a committee sitting upstairs'.[31] He then made a long and admittedly irrelevant digression, elaborately retailing his disagreements with Aberdeen about the reorganization of the war departments, and reading out many extracts from their letters.

It was a skilful speech, so phrased as to be clearly understood by the House as supporting Roebuck's motion, and proposing himself as Prime Minister, with the right ideas for remedying the prevailing 'evils', and Palmerston, as Secretary of State both *for* War and *at* War, to give effect to those ideas and win the war.

There were many sly digs at Aberdeen behind the conventional courtesies. He ended with a peroration almost crudely playing for the support of his old friends in the Whig ranks. Gladstone and Herbert thought he had carried the House with him.[32] Not so Aberdeen. 'He made a very elaborate and dexterous statement,' he reported to the Queen; 'but which, although very plausible, did not produce a great effect.'[33]

(*The Times*, while welcoming Lord John's conversion, suggested that he would have been more convincing if he had resigned the previous November. Now he only seemed to be running away from criticism by leaving his colleagues in the lurch. Since he had assented to the measures of the Government, it was unprecedented behaviour for him not to defend them.[34])

Palmerston replied to him; and his speech was from all accounts a feeble one. When he sat down Gladstone almost asked him whether there was nothing more to be said.[35] 'It had been decided that he should be followed by Mr Gladstone, who was in full possession of the subject,' Aberdeen told the Queen; 'but . . . it was decided that Lord Palmerston should follow Lord John, in order to prevent the appearance of a division in the Cabinet between the Whig and Peelite members. As Lord Palmerston was to act as Leader of the House the substitution of Mr Gladstone would have appeared strange. But the decision was unfortunate; for by all accounts the speech of Lord Palmerston was singularly unsuccessful.'[36] Palmerston, of course, may have been acting deliberately. There was no response from the Opposition benches, so no other minister was able to rise. Later on, however, in the debate on Roebuck's motion, Sir George Grey expressed his amazement at Lord John's action in strong terms. Such words from such a source must have been a great blow to Lord John, as Aberdeen suggested to the Queen.[37]

Immediately after Lord John's initial statement Roebuck had introduced his motion for a select committee 'to inquire into the condition of our army before Sebastopol, and into the conduct of those departments of the Government whose duty it has been to minister to the wants of the army'. Then an attack of the paralytic affliction from which he suffered overpowered him, and he sat down after a few minutes. This was another disaster for Aberdeen and his supporters. It put Sidney Herbert, who was to reply for the Government, in a very difficult position. He had been ready to defend their administration of the war against charges he could expect to be raised, but now no specific charges had been made. They were present in everyone's minds, for they had been made often enough, and loudly enough, but for him to introduce them into the debate was to frame the counts in the indictment himself. Still, he did his best, in the awkward circumstances.[38]

To begin with he stressed the serious disadvantages from which the British army suffered after forty years of peace. (*The Times* unfairly accused him of shifting the blame on to the soldiers in the Crimea.) He pointed out that Wellington's army had been in much the same situation as Raglan's in the early stages of the Peninsular War. He gave some impressive facts and figures to illustrate all that had been achieved. He refuted some of the untrue criticisms which had been going the rounds concerning deficiencies. He shifted the blame for certain misfortunes, if not on to the soldiers, on to the Almighty, saying, 'But when we talk of commanding the seas, we are apt to be rebuked by Him at whose breath the stormy wind arises, and we are visited by the terrible calamity which befell our transports a short time ago'. Then he pointed out that a select committee would face many difficulties, and that it would be futile to appoint one. After all, the Government knew what was wrong, and was taking steps to remedy the existing faults and deficiencies. He went into lengthy detail about what had already been done to that end, and what was in process of being done.

What Sidney Herbert could not say, however, or acknowledge, even by implication, was in the minds of everyone listening to him in the House, as well as haunting the public outside – that perhaps these misfortunes might not have come to pass at all if different men had been at the helm, either at home or overseas, or both; and that the Government which was now answering for them might not be able to rectify them quickly and forcefully. The tacit question was, above all, whether this Government and this Prime Minister could spur the troops to victory. Brave soldiers had been reduced to a pitiable state under their guidance. Might not the same men merely bring on new, or worse, disasters in the future?[39]

Against this implacable unspoken opposition even the valiant Sidney Herbert could do nothing. His speech made no impression, and it was obvious that had a division been taken on that Friday evening it would have gone against the Government. There was one forlorn hope – the week-end's pause for reflection. Perhaps calm thought about the supposedly unconstitutional nature of the resolution would influence most members against voting for it.

Sir John Young, Peel's Chief Whip, wrote to Gladstone on Sunday, saying he thought the adjournment would prove favourable to the Government. He had sensed a lessening of hostility as the debate continued. 'Some will stay away following Lord John's example,' he wrote, 'but the decision will really lie with the opposition. If they bring their men up – I mean Lord Derby's friends – and vote in a body they will have a majority.'[40]

On Monday 28 the two-day debate resumed. In its course five Liberals and twelve Conservatives spoke in support of the motion. Gladstone admitted to Aberdeen afterwards that he had never had so disagreeable a task as speaking in that House, feeling as he did that he had no sympathy anywhere.[41] He argued that the criticisms had been exaggerated, and all the achievements overlooked, defended Newcastle vigorously, and rejected the whole idea of a select committee. If their opponents wanted to get rid of the Government they had only to refuse to pass its measures. As to the future of the Government, he had given up hope, and did not seek to disguise it.

'Your inquiry will never take place as a real inquiry,' he declared; 'or, if it did, it would lead to nothing but confusion and disturbance, increased disaster, shame at home, weakness abroad; it would convey no consolation to those whom you seek to aid, but it would carry malignant joy to the hearts of the enemies of England, and, for my part, I ever shall rejoice, if this motion is tonight to be carried, that my last words, as a member of the Cabinet of the Earl of Aberdeen, had been words of solemn and earnest protest against a proceeding which has no foundation either in the constitution or in the practice of preceding Parliaments, which is useless and mischievous for the purpose which it appears to contemplate, and which in my judgment is full of danger to the power, dignity and usefulness of the Commons of England.'[42]

Palmerston wound up for the Government. His speech was short, slipshod and as pessimistic as Gladstone's. He, too, had clearly abandoned hope. Or was he again playing possum, remembering that there was an off-chance that he might yet prove to be Aberdeen's successor?

'So, I trust,' he ended, 'whatever may be the fate of the Government, whatever may be the decision of this night's debate, that when the House has settled what government it will have – when the House shall have given its confidence to any set of men who may be hereafter entrusted with the conduct of public affairs, they will give their support to that Government – that they will enable it to carry out the wishes and determination of the nation.'[43]

Roebuck made a brief contribution. Then the House divided. The motion was carried by 305 votes to 148, a majority of more then two to one.[44]

Next morning Gladstone called on Aberdeen before the midday Cabinet. He commented that the enormous majority had 'not only knocked us down but sent us down with such a whack, that one heard one's head thump as it struck the ground'. After some discussion about the debate they left for the last cabinet meeting. It was snowing heavily, as it had been all morning, and Aberdeen asked Gladstone to go with him in his carriage, but he preferred to trudge off through the snow, saying that 'it made him feel rural'.[45]

Aberdeen was determined to part friends with Lord John, and spoke with characteristic moderation and generosity of everyone and everything. He rejected as a matter of deliberate policy the presumption of conscious treachery of which his indignant colleagues were convinced. Now he was the only man to find anything to say in Lord John's defence, labouring to speak only the exact truth and make the fair judgement.

After the completion of the necessary sad formalities the Prime Minister, with his son, caught the two o'clock train for Windsor.

'The grey towers of the castle were relieved by a background of yet greyer and gloomier sky,' Arthur Gordon recorded, 'and the large damp snowflakes fell, slowly, thickly and sullenly round us as we walked up from the station. I parted from my father at the gate with a sigh. I watched him cross the court through the snow, and then passing through the Norman gate, and turning into the cloisters, I ran down the hundred steps and crossed the bridge to Eton.'[46]

Chapter 24

Procul Negotiis Non Beatus

On 30 January 1855 the Queen sent for Lord Derby.[1]

Two days later the Abercorns dined at Argyll House. With beautiful courtesy and self-forgetfulness, Aberdeen exerted himself all evening to lessen Lady Louisa's distress at the behaviour of her half-brother, Lord John, by saying everything he could in extenuation.[2] Harriet's offspring had caused another embarrassment, for Abercorn's brother, Lord Claud Hamilton, had voted in favour of Roebuck's motion.[3] Yet, to Arthur Gordon's indignation, he was to feel no inhibition about turning up to dinner at Argyll House within a week of the division. 'Claud is, I hope, comfortable,' his stepbrother confided to his diary. 'He has *not* got his office, and *has* overthrown His Lordship – His Lordship and the Duke of Newcastle alone.'[4]

By February 2 Derby had abandoned his attempt to form a government, because the Peelites had refused to join him. Next Lansdowne refused, on the grounds that he was seventy-five and crippled with gout.[5] The Queen then sent for Russell, who accepted his commission with alacrity. To his astonishment and mortification not one of his colleagues except Palmerston (to whom he had offered the leadership in the Commons) would serve under him; and his old friend Sir George Grey turned him down expressly because of his disapproval of his recent conduct.[6] Gladstone came from the Speaker's Dinner to Argyll House to describe his interview with Lord John, 'who he said was nervous and frightened to the last degree. His hand shook so that he almost dropped his hat.' Graham too gave him a bad reception, 'taxing him with all his vexatious conduct towards H[is] L[ordship] during the last few years'.[7] As for Argyll, he refused to see him at all. Arthur Gordon wrote caustically that it was rather like being kicked by a donkey for Lord John Russell to meet with a refusal from the Duke of Argyll – 'a refusal too of the most ignominious kind – Lord John wrote and asked him to come to Chesham Place. "I have nothing to say to him," cries the Duke. "I don't want to be talked over by Lady John. I'll write and say I don't want to see him and won't go" – nor did he!'[8] After twenty-four hours of unprecedented humiliation Russell gave up.[9] Never again, except for a few months more than ten years later, on Palmerston's death, was he Prime Minister. He had overthrown Aberdeen without achieving his objective.

On the night of February 3 Arthur Gordon was 'annoyed by ballad singers followed by a small mob taking up their station just outside the yard gates, pointing at the house and singing ditties about "old Aberdeen there", etc.'[10]

On February 4 the Queen at last sent for Palmerston, 'the inevitable', as he dubbed himself.[11] The Peelites Gladstone, Herbert, Graham and Argyll, declined to join his government out of loyalty to Aberdeen. ('I could disregard the prevailing nonsense about Palmerston,' Argyll wrote later, 'but I could not stoop to any, even seeming, acquiescence in the prevalent nonsense about Aberdeen.'[12]) By the next day Aberdeen was, if with painfully ambivalent feelings, persuading them to serve under Palmerston. On February 5 a meeting of the Peelites was arranged at the Admiralty for 10.30 a.m. Arthur persuaded his father not to go. Herbert, they knew, was wavering, but Graham and Gladstone 'were both vehement against union, and Herbert was sure to give way to them. His Lordship intended strongly to urge the union'. At about noon Gladstone sent word that the meeting had resolved that it could not decide without Aberdeen's presence, and that they had despatched a cab with the messenger to bring him down. 'So we bundled into the cab which took us to the Admiralty through the falling snow,' wrote Arthur. 'I . . . wrote a secret note to Gladstone reminding him that in HL's position he could but give one advice, and urging him to stand firm.' Did Aberdeen know of the existence of this note? Apparently not, for the entry goes on: 'HL did not return home till four o'clock. In spite of his urgent entreaties and efforts the proposals for union were unanimously rejected and separate letters written to Lord Palmerston to state their fears that it would be impossible to concur in his foreign policy. HL was annoyed and says reasonably enough that they should not have sent for him if they did not mean to take his advice. He declares too that it is a mistake'.[13]

Clarendon had suggested that the Peelites' objections might be overcome if Aberdeen himself would go into the Cabinet. The Queen and the Prince Consort were enthusiastically in favour, and Palmerston invited Aberdeen to join him.[14] Aberdeen's reaction surprised even his son by its violence and bitterness. Very early on the morning of February 6 he sent for Arthur, who 'found him sitting in the library in his grey flannel dressing-gown and white nightcap, writing'.

'Now there is really no sense in this, and I cannot imagine how you could seriously propose it,' he was saying, among other things, in a long letter to Sidney Herbert. 'You would expose me to gratuitous indignity, to which no one ought to expect me to submit . . . If at any future time my presence should ever be required in a cabinet, I should feel no objection to accept any office, or to enter it without an office. But to be the head of a cabinet today, and to become a subordinate member of the very same cabinet to-morrow would be a degradation to which I could never submit. I tell you plainly that I would rather die than do so; and, indeed, the sense of it would go far to kill me.'[15]

If Herbert told him, he said, that their keeping their present offices, without the slightest sacrifice, but on the contrary with the approval of everyone, depended at all on his taking such a step, 'I can only say that, as friends, I cannot believe it possible that you should be guilty of such mere wanton cruelty, without any rational object'.[16]

Crushing his personal feelings, Aberdeen exhorted his friends to think again, and remain in the Government to carry on the Queen's business. In the end, thanks to his efforts, the Peelites consented to join Palmerston.[17] 'Strange as it may seem,' he wrote that month to Mary, 'I never laboured more than to constitute the government of Lord Palmerston. Indeed, I received a letter of thanks from him, in which he says that he could never have succeeded without my assistance.'[18] And again, 'I have gained credit for generosity and magnanimity; but it is a strange event that I should be active in securing the success of the ministry of Lord Palmerston'.[19]

On the day on which Palmerston's election writ was moved for in the Commons on his acceptance of the premiership, Aberdeen was installed as a Knight of the Garter. From Windsor he wrote to Mary of the Queen's gesture of affection and compassion as he bent to kiss her hand: 'To my surprise, when I took hold of it to lift it to my lips, she squeezed my hand with a strong and significant pressure'.[20] 'In the evening too,' Arthur Gordon wrote in his diary, 'as she left the room she put out her hand as she passed him and laid it upon his. The Queen never shakes hands with a man, so he raised it again to his lips. This was his farewell.'[21] The Queen, indeed, could not do and say enough to express her feelings of loss and chagrin, but wrote, 'The pain has been to a certain extent lessened by the knowledge of *all* he has done to further the formation of this government in so loyal, noble and disinterested a manner, and by *his* friends retaining their posts, which is a *great* security against any possible dangers'.[22] Three days after they had bidden each other so tender – indeed, it seems, so tearful[23] – a farewell, the Queen wrote Aberdeen 'another very pretty letter making him a present of her bust by Marochetti'. Aberdeen accepted it gracefully, for his descendants, writing that 'for himself HM's image already exists in his heart'.[24]

In his letter to Mary written from Windsor Castle Aberdeen had given her a resumé of his overthrow, which, coming from him, and written to her to whom he was always frank, cannot fail to be of interest. 'Indeed, it is not easy to explain it,' he wrote, 'for it has been owing to a strong popular feeling, for which no real foundation exists. The sufferings of our army in the Crimea have been very great, and there has been much mismanagement on the spot. The public here, not very unnaturally, are persuaded that there has also been neglect and official misconduct in the management of the war in this country. Notice of a motion for a Committee of inquiry was given in the House of Commons. Lord John professed to think that it could not be resisted, and consequently resigned. A large number of his friends supported the motion, and the Government was defeated by a great majority. This was equivalent to a vote of censure, and made it necessary for us to resign.'[25]

Gladstone, like the Queen, was emotional, writing to Aberdeen: 'I feel as if a dear friend were dead: and I abhor the manner in which the end has been accomplished. Even the unbounded kindness of your letter cannot overpower the revulsion with which I look back on the past fortnight, and I have used the poor and feeble expedient of trying to shut my eyes upon the fact I loathed'. He ended, 'Your whole demeanour has been a living lesson to me: and I have never gone, with my vulnerable temper and impetuous moods, into your presence, without feeling the strong influence of your calm and settled spirit'.[26]

There was at this time, as there could hardly fail to be, an emotional atmosphere at Argyll House. To Arthur Gordon Palmerston was 'the great imposture which we know the new "vigorous" minister to be, and which must explode', and he was convinced that 'England will soon find out a charlatan'.[27] He gossiped with Mrs Gladstone, though he judged her 'a bore', and she told him, on the day Palmerston became Prime Minister, that she had watched 'the ancient dandy' come upstairs in his white gloves the night before. 'The stairs groaned under him,' she said, 'and he groaned as he mounted them.'[28] How much all this was a reflection of Aberdeen's own feelings we do not know, but one revealing entry in his son's diary seems to show that he was somewhat shaken from his normal calm:

'Sat up at home till HL came home from Lady Palmerston, where he had gone in the spiteful hope that he might meet Drummond who he intended to cut after his speech of yesterday. He says he would have stared straight into his face. By the way, Drummond's speech shows that a friendship of considerably more than forty years standing is no obstacle to a vigorous prosecution of hostilities.'[29]

Of course Arthur's choice of vocabulary may have been unfortunate, and Aberdeen himself would doubtless have used other phraseology.

For a time Aberdeen was still as occupied as when he had been Prime Minister, since Clarendon wrote to him almost daily, and kept him in close touch with cabinet discussions and despatches from abroad. Soon things changed, however.

On February 16 Palmerston was himself faced by Roebuck's motion for the appointment of the Committee of Inquiry. He asked the House to rescind the resolution, saying that he would investigate the conduct of the war himself as Prime Minister.[30] He had to retreat before an adamant House; but then found his Cabinet equally adamant in its opposition to a committee. Even his Whig ministers refused to accept his decision to agree to one, and the Peelites found it intolerably 'mischievous and unconstitutional'.[31] Gladstone in particular found it intolerable, having resigned with Aberdeen on the question of the Committee of Inquiry, simply to accept it under Palmerston, which would make the motion appear a device to get rid of Aberdeen. So on February 21 Gladstone, Herbert and Graham resigned, as a politically suicidal gesture of loyalty to Aberdeen, leaving the young Argyll the sole Peelite survivor in the Cabinet. This time Aberdeen did not put himself out to persuade the departed ministers to return. As for Palmerston, they had served their purpose in enabling him to form his Government, and he watched them go philosophically. Meanwhile Lord John had agreed to take office under Palmerston as Secretary for the Colonies, as well as to act as negotiator for peace in Vienna. By March 8, after a talk with Aberdeen about the peace terms, he had gone off to attend the Vienna Congress.

Now the small things of life took over for Aberdeen. To Mary, on February 7, he had written, 'I do not know how I shall bear being out of office. I have many recourses [sic], and many objects of interest; but after being occupied with great affairs it is not easy to subside to the trend of common occupation'.[32] It was the first time that he, who had always proclaimed the contrary, admitted this, and it was to Mary alone.

Only four months before, at the time of the Alma crisis, Arthur had described his father as being in fine physical form, remarkably so for a man of nearly seventy-one, not minding the cold, and still taking his excessively long walks at Haddo.[33] But on January 6 Aberdeen had been brought home by Sir James Graham after a severe attack of giddiness while talking to his friend. Dr Holland had pronounced it merely stomach trouble, and let him go out to dinner.[34] But he had written to Mary that she might not find him alive on her return.[35] He had had headaches and sore throats for many years. Now, however, he began to suffer from an almost constant succession of various illnesses which were probably the result of stress, conflict and disappointment – not only very bad headaches, sore throats and giddy attacks, but lumbago, indigestion and colds. By February 19 Arthur was writing, 'HL looks ill: I am afraid that the loss of office and absence of work begins [sic] to tell on him as I feared it would'.[36] The abrupt break told on Arthur himself, and he wrote, 'Clarendon sends plenty of infon, but it must be avowed that one looks instinctively for red boxes in the evening and that one cannot help feeling a little blank without them'.[37]

When Aberdeen was well enough for it he dined out – at the Palace, with Argyll, with Newcastle, with Clarendon, and, surprisingly often, with Palmerston.[38] But he had too much leisure all of a sudden. He tried to fill it with walks – in Regent's Park, where he sat in the conservatory and admired the azaleas; on the Hampstead Road, after a drive out; in the garden at Blackheath; to the British Museum, or to the National Gallery.[39] He visited the half-empty Crystal Palace building – and, remembering Mary, was moved to tears by a fine band suddenly playing 'Annie Laurie'.[40] He went to a Drawing Room and to a Palace concert. He sat to photographers.[41]

Aberdeen had always claimed to prefer being a spectator, but now, with the loss of face, he was touchy, sharing Arthur's outrage when Palmerston 'most unscrupulously stole our thunder' by 'appropriating credit for measures resolved on in Cabinet' before he succeeded as Prime Minister.[42] It worried him so much when the Peelite Cardwell told Arthur that 'he had but one fault to find with HL, he was too warlike, and ought to have resisted the Sebastopol expedition', that he sat up that night talking over with his son 'the different moments at which a resistance to the war

308

fever might have been possible'.[43]

To add to Aberdeen's distresses, it transpired that his affairs had been mismanaged while he had been unable to oversee them.[44] There was one debt of £3000 which Arthur found 'impossible to explain or understand'.[45] The loss of his £5000-a-year official salary did not help matters.[46] At home, not surprisingly, Aberdeen's temper was uncertain, even at mealtimes. 'HL,' his son complained on April 14, 'puts on a face of thunder if ever one ventures to ask a reason or an explanation, and though Uncle John and Hamilton [Admiral Baillie-Hamilton] argue, they cannot do so without a quarrel.'[47]

By May 10 Roebuck was moving for leave to examine Aberdeen, and he agreed.[48] He and Arthur watched Graham during his day-long evidence, Arthur approving Sir James's manner of 'rather putting down the committee' and 'meeting impertinent questions with cool answers'.[49] Next day, May 15, Aberdeen himself was examined at noon. 'He was a little confused and uncertain in his answers and had forgotten a good deal, but the Johnny part of the business came out pretty clearly,' his son recorded. His examination, mainly conducted by the relentless Layard, took only an hour. He was the last witness examined.[50]

Aberdeen lived for the return of Mary and Haddo and their eldest son, George – for Haddo, as the Queen had foretold, had made a remarkable recovery during his time abroad.[51] In December 1854 Aberdeen had ended a letter to Mary, 'But now I must tear myself away from you; and oh, how I wish that in doing so I could hold you for a moment to my heart'.[52] He had never ceased to assure her that his chief cause of regret at leaving office was that she and Haddo might no longer be treated as the children of a Prime Minister. (Arthur recorded on the day his father fell from power: 'HL's chief anxiety seems to be on account of the Haddos, who he fears will be ill-treated by the Pasha when the news of his fall reaches Egypt. I tell him they are civilized enough to know that English ex-Grand Viziers do not have their heads cut off'.[53]) He did everything he could to ensure that they enjoyed continued favour with the Pasha, including organizing a letter from Clarendon conveying hints of the Queen's special patronage.[54] Now the time was drawing near for their return. He had avoided visiting the Ranger's House at Blackheath since their departure, writing to Mary, 'It is too full of your presence to be endurable'[55]; but now he had it well cleaned and painted outside in readiness for them. On June 4 he was at Southampton to greet them. By two-thirty next day he and Mary and her son 'Dod' were back at home at

Argyll House. Haddo was on his way to the House of Commons to take his seat.[56]

On June 18 the Sebastopol Report was read, and laid on the table, at the House of Commons. (By coincidence it was followed by a debate on administrative reform, which had been adjourned after one night, during which Palmerston's ministry was severely criticized for doing nothing to ensure promotion by merit in the armed forces.[57]) The Report fell far short of what the critics of Aberdeen's government had hoped for, and of what the chairman of the Committee, Roebuck, and Layard had pressed for. The majority of the committee members had presented a moderate report, abstaining from strong individual criticisms. Indeed, General Peel, one of the committee members, later said in the Commons, 'The mistake of those who had been foremost in demanding inquiry into the sufferings of the Crimean army consists in the attempt to throw the blame upon individuals . . . What, then, were the causes of these hardships? . . . I believe that the chief cause was your commencement of a great war with little means . . . With that army, suffering much from sickness, you undertook a great military operation with no reserve whatever. The Government were not so responsible for that as the country, which raised the universal cry that the war should be carried on with vigour'. In fact, the blame lay with public opinion and the war party in the Cabinet which pandered to it. Whatever criticisms can be made of Aberdeen, no one could maintain that he was the puppet of public opinion.

There was, however, one paragraph in the Report which censured Aberdeen's government for having embarked on the Crimean expedition without adequate information as to the enemy's strength, and declared this to have been the main cause of the army's subsequent calamities. Having had his own draft of the Report itself, and of other violent paragraphs, all but unanimously rejected, Roebuck had succeeded in getting this paragraph inserted, thanks only to his own casting vote as Chairman, after a tie in which he had already voted. Undeterred by this, the implacable maverick tabled a motion 'coinciding with the Resolution of [the] Committee' to 'visit with severe reprehension every Member of [Aberdeen's] Cabinet'. That Cabinet's 'conduct of the Administration', the motion alleged, altering the paragraph with which it was supposed to coincide, was 'the first and chief cause of the calamities which befell the Army'.

The attitude of the Peelites now out of office is illustrated in a letter from Sidney Herbert – that knight *sans peur et sans reproche*, whom even the Roebuck Committee was shamed into commending in the Report – to Gladstone on 9 July 1855. It was written while Roebuck was deferring his motion from week to week, though Herbert was sure he had no intention of withdrawing it, 'his vanity and his acrimony being too strong, I think, for that'.

'I think we ought all to vote on Roebuck's motion. If it be meant as a censure of our policy, we naturally vote in maintenance of its soundness. If a censure on ourselves, we vote on it as we should do on any vote of non-confidence. We must consider how far we are to confine ourselves to a defence of our policy and proceedings, and how far we may criticise and throw dirt on the Committee – their leading questions, their acceptance of gossip and hearsay evidence, their pursuit of any subject which promised to be condemnatory, and their sudden dropping of any which looked as if it would turn out exculpatory if followed up; their bullying, Old-Bailey tone to Dr Menzies and the small fry contrasted with their studious civility to Newcastle, etc.; their opinion given against the policy of an expedition agreed on by France as well as by ourselves; their condemnation of Dr Hall, who is unheard; their non-examination of Mr Wreford,* seriously accused by other witnesses, and who was here in England, but not called; their departure from the evidence in some respects in their Report, and their condemnation implied of everything which, however successfully done, was a departure from routine and office forms.'

When Roebuck eventually moved his motion, on July 17, General Peel, who had voted in the Select Committee against inserting in its Report the paragraph on which the motion was based, moved 'the previous question', the effect of which manœuvre, as Disraeli put it, was 'to ask the House not to proceed with the controversy'. Voting in favour of this evasion, after a two-day debate, were Palmerston and Russell and the other Whig members of Aberdeen's Cabinet who were now again in office – naturally, since if the motion were carried they would individually be censured – supported by their Whig, Liberal and Radical followers.

Those voting for a debate on the substantive motion included some strange bedfellows – Roebuck, wanting his motion, which he moved in a characteristically vindictive speech, debated and carried; Disraeli, considering the ploy of moving the previous question 'ambiguous and unsatisfactory', and probably hoping with other Derbyites that the carrying of a motion censuring Palmerston might

---

* Mr Wreford, the Purveyor-General; Drs Hall and Menzies, doctors at Scutari.

pave the way for a Derbyite government; Aberdeen's former Peelite ministers, with nothing more to lose from the carrying of the motion, and much to gain from the opportunity to defend themselves at last to the House and the country; Aberdeen's erstwhile errant stepson, Lord Claud Hamilton, and, of course, his son, Arthur Gordon.

However, these variously motivated members were voted down by Palmerston's supporters, by 289 votes to 182. Thus did the Report of the Sebastopol Committee seep miserably into the sand.[58]

Within a month of the Haddos' return there was another dramatic arrival, as described by Arthur: 'About seven this morning a cab drove to the door. I felt convinced that it was Alex and so it was. He was an odd figure. Bearded and mustached [sic] – draped in a blue flannel shirt, loose dirty white holland trousers and coat, the seediest of neck handkerchiefs and laced half boots worn into holes and gaping wide open. I went to tell His Lordship of the arrival and also of my speech last night which is very accurately reported in the *Times*. Alex cut off his beard, dressed himself and came down to breakfast looking so like the Alex of old times that I was much vexed to see that His Lordship appeared to forget that he came from the Crimea and hardly even shook hands with him'.[59]

Aberdeen's coolness is a little hard to understand. He had been racked by anxiety for his son's safety after Alma, and since, regarding him as in deadly peril, 'both from disease and the enemy'.[60] Colonel Alexander Gordon had returned to his father's house and the young bride whom he had left pregnant in his care when he set off for war with the Prince Consort's charger. All had not been well between them at the time, for he had gravely displeased Aberdeen by presuming, at the ripe age of 35, to follow Haddo's example, and propose to a young lady without previously consulting his father. Although deeply involved in the events of Derby's three hundred days, which would culminate in his becoming Prime Minister, Aberdeen had found time to express to Admiral Baillie-Hamilton his disapproval of the forthcoming marriage to a daughter of Sir John Herschel, the eminent astronomer and Master of the Mint. 'On the score of prudence,' it was, he wrote, 'about as bad an affair as can well be.'[61] Miss Herschel, he told Haddo, had 'not a farthing'.[62] To the Admiral, again, he grumbled, 'I should certainly have wished for a little birth and a little money; but we must contrive to do without either'.[63] The liberal Aberdeen who was himself the grandson of a lady of what he would have considered very low birth – certainly so as compared with Sir John

Herschel's daughter – was in these matters more squeamish than the arrogant third earl, his grandfather.

Aberdeen was to find Alex's Caroline 'amicable' if 'a little of the *Cockney*',[64] and his displeasure did not prevent his liking the 'certainly very handsome' young woman, or being very kind to her.[65] He was gratified when the Queen offered to become the godmother of her infant daughter, Victoria Alberta Alexandrina, his granddaughter, in the father's absence.[66] Now, however, the battle-scarred hero of 38 himself returned to be treated like a recalcitrant schoolboy. Soon, however, Alex was to be in serious trouble. That October, again at the front, he was appointed Deputy Quarter-Master-General, and shortly afterwards he and other senior officers found themselves personally severely censured by the second report of the two Commissioners sent out by the Government to investigate conditions in the Crimea. The Government set up a Royal Commission to sit at Chelsea, investigate the allegations, and allow the officers a chance to vindicate themselves. This decision gave rise to a vicious attack on Alex in the Commons, led by Roebuck, in the course of which General Sir de Lacy Evans sneered at him as 'the Palace favourite' because he had been one of the Prince Consort's equerries before the war. The attack was repulsed with devastating and humiliating effect by his brother Arthur Gordon and his stepbrother Lord Claud Hamilton. Alex and his brother officers were eventually completely exonerated by the Royal Commission; but it was a time of great additional stress for Aberdeen, especially as there was much hostile publicity to be endured.[67]

That September, at last, Sebastopol was captured, and the following January the four points of Vienna were accepted. The Treaty of Paris was signed in March 1856. The war was over.

So for the thirteen months before peace was sounded by the heralds on 29 April 1856 Aberdeen watched from the sidelines as Palmerston guided the reins he had grown accustomed to hold, assessing the performance of 'the new "vigorous" minister' who was to correct all his errors of omission and commission.

Palmerston, he could see, was certainly busying himself about the details of the war, and the administration of the army. He was particularly interested in the forces still before Sebastopol, only 45,000 out of 250,000 of whom were British. He went about, inspecting cannon, shells and rifles. He showed interest in the soldiers' health, and in the cleanliness of the camp. But, as Aberdeen must have recognized, beyond such activities he failed in exactly the same respects as he himself had been accused of doing. To take Newcastle's place he appointed as Secretary for War Lord Panmure – known as 'the Bison', even slower and less imaginative than Newcastle, and determined to obstruct all change. There was a public outcry, calling for his head; but Palmerston refused to remove him. He would not remove Raglan from the supreme command, either, and when the unhappy old man died in June 1855 he appointed as his successor General Simpson. Simpson was so incompetent that after a few months he was induced to resign. Even then Palmerston did not pick a good man, refusing to fall in with the wishes of the public and the press, who wanted General Sir Colin Campbell, the son of a Scottish crofter, for Commander-in-Chief in the Crimea, and appointing General Codrington instead.

Only a few months after Palmerston succeeded Aberdeen, Ellenborough had given notice that he would move a vote of censure in the Lords, attacking the Government for its failure to remove incompetent administrators in the Crimea. That had forced Palmerston to take action, but he took as little as possible. He merely asked Panmure for a few changes, none of them in the top rank, and demanded the dismissal of the Quarter-Master-General, and his deputy, Colonel Alexander Gordon. That was as far as Palmerston meant to go. A few heads might fall, but the military system as a whole, including the army's aristocratic leadership, was to stand, and that despite persistent attacks by Henry Layard, speaking from personal experience as an observer in the Crimea. On 15 June 1855, Palmerston obstinately opposed Layard's motion categorically censuring the Government for adhering to the system of aristocratic privilege in the army, including the buying and selling of officers' commissions. He was pushed into setting up a committee of inqiury, but nothing came of it. No reforms were introduced while he was in power.

After the fall of Sebastopol Aberdeen constantly and heartily longed for peace, and his joy was unbounded whenever it looked possible. But all too soon he was writing, 'This great event ought to facilitate the work of peace; but the *Times* is determined it shall not; and the *Times* rules the Government'.[68] As time went on it became clear that Palmerston's contribution, far from winning the war speedily, was, probably, as historians now accept, to prolong it. The Queen, embarrassed by the British defeat at the Redan, in humiliating contrast with the French success at the Malakov,[69] which had led to the surrender of Sebastopol, was anxious to carry on the war for another campaign, in the hope of gaining some glory, even with forces so depleted that Europe was being scoured for mercenaries.[70] Palmerston, too, was reluctant to make peace on terms which both the French and Lord John were prepared to accept, and laid down more stringent conditions in 1855. Historians of weight agree, too, that peace might have been made eleven months earlier than it was. In fact, Aberdeen must have reflected, the change from him to Palmerston as Prime Minister apparently made no difference except to prolong the war. The final victory was due to the French army, by then so greatly superior in numbers to the British, though it was they who by their sacrifices and their valour at the beginning had made the end possible.

Aberdeen well knew that the major steps towards reforming the lamentable situation in the Crimea had already been taken when his Government fell. Supplies of huts and clothing which had been lacking had already arrived. The Balaclava railway was being built. Efficient new officers were organizing the unloading of cargoes in the harbour. A Land Transport Corps, and a reinforcement depot in Malta, were being set up. A telegraph cable was being laid across the Black Sea to the Crimea. The hospitals at Scutari had been revolutionized. Then, the separation of the War Office and the Colonial Office had taken place; the Commissariat had become a part of the War Office instead of part of the Treasury; and a new Board to co-ordinate all the independent army departments was being formed. The army was already showing signs of the results of all these improvements in its condition. Palmerston had inherited a machine which was geared for action; and did nothing to improve it.

Yet Aberdeen was capable of saying, and indeed did say, 'After all, we cannot expect justice in this world'.[71] Though it is clear today, and authoritatively accepted, that it was on the whole the army, and not the Government, which was to blame for the disasters in the Crimea, and Aberdeen would have known that to be so, he would have been the last to deny that it was the politicians who were ultimately responsible. Unjust though it might be, Aberdeen had to go, and he knew it. Even if Roebuck's motion had failed, he would almost certainly have been forced to do so. The nation required a war-leader, and, to put it mildly, this sad, wistful and tormented figure was no war-leader – no Chatham, no Churchill, no de Gaulle. Like Addington – and like Asquith and Chamberlain – Aberdeen had to give way to a man whose presence encouraged the nation to renewed self-confidence. It was a function which is all-important when called for, whatever the reality behind the façade, or 'image', of the replacement. Sidney Herbert wrote to Gladstone, 'I cannot name Lord Palmerston in the same breath as

Lord Aberdeen as a statesman, still less as Prime Minister'.[72] However, Palmerston had stepped into Aberdeen's shoes in 1855 not because he was a statesman, but because the nation believed in his fighting spirit, and in his determination to change all that was wrong.

Palmerston fulfilled one necessary rôle, and Aberdeen fulfilled another – that of scapegoat. That a Prime Minister who had taken office a mere fifteen months before war broke out, and in a time of settled peace, should be blamed for all the shortcomings of the military administration in the Crimea, which were directly due to forty-odd years of deliberate neglect and niggardliness since Waterloo, was patently unjust, if not absurd. Aberdeen probably realized that he had been the victim of a capricious House of Commons; of a Cabinet largely composed of overbearing personalities; of inherited difficulties which would have tested any man in his position to breaking-point; of the national war-fever which he had so often in the past succeeded in quelling, but which was whipped up by the war-correspondents and the press; and, above all, of the machinations of Lord John Russell. Before such onslaughts his virtues of tolerance and fair-mindedness, imperturbability in the face of public clamour, loyalty to his colleagues, fearlessness in adhering to unpopular opinions, conciliatoriness, and refusal to give way to prejudice and violent emotion were not only unavailing but positively harmful to him and his cause. Had the Crimean War not occurred his Coalition Government might well have survived to become powerful and popular, standing for free trade and moderate reform. In its path Aberdeen and his government were as much war casualties as any soldier dead in the field.

Chapter 25

The Last Years

With the examination and the Report both behind him,[1] and Mary, Haddo and George, as well as Alex, at home, Aberdeen seemed gradually to regain his equilibrium. By 4 October 1855 Arthur Gordon could write, 'HL is more gentle, more talkative, more thoughtful for others, and more caressing than I have ever known him. We live together nearly all day. I write in his room in the morning, walk with him before and after luncheon, and read in his room in the evening'.[2] Now, with peace and the passage of time, he might be expected to accommodate himself to his changed circumstances.

He was indeed, out of office though he was, exercising a surprisingly powerful influence on others, and notably on the Queen. 'His position with Her Majesty,' E. S. Dallas, leader writer on *The Times*, would write in his obituary notice, which would undoubtedly be vetted by Delane, 'was like that which Lord Melbourne occupied before him – the position rather of an instructor than of a mere adviser; and the private influence which he exerted over the Queen was but the type of an influence which he enjoyed in the legislature. The personal weight thus carried by a man who avoided all public appearance was something extraordinary and almost unaccountable . . . out of office he had more authority than half the Cabinet, and his opinions, if not immediately accepted, were always respected, and in the end generally triumphed.'[3]

Yet Aberdeen was far from happy. Behind his equable and controlled bearing in the face of the world were many stresses. The strains told at home, and Arthur Gordon seems to have borne the brunt of them. Arthur was sensitive, perhaps over-sensitive, and demanding of love. He too had suffered a cruel disappointment at the time of his father's fall. He had hoped for office in Palmerston's government, and looked for the India Board or the Colonies. Graham had 'rather relished'[4] the idea, and been willing to put it to Palmerston, until Admiral Baillie-Hamilton had suggested to him that it would look as if Aberdeen had made a bargain with Palmerston. Still Arthur hoped, but no offer came – and Lord John Russell, of all people, took the Colonies. By December 10, too, he had learned, as he put it, 'that Wells and Lord Londesborough were to eject me from my seat at Beverley'.[5] Now father and son, living in each other's pockets, began to get on each other's nerves. Such fond diary entries of the past as 'HL was very gracious',[6] or 'HL was conversible and kindly',[7] gave way to plaints. By June 1856 Arthur was writing, '72 and 26 were not meant always to live together,'[8] and on New Year's Day 1857 he was plunged in an abyss of gloom, declaring among other things that he wished 'that life itself were over'.

'January 1, 1857. Thursday. Another year! . . . Sympathy is ever closed to me at home, yet to that home I adhere and continue ungrudgingly to perform a service which brings no joy, which earns no thanks – and which is not prized for aught but its convenience. For all the year I have scarce ever left him, seldom for a day, but once for a week, and yet he believes that I neglect him, and am always out of the way, a notion carefully fostered by those who have an interest in fostering it – For many a week have we now lived alone together. [Here three-and-a-half lines are cut out of the diary page, which leads on to mid-sentence] of slowness and awkwardness. – Rarely is the silence broken and sharp are the rebuffs I get for making any endeavour to provoke conversation. In the 28th year of my age I am treated as a baby – watched and suspected. All my visions are passing away and oh when at last I am thrown on the world how will my ignorance hang about my neck like a mill stone! . . . Dressed – dinner – a silent evening – and was glad at 12 to throw myself again on my humble mattress on the floor.'[9]

At this time Aberdeen was facing the unhappy spectacle of the gradual extinction of the Peelites, whom he had led since Peel's death in 1850. By the autumn of 1856 he believed the group to be virtually extinct, and considered that it ought to be merged with the Liberal party. Now with 1857 came more signs of its growing weakness, with men like Gladstone feeling the lack of a leader under whom they might hope for office in the future. Gladstone had already played with the idea of reunion with the Conservatives, but Aberdeen and Graham had strongly, and effectively, opposed it.[10]

From the beginning Aberdeen had thought Palmerston's Government too weak to last, and now he looked for its defeat.[11] When Derby attacked it in the Lords on the China question, Aberdeen moved in with other Peelites to his support, but the motion was defeated. In the Commons, however, the Peelites followed his lead, and on 3 March 1857 combined with Radicals, Conservatives and some Liberals to bring the Government down. Palmerston, however, chose to ask the Queen for a dissolution. When he went to the country he gained a great majority, while Arthur Gordon and most of the other Peelites lost their seats. (Haddo was returned once more unopposed for Aberdeenshire.) Aberdeen had done the Peelites no favour. After the election the party was considered defunct. Sidney Herbert even suggested that the surviving Peelites should no longer sit together in Parliament, to show that they were disbanded, but Aberdeen would have none of it. 'I am not sure that it is sound or wise that friends should separate,' he said.[12]

That May the Indian Mutiny broke out.

Even so early Aberdeen seems to have been giving way to his feelings of guilt about the Crimean War, as is evident from a passage in Argyll's autobiography.

'I think that in the autumn of 1857 Aberdeen's mind was a little under the influence of a most natural irritation on account of Palmerston's sweeping success at the polls. In no other way can I account for a sentence in one of his letters, in which he said that we "deserved to be turned out for India, as much as we did before for the Crimean affair".'

Argyll, who, as he claimed, never allowed his love for Aberdeen and his veneration for his character to silence him on such occasions, replied that he could not understand that sentence, and that he had never admitted, and did not admit, that the Aberdeen Government deserved to be turned out for the Crimean disasters.[13]

By then Aberdeen was paying an annual autumnal visit to Balmoral, where he was welcomed more like a member of the family than like a subject. That October, rather to his consternation, the Queen paid him the honour of a personal visit to Haddo House. 'Neither my house, nor habits, can be at all adapted to receive such a visit,' he wrote wearily, 'but it has been offered in a very kind manner.'[14] Arranging the visit from Haddo House, Clarendon wrote to the Queen, remarking, 'His house is rather ugly, but very comfortable, tho' the grounds are extremely pretty and they have all been laid out by Ld A' – an aspersion on the beautiful classical mansion which reflects contemporary aberrations of taste.[15]

On the day only Aberdeen and his immediate family were at Haddo House to receive the Queen, but three hundred of his tenants on horseback under the 'command' of Col. Alex Gordon accompanied her brougham up the carriage drive – as they had welcomed Mary home after her marriage – and five thousand people gathered within the policies to greet her and the Prince

Consort. Inside, the royal visitors admired Aberdeen's Raphael, his Titians, his Tintoretto, his Vandyke, his Pannini, his Guido, his Kneller, his Lely, his Salvator Rosa, his Landseers, and the Lawrence portraits of his father-in-law Abercorn, Metternich, Melville, Kemble, and himself as a young man, as well as the de la Roche of Guizot and copies of Lawrences of Wellington, Canning, Castlereagh, Bathurst and Peel – and the four thousand volumes in the elegant Adam library. The Queen walked in the grounds, to see the obelisk commemorating the hero of Waterloo, the 300-acre deer-park with its 300 deer, the artificial lake, and Kemble's seat. That night the Queen, who had been in 'great good humour'[16] all day, slept in a room of the utmost simplicity, with window-curtains and bed-hangings, specially made for the visit, of white dimity lined with blue calico.[17]

Not long after the Queen's visit, however, Aberdeen was laid low by a sudden illness, and for two or three days his life was in danger. The Queen wrote to her Uncle Leopold, 'We had a great fright about poor dear Lord Aberdeen, who was taken very ill about 10 days ago with an Attack on his Stomach wh caused violent vomiting of blood, but the danger was quickly past and he is now much better'.[18] He rallied, but did not recover his strength. Early in November he complained to Admiral Baillie-Hamilton, 'I am so miserably weak, that I write with some difficulty . . . I have been obliged to give up the Comte de Paris, whom I expected at this time, as I could not possibly attend to him . . . to have a Prince, when I am unable to appear at breakfast, or dinner, would never do'. And to Jarnac, speaking of his favourite sport, he said, 'My otters are worn out, my hounds are worn out, and I am worn out too'.[19]

Aberdeen clearly faced the possibility that his death was approaching, for it was in that November of 1857 that he wrote in his own hand a codicil to his will, leaving the sole custody and disposal of his papers to his son Arthur, with discretion to publish them subject to certain conditions, which included supervisory powers to Graham and Gladstone.[20] He also put in hand the publication of a volume covering the years of his Foreign Secretaryship from 1841 to 1843, which was to appear the next year from a London publishing house.[21] The doctors sent him back to London in early December – 'contrary to my judgment,' he wrote, 'for I cannot imagine that anything can be better than the season here at this time'.[22] In London he reported himself as writing after breakfast 'with candles in the room, which the doctors wish to persuade me is coming to a better climate'.[23] However, he slowly improved.

His attitude to religion and the after-life, as expressed to a presumptuous enquirer in that year, was stoical rather than fervent. 'The language and conduct of what is usually called the religious world,' he wrote crisply, 'is not encouraging. If it did not excite pity, it could only produce disgust. Every man must bear his own burden, and I presume to judge no man. At my age and in my situation I naturally look at those subjects with increased awe and reverence, and with many failings and shortcomings, I must still endeavour to do my best.'[24]

He had forgiven Russell, as he had said to Hudson Gurney: 'In truth I am not bound to take up the cudgels for him. For he treated me very scurvily. I have, however, forgiven him, which it is now by no means a great effort to do, seeing that age and infirmity remove me from the possibility of any personal competition or interference with him, or anyone else'.[25]

Of course Aberdeen had always protested in this manner, and when the year 1858 dawned things looked hopeful – from the outside, at any rate – for his return to power. After the seccession of the Peelites he had once again become the head of a party which was small but powerful, since it held the balance in Parliament. When, as a result of the Orsini affair, Palmerston was defeated on the Conspiracy to Murder Bill, and Derby became Prime Minister, with Disraeli Chancellor of the Exchequer, his prospects seemed good. If Derby was driven from office the Queen meant to send for him. Aberdeen wrote scathingly of Palmerston to Argyll: 'It is . . . certainly comical that a man who for so many years had upbraided me for unworthy concessions to foreign powers should at last have been overthrown for an act of this kind. It is a lesson to be careful in making such accusations'.[26]

It was really too late, however. Despite his apparently renewed vigour, his regularly attending the Lords, and speaking with unusual frequency there, his strength was declining, and those closest to him believed that, though he might agree to form a cabinet, he would never again consent to lead one.[27] Derby's Government struggled on through another year. To Aberdeen was left such consolations as were provided by the visits of friends to his beloved Haddo, his trusteeship of the British Museum, and similar activities. That year he presented the British Museum with a gold ring inscribed with Anglo-Saxon runes, two swords, a pommel end of a sheath, and an ornamental pin in bronze. His gifts would continue to the year of his death, and after it the Museum would be given his collection of marbles, fragments of Persepolitan sculpture and plaster-casts of bas-reliefs of deities, gathered in 1803 during his happy and successful travels in Greece and Asia Minor as a young man of nineteen.[28] Though he may not himself have realized it, he had made his last speech in the Lords during the debate on the Scotch Universities Bill on 13 July 1858.[29]

That autumn and winter Aberdeen corresponded closely, frequently and confidentially with Argyll on the question of a new Reform Bill, and what Disraeli might do about it.[30] Despite Aberdeen's fears to the contrary, the Reform Bill was introduced on the last day of February 1859, by Disraeli. In March it was defeated, and after a general election, and Granville's failure to form a government, Palmerston became Prime Minister once again, with Lord John Russell as his Foreign Secretary. Haddo was again elected unopposed. France and Sardinia were at war with Austria; but he had not his father's interest in foreign affairs. In July the shy man braved the House to move an amendment to a motion for discontinuing the government grant of £100 to schools of art where nude models were employed.

'He had on one occasion been accidentally a witness of the mode of study pursued in the Government schools,' reported *The Times* of July 26, 'and he felt bound to say that he had never witnessed a more painful or scandalous exhibition. He brought forward the subject with feelings of sincere disgust . . . As far as art was concerned, he believed it was the opinion of the best writers on the subject that the introduction of the voluptuous school had occasioned the decay of art and the decline of public taste in ancient Greece; and that of the age of Phidias and Pericles not a single example of an undraped female figure was known to exist. It was quite unnecessary to give public aid to a mode of study which was evidently so attractive and remunerative as that to which he referred.'[31]

By early 1859 Aberdeen's health had markedly improved, and he seemed to be very nearly as strong as before his 1857 attack; but in August, at Haddo, an apparently trivial illness, which had confined him to his room for only a day or so, reduced him to his former state of weakness. By the winter he was back in London; but from then on it was a losing battle.

That year too saw the effective end of the Peelite party. The two were going out together.

In May 1860 Aberdeen had to bid farewell to his eldest son, who had had a relapse, and was setting off once again with Mary to seek a second miraculous cure in Egypt. Though weak and ill, Haddo had returned to the attack in his battle against nude models in the House of Commons. Lord Palmerston had opposed his motion, and it was heavily lost. Now he departed, and, ill as he was, journeyed up the Nile evangelizing. His father, at Haddo that summer, could not walk more than a few steps without help, or drive himself in his pony carriage. The man so strong in his youth that he had planted trees for nine hours a day, and taken seven-hour-long walks, struggled against the inevitable, but he was obviously dying. In response to news of his state, Mary sailed back to see him – a great undertaking for her, to leave a sick husband unattended across the seas, and make the double journey alone. 'Dearest Mary,' he had once written, 'living or dying, the recollection of you will always be deeply fixed in my heart.'[32] It could only be a brief visit, and by October 11 Mary was back in Egypt with Haddo. Delane, too, came to see his old friend, and bid him farewell. Late in October he was very ill, so much so that Lord John Russell, then Foreign Secretary, added to a letter of his to the Queen, 'Lord Aberdeen, Sir Henry Holland says, is speechless and is dying'. His only comment was a perfunctory one: 'This is a sad event'.[33]

However, it was not until December 14 that, at last, His Lordship died at Argyll House, his hands held by his son Arthur and his grandson George – Mary's 'Dod'. His stepsons, Abercorn and Lord Claud Hamilton, and his son, Rev. the Hon. Douglas, and his brother Admiral John, stood by. 'Life had become to him a weary, weary burden,' Arthur wrote to Mary, 'and the end was a painless release.'[34] Alex informed the Queen at once, so that she should have the news before the morning papers announced it.[35] Abercorn, too – who, it seems, had never left the fold despite the offence he had given, or ceased to love his stepfather – wrote within hours of his death to give the Queen details of 'the last days of our beloved Father'. Since the sixth he had been 'more or less unconscious,' he said, 'though on Sunday evening consciousness entirely returned for a time, and though unable to speak, he was tenderly affectionate. He did not suffer, which is a great comfort, and his death, which took place at a quarter to two this morning, was as calm and peaceable as that of a child falling asleep, and he is now in peace in that world where we are told "the spirits of just men are made perfect" '.[36]

All Aberdeen's papers, dating from a very early period, were found, as Alex reported on Christmas Day to his absent brother, the new Earl, 'so well arranged and put away, according to dates and subjects, that there can be little difficulty in finding what is wanted. On some packets are instructions to burn them without their being read'.[37] The man of many reticences took some secrets to the grave.

There was one minor secret to be revealed. An old black trunk had lain in His Lordship's bedroom for the past ten or twelve years. No one, except Alex, knew what was in it – not even Arthur. Aberdeen had kept jewellery and trinkets in it, and had occasionally gone to it to choose a present for someone – for Mary, among others. There were still several pieces in it when he died, and more jewellery and trinkets in drawers in different parts of the room. They were sealed up, and the black trunk was deposited at Coutts's Bank on Boxing Day in the new Earl's name. The devastated Arthur asked his eldest brother as a favour if he might be allowed to wear the only ring that was removed from his father's fingers.[38] (Forgotten were the times when he had found his ageing father intolerable. Now his grief was such that his brothers feared for him, accepting it that he had 'lost his all' in one who had been both father and mother to him since his infancy.[39]) The other rings on Aberdeen's fingers, his Catherine's, would be buried with him.

Aberdeen's death would leave a gap in the lives of others beside Arthur which would never be filled. They felt, as Croker had done, 'Of all the men I have known in my life, his regard for truth was the most strict and scrupulous'.[40] Thirty-four years after his death Gladstone would say, 'He is the man in public life of all others whom I have *loved*. I say emphatically *loved*. I have *loved* others, but never like him'.[41] Like Peel and Wellington in their lives, and like Argyll, they felt for him admiration and affection combined such as is seldom accorded to other men, and almost never by politician to politician.

His Lordship was gone. It was the Right Hon. Sir George Hamilton Gordon, KG, KT, PC, MA, FRS, FHS, FSA, fourth Earl of Aberdeen, Viscount Formartine, Lord Haddo, Methlic, Tarves and Kellie, in the peerage of Scotland, Viscount Gordon of Aberdeen, in the county of Aberdeen, in the peerage of the United Kingdom, and a baronet of Nova Scotia, Chancellor of King's College, Aberdeen, Lord-Lieutenant and Sheriff-Principal of Aberdeenshire, and Ranger of Greenwich Park, who must be buried; to whose funeral the Queen sent one of her state coaches, drawn by six horses, with postillions and grooms in dress liveries; and whose pall was borne by the Duke of Newcastle, the Earl of Clarendon, Sir James Graham, Gladstone, Cardwell, and the Earl of Dalkeith, representing his sick father in Scotland, the Duke of Buccleuch.[42] On a 'calm cold, hard, frosty day, with the ivy on the ruined walls of the old church powdered with snow',[43] he was laid to rest at

Stanmore, in the vault of Bentley Priory, his coffin resting on that of his daughter Frances, whose funeral he had not been able to bring himself to attend, and between those of his first wife Catherine and his second wife Harriet. Twenty-seven years before, when Harriet had died, he had given his instructions. But now Bentley Priory, seat of old Abercorn, was no longer in the family. When the Earl's coffin was deposited the vault was full; and it was then closed.[44] Of the orphaned family of five brothers and a sister, to whom he had been a father, only Admiral John, the youngest and most difficult, remained to bid him farewell.

Bishop Wilberforce had read the service. Afterwards he wrote to Arthur: 'I am most thankful I was with you at Stanmore, not only because I should ever after have so lamented my absence, but also because I would not for anything have missed that last and most impressive sight, which now is engraven in my memory for ever: Graham's tall kingly figure, with the snow falling on his head and his full countenance; Gladstone with his face *speaking*; Newcastle, you; and the light *within* that vault, and all that belonged to its opening and its closing'.[45]

Aberdeen, we know, always blamed himself, too harshly some thought, for the war. In January 1855 he had written to Mary, 'My conscience has never been quite at ease, in consequence of not having done enough to prevent it. Do you remember the Sunday at Blackheath, when I heard that the Emperor had accepted the Vienna Note, and believed that all was settled? That was a happy day; and perhaps the only one I have passed since I have been in office'.[46]

Now, after his death, it became tragically evident that his sense of guilt had gone far deeper than anyone had guessed. He who had built many new churches, manses and schools as part of his duty to his people, had rebuilt the manse of Methlic on a new site. The parish church remained, falling into ruin, but he had always refused to rebuild it, saying, 'I leave that for George,' to the mystification of all. Now his family found, written by him on various scraps of paper at different times, the quotation: 'And David said to Solomon, My son, as for me, it was in my mind to build an house unto the name of the Lord my God: but the word of the Lord came to me, saying Thou hast shed blood abundantly, and hast made great wars: Thou shalt not build an house unto my name, because thou hast shed much blood upon the earth in my sight (1 Chronicles, XXII, 7, 8)'.[47]

After Aberdeen's death a group of his friends commissioned Matthew Noble to produce a marble bust of him, and placed it in Westminster Abbey. The inscription is simple: 'George Gordon, fourth Earl of Aberdeen, KG, KT. Born January 28, 1784. Died December 14, 1860. Ambassador, Secretary of State, Prime Minister'. After it they who knew him best chose to add the one word ΔΙΚΑΙΟΤΑΤΟΣ – Most Just. That tribute brings to mind Plutarch's story of the Athenian who voted against Aristides, and who, when asked whether Aristides had ever done him any harm, replied, 'None at all; neither know I the man; but I am tired of hearing him everywhere called The Just'.[48]

Perhaps it is time that we forgave Aberdeen for his virtues, pardoned him for weaknesses which he would have considered strengths, and did full justice to one who was unjust to only one person in his life – himself.

The End

APPENDIX

Scottish Church Affairs

As the most prominent, powerful and respected Scotsman in public life and, as he put it, 'a sort of eldest son'[1] of the Established Church of Scotland, Lord Aberdeen was appealed to by its leaders to introduce a Bill in Parliament calculated to preclude a recurrence of a dispute which in the 1830s was already threatening to lead to the total disruption of that church.

The right of patrons, for the most part the large landowners, to appoint ministers to livings had been established in Scotland since the Reformation. It was enshrined in modified form in an Act of the United Kingdom Parliament passed shortly after the Union. On one side in the dispute that had arisen were those who recognized that the ultimate jurisdiction over such appointments was therefore vested in the civil courts. On the other were those who claimed exclusive jurisdiction for the General Assembly of the Church of Scotland. The latter prevailed upon the Assembly of 1834 to pass a Veto Act. This purported to prevent the 'intrusion' of a patron's appointee upon a congregation if a majority of it objected to him.

In the following year this Veto Act was applied in the parish of Auchterarder. However, the patron and appointee had the appointment upheld by the Court of Session and eventually by the House of Lords, which also declared the Veto Act *ultra vires* the Assembly.

Here, then, in Scotland was conflict between Church and State. Such conflict had long been settled in favour of the state in England and was by now beyond the comprehension of politicians south of the Border. In Scotland, however, it evoked such passion that the 'intrusionists', who recognized the supremacy of the civil law, were to be anathematized by the 'non-intrusionists' as denying 'the crowned Rights of Christ the Redeemer'. Further, 'intrusion', originally applied to the presentation of ministers by patrons, came to take on the extended meaning of the intrusion of the secular world into the spiritual domain through the instrument of the civil law.

Into this arena Aberdeen found it his painful and thankless duty to enter. He undertook to introduce in the Lords a Bill calculated to obviate the possibility of objectionable 'intrusion', without conceding the principle of the supremacy of the State over the Church.

At this stage there was no idea of abolishing patronage – not, it seems, that Aberdeen himself would have been particularly averse to doing so. Nor was patronage to be openly attacked by leaders of the Church until it had moved much farther along the road to disruption. However, to one looking back now it seems possible that it was really resentment against patronage that, at the deepest level, precipitated the Disruption. Patronage had survived from times when rule by an aristocratic landowning caste had been acceptable throughout Europe because the mighty and powerful, even when deficient in the gentler virtues, were felt to be the people's guarantors against lawless chaos such as tended to prevail everywhere after the collapse of the Roman Empire. The mighty were felt to be the protectors of those who huddled outside the castle wall. Insensibly, as law and order came to be taken for granted over the centuries, the profound unspoken universal craving for protection had given way to an equally profound resentment – articulated only by the radical element ever present in society – against being obliged to, as the phrase in common currency today has it, 'touch the forelock'. Latterly, popular reaction against the patronage system came to be held out as having been from the beginning the overt cause of the dispute leading to the Disruption. The prevalence of this myth – which may have revealed, as myths do, an inner truth obscured at the time by conventional forms – is illustrated in E. S. Dallas's obituary of Aberdeen in *The Times* two decades after the Disruption.[2] Dallas takes it for granted that the Disruption sprang directly and expressly from opposition in the Church to the system of patronage.

While engaged on framing his Bill Aberdeen, who had been a member of the General Assembly from 1818 to 1828, gained personal insight into the temper that had since developed in his Church, though he, like all the simpler souls concerned, was clearly oblivious of any submerged current of anti-patronage feeling.

He was the patron of the living of his own parish of Methlic. When the minister died in 1839 he presented the Reverend James Whyte, about whom he had made stringent enquiries. Rumours were circulated that Whyte had a skeleton in his cupboard, and a majority of the congregation therefore objected to him. In a sixteen-hour-long enquiry in the little kirk the rumour was proved to be completely false, and the objectors and their agent professed themselves satisfied. Still, at the instigation of 'a radical attorney in Aberdeen',[3] the congregation later persisted in their objection to their patron's 'intrusion' upon them of his appointee. The mere existence of a rumour of immorality, however false, rendered him unacceptable.

Aberdeen would not have presented Mr Whyte, he told the congregation (whose 'stupidity and obstinacy' he described as 'alarming')[4] had he known of the rumour, even had he also known it to be false. But, having presented him in good faith, for him to withdraw the presentation because of an allegation disproved beyond question would be unjust. It would blight an innocent man's whole career. Now 'no power on earth', Aberdeen said, would 'induce me to abandon him'.[5] His 'allocution produced a great effect' on the congregation, he told his adviser, the Dean of Faculty in the Scottish Law Courts, and added, 'I fairly confess that I never addressed the House of Lords with a tenth part of the interest which I felt on that occasion. Had I failed, considering the footing on which I have always stood with these people, I really should not have known what to do or what to have left'.[6] However, he was able to inform the Dean, he had won the day and the objectors had 'written to their radical agent in Aberdeen, and . . . given as the reason for retracting their mandate the feelings which they profess to entertain for myself'.[7] Nearly a week later he wrote again in characteristically candid and self-immolatory vein, evidently still moved by the experience, 'Certainly it required a strong stimulus for me to volunteer an oration in a church! . . . but I fear my self-love was . . . deeply wounded at the notion that their conduct exhibited a deficiency of deference towards myself . . . If the truth must be told, I very much fear that I was secretly even more interested for myself than for Mr Whyte'.[8]

Had Aberdeen failed to persuade the Methlic congregation, he and Mr Whyte would have been in the same position as the Auchterarder patron and presentee, with no recourse but to enforce their statutory rights in the civil courts. Such a situation was later to arise elsewhere. The Court in that case merely ordered the Presbytery of Strathbogie to carry out its statutory duty to enquire whether the presentee lawfully presented to them was or was not qualified for ordination, not presuming to require the Assembly to ordain him. The Assembly treated this as secular 'intrusion' into things spiritual, and forbade the Presbytery to obey the Court. The majority of the Presbytery resolved to obey. They examined the presentee and reported him qualified. For this the Assembly suspended them from all clerical functions.

Aberdeen's experience of the 'alarming stupidity and obstinacy' of which a congregation could be capable caused him, in framing his Bill, to give the power of rejecting an unacceptable 'intruded' presentee to the Presbytery. This body was one tier above the Kirk Session of the congregation and, consisting of all the ministers of parishes in an area and one lay member for each parish, might be presumed to be a safer tribunal.

The draft Bill met with the guarded approval of the General Assembly's Anti-Intrusion committee. It provided for the recognition of a Presbyterial veto instead of the popular veto which had been imposed by the *ultra vires* Veto Act passed by the Assembly. Before it was introduced certain amendments were suggested by anti-intrusion spokesmen. The most important one was to make it mandatory rather than discretionary for the Presbytery to reject a presentee if objected to by the congregation, even if no reasons for the objection were given to them. Aberdeen was persuaded to be inflexible in refusing amendments, partly so as to be able to claim independence from the Assembly, and partly in order to ensure that the Bill did not covertly enact a popular right of veto.

It was the Dean of Faculty, later Lord Justice Clerk, Aberdeen's adviser and confidant, with whom he had been corresponding over his Methlic presentation, who influenced him into adopting this attitude. (The Dean has been made the scapegoat of the anti-intrusionists. Lady Frances Balfour's treatment of Scottish Church affairs in her life of Aberdeen is a sustained attack on him as an overbearing and legalistic bigot who virtually caused the Disruption. Lady Frances was the daughter of the Duke of Argyll, who became Aberdeen's devoted admirer and owed a successful political career to the start Aberdeen had given him by choosing him as a young man of thirty to enter his Coalition Cabinet, when places were so hard-fought-for. She herself was requested by Aberdeen's family to write his life, and it is dutifully eulogistic of her father's benefactor. She may well have felt inhibited from venting on Aberdeen personally the passionate anti-intrusionist feelings she had imbibed from her father, and, even more strongly, from her grandfather, who was deeply involved in this emotive issue.)

Aberdeen has been criticized by his son on the ground that if only he had accepted the amendments the Assembly's support for the Bill would have been ensured. But on the day Aberdeen was introducing the Bill in the Lords, in high hopes of getting it on the Statute Books, the Church erupted against it in the Synod of Lothian and Tweeddale. Violent opposition to it from the anti-intrusionists was further manifested at the subsequent meeting of the Assembly. Accounts of these inflamed debates induce the conviction that any attempt to prevent the Disruption of the Church of Scotland by Aberdeen or any human agency, by any means whatever, was doomed from the start.

Political leaders understandably proclaim their ability to steer the ship of society by the rudder of rationality. In reality, however, they can do so only to a limited extent and in fair weather. In gales of popular passion beyond a certain force the ship no longer answers to the helm. For historians to say she would have done so if only the helmsman had twiddled the wheel a spoke or two this way or that is not even the wisdom of hindsight. It is fantasy.

Peel was eager to move the second reading of the Bill in the Commons, but with the Assembly against it, and with no support from the Whig government – Melbourne was bored and impatient with the whole question, and Russell feared the radicals in the Commons – Aberdeen abandoned it after its committee stage in the Lords.

Next, the extreme anti-intrusionists promoted a Bill which the Duke of Argyll tried to introduce in the Lords, with total lack of success. It provided for the abolition of patronage. This – although such abolition had not previously been mooted by the Assembly, and was never pressed upon Aberdeen – perhaps indicates the true nature of the current of feeling that was sweeping the Church inexorably towards the Disruption.

Aberdeen's Bill was resuscitated on the Tory Government's advent to office, under the aegis of Sir Robert Sinclair, and was actually accepted by the Assembly's non-intervention committee. But at the last moment the Committee withdrew its support. By an ill chance a Government spokesman had wrongly and inadvertently given the impression in a public speech that the Government was really intending to go much farther, and in effect to legitimize the Assembly's *ultra vires* Veto Bill. Not unnaturally the Assembly spurned the proffered cutlet, believing that the whole sheep was soon to be served up.

The debâcle, which it may well seem was fated from the beginning, followed. In May 1842 the General Assembly, going to the root of the trouble, passed its famous 'Claim of Right' resolution to the effect that all Acts of Parliament passed without the consent of the Church of Scotland, and sentences of the Courts 'in contravention of the . . . government discipline' of that Church (that is, purporting to deal with matters declared by the General Assembly to be within its sole jurisdiction as an Ecclesiastical Court) 'are and shall be null and void'.[9] In November an *ad hoc* convention of non-intrusionists pledged all who had voted for that resolution to secede from the Church if the 'Claim of Right' was rejected by the Government. The claim was rejected by both parties, being as Arthur Gordon said in his life of his father, 'one which no Civil Government or Legislature could admit on the part of an Established Church, or indeed any other'.[10]

After the convocation Aberdeen thought the time had come for legislation which would enable as large a proportion of the Assembly as possible to remain in the Established Church. He soon realized that, as he put it, he 'was the only person who desired it . . . chiefly with a wish to save these poor fellows if possible'.[11]

The schism – the secession at the fateful Assembly of May 1843, the great Disruption of the Church of Scotland – duly took place. It was mighty. There were very few 'poor fellows' left to save. As the rump of the Assembly, they resolved that the illegal Veto Act had been *ab initio* null and void. Then, to meet the continuing need for a provision against the intrusion, as Ministers, of unfit persons into the parishes of what was left of the Church of Scotland, Aberdeen reintroduced his original Bill. (The fact that even this Bill was strenuously objected to by the English Law Lords as giving too much power to the Church demonstrates how little chance there would have been of passing the sort of extreme Bill the old Assembly had desired.) It became law in August 1843, and remained in force until the abolition of patronage in the Established Church in Scotland by Lord Derby's Government in 1874.

References

Abbreviations used are as follows:

Ab.Corr.:	Aberdeen Correspondence.
Add.MSS.:	Manuscripts at the British Museum.
Am.Hist.R.:	The American Historical Review.
B. & E.:	Benson & Esher, *The Letters of Queen Victoria*, 1837–1861.
Camb.Hist.J.:	The Cambridge Historical Journal.
DNB:	The Dictionary of National Biography.
EHR:	English Historical Review.
HH:	Haddo House papers, followed by box number.
Hansard:	Hansard Parliamentary Debates (unless otherwise stated refers to 3rd series).
MS. Clar.:	Clarendon Papers, Bodleian Library.
PP:	Parliamentary Papers.
PRO:	Public Record Office.
RA:	Royal Archives.
SP:	State Papers.

CHAPTER 1 – SCION OF THE GORDONS

The main sources drawn on for the first two chapters are *Lord Aberdeen*, by Sir Arthur Gordon (bound proof); *The Earl of Aberdeen*, by Sir Arthur Gordon; *Fyvie Castle, Its Lairds and Their Times*, by A. W. M. Stirling; *House of Gordon*, by Dr J. M. Bulloch, Vol. I; *A Souvenir of Haddo House*, by Cosmo Gordon; and, above all, the Muniment Room at Haddo House, Aberdeenshire.

(1) *The Times*, 1 March 1875.
(2) Butterfield, *The Whig Interpretation of History, passim.*
(3) Cecil, *British Foreign Secretaries*, p. 91.
(4) Butterfield, *op cit*, p. 125.
(5) HH 1/27, 'Draft of a will in the third Earl's own hand'; University of Aberdeen Library MS 1164, Gordon of Cairnfield MS, *The Book of the Gordons*, X, 17–18, and MS 1061 *Sederunt Book of Trust of George Gordon, 3rd Earl of Aberdeen.*
(6) Croker Papers, II, p. 102, Duke of Wellington to Croker, 24 January 1831.
(7) Bulloch, *House of Gordon*, II, p. 68.
(8) HH 1/27, Draft of Third Earl's will.
(9) Gordon, *Aberdeen*, pp. 8–9.
(10) Meryon, *Lady Hester Stanhope*, I, pp. 4, 175; II, pp. 16, 17–18, 19; III, pp. 352–3; Gordon, *Aberdeen* (proofs), Chap. II, p. 7.
(11) Gordon, *Aberdeen* (proofs), Chap. II, p. 17.

(12) *The Times*, 15 December 1860, obituary; DNB (1890).
(13) Gordon, *Aberdeen*, p. 9.

CHAPTER 2 – 'THE TRAVELLED THANE' AT HOME

(1) Evans, *A History of the Society of Antiquaries*, p. 240.
(2) Broughton, *Recollections*, I, p. 23.
(3) Meryon, *Lady Hester Stanhope*, I, p. 188; II, pp. 69–70; III, pp. 342–4, and *passim*.
(4) Croker Papers, II, pp. 300–2, Aberdeen to Croker, 30 October 1836; Gordon, *Aberdeen*, p. 13.
(5) Gordon, *Aberdeen*, p. 13; Walford, *Greater London*, pp. 299f.
(6) Add.MSS. 43347, fos. 40 and 53–53b.
(7) Gordon, *Aberdeen* (proofs), Chap. II, pp. 14, 17.
(8) Balfour, *Life*, I, p. 38, Melville to Aberdeen, July 1805.
(9) *Private Correspondence of Lord Granville*, II, p. 94, Lady Bessborough to George Leveson-Gower, 25 July 1805.
(10) Bessborough, *Georgiana*, p. 273.
(11) Balfour, *Life*, I, p. 39, *Note*; DNB (1890).
(12) Gordon, *Aberdeen*, pp. 16–17, Diary, 24 January 1806.
(13) Balfour, *Life*, I, p. 45, Diary, 28 January 1806.
(14) *ibid*, Lady Melville to Aberdeen, 29 January 1806.
(15) Erskine May, *Parliamentary Practice* (6th ed.), ed. Fellowes and Cocks, pp. 10–11; Union with Scotland Act, 1806, arts. XXII and XXIII; *Acts of Parliament of Scotland*, 1707, C.8; *Union with Ireland Act*, 1800, art. 4.
(16) Balfour, *Life*, I, p. 49, Aberdeen's Journal, 15 February 1806.
(17) Add.MSS. 43225, fos. 12–13, Abercorn to Aberdeen, 25 November 1806.
(18) *ibid* (undated).
(19) *Journal of Elizabeth, Lady Holland*, II, p. 191, 12 December 1806.
(20) *Journals of the House of Lords*, XLVI.6.
(21) Hansard, IX, 352–4.
(22) HH 1/29, Lady Haddo to Lord Abercorn, 27 September 1806.
(23) HH 1/29, Abercorn to Aberdeen, 14 August 1806.
(24) Balfour, *Life*, I, p. 50, Aberdeen's Journal.
(25) Derry, *Castlereagh*, pp. 109–10.
(26) Greville, *Diary*, II, p. 414.
(27) Balfour, *Life*, I, p. 62, Aberdeen to the Rev. G. Whittington, no date, but from internal evidence probably 26 March 1807.
(28) *ibid*, I, p. 64, Canning to Aberdeen, 27 April 1807.
(29) Dixon, *Canning*, p. 108 [Canning Papers, Leeds, Box 31].
(30) Balfour, *Life*, I, p. 65.

CHAPTER 3 – '*VERISSIMA, DULCISSIMA IMAGO*'

(1) Hansard (2nd ser.), XVIII, 1148–57.
(2) HH 1/35, Aberdeen to Major the Hon. A. Gordon, 8 June 1811 (Copy), Hansard (2nd ser.), XX, 672–3.
(3) HH 1/35, 14 July 1811.

(4)   *ibid*, 30 April 1811.
(5)   *ibid*, 9 April 1811; and see 13 February, 13 March 1811.
(6)   *ibid*, 4 June 1811; 30 April 1811.
(7)   *ibid*, 23 August 1810; 13 February, 13 March 1811; 25 August 1811.
(8)   *ibid*, 4 February 1812.
(9)   *ibid*, 10 October 1811; 23 August 1810; 13 March, 4, 9 April 1811.
(10) HH 1/35, Major Gordon to Aberdeen, 31 July, 13 August 1809.
(11) *ibid*, from Quinta, 30 May 1811.
(12) HH 1/35, Aberdeen to Major Gordon, 10 October 1811.
(13) HH 1/35, Major Gordon to Aberdeen, 27 November 1811.
(14) *ibid*, 26 January 1811.
(15) HH 1/35, Aberdeen to Major Gordon, 7 November, 1 December 1810,
      1 January, 13 February, 13 March, 4, 30 April, 4 June, and *passim* on
      King's madness; 25 July, 1 December 1810, 13 February, 13 March,
      4 April, 10, 21 October, 25 November 1811, and *passim* on Peninsular
      Campaign; 25 November 1811, 7 January 1812, and *passim* on Prince
      of Wales.
(16) *ibid*, 13 February 1811; Hansard (2nd ser.), XVIII, 1148–54.
(17) *ibid*, 9 April 1811.
(18) *ibid*, 8 June 1811.
(19) *ibid*, 4 February 1812; and see 8 June 1811; Gash, *Mr Secretary Peel*,
      p. 138f.
(20) Gordon, *Aberdeen*, p. 314 (see also p. 103).
(21) Creevey Papers, I, p. 173, Creevey to Mrs Creevey, 19 October 1812.
(22) HH 1/35, Aberdeen to Major A. Gordon, 31 December 1811.
(23) *ibid*, 7 January 1812.
(24) *ibid*, 25 July, 23 August, 1 December 1810; 13 February, 4 June,
      26 August 1811.
(25) *ibid*, 1 December 1810.
(26) *ibid*, 1 January 1811.
(27) *ibid*, 30 April 1811.
(28) *ibid*, 26 August, 10 October 1811.
(29) *ibid*, 10 October 1811.
(30) *ibid*, 25 November 1811.
(31) *ibid*, 31 December 1811.
(32) *ibid*, 4 February 1812.
(33) Gordon, *Aberdeen*, p. 18.
(34) Gordon, *Aberdeen* (proofs), Chap. II, p. 23.
(35) Gordon, *Aberdeen*, pp. 18–19.
(36) HH 1/35, Aberdeen to Major A. Gordon, 8 August 1812.
(37) *ibid*, 8 August 1812.
(38) *ibid*, 7 December 1812.
(39) *Lady Bessborough and Her Family Circle*, p. 230.
(40) HH 1/35, Aberdeen to Major A. Gordon, 14 December 1812.
(41) *ibid*, 8 October, 7 December 1812; 9 February 1813.
(42) Add.MSS. 43225, f. 26, Aberdeen to Abercorn, 16 July 1813; Gordon,
      Aberdeen (proofs), Chap. III, p. 2.
(43) *ibid*, f. 25, 3 May 1813.
(44) Gordon, *Aberdeen* (proofs), Chap. V, p. 1.
(45) Gordon, *Aberdeen*, p. 313.
(46) *ibid*, p. 319.
(47) HH 1/28, Aberdeen to Lady Maria Hamilton, 29 July 1813.

(48) Ilchester, *Journal of Elizabeth Lady Holland*, I, p. 97.
(49) Gordon, *Aberdeen* (proofs), Chap. V, p. 1.
(50) Webster, *Foreign Policy of Castlereagh*, p. 151.
(51) Add.MSS. 43225, f. 25, Aberdeen to Abercorn, 16 July 1813.
(52) HH 1/28, Aberdeen to Lady Maria Hamilton, 29 July 1813.
(53) *ibid.*

CHAPTER 4 – 'THE DIN OF WAR'

(1) Webster, *Foreign Policy of Castlereagh*, p. 151.
(2) Add.MSS. 43225, fos. 25, 26, Aberdeen to Abercorn, 3 May, 16 July 1813.
(3) Gordon, *Aberdeen* (proofs), Chap. III, pp. 2–3.
(4) Webster, *British Diplomacy 1813–15* (Select Documents Dealing with the Reconstruction of Europe), pp. 94–7.
(5) HH 1/28, Aberdeen to Lady Maria Hamilton, 29 July 1813.
(6) Balfour, *Life*, I, p. 72.
(7) *ibid*, p. 73.
(8) Metternich, *Mémoires*, Napier translation, Vol. I, p. 192; Nicolson, *Congress of Vienna*, p. 43.
(9) Webster, *British Diplomacy*, pp. 76–9, Stewart to Castlereagh, 12, 20 August 1813; Jackson to Stewart, 12 August 1813; Webster, *Foreign Policy of Castlereagh*, p. 149.
(10) Add.MSS. 43225, fos. 98–9, Aberdeen to Lady Maria Hamilton, Ystadt, 19 August 1813.
(11) *ibid*, fos. 100–1, Breslau, 27 August 1813.
(12) *ibid.*
(13) *ibid.*
(14) *ibid*, Prague, 1 September 1813.
(15) *ibid.*
(16) *ibid*, Teplitz, 4 September 1813.
(17) HH 1/32, Aberdeen to Lady Jane Gordon, 7, 19 September 1813.
(18) Add.MSS. 43225, f. 103, Aberdeen to Lady Maria Hamilton, 6 September 1813.
(19) *ibid*, f. 25, Aberdeen to Abercorn, 3 May 1813.
(20) Add.MSS. 43073, fos. 305–9, Aberdeen to Castlereagh, Teplitz, 12 September 1813.
(21) Add.MSS. 43225, f. 29, Abercorn to Aberdeen, 22 July 1813.
(22) *ibid* 43074, f. 89, Aberdeen to Castlereagh, Teplitz, 23 September 1813.
(23) *ibid.*
(24) *ibid* 43073, fos. 285–6, Castlereagh to Aberdeen, St James's Square, 1 September 1813.
(25) *ibid*, fos. 293–4, Aberdeen to Castlereagh (Private), Teplitz, 7 September 1813.
(26) *ibid*, fos. 305–9, Aberdeen to Castlereagh, Teplitz, 7 September 1813.
(27) *ibid*, fos. 317–20, Aberdeen to Castlereagh, Prague, 14 September 1813.
(28) *ibid.*
(29) Add.MSS. 43225, fos. 104–5, Aberdeen to Lady Maria Hamilton, 19 September 1813.
(30) Add.MSS. 43074, f. 1, Aberdeen to Sir Charles Stewart, Teplitz, 18 September 1813.

(31) Add.MSS. 43225, fos. 104–5, Aberdeen to Lady Maria Hamilton, 19 September 1813.
(32) Balfour, *Life*, p. 99, Aberdeen to Harrowby, 23 September 1813.

CHAPTER 5 – THE FIELD OF LEIPZIG

(1) Add.MSS. 43225, f. 124, Aberdeen to Lady Maria Hamilton, Dornheim, 27 October 1813.
(2) *ibid*, f. 115, Comotau, 10 October, 1813.
(3) Add.MSS. 43074, fos. 202–3 and 204–5, Aberdeen to Castlereagh, Teplitz, 1 October 1813.
(4) Balfour, *Life*, Vol. I, pp. 108–9.
(5) Add.MSS. 43225, f. 112, Aberdeen to Lady Maria Hamilton, Comotau, 8 October 1813.
(6) Add.MSS. 43074, fos. 219–22, and 223–4, 227–30, Aberdeen to Castlereagh, Comotau, 9 October 1813.
(7) Add.MSS. 43225, f. 116, Aberdeen to Lady Maria Hamilton, Marienberg, 15 October 1813.
(8) Add.MSS. 43074, f. 89, Aberdeen to Castlereagh, Teplitz, 23 September 1813.
(9) Cronin, *Napoleon*, p. 348f.
(10) Add.MSS. 43225, f. 119, Aberdeen to Lady Maria Hamilton, Chemnitz, 16 October 1813.
(11) *ibid*, fos. 120–5, Altenburgh, 18 October [1813].
(12) *ibid*, f. 120.
(13) *ibid*, f. 121.
(14) *ibid*, f. 121, Rotha, 20 October [1813].
(15) *ibid*, f. 130, Hanau, 5 November 1813.
(16) Cronin, *Napoleon*, p. 35.

CHAPTER 6 – 'HEARTBURNINGS ENOUGH'

(1) Wittichen, *Briefe von und an F. von Gentz*, III, pp. 134, 149.
(2) Balfour, *Life*, I, p. 137.
(3) Mendelssohn – Bartholdy, *Briefe von Gentz an Pilat*, I, 21; Webster, *Foreign Policy of Castlereagh*, pp. 126–7.
(4) Webster, *Foreign Policy of Castlereagh*, pp. 126–7 (Stewart to Cooke, 20 April 1813).
(5) Add.MSS. 43225, f. 102, Aberdeen to Lady Maria Hamilton, Teplitz, 4 September 1813.
(6) Gordon, *Aberdeen*, p. 33.
(7) Add.MSS. 43225, f. 109, Aberdeen to Lady Maria Hamilton, Teplitz, 29 September 1813.
(8) *ibid*, f. 134, Frankfort, 15 November 1813.
(9) *ibid*, fos. 42–3, Aberdeen to Abercorn, Frankfort, 4 December 1813.
(10) Webster, *British Diplomacy*, pp. 12–13; Webster, *Foreign Policy of Castlereagh*, p. 147; Castlereagh to Cathcart, 13, 14 July [1813].
(11) Nicolson, *Congress of Vienna*, pp. 60–1.
(12) *ibid*.
(13) Gordon, *Aberdeen*, p. 39.

(14) Londonderry, *Correspondence, Despatches and Other Papers of Viscount Castlereagh*, IC, pp. 75–6 (see also p. 90), Castlereagh to Aberdeen, 13 November, 7 December 1813.
(15) Gordon, *Aberdeen*, p. 42, Aberdeen to Castlereagh, 4 December 1813.
(16) Balfour, *Life*, I, p. 144.
(17) *ibid*, pp. 146–7, Aberdeen to Castlereagh, Frankfort, 11 November 1813.
(18) *ibid*, pp. 154–5.
(19) *ibid*, p. 156, Aberdeen to Castlereagh, Frankfort, 12 November 1813.
(20) Add.MSS. 43225, f. 135, Aberdeen to Lady Maria Hamilton, Frankfort, 15 November 1813.

CHAPTER 7 – DISAPPOINTED HOPES

(1) HH 1/28, Aberdeen to Lady Maria Hamilton, Leipzig, 22 October 1813; Jena, 25 October 1813.
(2) *ibid*, Smalhalden, 31 October 1813.
(3) Add.MSS. 43225, f. 135, Aberdeen to Lady Maria Hamilton, 24 November 1813.
(4) *ibid*.
(5) *ibid*.
(6) *ibid* 43075, fos. 166–7, Aberdeen to Castlereagh, Frankfort, 12 November 1813.
(7) *ibid*, fos. 209–10, Aberdeen to Castlereagh, Frankfort, 25 November 1813.
(8) *ibid*, f. 217, Aberdeen to Castlereagh, Frankfort, 28 November 1813.
(9) Webster, *Foreign Policy of Castlereagh*, p. 157f. Add.MSS. 43225, fos. 42–3; Aberdeen to Abercorn, 4 December 1813.
(10) Balfour, *Life*, I, p. 166.
(11) Add.MSS. 43225, f. 140, Aberdeen to Lady Maria Hamilton, Frankfort, 28 November 1813.
(12) *ibid*.
(13) Add.MSS. 43225, f. 42, Aberdeen to Abercorn, Frankfort, 4 December 1813.
(14) *ibid*.
(15) Balfour, *Life*, I, p. 173, Aberdeen to Harrowby, Freyburg, 24 December 1813.
(16) *ibid*, pp. 173–4.
(17) *ibid*, p. 174.
(18) Add.MSS. 43225, f. 46, Abercorn to Aberdeen, 5 December 1813.
(19) Balfour, *Life*, I, p. 174.
(20) *ibid*, pp. 174–5.
(21) *ibid*, p. 175.
(22) Add.MSS. 43076, Aberdeen to Harrowby, 17 January 1814.
(23) Add.MSS. 43225, f. 141, Aberdeen to Lady Maria Hamilton, Karlsruhe, 15 December 1813.
(24) *ibid*, f. 142, Freyburg.
(25) *ibid*, f. 154, 18 December 1813.
(26) HH 1/28, Aberdeen to Lady Maria Hamilton, Freyburg, 23 December 1813.
(27) *ibid*, 25 December 1813.

CHAPTER 8 – 'VIVE LA PAIX! VIVE QUI VOUDRA!'

(1) Gordon, *Aberdeen* (proofs), Chap. III, p. 51.
(2) *ibid*, p. 54.
(3) *ibid*, p. 54.
(4) *ibid*.
(5) *ibid*, p. 57.
(6) *ibid*.
(7) *ibid*, p. 60; Hansard (2nd ser.), Vol. XXII, 415
(8) *ibid*, p. 61.
(9) *ibid*, p. 62.
(10) Londonderry, *Correspondence*, Vol. IX, p. 298, Aberdeen to Castlereagh, Châtillon-sur-Seine, 28 February 1814.
(11) *ibid*, p. 297.
(12) *ibid*, p. 334, 10 March 1814.
(13) Gordon, *Aberdeen* (proofs), Chap. III, p. 65.
(14) *ibid*, p. 65.
(15) *ibid*, p. 66.
(16) *ibid*, pp. 66–7.
(17) *ibid*, p. 67.
(18) *ibid*.
(19) Nicolson, *Congress of Vienna*, p. 99; Balfour, *Life*, I, p. 189.
(20) Seton-Watson, *Britain in Europe*, p. 129.

CHAPTER 9 – 'MOST DEAR AND SWEET LOVE'

(1) HH 1/35. Aberdeen to Major A. Gordon, 17 November 1810.
(2) Gordon, *Aberdeen* (proofs), Chap. V, p. 1.
(3) *ibid*, p. 2.
(4) Bulloch, *House of Gordon*, §196. (*Note:* Wellington's letter is inaccurately reported.)
(5) Creevey Papers, Vol. 1, p. 236, *footnote*.
(6) Edgecumbe, *Diary of Frances Lady Shelley*, Vol. 1, pp. 99–144.
(7) Wellington's letter is on display in a glass case in the Muniment Room at Haddo House, Aberdeenshire.
(8) HH 1/24. *Notes on Lieut. Col. the Hon. Sir Alexander Gordon, KCB, Scots Guards, ADC to the Duke of Wellington, and on the Monument erected to his Memory on the Field of Waterloo*, by the Marchioness of Aberdeen and Temair (reprinted from *The Deeside Field*, sixth number 1933).
(9) HH 1/32, Aberdeen to Lady Aberdeen, 16, 25, 26, 29 September 1821; 1, 6, 8 September 1822.
(10) *ibid*, 20, 29 October 1820.
(11) *ibid*, n.d. probably 10 October 1820.
(12) HH 1/32, Aberdeen to Lady Jane Gordon, n.d. probably June 1820.
(13) Gordon, *Aberdeen*, p. 67.
(14) *London Gazette*, 1818, 2225–6.
(15) Gordon, *Aberdeen* (proofs), Chap. V, p. 2.
(16) Add.MSS. 43225, f. 38, Aberdeen to Abercorn, Gera, 25 October 1813.
(17) Gordon, *Aberdeen* (proofs), Chap. V, p. 16.

(18) HH 1/28, Aberdeen to Lady Maria Hamilton, 29 July 1813.
(19) HH 1/32, Aberdeen to Lady Aberdeen, 30 August 1822.
(20) *ibid*, 9 September 1822.
(21) *ibid*, 17 September 1822.
(22) *ibid*, 20 September 1822.
(23) *ibid*, 7, 10 January 1825, Nice.
(24) HH 1/4, Diary of Alice Gordon, 16 November, 4 December 1825.
(25) HH 1/32, Aberdeen to Lady Aberdeen, 13 December 1825.
(26) *ibid*.
(27) HH 1/37, Aberdeen to Lady Aberdeen, 29 January 1826.
(28) *ibid*, 7 February 1826.
(29) *ibid*, 9 February 1826.
(30) *ibid*, 21 February 1826.
(31) *ibid*, 24 February 1826.
(32) Creevey Papers, Vol. 1, p. 306 (Creevey to Miss Ord, 16 August 1820).
(33) HH 1/32, Aberdeen to Lady Aberdeen, 18 October 1820.
(34) *ibid*, 20 October 1820.
(35) Hansard (2nd ser.), XIII, 662f.
(36) Hansard (2nd ser.), XI, 959f.
(37) Gordon, *Aberdeen*, p. 75.
(38) Longford, *Wellington*, p. 154.
(39) *ibid*, pp. 160–3.
(40) *ibid*.
(41) Broughton, *Recollections*, Vol. III, p. 274.

CHAPTER 10 – FOREIGN SECRETARY

(1) Gash, *Mr Secretary Peel*, p. 277; Walpole Society, Vol. 39, 1964.
(2) Balfour, *Life*, Vol. I. Note on illustration of Lady Aberdeen's portrait by Lawrence, opposite p. 160.
(3) Robinson, *Princess Lieven's London Letters*, p. 125. Princess Lieven to Benckendorff, 16, 28 March 1828.
(4) RA B3/79, and B. & E., Vol. I, p. 451, Lord Melbourne to the Queen, 7 November 1841.
(5) B. & E., Vol. I, p. 289. *Footnote*.
(6) PRO FO 181/78, Aberdeen to Heytesbury, 31 October 1829; PP (347) 1854, Vol. XXXII, 1–5; extract reprinted in Bourne, *Foreign Policy*, Selected Document No. 4, pp. 210–15.
(7) Hansard (2nd ser.), XXII, 415 (12 February 1830).
(8) Gordon, *Aberdeen* (proofs), Chap. VI, pp. 23–6.
(9) *ibid*, p. 26.
(10) Bartlett, *Great Britain and Sea Power*, p. 80; Dakin, *Greek Struggle*, p. 274, Wellington to Aberdeen, 4 October 1829 (Texts inconsistent).
(11) Cecil, *British Foreign Secretaries*, p. 108.
(12) Parker, *Peel*, Vol. II, pp. 157–9.
(13) Add.MSS. 43059, Wellington to Aberdeen, 14, 17 August 1830; Aberdeen to Wellington, 16, 27 August 1830. Extract from Wellington to Aberdeen, 14 August 1830, reprinted in Bourne, *Foreign Policy*, Selected Document No. 5, p. 215.
(14) Balfour, *Life*, Vol. I, p. 271.
(15) *ibid*, p. 278.

(16) *ibid*, p. 279.
(17) Gordon, *Aberdeen*, p. 104.
(18) Longford, *Wellington*, p. 237.
(19) Balfour, *Life*, Vol. I, p. 279.
(20) Banford and Wellington, *Journals of Mrs Arbuthnot*, Vol. II, p. 373.
(21) Connell, *Regina v. Palmerston*, pp. 120–1, Prince Albert's Memo., 11 July 1850; Greville, *Diary* (Wilson ed.), Vol. II, pp. 88–9, 28 August 1853; Fulford, *The Prince Consort*, p. 61 n.
(22) HH 1/32, Aberdeen to Lady Aberdeen, 26 September, 12 October 1821.
(23) Gordon, *Aberdeen*, p. 113.
(24) Jones Parry, *Corr.*, Vol. I, p. 9, Aberdeen to Princess Lieven, 25 November 1832.

CHAPTER 11 – THE YEARS THE LOCUST HATH EATEN

(1) Jones Parry, *Corr.*, Vol. I, p. 3, Aberdeen to Lieven, 26 September 1832.
(2) Parker, *Politics in the Age of Peel*, Vol. III, p. 373.
(3) Jones Parry, *Corr.*, Vol. I, p. 21, Aberdeen to Lieven, 22 November 1834.
(4) *ibid*, Introduction, Vol. I, Lieven to General Benckendorff, 18 June 1829.
(5) *ibid*.
(6) Kriegel, *Holland House Diaries*, pp. 24, 48, 118: *Diary*, 5 August, 4 September 1831, 26 January 1832, and Hansard, IX, 891–2.
(7) Jones Parry, *Corr.*, Vol. I, p. 3, Aberdeen to Lieven, 26 September 1832.
(8) *ibid*, p. 8, 8 September 1835.
(9) Gordon, *Aberdeen*, pp. 105–6.
(10) Bagehot, *English Constitution*, p. 128.
(11) Parker, *Peel*, Vol. II, pp. 211–12. Aberdeen to Peel, 25 January 1833.
(12) *ibid*, pp. 126, 142.
(13) Jones Parry, *Corr.*, Vol. I, p. 8f., Aberdeen to Lieven, 25 November 1832.
(14) HH 1/32. Aberdeen to Lady Aberdeen, 4 September 1822.
(15) HH 1/35, Aberdeen to Major A. Gordon, 17 November 1810.
(16) HH 1/37, Aberdeen to Lady Aberdeen, 15 January 1825, Nice.
(17) *ibid*, 31 January 1825.
(18) HH 1/28, Aberdeen to Haddo, 17 July 1833.
(19) HH 1/32, *ibid*, 15 October 1833.
(20) *ibid*, 26 October 1833.
(21) *ibid*, 15 July 1831.
(22) *ibid*, Aberdeen to Lady Aberdeen, 30 August 1822.
(23) *ibid*, Aberdeen to Haddo, 21 April 1834.
(24) *ibid*, Aberdeen to Haddo, 28 April 1834.
(25) Jones Parry, *Corr.*, Vol. I, p. 17, Aberdeen to Lieven, 27 April 1834.
(26) Balfour, *Life*, Vol. II, p. 10, Aberdeen to Hudson Gurney, 14 December 1833.
(27) Gordon, *Aberdeen*, pp. 115–16.
(28) *Edinburgh Review*, October 1883, p. 573.

REFERENCES

(29) Broughton, *Recollections*, Vol. V, pp. 153–4.
(30) Gurwood, *Duke of Wellington's Speeches*, p. 546.
(31) Parker, *Peel*, Vol. II, p. 232, Arbuthnot to Aberdeen, 2 May 1834.
(32) *ibid*, Aberdeen to Peel, 5 May 1834, pp. 233–5.
(33) Add.MSS. 40312 f. 178; and Parker, *Peel*, Vol. II, pp. 232–3.
(34) Gordon, *Aberdeen*, p. 109.
(35) Jones Parry, *Corr.*, Vol. I, p. 23f., Aberdeen to Lieven, 19 December 1834.
(36) Gordon, *Aberdeen*, p. 110.
(37) Jones Parry, *Corr.*, Vol. I, p. 34, Aberdeen to Lieven, 30 July 1835.
(38) *ibid*, Vol. I, p. 31, 16 June 1835.
(39) *The Times*, 6 October 1837.
(40) Jones Parry, *Corr.*, Vol. I, p. 121, Aberdeen to Lieven, 4 November, 1 December 1838.
(41) *ibid*, pp. 33–6, 30 July 1835.
(42) *ibid*, p. 106, 16 April 1838.
(43) Gordon, *Aberdeen*, p. 118.
(44) B. & E., Vol. I, p. 220, Queen to King of Belgians, 14 May 1839.
(45) *ibid*, Vol. I, p. 200, Queen to Melbourne, 8 May 1839.
(46) Gordon, *Aberdeen*, p. 115.
(47) *ibid*, p. 116.
(48) Gash, *Peel*, p. 287.
(49) B. & E., Vol. I, p. 539, Queen to Melbourne, 10 September 1842.
(50) Jones Parry, *Corr.*, Vol. I, p. 42, Aberdeen to Lieven, 16 September 1838.
(51) HH 1/28, Aberdeen to Haddo, 24 September 1840.
(52) Balfour, *Life*, Appendix, p. 332, Aberdeen to an unknown person.
(53) Jones Parry, *Corr.*, Vol. II, pp. 151–2, Aberdeen to Lieven, 9 November 1840.
(54) Balfour, *Life*, Appendix, Vol. II, p. 328, Aberdeen to Lady Haddo, 12 September 1844.
(55) *ibid*, p. 328, 18 September 1844.
(56) HH 1/19, Aberdeen to Lady Haddo, Christmas Day 1854 (copy).
(57) HH 1/35, Aberdeen to Lady Haddo, 25 September 1854.
(58) HH 1/35, Smithfield show, 9 December 1848; Queen's Ball, 28 June 1845; HH 1/29, headaches, 21 January, 25 February, 1 May 1847 and *passim*; reading his speeches, 23 March 1849; children's ailments, 31 December 1850, 22 March 1853 and *passim*, Aberdeen to Lady Haddo.
(59) HH 1/29, Aberdeen to Lady Haddo, 2 August 1849.
(60) HH 1/19, Aberdeen to Lady Haddo, 4 August 1845.
(61) *ibid*, 28 August 1855.
(62) *ibid*, 30 September, 4 October 1853.
(63) *ibid*, 4 October 1853.
(64) *ibid*, 4 August 1845.
(65) *ibid*, 2 June 1845, 12 September 1853.
(66) Gordon, *Diary*, 10 December 1855.
(67) HH 1/32, Aberdeen to Haddo, 22 February 1835.
(68) *ibid*, 20 June 1834.
(69) Balfour, *Life*, Vol. I, pp. 214–15.
(70) Add.MSS. 43061, fos. 220, 234; Add.MSS. 40617, f. 54, 20 June 1834, 1 July 1837, 25 December 1838, 22 February 1835, 11 December 1838.

REFERENCES

(71) Add.MSS. 40617, fos. 70–2, 91; Add.MSS. 40427, f. 157. See also HH 1/32, Aberdeen to Captain Baillie-Hamilton, 30 May 1849.
(72) Gash, *Politics in the Age of Peel*, pp. 166–9.
(73) Jones Parry, *Corr.*, Vol. I, pp. 80f., Aberdeen to Lieven, 6 October 1837.
(74) Gordon, *Aberdeen*, p. 211.
(75) *ibid*, p. 137.
(76) *The Times*, 15 December 1860.
(77) Jones Parry, *Corr.*, Vol. I, pp. 138–9, Aberdeen to Lieven, 24 April 1840.
(78) Parker, *Peel*, Vol. II, pp. 462–5.
(79) Parker, *Peel*, Vol. II, p. 486, Disraeli to Peel, 5 September 1841.
(80) Jones Parry, *Corr.*, Vol. I, p. 178, Aberdeen to Lieven, 7 September 1841.
(81) *ibid*, p. 184, 19 October 1841.
(82) B. & E., Vol. I, p. 409, Melbourne to Queen, 12 September 1841.

CHAPTER 12 – *L'ENTENTE PEU AMICALE*

(1) Frothingham, *Edward Everett*, p. 188.
(2) Gordon, *Aberdeen*, pp. 152–3; see also Guizot, *Sir Robert Peel*, pp. 82–3, 142.
(3) Gash, *Peel*, p. 497.
(4) Jones, *Aberdeen and the Americas*, p. 3; see also Martin, *Prince Consort*, Vol. I, p. 267.
(5) Gash, *Peel*, p. 498.
(6) Jones Parry, *Corr.*, Vol. I, p. 116, Aberdeen to Lieven, 4 November 1838.
(7) *ibid*, p. 177, 7 September 1841.
(8) *ibid*, p. 151, 9 November 1840; p. 177, 7 September 1841.
(9) Cook, *Delane*, p. 15.
(10) Jones Parry, *Corr.*, Vol. I, p. 133, Aberdeen to Lieven, 10 February 1840.
(11) *ibid*, p. 151. See also Balfour, *Life*, Vol. II, pp. 106–7, 123; and Greville, *Letters*, p. 43, Greville to Reeve, 27 October 1840.
(12) Jones Parry, *Corr.*, Vol. I, p. 174, Aberdeen to Lieven, 6 July 1841.
(13) *Correspondence relative to the Society Islands*, p. 78.
(14) Lovett, *London Missionary Society*, Vol. I, pp. 299, 314, 325; *The Times*, 17, 24 August 1844 and *passim*.
(15) Pritchard, *Polynesian Reminiscences*, p. 34; *Corr.*, p. 41, Pomare to George IV, 5 October 1826 [*sic*, error for 1825].
(16) Lovett, *LMS*, Vol. I, pp. 13f, 127–34, 146, 237; *Corr.*, pp. 1, 3–5, 10, 24; *Poly. Rems.*, p. 4, Canning to Pomare, 3 March 1827.
(17) Russier, *Le Partage*, Vol. I, pp. 125–7; Pritchard, *Queen Pomare*, pp. 18–21; Pritchard, *Poly. Rems.*, pp. 4–7; LMS, *Jubilee Services*, pp. 64–5, 75f, 129–30; *Corr.*, pp. 26f, 42, 57–9.
(18) Pritchard, *Poly. Rems.*, pp. 7–8; *Corr.*, pp. 61–74.
(19) *Corr.*, pp. 61–74; *Poly. Rems.*, pp. 8–17.
(20) *Corr.*, pp. 68, 70, 74–7; *Poly. Rems.*, pp. 17–18. (Pomare to Queen Victoria, 8 November 1838.)
(21) *Corr.*, pp. 88–92, 107–8, 112, 124; *Poly. Rems.*, pp. 22–3.

(22) *Corr.*, pp. 141, 143, 146–55; *Poly. Rems.*, pp. 25–30.

(23) *Poly. Rems.*, p. 35.

(24) Guizot, *Peel*, pp. 164–7; Hansard, LXVIII, 1, 3, 40, 1001; LXIX, 566; LXXI, 492; *The Times*, 2, 13 March 1843, 1 April 1843.

(25) *Corr.*, pp. 210–17, 222, 226–9; Bastide, *Revue*, Vol. XXI, Pt III, pp. 165–7; *Poly. Rems.*, pp. 37–9.

(26) *Corr.*, pp. 164–6, 216–17, 226, 254–7, 260–3, 271–2, 276–7, 306–10, 324; *Poly. Rems.*, pp. 42–7; Guizot, *Peel*, Vol. II, pp. 79–80; Bastide, *Revue*, Vol. XXVII, Pt III, pp. 76–81; *The Times*, 8 August 1844.

(27) *The Times*, 8 August 1844.

(28) Hansard, LXXVI, 1575–6; Parker, *Peel*, Vol. III, pp. 394–5, Peel to Aberdeen, 12 August 1844.

(29) Add.MSS. 43211, Aberdeen to Robert Gordon, *Private*, 24 May, 2 November, 24 November 1842, 3 February 1843; Gordon to Aberdeen, *Private*, 3 November 1842, 15 December 1853; Aberdeen to Peel, *Private*, 15 December 1843; Add.MSS. 43062, Peel to Aberdeen, 30 September 1842.

(30) Jones Parry, *Corr.*, Vol. I, p. 223, Aberdeen to Lieven, 2 February 1844.

(31) Parker, *Peel*, Vol. III, pp. 401–2, 18 September 1845.

(32) Add.MSS. 43133, Guizot to Jarnac, 8 August 1844; FO 27/699, Cowley to Aberdeen, No. 396, 4 August 1844; No. 397, 5 August 1844; No. 400, 5 August 1844, *Secret*; 7 August 1844 and enclosures; *The Times*, 3, 4 August 1844.

(33) Add.MSS. 43130, Cowley to Aberdeen, *Private*, 23, 26, 28, 30 August 1844; Add.MSS. 43053, Lieven to Aberdeen, 1 September 1844; Add. MSS. 40454, Aberdeen to Peel, 1 September 1844; Jarnac, *Révue des Deux Mondes*, Vol. XXXIV, p. 456.

(34) Add.MSS. 43130, Draft despatch, n.d., August 1844, marked 'not sent'.

(35) Hansard, LXXVII, 113–18.

(36) Add.MSS. 43133, Guizot to Jarnac, 2, 9 September 1844; 43130, Cowley to Aberdeen, 4 September 1844; 40454, Aberdeen to Peel, 1, 16, 21 September 1844; 40450, Graham to Peel, 16 September 1845; 43054, Peel to Aberdeen, 19 September 1844; *Corr.*, pp. 558, 572, 599; *Poly. Rems.*, p. 48; Jarnac, *Révue des Deux Mondes*, Vol. XXXIV, p. 457.

(37) Add.MSS. 43133, Jarnac to Aberdeen, 12 September, 20 December 1844; Aberdeen to Jarnac, 20 September 1844; Guizot to Jarnac, 9 September, 26 November 1844; 40454, Aberdeen to Peel, 18, 22 October 1844; 43064, Peel to Aberdeen, 20 October 1844.

(38) Jones Parry, *Corr.*, Vol. I, pp. 230f., Aberdeen to Lieven, 6 September 1844; Gordon, *Aberdeen* (proofs), Chap. IX, p. 8.

(39) RA Y91/59, Queen to King of Belgians, 15 September 1844.

(40) *Times Archives*, Vol. II, Delane Correspondence, Aberdeen to Delane, 15 January 1845.

(41) Gordon, *Aberdeen*, p. 159.

(42) Gordon, *Aberdeen*, pp. 160–1, Aberdeen to Lyons, 11 November 1844.

(43) *ibid*, p. 161.

(44) PRO FO 17/53, Aberdeen to Pottinger, 4 November 1841.

(45) PRO FO 17/57, Pottinger to Aberdeen, 29 August 1842.

(46) Add.MSS. 40467, f. 303, Peel to Stanley, 23 November 1842.

(47) Add.MSS. 43198, f. 403, Davis to Aberdeen, 28 September 1846.

CHAPTER 13 – THE SPANISH MARRIAGES

(1) Hansard, XXXII, 387–92.

(2) FO 27/629–31, Bulwer to Aberdeen, 25 October, 8 November 1841; Cowley to Aberdeen, 3, 24 December 1841.

(3) Add.MSS. 40460, Peel to Wellington, 25 August 1843; Wellington to Peel, 25 August 1853; *ibid* 40453, Aberdeen to Peel, 18 August 1843; Guizot, *Mémoires*, Vol. VI, pp. 187–9; Martin, *Prince Consort*, Vol. I, pp. 172–83.

(4) Add.MSS. 40453, Guizot, *Mémoires*, Vol. VI, p. 194; Martin, *Prince Consort*, Vol. I, pp. 181, 183, Prince Albert to Stockmar, 10 September 1843.

(5) Add.MSS. 40453, Aberdeen to Peel, 6 September 1843; *ibid* 43211, Aberdeen to Gordon, 16 October 1843, and *ibid* 40454, Aberdeen to Peel, 19 October, 5 December 1843; *ibid* 43063, Peel to Aberdeen, 7 December 1843.

(6) Guyot, *La Première Entente Cordiale*, pp. 253–4; Jones, *Aberdeen and the Americas*, Foreword by Marjorie Pentland, p. XII; Jarnac, *Révue des Deux Mondes*, Vol. XXXIV, pp. 451–2. (1 July 1861 issue, article *Lord Aberdeen*.)

(7) Cook, *Delane*, p. 7.

(8) Ridley, *Palmerston*, p. 309.

(9) Add.MSS. 40455, Aberdeen to Peel, 8 September, 9 October 1845; *ibid* 43128, Aberdeen to Metternich, 20 September 1845; Gordon, *Aberdeen*, p. 163.

(10) Add.MSS. 40455, Louis Philippe to Queen of Belgians.

(11) Add.MSS. 40454, Aberdeen to Peel, 31 December 1844; *ibid* 40461, Peel to Wellington, 4, 12 January 1845; Wellington to Peel, 7 January 1845; *ibid* 43060, Aberdeen to Wellington, 14 January 1845; Wellington to Aberdeen, 15 January 1845.

(12) Add.MSS. 40455, Aberdeen to Peel, 18 September 1845; Parker, *Peel*, Vol. III, pp. 401–2, Aberdeen to Peel, 18 September 1845 (text abridged); also Gordon, *Aberdeen*, pp. 174–6 (text correct, but wrongly dated 28 September 1845). Letter reprinted in Bourne, *Foreign Policy*, Selected Document No. 36, pp. 264–7.

(13) Add.MSS. 43064, Peel to Aberdeen, 20 September 1845; Parker, *Peel*, Vol. III, pp. 402–3.

(14) Add.MSS. 40461, Wellington to Peel, 22 September 1845; Parker, *Peel*, Vol. III, p. 404.

(15) Parker, *Peel*, Vol. III, pp. 407–8; Add.MSS. 40451, Peel to Graham, 21 September 1845; Graham to Peel, 22 September 1845.

(16) Add.MSS. 43064, Peel to Aberdeen.

(17) Gordon, *Aberdeen* (proofs), Chap. IX, p. 49, Aberdeen to Guizot, 20 October 1845.

(18) *ibid*, p. 25.

(19) Add.MSS. 43147, Aberdeen to Bulwer, 7, 18, 19 May 1846; *ibid* 43045, Victoria to Albert, 18, 21 May 1845; Gordon, *Aberdeen* (proofs), Chap. IX, p. 25–6.

(20) Add.MSS. 43147, Bulwer to Aberdeen, 24 April, 6, 19 May 1846; PRO FO 72/697, No. 57, Bulwer to Aberdeen, 24 April 1846; Add.MSS. 43133, Guizot to St Aulaire, 6 June 1846.

(21) Gordon, *Aberdeen* (proofs), Chap. IX, pp. 279.
(22) Jones Parry, *Spanish Marriages*, p. 271 [Bresson, 3, 5 April 1846, Val Richer MSS; Bulwer, 4 April 1846, Add.MSS.].
(23) PRO FO 72/694, Palmerston to Bulwer, 19 July 1846.
(24) Bell, *Palmerston*, Vol. I, 378.
(25) B. & E., *Letters*, Vol. II, p. 122, Queen to King of Belgians, 14 September 1846.
(26) *The Times Archives*, Aberdeen to Delane, 14 October 1846; Greville, *Memoirs*, Vol. V, p. 439.
(27) Add.MSS. 48577; Bell, *Palmerston*, Vol. I, p. 389; *Cracow Papers*, pp. 39–42, 49, 50–4; Czartoryski, *Memoirs*, Vol. II, pp. 348–9; Greville, *Memoirs*, Vol. V, pp. 436–8; Bourne, *Foreign Policy*, pp. 61–2; Martin, *Prince Consort*, Vol. I, pp. 378–81.
(28) Balfour, *Life*, Vol. II, p. 136, Aberdeen to Lieven, 21 December 1846.
(29) Jones Parry, *Spanish Marriages*, pp. 334–6.
(30) *ibid*, p. 335. [Jarnac to Aberdeen, 3 November 1846, Add.MSS.]
(31) Webster, *Foreign Policy of Castlereagh*, p. 496.
(32) Jones Parry, *Spanish Marriages*, p. 336. [Bulwer to Aberdeen, 8 July 1846, Add.MSS.]

CHAPTER 14 – AMERICAN PROBLEMS

(1) Tyler, *Letters and Times*, Vol. II, p. 205; Dubois, *Suppression of African Slave Trade*, p. 141.
(2) Add.MSS. 43189, Aberdeen to Clarendon, 5 November 1854.
(3) SP, Vol. XVIII, pp. 1249–57; Lucas, *Boundary Line of Canada*, pp. 11–12.
(4) Add.MSS. 43123, Aberdeen to Ashburton, 9 February, 31 March 1842; PRO FO 5/378, 26 May 1842 (draft).
(5) PRO FO 5/378, Aberdeen to Ashburton, No. 2, 8 February 1842.
(6) Add.MSS. 43060, Wellington to Aberdeen, 8 February 1842 (three letters).
(7) Add.MSS. 43123, Aberdeen to Ashburton, 9 February 1842.
(8) *ibid*, Ashburton to Aberdeen, 10 February 1842.
(9) *ibid*, Aberdeen to Ashburton, 31 March 1842.
(10) Add.MSS. 43123, Ashburton to Aberdeen, 26 April 1842, enc. Gallatin to Ashburton, 21 April 1842.
(11) PRO FO 5/378, 26 May 1842 (draft).
(12) Add.MSS. 43060, Wellington memorandum, 8 February 1842; Add. MSS. 43123, 24 February–9 March 1842, Opinions of the Military Authorities, Sir James Kempt, Sir Howard Douglas, Lord Seaton and Sir George Murray.
(13) Hansard, LXVII, 247–8; Watt, *Case of Alexander McLeod*, p. 1162f.
(14) Add.MSS. 48495, Palmerston to Fox, Nos. 4 and 5, 9 February 1841; Ashley, *Palmerston*, Vol. I, p. 408. See also Palmerston to Sir William Temple, Ashley, *Palmerston*, Vol. I, p. 406, 9 February 1841.
(15) PRO FO 5/262–3, Fox to Aberdeen, No. 82, 28 August; No. 84, 12 September; No. 91, 25 September; No. 98, 28 September; No. 100, 29 September; No. 112, 12 October 1841; Tyler, *Letters and Times*, Vol. II, pp. 206–15; Watt, *Alexander McLeod*, pp. 145–67.

REFERENCES

(16) PRO FO 5/383-4, Fox to Aberdeen, No. 114, 13 October; No. 118, 26 October 1841.
(17) Add.MSS. 43123, Ashburton to Aberdeen, 29 June, 28 July, 9 August 1842; PRO FO 5/379-80, Ashburton to Aberdeen, No. 6, 12 May; No. 14, 28 July; No. 20, 9 August 1842.
(18) Add.MSS. 43123, Aberdeen to Ashburton, 31 March, 3 June 1842; PRO FO 5/379-80, Ashburton to Aberdeen, No. 2, 25 April; No. 5, 28 April and enclosure; No. 6, 12 May; No. 12, 29 June; No. 18, 9 August 1842.
(19) Add.MSS. 43123, Aberdeen to Ashburton, 26 September 1842; extract from letter reprinted in Bourne, Foreign Policy, Selected Document No. 30, pp. 255-6.
(20) Chamberlain, Character of Foreign Policy, Chap. III, passim.
(21) Jones, American Problem, p. 25.
(22) Hansard, LXVII, 1164-1218; The Times, 22 March 1843; Bell, Palmerston, Vol. I, pp. 334-5.
(23) Add.MSS. 49964, Bankhead to Palmerston, 13 July 1831.
(24) Gordon, Aberdeen, p. 322.
(25) ibid.
(26) Add.MSS. 43064, Peel to Aberdeen, 23 February 1845; ibid 40455, Aberdeen to Wellington, 2 March 1845; Merk, Oregon Pioneers, pp. 681-9.
(27) Add.MSS. 43123, Ashburton to Aberdeen, 26 April 1842.
(28) Add.MSS. 43123, Gratton, 30 September, 1, 16 November 1844; PRO FO 5/405, 406, 409, Pakenham to Aberdeen, No. 54, 26 May; No. 76, 27 June; No. 122, 13 November 1844; Quaife, Polk's Diary, Vol. I, pp. xiii-xiv, xxviii-xxix. See also Jacobs, Winning Oregon, pp. 169-76.
(29) Richardson, Messages, Vol. V, p. 2331.
(30) Hansard, LXXIX, 193-9.
(31) Hansard, LXXIX, 115-24; Jones Parry, Corr., Aberdeen to Lieven, Vol. I, p. 240, 12 April 1845.
(32) Add.MSS. 43064, Peel to Aberdeen, 19 August 1845; ibid 40455, Aberdeen to Peel, 29 August 1845. See also ibid 43065, Peel to Aberdeen, 2 October 1845, Aberdeen to Peel, 3 October 1845; ibid 43123, Aberdeen to Pakenham, 3 October 1845.
(33) ibid.
(34) Add.MSS. 43123, Everett to Aberdeen, 10 December 1845, Aberdeen to Everett, 3 January 1846; Richardson, Messages, Vol. V, pp. 2242-9.
(35) Gordon, Aberdeen, p. 181.
(36) Bell, Palmerston, Vol. I, p. 253; Ward and Gooch, Cambridge History, Vol. II, 259n; Merk, British Party Politics, Vol. XXXVII, p. 653.
(37) Hansard, LXXXVII, 1049-53.
(38) Hansard, LXXXVII, 1057; The Times, 30 June 1846.
(39) Add.MSS. 43239, Croker to Aberdeen, 13 May 1846.
(40) Add.MSS. 48575, Palmerston to Pakenham, 18 July, 15, 18 August, 31 October 1846; Pakenham to Aberdeen, 28 June 1846; Pakenham to Palmerston, 23 November 1846; ibid 49968, Palmerston to Bankhead, 15, 24 August, 31 October 1846; ibid 49968, Bankhead to Palmerston, 30 December 1846; Rives, Mexican Diplomacy, pp. 274-94. See also Adams, British Interests and Activities in Texas, 1838-1846, pp. 224-42, 234-63.
(41) Ridley, Palmerston, pp. 303-6.

(42) Add.MSS. 43127, Aberdeen to Ouseley, 4 March 1846.
(43) Ferns, *Britain and Argentina*, p. 225.
(44) RA C28/61, 27 December 1852.
(45) Hansard, LXXXVII, 1049-5 (29 June 1846).
(46) Add.MSS. 43045, Queen to Aberdeen, 29 June 1846 (see also *ibid* 43053, Lieven to Aberdeen, 1 July 1846.)
(47) *ibid.*
(48) Balfour, *Life*, Vol. II, p. 135.
(49) Jones Parry, *Corr.*, Vol. I, pp. 257-8, Aberdeen to Lieven, 26 June 1846.
(50) Add.MSS. 43123, Aberdeen to Pakenham, 30 June 1846.
(51) SP Vol. XXXIII, pp. 4-18; Guizot, *Mémoires*, Vol. VI, pp. 238-41.
(52) Dalling and Ashley, *Palmerston*, II, pp. 375, 377, Palmerston to Bulwer, 10 August 1841; 1879 edition, Vol. I, p. 411.
(53) Ridley, *Palmerston*, p. 282.
(54) RA B4/7, Aberdeen to Queen, 20 December 1841.
(55) RA B4/28, Aberdeen to Queen, 28 January 1842.
(56) RA B4/29, Aberdeen to Queen, 28 January 1842.
(57) RA B8/19, Aberdeen to Queen, 29 January 1844. (See also RA B4/49, Aberdeen to Queen, 21 February 1842; RA B6/25, Aberdeen to Queen, 16 January 1843.)
(58) Letter to author.
(59) RA Y92/44, Queen to King of Belgians, 7 July 1846.
(60) *ibid.*
(61) Jones Parry, *Corr.*, Vol. I, p. 178, Aberdeen to Lieven, 7 September 1841.
(62) Gordon, *Aberdeen*, p. 185.
(63) Gordon, *Herbert*, Vol. I, pp. 43-55.
(64) Walpole, *Russell*, Vol. I, pp. 422-4; Gordon, *Herbert*, Vol. I, pp. 50-5 (Herbert's Memo.).
(65) Cook, *Delane*, pp. 20-6; Gordon, *Herbert*, Vol. I, pp. 61-3; *The Times*, 4 December 1845.
(66) Gordon, *Herbert*, Vol. I, pp. 55-60.
(67) Walpole, *Russell*, Vol. I, pp. 428-35, quoting Grey to Russell, 16 December 1845; Palmerston to Russell, 19 December 1845; Grey to Russell, 19 December 1845; Russell to Grey, 21 December 1845.
(68) Add.MSS. 43134, Aberdeen to Guizot, 5 May 1846; Merk, *British Party Politics*, p. 674.
(69) Jones Parry, *Corr.*, Vol I, p. 251, Aberdeen to Lieven, 5 May 1846; Greville, *Memoirs*, Vol. V, pp. 388-9; Dalling and Ashley, *Palmerston*, Vol. III, pp. 192-3, and 1879 edition, Vol. I, pp. 498-9; Bell, *Palmerston*, Vol. I, p. 366; *The Times*, 29 June 1846; *The Spectator*, 18 April 1846.

CHAPTER 15 – CINCINNATUS RECALLED

For the details of Aberdeen's life at Haddo used in this chapter I am mainly indebted to *The Earl of Aberdeen* by Sir Arthur Gordon, pp. 188–194, and to the article written after his death by the Comte de Jarnac. (*Révue des Deux Mondes*, Vol. XXXIV, 1 July 1861, pp. 429–71.)

REFERENCES

(1) Jones Parry, *Corr.*, Vol. I, p. 260, Aberdeen to Lieven, 27 August 1846.
(2) *The Times*, 25, 27 August 1846.
(3) HH 1/32, Aberdeen to Baillie-Hamilton, 8 September 1846.
(4) *ibid*, 10 September 1846.
(5) *ibid*, 28 September 1846.
(6) *ibid*, 3 November 1846. See also Add.MSS. 43225, fos. 211–12, Aberdeen to Baillie-Hamilton, 14 September 1846.
(7) Balfour, *Life*, Vol. II, p. 10, Aberdeen to Hudson Gurney, 14 December 1833.
(8) Balfour, *Life*, Vol. I, pp. 200–1, Aberdeen to Hudson Gurney.
(9) British Museum minutes of Standing Committee, 9 May 1818, p. 2697.
(10) Jones Parry, *Corr.*, Vol. I, p. 257f., Aberdeen to Lieven, 26 June 1846.
(11) Gordon, *Aberdeen*, p. 319.
(12) HH 1/19 and 1/29. See, e.g. Aberdeen to Lady Haddo, 21, 26 January, 6, 10, 25 February, 10, 28 March, 1 May, 11 August 1847.
(13) Gordon, *Aberdeen*, p. 318.
(14) Croker Papers, Vol. III, pp. 180–1, Aberdeen to Croker, 1 September 1846.
(15) Gordon, *Aberdeen*, p. 319.
(16) Argyll, *Memoirs*, Vol. I, p. 184.
(17) Gordon, *Aberdeen*, p. 320.
(18) HH 1/28, Aberdeen to Lady Haddo, 8 August 1845.
(19) Gordon, *Aberdeen*, pp. 191–2; Jarnac, *Révue des Deux Mondes*, Vol. XXXIV, pp. 446–7.
(20) Balfour, *Life*, II, p. 151.
(21) Gordon, *Aberdeen*, p. 127, Aberdeen to John Hope, Dean of Faculty, 17 September 1839.
(22) Gordon, *Souvenir of Haddo House* (1958).
(23) Elliott, *Memoirs of Lord Haddo*, pp. 19–20, Diary, 24 January 1849.
(24) *ibid*, 4 June 1849.
(25) HH 1/29, Aberdeen to Lady Haddo, 28 March 1847.
(26) *ibid*, 5 April 1847.
(27) Elliott, *Memoirs*, pp. 56–7, Diary, 4, 7 June 1849.
(28) Jones Parry, *Corr.*, Vol. I, p. 289, Aberdeen to Lieven, 17 November 1847.
(29) Jones Parry, *Spanish Marriages*, pp. 19, 106.
(30) Martin, *Prince Consort*, Vol. II, p. 109, Prince Albert to Dowager Duchess of Coburg, 11 September 1848.
(31) Jones Parry, *Corr.*, Vol. I, p. 289, Aberdeen to Lieven, 17 November 1847.
(32) Martin, *Prince Consort*, Vol. II, pp. 107–9, 461, 505.
(33) HH 1/29, Aberdeen to Lady Haddo, 24 April 1847.
(34) Balfour, *Life*, Vol. II, p. 324.
(35) HH 1/32, Aberdeen to Baillie-Hamilton, 29 November 1848.
(36) Walford, *Greater London*, Vol. I, pp. 299–302.
(37) HH 1/28, Aberdeen to Abercorn, 20 April 1850 (copy).
(38) *ibid*, 2 October 1850 (copy).
(39) Argyll, *Memoirs*, Vol. I, p. 301.
(40) Jones Parry, *Corr.*, Vol. II, p. 296, Aberdeen to Lieven, 16 August 1848.

(41) *ibid*, p. 316, 18 August 1849.
(42) *ibid*, p. 328, 26 September 1849.
(43) *ibid*, p. 351, 16 December 1849.
(44) *ibid*, p. 347, 19 November 1849.
(45) Add.MSS. 40455, 490, Aberdeen to Peel, 4 April 1850; Parker, *Peel*, Vol. III, p. 540.
(46) Add.MSS. 43065, 420–7, Peel to Aberdeen, 2 April 1850.
(47) Gash, *Peel*, p. 652; B. & E., Vol. II, p. 288, Russell to Prince Albert, 18 May 1850. See also Russell to Palmerston, Private, 22 May 1850, reprinted in Bourne, *Foreign Policy*, Selected Document No. 53, pp. 299–301.
(48) B. & E., Vol. II, p. 295, Russell to Queen, 22 June 1850.
(49) Hansard, CXII, 1350–62.
(50) *ibid*; and see Malmesbury, *Memoirs*, p. 194.
(51) Parker, *Peel*, Vol. III, pp. 541–4.
(52) Greville, *Diary*, Vol. II, pp. 81–2, 11 June 1829, 12 May 1834; Ridley, *Palmerston*, pp. 153–4.
(53) Hansard, CXII, 380–444. Partly reprinted in Bourne, *Foreign Policy*, Selected Document No. 54, pp. 301–2.
(54) Jones Parry, *Corr.*, Vol. II, p. 468, Aberdeen to Lieven, 17 May 1850.
(55) *ibid*, p. 497, 26 June 1850.
(56) *ibid*, p. 583, 14 June 1851; Ridley, *Palmerston*, p. 385.
(57) Gordon, *Aberdeen*, p. 197.
(58) HH 1/29, Aberdeen to Lady Haddo, 4 July 1850.
(59) Parker, *Peel*, Vol. III, pp. 555–6, Lady Peel to Aberdeen, 2 August 1850.
(60) *ibid*, p. 556, Aberdeen to Lady Peel, 15 August 1850.
(61) Gordon, *Herbert*, Vol. I, p. 144.
(62) Martineau, *Newcastle*, p. 106.
(63) Gordon, *Herbert*, Vol. I, p. 130.
(64) *ibid*, p. 145, Newcastle to Herbert, 27 October 1851.
(65) Cook, *Delane*, p. 41.
(66) Jones Parry, *Corr.*, Vol. II, p. 545, Aberdeen to Lieven, 17 February 1851.
(67) B. & E., Vol. II, pp. 349–50, Prince Albert's Memo., 22 February 1851.
(68) Gordon, *Aberdeen*, p. 199.
(69) *ibid*, p. 198.
(70) B. & E., Vol. II, p. 354, Prince Albert's Memo., 23 February 1851.
(71) *ibid*, pp. 352–7.
(72) *ibid*, p. 356, Prince Albert's Memo., 23 February 1851.
(73) *ibid*, p. 356.
(74) *ibid*, p. 358, Prince Albert's Memo., 23 February 1851.
(75) *ibid*, p. 359, Prince Albert's Memo., 24 February 1851.
(76) *ibid*, pp. 360–1; Walpole, *Russell*, Vol. II, pp. 124–7.
(77) Russell, *Recollections*, p. 257.
(78) B. & E., Vol. II, p. 361, Prince Albert's Memo., 25 February 1851.
(79) *ibid*, p. 360, Queen to Russell, 24 February 1851; Queen to King of Belgians, 25 February 1851.
(80) Gordon, *Aberdeen*, p. 200.
(81) B. & E., Vol. II, p. 362, Prince Albert's Memo., 25 February 1851.
(82) Hansard, CXIV, 999–1000.

(83) *ibid*, CXVIII, 1072–93.
(84) Gordon, *Aberdeen*, p. 202, Aberdeen to Gordon.
(85) B. & E., Vol. II, p. 364, Prince Albert's Memo., 25 February 1851.
(86) *ibid*, pp. 374–5, Prince Albert's Memo., 2 March 1851.
(87) *ibid*, p. 375.
(88) *ibid*, pp. 376–7, Prince Albert's Memo., 3 March 1851.
(89) *ibid*, p. 376.
(90) *ibid*, p. 377.
(91) B. & E., Vol. II, pp. 439–40. The Marquis of Normanby to Col. Phipps, 5 February 1852. See also RA A79/44, Queen to Russell (draft), 12 August 1850, and RA A79/46, Palmerston to Russell, 13 August 1850.
(92) Gordon, *Aberdeen*, pp. 205–6; Southgate, *Whigs*, p. 230; Walpole, *Russell*, Vol. II, p. 143.
(93) B. & E., Vol. II, p. 445, Prince Albert's Memo., 21 February 1852.
(94) Malmesbury, *Memoirs*, pp. 12–13, 21 February 1852.
(95) Ridley, Palmerston, p. 402.
(96) Maxwell, *Clarendon*, Vol. I, p. 345.
(97) Argyll, *Memoirs*, Vol. I, p. 365.
(98) Gordon, *Aberdeen*, p. 206.
(99) *ibid*, p. 209.
(100) Walpole, *Russell*, Vol. II, p. 161.
(101) RA C28/1, Prince Albert's Memo., 18 December 1852.
(102) *ibid*.
(103) Parker, *Graham*, Vol. II, p. 192, Diary, 20 December 1852; B. & E., Vol. II, pp. 507, 509–10, Queen to Derby, 21 December 1852, Derby to Queen, 22 December 1852.
(104) Argyll, *Memoirs*, Vol. 1, p. 369.
(105) Conacher, *Peel and the Peelites*, p. 452.
(106) Walpole, *Russell*, Vol. II, p. 161; RA C28/4 and 5, Lansdowne to Queen, Aberdeen to Queen, 18 December 1852.
(107) Parker, *Graham*, Vol. II, pp. 190–1.
(108) *ibid*, pp. 192–4.
(109) Walpole, *Russell*, Vol. II, p. 161.
(110) *ibid*, pp. 169–70, and RA C28/93, Aberdeen to Russell, 21 January 1853.
(111) Parker, *Graham*, Vol. II, p. 193.
(112) Argyll, *Memoirs*, Vol. I, pp. 362–3.
(113) RA C28/13, Prince Albert's Memo., 19 December 1852 (copy).
(114) *ibid*.
(115) Parker, *Graham*, Vol. II, pp. 192–3.
(116) *ibid*, p. 194; RA C28/21, Aberdeen to Queen, undated.
(117) RA C28/14, Queen to Russell, 19 December 1852.
(118) Walpole, *Russell*, Vol. II, pp. 162–3.
(119) Parker, *Graham*, Vol. II, pp. 194–5, Diary, 20, 21 December 1852; RA C28/31, Aberdeen to Queen, 20 December 1852; Prest, *Russell*, p. 354.
(120) Prest, *Russell*, p. 354. [Russell Papers, 118A, Lady John Russell to Doddy, 15 July 1895.]
(121) Maxwell, *Clarendon*, Vol. II, p. 21; Prest, *Russell*, p. 354. [Russell Papers 11F, Wood to Russell, 7 December 1854.]
(122) Walpole, *Russell*, Vol. II, p. 157; Southgate, *Whigs*, p. 236.

(123) Parker, *Graham*, Vol. II, p. 180.
(124) *ibid*, p. 194.
(125) Southgate, *Whigs*, p. 239.
(126) Morley, *Gladstone*, Vol. I, p. 446.
(127) RA C28/53, Queen's Memo., 25 December 1852.
(128) Parker, *Graham*, Vol. II, pp. 199–200.
(129) *ibid*, p. 200.
(130) Ward, *Graham*, p. 269.
(131) Argyll, *Memoirs*, Vol. I, p. 373.
(132) Parker, *Graham*, Vol. II, p. 195, Diary, 21 December 1852; Reeve, *Memoirs*, Vol. I, p. 269.
(133) RA C28/38, Prince Albert's Memo., dictated to the Queen, 22 December 1852.
(134) RA C28/53, Queen's Memo., 25 December 1852.
(135) RA C28/65, Prince Albert's Memo., dictated to the Queen, 28 December 1852.
(136) Argyll, *Memoirs*, Vol. I, p. 380.
(137) Cook, *Delane*, p. 61.
(138) Parker, *Graham*, Vol. II, p. 197, Diary, 23 December 1852; and see Greville, *Diary*, Vol. II, p. 414, 24 December 1852.
(139) Maxwell, *Clarendon*, Vol. I, p. 354–5, Londonderry to Clarendon, 26 December 1852.
(140) B. & E., Vol. II, p. 478, Queen to King of Belgians, 17 September 1852.
(141) Martin, *Prince Consort*, Vol. II, p. 483, Queen to King of Belgians, 28 December 1852.
(142) *The Times*, 25 December 1852.
(143) Maxwell, *Clarendon*, Vol. I, p. 355.

CHAPTER 16 – 'CHAINED TO THE OAR'

(1) Conacher, *Coalition*, p. 21. [Minto Papers, Acc. 2794, Box 136 (National Library of Scotland), dated 'Xmas Day' 1852].
(2) Malmesbury, *Memoirs*, pp. 307–8, 29 May 1853.
(3) *ibid*, p. 308, 3 June 1853.
(4) Gordon, *Aberdeen*, p. 224; Herkless, *Stratford*, p. 510, MS. Clar., Dep. C4, Aberdeen to Clarendon, 5 June 1853.
(5) *ibid*.
(6) Greville, *Diary*, Vol. I, p. 413.
(7) Ab.Corr., 1852–5, pp. 158–60, 4 July 1853.
(8) Croker Papers, Vol. III, pp. 298–9, Lord Strangford to Croker, 5 December 1853.
(9) Argyll, *Memoirs*, Vol. I, p. 438.
(10) Conacher, *Coalition*, p. 267.
(11) MS. Clar. Dep. C4, fos. 48–9, 5 July 1853.
(12) Gordon, *Aberdeen*, pp. 225–7. Minute by Aberdeen.
(13) *ibid*, p. 234.
(14) Jones Parry, *Corr.*, Vol. II, p. 600, Aberdeen to Lieven, 14 November 1851.
(15) Argyll, *Memoirs*, p. 364, October 1852.
(16) Greville, *Memoirs*, Vol. VII, p. 80.

REFERENCES

(17) Add.MSS. 43070, 12 August 1853.
(18) Jones Parry, *Corr.*, Vol. II, p. 646f., Aberdeen to Lieven, 8 September 1853; Add.MSS. 43251, 217–18, 8 September 1853.
(19) B. & E., Vol. II, pp. 557–8, Prince Albert's Memo., 16 October 1853.
(20) Add.MSS. 43070, 372–5, 12 August 1853.
(21) HH 1/19, Aberdeen to Lady Haddo, 10 September 1853.
(22) Graham Papers, Aberdeen to Graham, 22 September 1853 (Confidential).
(23) *ibid*, 22 September 1853.
(24) Ab.Corr., 1852–5, pp. 275–6, and B. & E., Vol. II, p. 551, Aberdeen to Queen, 6 October 1853.
(25) B. & E., Vol. II, p. 552, Aberdeen to Queen, 7 October 1853.
(26) Conacher, *Coalition*, p. 265.
(27) Gordon, *Aberdeen*, p. 232, Aberdeen to Gladstone, 17 October 1853.
(28) Graham Papers, 22 September 1853.
(29) Greville, *Memoirs*, Vol. VII, p. 91.
(30) *ibid*, pp. 96–7.
(31) Graham Papers, Clarendon to Graham, Private, 22 September 1853.
(32) MS. Clar. Dep. C3, 431–4, 27 September 1853.
(33) Greville, *Memoirs*, Vol. VII, p. 98.
(34) B. & E., Vol. II, p. 558, Prince Albert's Memo., 16 October 1853.
(35) HH 1/19, Aberdeen to Lady Haddo, 30 September 1853. See also *ibid*, 4 October 1853.
(36) Ab.Corr., 1852–5, pp. 264–5, 3 October 1853.
(37) *ibid*, pp. 285–6.
(38) *ibid*, p. 272, 5 October 1853.
(39) Graham Papers, Aberdeen to Graham, 6 October 1853.
(40) MS. Clar. Dep. C3, 187–92, Palmerston to Graham, 14 October 1853.
(41) Maxwell, *Clarendon*, Vol. II, p. 26, Clarendon to G. C. Lewis, 9 October 1853.
(42) Ab.Corr., 1852–5, pp. 289–92, 10 October 1853; B. & E., Vol. II, pp. 552–4, Prince Albert's Memo., 10 October 1853.

CHAPTER 17 – 'ODD TEMPERS AND QUEER WAYS'

(1) MS. Clar. Dep. 64, 102, Aberdeen to Clarendon, 12 October 1853.
(2) *ibid*, Dep. C3, 473–81.
(3) Martin, *Prince Consort*, Vol. II, pp. 530–2.
(4) Gordon, *Aberdeen*, p. 237.
(5) Greville, *Diary*, Vol. I, p. 474, 27 November 1853.
(6) Add.MSS. 43069, Palmerston to Lansdowne, 8 December 1853; *ibid* 43251, 389–91.
(7) Add.MSS. 43069, Palmerston to Aberdeen, 10 December 1853.
(8) Graham Papers, Aberdeen to Graham, 10 December 1853.
(9) Ab.Corr., 1852–5, pp. 393–4, Graham to Aberdeen, 10 December 1853.
(10) *ibid* 43069, Aberdeen to Palmerston, 11 December 1853; *ibid* 43251, 397–8.
(11) *ibid* 43251, 404, 13 December 1853.
(12) Maxwell, *Clarendon*, Vol. II, p. 36, Lady Clarendon's Journal, 20 December 1853; Bell, *Palmerston*, Vol. II, pp. 97–8; Martin, *Triumph*, pp. 190–8.

(13) Add.MSS. 43069, Palmerston to Aberdeen, 14 December 1853; *ibid* 43251, 14 December 1853; Maxwell, *Clarendon*, Vol. II, p. 36.
(14) Ab.Corr., 1852–5, pp. 402–3, Aberdeen to Russell, 13 December 1853.
(15) MS. Clar. Dep. C4, 270–3, Graham to Clarendon, 13 December 1853.
(16) Gooch, *Later Corr.*, Vol. II, p. 155, Aberdeen to Russell, 20 December 1853.
(17) Ab.Corr., 1852–5, pp. 416–17.
(18) *ibid*, pp. 425–6, 22 December 1853.
(19) Maxwell, *Clarendon*, Vol. II, pp. 31–2, Clarendon to Lady Clarendon, 22 November 1853.
(20) MS. Clar. Dep. C3, 83–7.
(21) Gordon, *Aberdeen*, pp. 224–5, 253–4.
(22) Maxwell, *Clarendon*, Vol. II, p. 37, Lady Clarendon's Journal, 12 January 1854.
(23) Greville, *Diary*, Vol. II, pp. 376–8, 15 January 1854.
(24) PRO 30/22/11/C, 744–5, Clarendon to Aberdeen, 17 February 1854.
(25) Jones Parry, Vol. II, p. 63, Lieven to Aberdeen, 7 January 1854.
(26) Martin, *Triumph*, p. 30.
(27) Gordon, *Herbert*, Vol. I, p. 182.
(28) Conacher, *Coalition*, pp. 325–8.
(29) Add.MSS. 44778, 167–74, Memo. 111, 26 February 1854; Morley, *Gladstone*, Vol. II, pp. 491–2.
(30) Ab.Corr., 1854–5, pp. 61–2, Russell to Aberdeen, 3 March 1854.
(31) *ibid*, p. 62, Aberdeen to Russell, 3 March 1854.
(32) Gordon, *Aberdeen*, p. 257, Aberdeen to Russell.
(33) Gladstone, EHR, Vol. II, 1887 ('The History of 1852–60 and Greville's Latest Journals'); Argyll, *Edinburgh Review*, C, No. 203 (1854), pp. 1–43; Clarendon, *Edinburgh Review*, CXVII (1853), pp. 307–52.
(34) HH 1/19, Aberdeen to Lady Haddo, 22 March 1854.
(35) Trevelyan, *Bright*, pp. 232–3.

CHAPTER 18 – A RUSSELL AT HOME AND A RUSSELL ABROAD

(1) Ab.Corr., 1854–5, p. 93, 4 April 1854.
(2) Greville, *Memoirs*, Vol. VII, p. 153, 15 April 1854.
(3) B. & E., Vol. III, p. 25, Queen to Russell, 9 April 1854.
(4) *ibid*, Russell to Queen, 9 April 1854.
(5) PRO 30/22/11/C, 949–54, 10 April 1854.
(6) B. & E., Vol. III, p. 27, Prince Albert's Memo., 10 April 1854.
(7) *ibid*.
(8) *ibid*, p. 29.
(9) *ibid*, p. 28.
(10) *ibid*.
(11) *ibid*.
(12) Greville, *Memoirs*, Vol. VII, p. 153, 15 April 1854.
(13) PRO 30/22/11/C, 955–8, 11 April 1854.
(14) Greville, *Memoirs*, Vol. VII, p. 154, 15 April 1854; B. & E., Vol. III, p. 28, footnote; *Annual Register* 1854, p. 120; Argyll, *Memoirs*, Vol. I, p. 478.
(15) Hansard, CXXXI, 376.
(16) *ibid*.

(17) Hansard, CXXXII, 649.
(18) *ibid*, 665–9.
(19) Ab.Corr., 1854–5, pp. 107–8.
(20) RA G13/61, Aberdeen to Queen, 28 May 1854.
(21) Add.MSS. 44778, 183–4, 8 June 1854.
(22) Ab.Corr., 1854–5, p. 148, 8 June 1854.
(23) Hansard, CXXXV, 915–31.
(24) Russell, *The War*, pp. 70–1.
(25) *ibid*, pp. 143–4.

CHAPTER 19 – TO SEBASTOPOL

(1) Graham Papers, Graham to Raglan, Private, 8 May 1854; Parker, *Graham*, Vol. II, pp. 242–4.
(2) Kinglake, *Invasion*, Vol. II, p. 249, and note p. 407.
(3) Martin, *Prince Consort*, Vol. III, pp. 73–80; Gordon, *Aberdeen*, p. 259; and see Greville, *Diary*, Vol. II, p. 503, 21 June 1854.
(4) Gordon, *Aberdeen*, p. 259.
(5) RA G14/36, Queen to Aberdeen, 26 June 1854; Add.MSS. 43253, 150, 26 June 1854; see also Martin, *Prince Consort*, Vol. III, pp. 77–8.
(6) Ab.Corr., 1854–5, p. 156, Clarendon to Aberdeen, 26 June 1854.
(7) Hansard, CXXXV, 535–50.
(8) *ibid*, 598–613.
(9) *ibid*, 613–90.
(10) *ibid*, 680.
(11) *ibid*, 709–16.
(12) *ibid*, 716f.
(13) *ibid*, 766.
(14) HH 1/19, Aberdeen to Lady Haddo, 9 August 1854; Arthur Gordon's Diary, entries for 12, 15 July 1854, 14, 15, 16 August 1857.
(15) Ab.Corr., 1854–5, p. 177, Aberdeen to Graham, 26 July 1854 (copy). Copy in Graham Papers with note by C. S. Parker about Lord Stanmore's attitude to publication.
(16) Add.MSS. 44319, 58, Arthur Gordon to Gladstone, 'Monday, 3 p.m.'.
(17) *ibid*, 60–1, Gladstone to Gordon, 24 July 1854.
(18) Hansard, CXXXV, 1522–33.
(19) Elliott, *Memoirs*, p. 68f., Lord Haddo's Diary, 2 September 1853.
(20) *ibid*, Haddo to Aberdeen, 8 August 1853.
(21) RA A23/143, Aberdeen to Queen, 28 August 1854; see also RA A23/105, Aberdeen to Queen, 22 May 1854; RA A23/143 & 144, Aberdeen to Queen, 28, 31 August 1854.
(22) Balfour, *Life*, Vol. II, p. 235.
(23) Add.MSS. 43254, 209–10, Newcastle to Aberdeen, 7 September 1854.
(24) Balfour, *Life*, Vol. II, p. 241, Aberdeen to Argyll, 30 August 1854.
(25) *ibid*, p. 244, Gordon to Aberdeen, March 1855.
(26) *ibid*, p. 241, Aberdeen to Argyll, 30 August 1854.
(27) *ibid*.
(28) *ibid*.

CHAPTER 20 – 'ANXIETY AND SUSPENSE'

(1) Ab.Corr., 1854–5, p. 221, Newcastle to Aberdeen, 28 September 1854.
(2) Wrottesley, *Burgoyne*, Vol. II, p. 734.
(3) *ibid*, p. 77.
(4) Balfour, *Life*, Vol. II, p. 243, Clarendon to Aberdeen, 14 September 1854.
(5) RA Y183/89, Prince Albert to Aberdeen, 17 September 1854.
(6) RA Y183/89 & 91, Queen to Aberdeen, 22, 25 September 1854.
(7) RA A23/144, Aberdeen to Queen, 31 August 1854.
(8) Arthur Gordon, *Diary*, 28 September 1854.
(9) Balfour, *Life*, Vol. II, p. 248, Lord Raglan's telegram, Sunday, 1 October 1854. (See also RA G17/63, Aberdeen to Queen, 1 October 1854.)
(10) Ab.Corr., 1854–5, pp. 225–6, Graham to Aberdeen, 30 September 1854.
(11) RA G17/83, Aberdeen to Queen, 6 October 1854; and RA G17/86, Queen to Aberdeen, 7 October 1854.
(12) RA G17/79, Aberdeen to Queen, 4 October 1854; and RA G17/83, Aberdeen to Queen, 6 October 1854.
(13) MS. Clar. C15, fos. 613–14, Russell to Clarendon, 9 October 1854; Gooch, *Later Corr.*, Vol. II, pp. 171–2, Clarendon to Russell, 11 October 1854; Greville, *Memoirs*, Vol. VII, p. 59.
(14) Ab.Corr., 1854–5, pp. 235–7, Graham to Aberdeen, 4 October 1854.
(15) RA G17/83, Aberdeen to Queen, 6 October 1854.
(16) Ab.Corr., 1854–5, p. 238, Graham to Aberdeen, 3 October 1854; RA G17/89, Prince Albert's Memo., 7 October 1854; Add.MSS. 44319, Arthur Gordon to Gladstone, 19 October 1854.
(17) Ab.Corr., 1854–5, p. 239, Aberdeen to Graham, 6 October 1854.
(18) Add.MSS. 44319, 77–8, Gladstone to Arthur Gordon, 12 October 1854.
(19) Ab.Corr., 1852–5, p. 351, Aberdeen to Russell, 12 November 1853.
(20) Add.MSS. 43225, fos. 257–8, Major the Hon. A. Gordon to Aberdeen, 18 October 1854.
(21) Martineau, *Newcastle*, pp. 166–7.
(22) Graham Papers, Graham to Dundas, 25 October 1854 (copy).
(23) *ibid*, Graham to Lyons, 4 December 1854 (copy).
(24) Argyll, *Memoirs*, Vol. I, p. 499.
(25) Maxwell, *Clarendon*, Vol. II, p. 47.
(26) Arthur Gordon, *Diary*, 7 November 1854. See also Greville, *Diary*, Vol. II, p. 504, 2 October 1854.
(27) RA Y183/95, Prince Albert to Aberdeen, 11 November 1854.
(28) Arthur Gordon, *Diary*, 22 November 1854.
(29) Add.MSS. 43225, fos. 270–1, Major the Hon. A. Gordon to Aberdeen, 8 November 1854.
(30) Balfour, *Life*, Vol. II, p. 244.
(31) Add.MSS. 43225, fos. 270–1, Major the Hon. A. Gordon to Aberdeen, 8 November 1854.
(32) *ibid*, fos. 273–4, Major the Hon. A. Gordon to Aberdeen, 13 November 1854.
(33) *ibid*, fos. 276–7, 17 November 1854.
(34) HH 1/19, Aberdeen to Lady Haddo, 24 November 1854.
(35) *Annual Register*, 1854, pp. 398–402.

(36) Martineau, *Newcastle*, pp. 229–30, Newcastle to Raglan, 22 December 1854.
(37) *ibid*, pp. 236–7, Newcastle to Raglan, 1 January 1855.
(38) *ibid*, pp. 240–1, Newcastle to Raglan, 26 January 1855.

CHAPTER 21 – A STORMY SESSION

(1) Arthur Gordon, *Diary*, 23 June 1854.
(2) Ab.Corr., 1854–5, p. 267, Russell to Aberdeen, 3 November 1854.
(3) *ibid* 43068, pp. 179–84; Walpole, *Russell*, Vol. II, p. 233, Russell to Aberdeen, 14 November 1854.
(4) Add.MSS. 43068, 187–8, Russell to Aberdeen, 18 November 1854; RA A84/4 (copy).
(5) Gordon, *Aberdeen*, p. 278.
(6) Martin, *Prince Consort*, Vol. III, pp. 196–7, Aberdeen to Russell, 24 November 1854.
(7) RA A84/5, Aberdeen to Russell, 21 November 1854 (copy).
(8) RA A84/1–6 (copies), Aberdeen to Queen, 23 November 1854; Russell to Aberdeen, 17 November 1854; Aberdeen to Russell, 18 November, 1854; Russell to Aberdeen, 18 November 1854; Aberdeen to Russell, 21 November 1854; Russell to Aberdeen, 23 November 1854; Aberdeen to Queen, 24 November 1854; Add.MSS. 38080, 102–4, 21 November 1854; *ibid* 43068, 198–206; PRO 30/22/11/F, 1781–3; Gooch, *Later Corr.*, Vol. II, pp. 174–6, 28 November 1854, Russell to Aberdeen, and Aberdeen to Russell, 30 November 1854.
(9) RA A84/10, Prince Albert's Memo., 27 November 1854 (copy).
(10) RA A84/8, Queen to Aberdeen, 25 November 1854 (copy).
(11) Argyll, *Memoirs*, Vol. II, pp. 508–10.
(12) Add.MSS. 43191, 270–4, Graham to Aberdeen, 5 December 1854.
(13) Argyll, *Memoirs*, Vol. II, pp. 508–10.
(14) *ibid*, p. 509.
(15) *ibid*, p. 510.
(16) *ibid*.
(17) *ibid*.
(18) Maxwell, *Clarendon*, Vol. II, p. 4.
(19) Add.MSS. 44778, 188–90, Gladstone Memorandum, 6 December 1854.
(20) Maxwell, *Clarendon*, Vol. II, p. 53, Clarendon to Lady Clarendon.
(21) *ibid*, p. 53, Lady Clarendon's Journal, December 1854.
(22) PRO 30/22/11/F, 1886–95, Wood to Russell, 7 December 1854.
(23) Maxwell, *Clarendon*, Vol. II, p. 54.
(24) RA A84/20, Prince Albert's Memo., 9 December 1854.
(25) *ibid*.
(26) RA A84/21, Aberdeen to Queen, 9 December 1854.
(27) Walpole, *Russell*, Vol. II, p. 237.
(28) RA A84/24, Aberdeen to Queen, 16 December 1854.
(29) *ibid*.
(30) HH 1/29, Aberdeen to Lady Haddo, 6 December 1854.
(31) Ab.Corr., 1854–5, pp. 249–51, Clarendon to Aberdeen, 8 October 1854.
(32) MS. Clar. Dep. C14, f. 88, 25 September 1854.
(33) PP 1854–5, IX, Pt II, Third Report, Appendix, 473, 479. See also evidence of Duke of Newcastle, *ibid*, p. 188.

(34) Hansard, CXXXVI, 135, 12 December 1854.
(35) *ibid*, 136–7.
(36) PP 1854–5, IX, Pt II, Third Report, Appendix, 470.
(37) Ab.Corr., 1854–5, pp. 272–4.
(38) PP 1854–5, IX, Pt III, Fourth Report, Appendix, 335–8.
(39) RA G18/134, Aberdeen to Queen, 10 November 1854; Maxwell, *Clarendon*, Vol. II, pp. 49–50; MS. Clar. C15, 248, 19 November 1854.
(40) Hansard, CXXXVI, 1–3.
(41) RA G20/112, 12 December 1854; *The Times*, 13 December 1854.
(42) *The Times*, 13 December 1854; Greville, *Memoirs*, Vol. VII, p. 210; Hansard, CXXXVI, 36–74.
(43) Hansard, CXXXVI, 136.
(44) *ibid*, 215–23.
(45) *ibid*, 197–215.
(46) HH 1/19, Aberdeen to Lady Haddo, 25 December 1854 (copy).
(47) *The Times*, 12 December 1854.
(48) *ibid*, 19 December 1854.
(49) *ibid*, 23 December 1854.
(50) *ibid*, 26 December 1854.
(51) *ibid*, 30 December 1854.
(52) *ibid*.
(53) Greville, *Memoirs*, Vol. VII, p. 214, 31 December 1854.

CHAPTER 22 – 'TREACHERY AND DECEIT'

(1) HH 1/29, Aberdeen to Lady Haddo, 7 January 1855.
(2) RA M54/4, Wilberforce to Prince Albert, 16 May 1854.
(3) RA G22/5, Queen to Aberdeen, 10 January 1855.
(4) RA G22/6, Aberdeen to Queen, 10 January 1855.
(5) RA G22/10, Aberdeen to Queen, 11 January 1855.
(6) RA G22/11 (draft), Queen to Aberdeen, 11 January 1855.
(7) RA G22/41, Aberdeen to Queen, 13 January 1855.
(8) Gordon, *Herbert*, Vol. I, pp. 303–6, Herbert to Newcastle, 8 January 1855; PRO 30/22/A, 30–3.
(9) Argyll, *Memoirs*, Vol. I, p. 513.
(10) PRO 30/22/11F, 1941–4, Granville to Raglan, 23 December 1854.
(11) *ibid*, 1808–9, Granville to Raglan, n.d.
(12) PRO 30/22/12/A, 18–19, Clarendon to Russell, 2 January 1855.
(13) Martineau, *Newcastle*, pp. 224–5.
(14) *ibid*, pp. 225–6.
(15) Walpole, *Russell*, Vol. II, pp. 238–40, Russell's Memorandum.
(16) PRO 30/22/12/A, 14–17, Russell to Aberdeen, unfinished.
(17) RA G21/73, Aberdeen to Queen, 2 January 1855.
(18) Walpole, *Russell*, Vol. II, p. 240.
(19) PRO 30/22/12/A, 44–5, Aberdeen to Russell, 4 January 1855; see also Walpole, *Russell*, Vol. II, p. 240.
(20) PRO 30/22/12/A, 34–41, Herbert's comments on Russell's Memorandum, 3 January 1855.
(21) *ibid*, 34–41, 3 January 1855; *ibid*, 46–9, 6 January 1855.
(22) Gordon, *Herbert*, Vol. I, pp. 318–25.
(23) RA G22/21, Aberdeen to Queen, 11 January 1855; PRO WO/6/70/84,

No. 202. Draft despatch, 6 January 1855, read to Cabinet, 11 January 1855.

(24) Martineau, *Newcastle*, pp. 240–4.
(25) Graham Papers, Herbert to Graham, Private, 7 January 1855.
(26) RA G21/111, Aberdeen to Queen, 9 January 1855; PRO 30/22/12/A, 57–60, Clarendon to Russell, 8 January 1855; RA G22/33, Queen to Aberdeen, 13 January 1855.
(27) HH 1/29, Aberdeen to Lady Haddo, 9 January 1855.
(28) Argyll, *Memoirs*, Vol. I, p. 516.
(29) *The Times*, 20 January 1855.
(30) *ibid.*
(31) *ibid*, 22 January 1855.
(32) *ibid*, 23 January 1855.
(33) Conacher, *Coalition*, p. 531.
(34) Morley, *Gladstone*, Vol. I, p. 521; Gordon, *Aberdeen*, pp. 280–2; Gordon, *Herbert*, Vol. I, p. 245; Martineau, *Newcastle*, p. 252.
(35) Gordon, *Aberdeen*, p. 281; Gordon, *Herbert*, Vol. I, p. 246.
(36) Morley, *Gladstone*, Vol. I, p. 521; Gordon, *Aberdeen*, pp. 280–2; Gordon, *Herbert*, pp. 245–6; Martineau, *Newcastle*, p. 252.
(37) Arthur Gordon, *Diary*, 22 January 1855.
(38) *ibid.*
(39) *ibid.*
(40) *ibid.*
(41) *ibid.*
(42) *ibid*, 23 January 1855.
(43) *ibid.*
(44) *ibid*, 22 January 1855.
(45) *ibid.*
(46) *ibid*, 23 January 1855.
(47) Walpole, *Russell*, Vol. II, p. 242.
(48) PRO 30/22/12/A, 2–8. See also Walpole, *Russell*, Vol. II, p. 243.
(49) Ab.Corr., 1855–60, p. 2, Russell to Aberdeen, 23 January 1855.
(50) RA A84/27, Russell to Queen, 24 January 1855 (copy); RA G22/89, Queen to Russell, 24 January 1855 (draft).
(51) Fitzmaurice, *Granville*, Vol. I, p. 90.

CHAPTER 23 – THE FALL

(1) Argyll, *Memoirs*, Vol. I, pp. 516–17.
(2) RA G23/1, Prince Albert's Memo., 25 January 1855.
(3) RA A84/35, Palmerston to Russell, 24 January 1855; PRO 30/22/12A, 108–9, 24 January 1855; and see Ashley, *Palmerston*, Vol. II, pp. 301–2.
(4) Argyll, *Memoirs*, Vol. I, p. 517.
(5) RA G23/1 and RA A84/30, Prince Albert's Memo., 25 January 1855.
(6) *ibid*; Maxwell, *Clarendon*, Vol. II, pp. 56–6; Add.MSS. 44745, 22–8, Gladstone Memorandum on Cabinet meeting of 24 January 1855, 9 March 1855; Morley, *Gladstone*, Vol. I, p. 522.
(7) Ab.Corr., 1855–60, p. 3, Wood to Aberdeen, 24 January 1855.
(8) RA G23/1 and RA A84/30, Prince Albert's Memo. (copy), 25 January 1855.

(9) RA G22/89 (draft), Queen to Russell, 24 January 1855.
(10) RA G23/2 and RA A84/31, Russell to Queen, 25 January 1855.
(11) RA G23/4 and RA A84/33, Queen to Russell, 25 January 1855.
(12) Gordon, *Aberdeen*, pp. 282-3.
(13) *ibid*, p. 283.
(14) *ibid.*
(15) *ibid.*
(16) RA G23/5 and RA A84/34, Prince Albert's Memo., 25 January 1855.
(17) Argyll, *Memoirs*, Vol. I, p. 518.
(18) Add.MSS. 44745, 28-9, Gladstone Memorandum, 9 March 1855.
(19) RA G23/5 and RA A84/34, Prince Albert's Memo., 25 January 1855.
(20) Argyll, *Memoirs*, Vol. I, p. 518.
(21) Add.MSS. 44745, 130, Gladstone Memorandum, 25 January 1855.
(22) Conacher, *Coalition*, p. 537.
(23) Ab.Corr., 1855-60, p. 4, Dawkins to Gordon, 25 January 1855; Gooch, *Later Corr.*, Vol. II, p. 182, 9 February 1855, Russell to Grey.
(24) Gordon, *Aberdeen*, p. 283.
(25) Argyll, *Memoirs*, Vol. I, p. 519.
(26) *ibid.*
(27) Hansard, CXXXVI, 941-3.
(28) *The Times*, 26 January 1855.
(29) Hansard, CXXXVI, 943-4.
(30) *The Times*, 27 January 1855.
(31) Hansard, CXXXVI, 960-74.
(32) Add.MSS. 44745, 31-2, Gladstone Memorandum, 9 March 1855.
(33) RA G23/17, Aberdeen to Queen, 27 January 1855.
(34) *The Times*, 27 January 1855.
(35) Morley, *Gladstone*, Vol. I, p. 523.
(36) RA G23/17, Aberdeen to Queen, 27 January 1855.
(37) Hansard, CXXXVI, 1039; RA G23/17, Aberdeen to Queen, 27 January 1855; Croker Papers, Vol. III, pp. 323-4, Lonsdale to Croker.
(38) Hansard, CXXXVI, 979-82 and 982-1002; RA A84/43, Palmerston to Queen, 26 January 1855.
(39) Hansard, CXXXVI, 989.
(40) Add.MSS. 44237, 245-6, Young to Gladstone, 27 January 1855.
(41) Hansard, CXXXVI, 1178-1206; Add.MSS. 43255, p. 8; Arthur Gordon, Diary, 30 January 1855.
(42) Hansard, CXXXVI, 1205-6.
(43) *ibid*, 1222-6.
(44) *ibid*, 1230-3.
(45) Arthur Gordon, *Diary*, 30 January 1855.
(46) *ibid.*

CHAPTER 24 – *PROCUL NEGOTIIS NON BEATUS*

(1) Greville, *Diary*, Vol. II, pp. 512-13, 4 February 1855.
(2) Arthur Gordon, *Diary*, 1 February 1855.
(3) Hansard, CXXXVI, 1230-3.
(4) Arthur Gordon, *Diary*, 7 February, 1855.
(5) Gordon, *Aberdeen*, p. 287; HH 1/29, Aberdeen to Lady Haddo, 7 February 1855; RA Y183/112, Prince Albert to Aberdeen, 1 February 1855.

REFERENCES

(6) Gordon, *Aberdeen*, pp. 287–8.
(7) Arthur Gordon, *Diary*, 3 February 1855.
(8) *ibid*, 4 February 1855.
(9) *ibid*; RA Y183/114, Queen to Aberdeen, 4 February 1855.
(10) Arthur Gordon, *Diary*, 3 February 1855.
(11) Dalling & Ashley, *Palmerston*, Vol. V, p. 77, and 1879 edition, Vol. II, p. 306, Palmerston to Temple, 15 February 1855; see also Monypenny & Buckle, *Disraeli*, Vol. I, p. 1383, Disraeli to the Dowager Lady Londonderry, 2 February 1855.
(12) Argyll, *Memoirs*, Vol. I, pp. 527–8.
(13) Arthur Gordon, *Diary*, 5 February 1855.
(14) RA Y183/113, Prince Albert to Aberdeen, 6 February 1855.
(15) Arthur Gordon, *Diary*, 6 February 1855; Gordon, *Aberdeen* (proofs), Chap. XIII, pp. 3–5; B. & E., Vol. III, pp. 126–7.
(16) Arthur Gordon, *Diary*, 6 February 1855; Gordon, *Aberdeen* (proofs), Chap. XIII, p. 4; B. & E., Vol. III, p. 127, Aberdeen to Herbert, 6 February 1855.
(17) Argyll, *Memoirs*, Vol. I, pp. 528–30.
(18) HH 1/29, Aberdeen to Lady Haddo, 24 February 1855; Ashley, *Palmerston*, Vol. II, p. 80.
(19) HH 1/29, Aberdeen to Lady Haddo, 7 February 1855 (copy).
(20) *ibid*.
(21) Arthur Gordon, *Diary*, 8 February 1855.
(22) B. & E., Vol. III, p. 129, Queen to Aberdeen, 7 February 1855.
(23) HH 1/29, Aberdeen to Lady Haddo, 9 February 1855.
(24) Arthur Gordon, *Diary*, 10 February 1855 (inaccurate); RA F38/28, Aberdeen to Queen, 10 February 1855.
(25) HH 1/29, Aberdeen to Lady Haddo, 7 February 1855 (copy).
(26) Gordon, *Aberdeen*, pp. 292–3, 10 February 1855.
(27) *ibid*, 4 February 1855.
(28) *ibid*, 5 February 1855.
(29) *ibid*, 24 February 1855.
(30) Hansard, CXXXVI, 1424; Argyll, *Memoirs*, Vol. I, p. 536.
(31) HH 1/29, Aberdeen to Lady Haddo, 8 March 1855.
(32) *ibid*, 7 February 1855.
(33) HH 1/35, Arthur Gordon to Lady Haddo, n.d., but dated from internal evidence.
(34) *ibid*, 6 January 1855.
(35) HH 1/29, Aberdeen to Lady Haddo, no date, but from internal evidence written 7 January 1855.
(36) Arthur Gordon, *Diary*, 19 February 1855.
(37) *ibid*, 14 February 1855.
(38) *ibid*, 24 March, 8 May, 26 May 1855 and *passim*.
(39) *ibid*, 29 April, 8, 16, 24 May 1855 and *passim*.
(40) HH 1/29, Aberdeen to Lady Haddo, 25 April 1855.
(41) Arthur Gordon, *Diary*, 6, 8, 20, 21 June 1855 and *passim*.
(42) *ibid*, 16 February 1855.
(43) *ibid*, 24 March 1855.
(44) HH 1/19, Aberdeen to Lady Haddo, 28 August 1855.
(45) Arthur Gordon, *Diary*, 24 March 1855.
(46) *ibid*, 24 March 1855; HH 1/19, Aberdeen to Lady Haddo, 28 August 1855.
(47) Arthur Gordon, *Diary*, 14 April 1855.

(48) *ibid*, 10 May 1855.
(49) *ibid*, 14 May 1855.
(50) *ibid*, 15 May 1855; see Martineau, *Newcastle*, pp. 187–94.
(51) Balfour, *Life*, Vol. II, p. 234.
(52) HH 1/35, Aberdeen to Lady Haddo, 24 November 1854.
(53) Arthur Gordon, *Diary*, 30 January 1855.
(54) HH 1/35, Aberdeen to Lady Haddo, 24 November 1854; HH 1/29, Aberdeen to Lady Haddo, 7 February 1855 (copy); HH 1/19, Aberdeen to Lady Haddo, 24 March 1855.
(55) HH 1/35, Aberdeen to Lady Haddo, 25 September 1854.
(56) Arthur Gordon, *Diary*, 5 June 1855.
(57) *ibid*, 18 June 1855.
(58) Martineau, *Newcastle*, pp. 192–3; Martin, *Prince Consort*, Vol. III, pp. 217–18; Hansard, CXXXIX, 968, Peel's speech; debate, 964–118f.; Gordon, *Herbert*, Vol. I, pp. 443–56.
(59) Arthur Gordon, *Diary*, 16 July 1855.
(60) HH 1/35, Aberdeen to Lady Haddo, n.d., December 1854; see also *ibid*, Aberdeen to Lady Haddo, 24 November 1854.
(61) HH 1/32, Aberdeen to Baillie-Hamilton, 1 November 1852.
(62) HH 1/28, Aberdeen to Haddo, 23 October 1852.
(63) HH 1/32, Aberdeen to Baillie-Hamilton, 12 November 1852.
(64) HH 1/19, Aberdeen to Lady Haddo, 28 August 1855.
(65) HH 1/32, Aberdeen to Baillie-Hamilton, 12 November 1852.
(66) RA A23/22, Aberdeen to Queen, 27 July 1854; RA A23/152, Aberdeen to Queen, 3 November 1854.
(67) Martin, *Prince Consort*, Vol. III, pp. 452–7, 499–500.
(68) HH 1/29, Aberdeen to Lady Haddo, 26 September 1855; HH 1/19, Aberdeen to Lady Haddo, 2 December 1855.
(69) Greville, *Diary*, Vol. II, p. 495, 20 February 1855; *ibid*, p. 493, 23 June 1855.
(70) Balfour, *Life*, Vol. II, p. 315.
(71) *ibid*, p. 317, Aberdeen to Hudson Gurney.
(72) Gordon, *Herbert*, Vol. I, p. 254, Herbert to Gladstone, 4 February 1855.

CHAPTER 25 – THE LAST YEARS

(1) Martineau, *Newcastle*, pp. 187–94.
(2) Arthur Gordon, *Diary*, 4 October 1855.
(3) *The Times*, 15 December 1860.
(4) Arthur Gordon, *Diary*, 7 February 1855.
(5) *ibid*, 7 December 1855.
(6) *ibid*, 8 August 1854.
(7) *ibid*, 15 November 1854.
(8) *ibid*, 11 June 1856.
(9) *ibid*, 1 January 1857.
(10) Add.MSS. 44089, Gladstone to Aberdeen, 31 March 1857; *ibid*, Aberdeen to Gladstone, 31 March 1857; *ibid*, Gladstone to Aberdeen, 4 April 1857; *ibid*, Aberdeen to Gladstone, 8 April 1857; Add.MSS. 43179, Herbert to Aberdeen, 12 April 1857; Jones and Erickson, *The Peelites*, pp. 206–9.

REFERENCES

(11) HH 1/29, Aberdeen to Lady Haddo, 24 February 1855.
(12) Add.MSS. 43179, Aberdeen to Herbert, 18 April 1857.
(13) Argyll, *Memoirs*, Vol. II, p. 91.
(14) Balfour, *Life*, Vol. II, p. 320.
(15) RA B16/79, Clarendon to Queen, 14 September 1857.
(16) Balfour, *Life*, Vol. II, p. 321.
(17) Gordon, *Aberdeen*, p. 305; *Illustrated London News*, 24 October 1857; HH 1/23, *Banffshire Journal*, 20 October 1857; RA *Queen Victoria's Journal*, 14 October 1857.
(18) RA Y102/36, Queen to King of Belgians, 3 November 1857; see also RA *Queen Victoria's Journal*, 26 October 1857.
(19) HH 1/32, Aberdeen to Baillie-Hamilton, 7 November 1857; Jarnac, *Révue des Deux Mondes*, Vol. XXXIV, p. 470.
(20) Catalogue of Additions to MSS in British Museum 1931–5, pub. 1967 by Trustees of British Museum, p. 88.
(21) *ibid*. Volume printed by Harrison & Sons, London, in 1858.
(22) Balfour, *Life*, Vol. II, p. 321.
(23) *ibid*.
(24) HH 1/32, Aberdeen to Baillie-Hamilton, 3 February 1858.
(25) Balfour, *Life*, Vol. II, p. 317, Aberdeen to Hudson Gurney. See also Add.MSS. 43329, f. 87, Aberdeen to Graham, 27 December 1856.
(26) Argyll, *Memoirs*, Vol. I, pp. 108–9.
(27) RA *Queen Victoria's Journal*, 21 April 1858; Gordon, *Aberdeen*, p. 301.
(28) Official Reports of British Museum, Vol. 66, pp. 226–31; Vol. 66, Re. No. 4076; Letter Books and Original Papers, Vol. LXIX, f. 437, 20 April 1861, Reg. No. 4625.
(29) Hansard, CLI, 1359–61.
(30) Argyll, *Memoirs*, Vol. I, p. 123, Argyll to Aberdeen, 31 August 1858.
(31) *The Times*, 26 July 1859.
(32) HH 1/29, Aberdeen to Lady Haddo, January 1855, n.d., but from internal evidence written on 7 January 1855.
(33) RA Z467/69, Russell to Queen, 27 October 1860; see also RA *Queen Victoria's Journal*, 29 November 1860.
(34) HH 1/28, Arthur Gordon to Lady Haddo, 18 December 1860.
(35) RA M54/172, Col. the Hon. A. Gordon to Col. Thomas Biddulph, 14 December 1860.
(36) RA F38/48, Abercorn to Queen, 14 December 1860; see also RA *Queen Victoria's Journal*, 14 December 1860.
(37) HH 1/28, Col. the Hon. A. Gordon to Lord Haddo, Christmas Day, 1860.
(38) HH 1/28, Col. the Hon. A. Gordon to Lord Haddo, 25 December 1860.
(39) *ibid*, Canon the Hon. Douglas Hamilton-Gordon to Lady Haddo, 17 December 1860.
(40) Croker Papers, Vol. II, p. 30.
(41) *Victorian Studies*, Vol. II, pp. 155–60, Account of a visit to the Gladstones in 1894, by Lady Aberdeen.
(42) Obituaries in *The Times*, 15 December 1860; *Illustrated London News*, 29 December 1860 (various inaccuracies).
(43) HH 1/28, Arthur Gordon to Lady Haddo, 26 December 1860.
(44) *ibid*, Col. the Hon. A. Gordon to Lord Haddo, 25 December 1860.

(45) Gordon, *Aberdeen*, p. 307.
(46) HH 1/29, Aberdeen to Lady Haddo, 9 January 1855.
(47) Gordon, *Aberdeen*, pp. 302–3.
(48) Plutarch, Translation by John Dryden, revised by Arthur Hugh Clough, Modern Library Giant Edition, p. 396; Bartlett, *Dictionary of Quotations*, p. 1112.

APPENDIX – SCOTTISH CHURCH AFFAIRS

(1)   Gordon, *Aberdeen* (proofs), Chap. VIII, p. 6.
(2)   *The Times*, 15 December 1860.
(3)   Gordon, *Aberdeen*, p. 126 ('Roguish' for 'radical' in proofs, Chap. VIII, p. 6).
(4)   Gordon, *Aberdeen* (proofs), Chap. VIII, p. 8.
(5)   *ibid.*
(6)   *ibid*, p. 7.
(7)   *ibid.*
(8)   *ibid*, p. 8.
(9)   *ibid*, p. 40.
(10) Gordon, *Aberdeen*, p. 150.
(11) *ibid.*

See also Add.MSS. 43329, *passim.*

Selected Bibliography

MAIN MANUSCRIPT SOURCES

Aberdeen Papers at Haddo House, Aberdeenshire.
Aberdeen Papers, British Museum, Add.MSS. 43039–43358.
Gladstone Papers, British Museum, Add. MSS. 43649–50.
Peel Papers, British Museum, Add.MSS. 40181–40617.
Public Record Office.
Graham Papers, Cambridge University Library (microfilm).
Clarendon Papers, Bodleian Library, Oxford.
The Diaries of Arthur Gordon, later Lord Stanmore.
The Archives of *The Times* newspaper.
The Royal Archives, Windsor Castle.
MSS records at the Society of Antiquaries.

PRINTED BUT UNPUBLISHED SOURCES

The Fourth Earl of Aberdeen, by Lord Stanmore, proof copy.
The Correspondence of Lord Aberdeen, privately printed by Lord Stanmore (British Museum, 9 vols.).
Correspondence relative to the Society Islands, 1822–46, privately printed for the use of the Cabinet.

NEWSPAPERS AND PERIODICALS

The Times, Morning Chronicle, Morning Post, Morning Herald, Daily News, Spectator, Political Examiner, Edinburgh Review, Révue des Deux Mondes, Punch, etc.

REFERENCE WORKS

Hansard's Parliamentary Debates.
British and Foreign State Papers.
British Parliamentary Papers.
MILLER, D. Hunter, *Treaties and Other International Acts of the United States of America*, Vols. IV and V, published by the Department of State, Washington, 1934–7.
RICHARDSON, J. D., *Messages and Papers of the Presidents*, Vols. IV, V and VI, NY, n.d.
USA Executive Documents.

365

SELECTED BIBLIOGRAPHY

USA Senate Documents.
DOD, C. R., *Electoral Facts, 1832–1852* (London, 1853).
The Annual Register.
The Encyclopaedia Britannica.
Dictionary of National Biography.
Burke's Peerage.

PRINTED SOURCES

ABERDEEN, fourth Earl, see BALFOUR and STANMORE. (Gloucester, Mass., 1963).
ACLAND, H. H. Dyke, and RANSOME, C.: *Political History of England* (London, 1882).
ADAMS, E. D.: *British Interests and Activities in Texas, 1838–1846*
AIRLIE, Mabell, Countess of: *Lady Palmerston and her Times* (London, 1922).
ANDERSON, M. S.: *The Eastern Question, 1774–1923* (London, 1966).
ANDERSON, O.: *A Liberal State at War* (London, 1967).
ARGYLL, Dowager Duchess of: *George Douglas, eighth Duke of Argyll, Autobiography and Memoirs* (London, 1906).
ASHLEY, E.: *The Life and Correspondence of Henry John Temple, Viscount Palmerston* (London, 1879).
BAGEHOT, Walter: *The English Constitution* (London, 1928).
BALFOUR, Lady Frances: *The Life of George, fourth Earl of Aberdeen* (London, n.d. but pub. 1923).
BANDINEL, J.: *Some Account of the Trade in Slaves from Africa* (London, 1842). (Dedicated to Lord Aberdeen.)
BANFORD, F., and WELLINGTON, Duke of: *The Journals of Mrs Arbuthnot, 1820–1832* (London, 1950).
BARTLETT, C. J.: *Castlereagh* (London, 1966); *Great Britain and Sea Power, 1815–1853* (Oxford, 1963).
BASTIDE, L.: *'L'expédition de Tahiti 1843–47', Revue de l'histoire des colonies françaises*, Vol. 21, pt 3 (Paris, 1933) (pp. 157–80).
BEASLEY, W. G.: *Great Britain and the Opening of Japan, 1834–1858* (London, 1951).
BELL, H. C. F.: *Lord Palmerston* (London, 1936).
BENSON, A. C., and ESHER, Viscount: *The Letters of Queen Victoria, 1837–1861* (London, 1907).
BENTLEY, Nicolas: *Russell's Despatches from the Crimea, 1854–6* (London, 1966).
BESSBOROUGH, Earl of: *Lady Bessborough and her Circle* (London, 1940); *Georgiana, Extracts from the Correspondence of Georgiana, Duchess of Devonshire* (London, 1955).
BETHELL, L.: *The Abolition of the Brazilian Slave Trade, 1807–1859* (Cambridge, 1970).
BINDOFF, S. T.: *The Scheldt Question to 1839* (London, 1970).
BLAKE, Robert: *Disraeli* (London 1966).
BLAKE, Robert: *The Conservative Party from Peel to Churchill* (London, 1970).
BOURNE, K.: *The Foreign Policy of Victorian England, 1830–1902* (Oxford, 1970); *Britain and the Balance of Power in North America, 1815–1908* (London, 1967).

BROSSARD, A. de: *Républiques de la Plata dans leur rapports avec la France et l'Angleterre* (Paris, 1850).

BROUGHTON, Lord (J. C. Hobhouse): *Recollections of a Long Life*, ed. Lady Dorchester (London, 1911).

BUCHANAN, James: *The Works of James Buchanan, comprising his speeches, state papers and private correspondence*, ed. J. B. Moore (Philadelphia, 1908–11).

BULLEN, Roger: *Palmerston, Guizot, and the Collapse of the Entente Cordiale* (London, 1974).

BULWER: see DALLING and ASHLEY, and PALMERSTON.

BUTTERFIELD, Sir H.: *The Whig Interpretation of History* (London, 1950).

BUXTON, T. F.: *The African Slave Trade and its Remedy* (London, 1840).

CADY, J. F.: *Foreign Intervention in the Rio de la Plata, 1835–1850* (Philadelphia, 1929).

Cambridge History of British Foreign Policy, 1783–1919, ed. Ward and Gooch (Cambridge, 1922–3).

Cambridge Modern History, ed. Ward, Prothero, Leathes (Cambridge, 1907–10).

CANNING: see PETRIE, DIXON, HINDE.

CASS, L.: *An Examination of the questions now in discussion concerning the Right of Search* (Baltimore, 1842).

CASTLEREAGH, Viscount: *Correspondence, Despatches and Other Papers of Viscount Castlereagh* (London, 1851–3) (Vols. VIII–XII); and see WEBSTER.

CECIL, Algernon: *British Foreign Secretaries, 1807–1916* (London, 1927).

CHAMBERLAIN, M. E.: *The Character of the Foreign Policy of the Earl of Aberdeen, 1841–6* (unpublished Oxford D.Phil. thesis, 1960).

CHAPMAN, J. K.: *The Career of Arthur Hamilton-Gordon, first Lord Stanmore, 1829–1912* (Toronto, 1964).

CLARENDON: see MAXWELL.

CLARKSON, T.: *History of Abolition* (London, 1839).

COLCHESTER, Lord: *The Earl of Ellenborough, a Political Diary, 1828–30* (London, 1881).

CONACHER, J. B.: *The Aberdeen Coalition, 1852–1855, A Study in mid-nineteenth-century party politics* (London, 1968); *Peel and the Peelites, 1846–1850*, EHR LXXIII, 1958, (pp. 431–52).

CONNELL, B.: *Portrait of a Whig Peer* (London, 1957); *Regina v. Palmerston* (London, 1962).

COOK, Sir E.: *Delane of the Times* (London, 1915).

COOPER, Rt. Hon. Duff: *Talleyrand* (London, 1932).

COSTIN, W. C.: *Great Britain and China, 1833–1860* (Oxford, 1937).

COURTNEY, Lord: *The Working Constitution of the U.K.* (London, 1901).

CRACOW PAPERS: *Papers relative to the Suppression by the Governments of Austria, Prussia and Russia of the Free State of Cracow* (Parliamentary Papers, 1847).

CRAWLEY, C. W.: *The Question of Greek Independence, 1821–1833* (London, 1930).

CREEVEY, Thomas: *The Creevey Papers*, ed. Sir H. Maxwell (London, 1923).

CRONIN, Vincent: *Napoleon* (London, 1971).

CZARTORYSKI, Prince A.: *Memoirs of Prince Adam Czartoryski*, ed. A. Gielgud (London, 1888).

DAKIN, D.: *The Struggle for Greek Independence, 1821–1833* (London, 1973).
DALLING: see PALMERSTON.
DELANE: see COOK.
DERRY, J. W.: *Castlereagh* (London, 1976).
DIXON, P.: *Canning, Politician and Statesman* (London, 1976).
DOUGLAS, S. (Lord Glenbervie): *Diaries of Sylvester Douglas*, ed. F. Bickley (London, 1928).
DUBOIS, W. E. B.: *The Suppression of the African Slave Trade to the United States of America* (Cambridge, USA, 1896).
EDGECUMBE, R.: *The Diary of Frances Lady Shelley* (London, 1912).
ELLENBOROUGH: see COLCHESTER.
EVANS, J.: *A History of the Society of Antiquaries* (London, 1956).
FALCONER, T.: *The Oregon Question* (London, 1848).
FERNS, H. S.: *Britain and Argentina in the Nineteenth Century* (London, 1960).
FITZGERALD, Percy: *The Life and Times of William IV* (London, 1884).
FITZMAURICE, Lord Edmond: *The Life of Granville George Leveson-Gower, second Earl of Granville, 1815–1891* (London, 1905).
FOOTE, A. H.: *Africa and the American Flag* (New York, 1853).
FROTHINGHAM, P. R.: *Edward Everett* (Boston, 1925).
GASH, Norman: *Mr Secretary Peel, The Life of Sir Robert Peel to 1830* (London, 1961); *Sir Robert Peel after 1830* (London, 1972); *Politics in the Age of Peel* (London, 1953).
GLADSTONE: see MORLEY.
GOOCH: see RUSSELL.
GORDON: see STANMORE.
GRAHAM: see PARKER.
GRANVILLE: *The Private Correspondence of Lord Granville Leveson-Gower, 1781–1821*, ed. Countess Granville (London, 1916).
GREENHOW, Robert: *The History of Oregon and California and the other Territories of the North West Coast of North America* (London, 1844).
GREVILLE, C. C. F.: *The Greville Memoirs*, ed. H. Reeve (London, 1887); *The Greville Diary*, ed. P. W. Wilson (London, 1927); *The Greville Memoirs*, VI and VII, ed. L. Strachey and R. Fulford (London, 1938).
GUIZOT, F.: *Mémoires pour servir à l'histoire de mon temps* (Paris, 1856–7); *Memoirs of Sir Robert Peel* (London, 1857).
GURWOOD, Col.: *Speeches of the Duke of Wellington in Parliament. Collected by Col. Gurwood* (London, 1854).
GUYOT, R.: *La Première Entente Cordiale, 1830–1846* (Paris, 1926).
HADDO: *Memoirs of Lord Haddo, later the fifth Earl of Aberdeen*, by the Rev. E. B. Elliott (London, 1866).
HALL, J. R.: *England and the Orleans Monarchy* (London, 1912).
HALLAM, Henry: *The History of the English Constituency* (London, 1867).
HERBERT: see STANMORE.
HERKLESS, J. L.: *Stratford, the Cabinet, and the Outbreak of the Crimean War*. Hist. Journal, 1975, pp. 497f.
HERTSTET, Sir E.: *Recollections of the Old Foreign Office* (London, 1901).
HINDE, W.: *George Canning* (London, 1973).
HOBHOUSE: see BROUGHTON.

HOPE, W. B.: *The Diary of Benjamin Robert Haydon* (Harvard, 1963).

HOWARD, Christopher: *Britain and the Casus Belli* (London, 1974).

ILCHESTER, The Earl of: *Journal of the Hon. Henry Edward Fox, fourth and last Lord Holland, 1818–1830* (London, 1923); *Chronicles of Holland House, 1820–1900* (London, 1937); *The Journals of Lady Holland* (London, 1908); *Elizabeth Lady Holland to her son* (London, 1946).

JACOBS, M. C.: *Winning Oregon* (Idaho, 1938).

JAGOW, K.: *Letters of the Prince Consort, 1831–1861* (London, 1938).

JARNAC, Comte de: *Révue des Deux Mondes*, Vol. XXXIV, 1 July 1861, pp. 429–71 (*Lord Aberdeen, Souvenirs et Papiers Diplomatiques*).

JOINVILLE, Prince de: *Notes sur les forces navales de la France* (Paris, 1844).

JONES PARRY, E.: *The Spanish Marriages, 1841–6* (London, 1936): and see LIEVEN.

JONES, W. D.: *The Peelites, 1846–1857*, in collaboration with Arvel B. Erickson (Ohio, 1972); *Lord Derby and Victorian Conservatism* (Oxford, 1956); *Lord Aberdeen and the Americas* (Athens, Georgia, 1958); *The American Problem in British Diplomacy, 1841–1861* (Athens, Georgia, 1974); *The Origins and Passage of Lord Aberdeen's Act* (*The Hispanic American Historical Review*, Vol. XLII, No. 4, November 1962).

KINGLAKE, A. W.: *The Invasion of the Crimea* (Edinburgh, 1877).

KRIEGEL, A. D.: *The Holland House Diaries, 1831–1840* (London, 1977).

LAUGHTON, J. K.: see REEVE.

LAYARD, Sir H.: *Sir Henry Layard's Autobiography*, ed. W. Bruce (London, 1903).

LEVER, T.: see PALMERSTON.

LIEVEN, Princess Dorothea: *Letters of Princess Lieven during her Residence in London, 1812–1834*, ed. L. G. Robinson (London, 1902); *Correspondence of Lord Aberdeen and Princess Lieven, 1832–1854*, ed. E. Jones Parry (London, 1938); and see QUENNELL.

LONDON MISSIONARY SOCIETY: *Jubilee Services* (London, 1848).

LONGFORD, Elizabeth: *Wellington, Pillar of State* (London, 1972).

LOVETT, R.: *History of the London Missionary Society* (London, 1899).

LUCAS, C. P.: *The Boundary Line of Canada: Memo. for the Colonial Office* (London, 1966).

McCORD, Norman: *The Anti-Corn Law League, 1838–1846* (London, 1975).

MAGNUS, Philip: *Gladstone* (London, 1954).

MALMESBURY, The Third Earl of: *Memoirs of an Ex-Minister, an Autobiography* (London, 1885).

MARTIN, Kingsley: *The Triumph of Lord Palmerston* (Revised ed., London, 1963).

MARTIN, Sir Theodore: *Life of HRH the Prince Consort* (London, 1875).

MARTINEAU, John: *The Life of Henry Pelham, fifth Duke of Newcastle, 1811–64* (London, 1908).

MAXWELL, Sir H.: *The Life and Letters of George William Frederick, fourth Earl of Clarendon* (London, 1913).

MAY, T. E.: *The Constitutional History of England* (London, 1863).

MERK, F.: *The Oregon Pioneers of the Boundary* (*Am. Hist. Review*, July 1924, pp. 681–9); *British Party Politics and the Oregon Treaty*, ibid (July 1932, pp. 653–77); *The Oregon Question* (Cambridge, Mass., 1967).

MERYON, Charles: *Memoirs of the Lady Hester Stanhope* (London, 1845).

METTERNICH, Prince de: *Mémoires, Documents et Ecrits divers laissés par le Prince de Metternich*, ed. Prince R. de Metternich (Paris, 1880–4). Also English translation by Mrs A. Napier, Vols. I–V (London, 1880–2).

MINTO, Earl of: *Life and Letters of Sir Gilbert Elliott, first Earl of Minto*, ed. The Countess of Minto (London, 1874).

MONYPENNY, W. F., and BUCKLE, G. E.: *The Life of Benjamin Disraeli, Earl of Beaconsfield* (London, 1929).

MORLEY, J.: *The Life of William Ewart Gladstone* (London, 1903).

NAMIER, L. B.: *Basic Factors in nineteenth-century European History* (London, 1952).

NEVINS, A.: *Polk, the Diary of a President* (New York, 1929); *American Social History as Recorded by British Travellers* (New York, 1923).

NICOLSON, Harold: *The Congress of Vienna* (London, 1961) (University Paperback Edition).

PALMER, Alan: *Metternich, Councillor of Europe* (London, 1972).

PALMERSTON: *The Letters of Lady Palmerston*, ed. Tresham Lever (London, 1957); *The Life and Times of Viscount Palmerston*, ed. J. E. Ritchie (London, 1866); *Lord Palmerston*, by H. G. F. Bell (London, 1936); *The Life of Henry John Temple, Viscount Palmerston*, by Sir Henry Lytton Bulwer, ed. E. Ashley (London, 1870–4, 1876), and 'improved' edition, ed. E. Ashley (London, 1879, 2 vols.); *Palmerston*, by Jasper Ridley (London 1970).

PARKER, C. S.: *Sir Robert Peel, from his Private Papers* (London 1899); *The Life and Letters of Sir James Graham, 1792–1861* (London, 1907).

PETRIE, Sir Charles: *George Canning* (London, 1946).

PLATT, D. C. M.: *Finance, Trade and Politics in British Foreign Policy, 1815–1914* (Oxford, 1968).

PREST, John: *Lord John Russell* (London, 1972).

PRICE, C.: *The Letters of Richard Brinsley Sheridan* (Oxford, 1966).

PRITCHARD, G.: *Queen Pomare and her Country* (London, 1879).

PRITCHARD, W. T.: *Polynesian Reminiscences* (London, 1866).

QUAIFE, M. M.: *The Diary of James J. Polk During his Presidency, 1845–1849* (Chicago, 1910).

QUENNELL, P.: *The Private Letters of Princess Lieven to Prince Metternich* (London, 1937).

REEVE, H.: *Memoirs of the Life and Correspondence of Henry Reeve, CB, DCL*, ed. J. K. Laughton (London, 1898).

RIDLEY: see PALMERSTON.

RITCHIE: see PALMERSTON.

RIVES, G. L.: *Mexican diplomacy on the eve of war with the United States* (*Am. Hist. Review*, Vol. XVIII) (London, January 1913).

RUSSELL, W. H.: *The War from the Landing at Gallipoli to the death of Lord Raglan* (London, 1855).

RUSSELL, Lord John: *The Early Correspondence of Lord John Russell, 1805–1840*, ed. R. Russell (London, 1913); *The Later Correspondence of Lord John Russell, 1840–1878*, ed. G. P. Gooch (London, 1925).

RUSSIER, H.: *Le Partage de l'Océanie* (Paris, 1905).

SETON-WATSON, R. W.: *Britain in Europe, 1789–1914* (Cambridge, 1937).

SOUTHGATE, D.: *'The Most English Minister'* . . . *The Policies and Politics of Palmerston* (London, 1966).

SPANISH PAPERS: *Papers Relative to the Affairs of Spain and Correspondence between Sir Henry Bulwer and the Duke of Sotomayor* (PP, 1948).

STANMORE, Lord: *Sidney Herbert, Lord Herbert of Lea – a Memoir* (London, 1906); *The Earl of Aberdeen,* as Sir Arthur Gordon (London, 1894).

STIRLING, A. M. W.: *Fyvie Castle, its Lairds and their Times* (London, 1928).

SURTEES, V.: *Charlotte Canning* (London, 1975).

TAYLOR, A. J. P.: *The Struggle for Mastery in Europe, 1848–1918* (Oxford, 1954).

TEMPERLEY, Professor Harold: *The Foreign Policy of Canning, 1822– 1827* (London, 1925); *England and the Near East – the Crimea* (London, 1936); *British Anti-Slavery, 1833–1870* (London, 1972).

TREVELYAN, G. M.: *The Life of John Bright* (London, 1913).

TYLER, L. G.: *Letters and Times of the Tylers* (Virginia, 1884).

VON STOCKMAR, E.: *Memoirs of Baron Stockmar,* trans. Max Muller (London, 1872–3).

WALFORD, Edward: *Greater London* (London, 1898).

WALPOLE, Spencer: *Life of Lord John Russell* (London, 1889).

WARD, J. T.: *Sir James Graham* (London, 1967).

WARD, W. G. F.: *The Royal Navy and the Slavers* (London, 1969).

WATT, A.: *The Case of Alexander McLeod* (*Cambridge Hist. Review,* XII, June 1931).

WEBSTER, Sir C.: *The Foreign Policy of Castlereagh, 1812–1815,* and *1815–1822* (London, 1931 and 1934); *The Foreign Policy of Lord Palmerston, 1830–1841* (London, 1957 and 1969); *British Diplomacy, 1813–15, Select Documents Dealing with the Reconstruction of Europe* (London, 1921); *The Congress of Vienna* (London, 1937).

WEINER, Margery: *The Sovereign Remedy, Europe after Waterloo* (London, 1971).

WOODHOUSE, C. M.: *Capodestria, the Founder of Greek Independence* (London, 1973).

WROTTESLEY, Lt-Col. G.: *Life and Correspondence of Field-Marshal Sir John Burgoyne* (London, 1873).

ZIEGLER, Philip: *William IV* (London, 1971); *Melbourne* (London, 1976).

Index

Abdülmecid I, Sultan of Turkey, 212, 214, 215, 216, 220, 229, 230, 231, 232, 237

Abercorn, John James, 9th Earl and 1st Marquess of, 25–6, 27, 31, 32, 41, 44, 46, 66, 79, 80, 85, 87, 95–6, 99–100, 192, 320, 325

Abercorn, Lady, 26, 39, 45

Abercorn, James, 2nd Marquess of. *See* Hamilton, James, Viscount.

Aberdeen Act, 178

Aberdeen, Catherine, Countess of (née Hamilton), 1st wife of 4th Earl of, 25–7, 28, 30–1, 38–40, 41, 97, 100, 111, 128, 192, 198, 324, 325

Aberdeen, Sir George Gordon of Haddo, 3rd Baronet, later Lord Haddo, 1st Earl of, 15

Aberdeen, George Gordon, 3rd Earl of, 16–18, 19, 20

ABERDEEN, GEORGE GORDON, 4th EARL OF (1784–1860):
reputation, 13–14; birth and ancestry, 14–18; childhood, 18–20; at Harrow, 19; at Cambridge, 20; succeeds to earldom, 20; travels, 21–5; at Bentley Priory, 25–6; courtship of Lady Catherine Hamilton, 25–6; first visit to Haddo House, 27–8; happy marriage, 28; attempts to enter Parliament, 29–30; becomes Scottish representative peer, 30; birth of three daughters, 31; no orator, 31; refuses embassy posts, 31–2, 36, 40; Knight of the Thistle, 32; F.R.S., 32; activity in Parliament, 33, 36, 121, 125, 126, 193, 321; and his brothers, 33–9; wife's illness and death, 39; his mourning, 39–40; trustee of British Museum, 40, 186, 321; and Anne Cavendish, 41–5; and Lady Maria Hamilton, 41–2; accepts mission to Vienna, 44
Ambassador Extraordinary to Vienna (1813–1814).
Second marriage, 95–106, 127–8; deaths of Lady Caroline, Lady Jane and Lady Alice Gordon, 100, 104, 110; invited by Wellington to join government, 108

Foreign Secretary (1828–1830):
Russo-Turkish war and Greek independence, 111–17; recognition of Louis Philippe 1830, 118; Belgian revolt, 119–20; and Wellington on reform, 120–1; fall of government, 121; contrasted with Palmerston, 121–3

Agrees to be Wellington's Foreign Secretary, 126; death of second wife, 127; death of Lady Frances Gordon, 128; death of Sir Charles Gordon, 129; his austerity, 129; active in healing breach between Peel and Wellington, 129–31; summoned by Wellington November 1834, 131; Secretary of State for War and the Colonies in Peel's government, 131–2; rebuked by Wellington for absenteeism, 133; head of Scottish Conservatives, 133; attitude to Lord and Lady Haddo, 134–6; on Scottish Church affairs, 138, 327–32; on Palmerston's handling of foreign affairs, 138, 139; fall of Melbourne government, 139; becomes Foreign Secretary, 140
Foreign Secretary (1841–1846):
Appoints brother Robert to Vienna, 140; appoints brother William a Lord of the Admiralty, 140; relationship with Peel and Wellington, 141–2; *entente cordiale* with France, 142; friendship with Guizot, 143; Tahiti affair, 144–8; revolution in Greece, 148; China, and acquisition of Hong Kong, 149–50; Spanish Marriages, 157–65; American problems summarized, 166; Ashburton's mission, 167; Maine boundary, 167–71; *Caroline* incident, 169–70; *Creole* incident, 167, 170; suppression of slave trade, 170; Oregon boundary, 172–5, 179; value of *entente cordiale*, 175; Mexico offers California to Britain, 175–6; Argentinian troubles, 176–8; Brazilian slave trade, 178–9; slave trade treaty with Portugal, 179; and France, 180–1; achievements summarized, 181–2; Queen's estima-

tion of Aberdeen, 179; departure from office, 184

'Edinburgh' Letter, 183; Peel's hundred days, 184; retirement in Scotland, 185–211; and Peel's death, 197–8; leader of Peelites, 198–9; and Ecclesiastical Titles Bill, 199–200, 201, 202; Russell's resignation and Derby's approaches, 200–1, 202; defeat of Derby government, 203; Aberdeen declines to form government, 201; qualifications as Prime Minister, 204–5; Aberdeen summoned with Lansdowne, 205; crucial meeting with Russell, 205; Aberdeen kisses hands, 206; offices for Peelites and Whigs, 208–9; Aberdeen's Cabinet, 209–10

Prime Minister (1852–1855):
Russia and Turkey, 212–15; efforts to avert war, 215–20; home affairs and reform 220; peace in balance, 224; Russell's impatience, 224; Turkey declares war on Russia, 225; Olmütz proposals, 225–6; public war fever, 227; Royal view, 227; Cabinet divisions, 227; Battle of Sinope, 231; Russell and Palmerston differ on reform, 232; Palmerston resigns, 233; Palmerston rejoins Cabinet, 234; war fever spreads to Parliament, 235–6; burnt in effigy, 236; France and Britain declare war on Russia, 236; Aberdeen's sense of guilt, 236–8; domestic priorities, 238; Britain's army built up, 239; difficulties with Russell, 240–1; W. H. Russell of *The Times*, 243–51; inadequacy of defence departments, 243–6; Newcastle's defensiveness, 246; Russell's offensiveness, 246–7; re-organization, 248; plight of British forces, 249; W. H. Russell's despatches, 250; plans for taking Sebastopol, 252–3; Aberdeen's tactless honesty, 253; Queen's rebuke, 253–4; Aberdeen castigated in Commons 254–5; Haddo's illness, 255–7; Raglan to the Crimea, 257–60; the Alma, 261; more difficulties with Russell, 263–4; Balaclava, 266; Inkerman, 267; Alexander Gordon's letters, 267–8; mismanagement and ill luck, 269; disease, 269–70; whom to blame?, 270; more difficulties with Russell, 271–6; diplomatic problems, 276–7; Parliamentary criticisms, 278; *The Times* hostile, 279–80; Aberdeen's opinion of Russell, 281; the Garter, 281–2; Government baffled by Crimean problems, 283; Russell's constructive criticisms, 284–5; *The Times* attacks, 287, 288; Roebuck's motion, 289; Russell resigns, 290–2; Cabinet condemns Russell, 293; Cabinet decides to resign, 294; Queen foils minister's resignations, 296; Cabinet members' 'personal honour', 298; Russell's resignation statement, 299; debate on Roebuck motion, 299, 301; motion carried, 302; Aberdeen's resignation, 302; refuses to join new government, 304–5

The last years (1855–1860):
Illnesses, 308, 320, 321, 322; Roebuck's inquiry, 309; Sebastopol Report, 310–12; return of son from Crimea, 312–13; Palmerston compared with Aberdeen as Prime Minister, 314–16; Aberdeen and Queen, 317; extinction of Peelites, 318; Queen's visit to Haddo House, 319–20; Aberdeen and religion, 321; his death, 323

Aberdeen, Harriet, Countess of, 2nd wife of 4th Earl of, 38, 95–7, 106, 110, 127–8, 303, 325

Aberdeen, William, Lord Haddo, later 2nd Earl of, 15–16

Addington, Henry, 1st Viscount Sidmouth, 21, 192, 316

Adelaide, Queen Dowager, widow of William IV, 192–3

Adrianople, Treaty of (1829), 115–16

Airey, Richard, later Lord, General, 284

Aix-la-Chapelle, Congress of, 118, 124

Albany, Louisa, Countess of, 24

Albert, Prince, of Saxe-Coburg-Gotha, 121–2, 179, 195–6, 200–1, 203, 206, 209, 222, 227, 236, 240–1, 267, 275, 277, 281, 296–7, 304, 313, 320

Alexander I, Czar of Russia, 22, 49, 50, 55, 56, 60, 66, 67, 69, 72, 84–5, 87–90, 92

Alfieri, Vittorio, Count, 24

Algeria, 148

Alma, Battle of the, 260–1, 262, 272, 308, 312

Almack's, 121

Altenburgh, 63, 64

Althorp, John Charles, Viscount, later 3rd Earl Spencer, 19

America, HMS, 185

Amiens, Treaty of, 21

Anstey, Thomas Chisholm, 194

Antiquaries, Society of, 185–6

Antwerp, 70, 72

Arbuthnot, Charles, 130–1
Arbuthnot, Mrs Harriet, 130
Argentina, 176–8, 181
Argyll, George Douglas Campbell, 8th
  Duke of, 186–7, 193–4, 203, 204,
  206, 209, 218, 221, 236, 237, 252,
  258, 266, 330
Argyll, John Douglas Edward Henry
  Campbell, 7th Duke of, 330, 331
Argyll House, 39, 95, 98, 106, 134, 193,
  209, 290, 291, 303, 306, 310, 323
Ashburnham, Lord L., 97
Ashburton, Alexander Baring, 1st
  Baron, 167–71, 172, 174
Asquith, Herbert Henry, 1st Earl of
  Oxford and Asquith, 316
Athenian Society, 24
Athens, 24, 25, 195, 276
Auchterarder, 327, 329
Austria, 41, 46–9, 51, 54–6, 67, 71–2,
  74, 79, 92, 118, 139, 232, 236, 256,
  277, 322

Bagehot, Walter, 126
Baillie-Hamilton, William Alexander,
  Admiral, 185, 309, 313, 317, 320
Baird, Sir David, General, 14, 16
Balaclava, 262, 266, 268, 269, 270, 283,
  285, 286–7, 288, 315
Balaclava, Battle of, 266, 269, 272
Balfour, Lady Frances, 330
Balkans, 222, 233, 235
Balmoral Castle, 124, 191, 260, 319
Barante, Guillaume Prosper Brugière
  de, Baron, 187
Barclay de Tolly, Mikhaïl Bogdano-
  vitch, Prince Marshal, 56
Baring, Mrs, 255
Bartlett, C. J., 117
Bathurst, Henry, 3rd Earl, 320
Bautzen, Battle of, 63, 67
Bavaria, 60, 61, 68, 72
Beauharnais, Hortense de, Queen of
  Holland, 22
Bedchamber Crisis, 133, 134
Bedford, Francis, 7th Duke of, 203–4,
  224, 240–1
Bedford, John Russell, 6th Duke of,
  125, 203
Belgium, 119, 120, 127, 142
Bellerophon, HMS, 97
Bennigsen, Levin August, Count von,
  General, 60, 62, 63
Bentley Priory, Stanmore, 25–6, 96, 98,
  100, 132, 192–3, 324–5
Berlin, 48, 49, 50, 51, 60–1
Bernadotte, Charles Jean-Baptiste,
  later Charles XIV, King of Sweden
  and Norway, 49, 51, 52, 63, 71, 72,
  88, 92

Berry, Charles, Duc de, 153
Bill of Pains and Penalties, 106
Black Sea, 218, 222, 226–7, 232–6, 249,
  258, 263, 264, 315
Blücher, Gebhard Leberecht von,
  Field Marshal, 49, 51–2, 61–4, 90
Bohemia, 49–51
Bonham, Philip, 136
Brand, Mrs Susan, 121–2
Brazil, 178–9; slave-grown sugar, 139
Breadalbane, Eliza, Lady, 133
Breslau, 48, 51, 52
Bresson, Charles, Count, 160, 162
Bright, John, 238
Brighton, 80, 98, 159
British Museum, 13, 25, 40, 186, 321–2
Brougham, Henry Peter, 1st Baron
  Brougham and Vaux, 121, 209
Brunnow, Philippe Ivanovitch, Baron,
  then Count, de, 213, 226
Buccleuch, Walter Francis Scott, 5th
  Duke of Buccleuch and 7th Duke of
  Queensberry, 133, 183, 324
Buchan Ness, 135, 138, 185
Buchanan, James, 174
Bucharest, 261
Buenos Aires, 176–7
Bulwer, William Henry Lytton Earle,
  Baron Dalling and Bulwer, 160–2
  passim, 163, 165, 180
Buol, Karl, Count von Buol-Schauen-
  stein, General, 220, 223, 229–32
Burdett's Relief Bill, 107
Burghersh, John, Lord, later 11th Earl
  of Westmorland, 73
Burgoyne, Sir John Fox, Major-
  General, 244, 259, 262
Burke, Edmund, 20
Butterfield, Sir Herbert, 14
Byron, Catherine, Mrs, 17
Byron, George Gordon, 6th Baron,
  19, 21, 24, 112
Byron, "Mad Jack", 17

Calamita Bay, 259
California, 166, 175–6
Cambridge University, St John's
  College, 20; university seat, 29–30
Campbell, Sir Colin, Baron Clyde,
  Field-Marshal, 314
Canada, 132
Canning, Charles John, Earl Canning,
  248
Canning, George (1770–1827), 31, 32,
  108, 111, 112, 117, 124, 144, 151, 152,
  172, 178, 192, 320
Canning, Sir Stratford, 1st Viscount
  Stratford de Redcliffe, 114, 213, 214,
  216, 217, 218, 220, 222, 223, 224,

228, 229, 231, 232, 234, 235, 261, 269
Canrobert, Certain, General, 287
Canton, 149
Capodistrias, Ioannis, Count, 112, 115, 116–17
Cardigan, James Thomas Brudenell, 7th Earl of, 282
Cardwell, Edward, 1st Viscount, 308, 324
Carlos, Charles de Bourbon, Don, 132, 151, 152
Caroline, 166, 167, 169, 170
Caroline, Amelia Elizabeth, Queen of George IV, 106
Castlereagh, Robert Stewart, 2nd Marquis of Londonderry, better known as Viscount Castlereagh, 31, 41–2, 44, 46–7, 49, 55, 57, 60–2, 66–8, 75, 77, 79–94, 100, 107, 164, 320
Cathcart, Lord, General Sir William Schaw, later 1st Earl Cathcart, 54–5, 59, 66–8, 76–7, 79, 86, 87
Catherine II, Empress of Russia, 22
Caulaincourt, Armand Marquis de, Duc de Vicenza, 87, 88, 89, 90, 91
Cavendish, Anne, 41, 42, 44, 76, 95
Cavendish, Lady George, wife of Lord George, 41, 44, 76
Cavendish, Lord George, 41, 76
Chamberlain, Arthur Neville, 316
Charlemagne, 212
Charles II, King of Great Britain and Ireland, 15
Charles X, King of France, 117, 143
Charles Edward Louis Philip Casimir Stewart, the Young Pretender, 24
Charles, Hippolyte, 21–2
Charlotte Augusta, Princess, 116
Chartists, 133
Château d'Eu, 154, 155, 156, 157, 162, 187
Chatham, William Pitt, 1st Earl of, 316
Châtillon, 86, 87, 89, 90, 91
Chaumont, Treaty of, 90
China, 139, 149–50, 180, 239
Churchill, Sir Winston, 316
Chusan, 149
Claim of Right, 331
Clanricarde, Ulick John de Burgh, 14th Earl and 1st Marquis of, 256
Clarendon, George William Frederick Villiers, 4th Earl of Clarendon and 4th Baron Hyde, 14, 207, 210–11, 213–14, 216–18, 220, 222–4, 226, 228–9, 231, 233–5, 237, 254, 256, 259, 262, 266, 271, 273–4, 277–8, 284, 289, 294, 297, 304, 307–9, 319, 324

Codrington, Sir Edward, Admiral, 108, 111–12
Codrington, Sir William, General, 314
Comotau, 61, 62
Conacher, Professor J. B., 204–5, 218, 223
Confederation of the Rhine, 48, 60, 68, 89
Conspiracy to Murder Bill, 321
Constantinople, 36, 114, 115, 213, 214, 215, 216, 217, 219, 224, 225, 229, 230, 232, 235, 249, 261, 262
Convention of Joint Occupancy, 172, 174
Corfu, 25
Corn Laws, repeal of, 161, 175, 179, 182, 184, 187, 195, 198, 200
Coutts's bank, 41, 193, 324
Cowley, Henry Wellesley, 1st Baron, 214
Cowper, Amelia (known as Emily) Lamb, Countess, later Lady Palmerston, 121, 125, 197
Cracow, 163
Cranworth, Sir Robert Monsey Rolfe, Baron, 210
Craonne, Battle of, 90
Creevey, Thomas, 36–7
Creole, 167, 170
Crete, 213
Crewe, Frances Anne, Lady, daughter of Fulke Greville, 20
Crimean War, 212–314
Croker, John Wilson, 175, 186, 217–18, 324
Cunard, Sir Samuel, 278
Cyndus, HMS, 48
Crystal Palace, 308

Dalkeith, William Henry Walter, Lord, later 6th Duke of Buccleuch, 324
Dallas, Eneas, Sweetland, 317, 328
Dalmatia, 25
Danube, 230, 233, 237, 249
Danubian Principalities (Moldavia and Wallachia), 115, 213, 216, 218, 222, 225, 226, 229, 230, 236, 256, 257, 277
Dardanelles, 113, 115, 117, 214–19, 222, 226, 229–30, 235, 237
D'Aubigny, Captain, 145
D'Aumâle, Henri Eugène Philippe d'Orleans, Duc, 154
Davis, Sir John Francis, 149
De Grey, Thomas Philip de Grey, Earl de Grey, 19
Delane, John Thaddeus, 142–3, 147, 162, 183, 211, 243, 250, 262, 269, 317, 323
Denmark, 68, 72, 74, 77
Derby, Edward George Geoffrey

Smith Stanley, 14th Earl of Derby, 183, 191, 195, 197, 200, 201, 202, 203, 204, 278, 301, 303, 318, 321, 332

Devonshire, William George Spencer Cavendish, 6th Duke of Devonshire, 41, 44

Dijon, 89, 92

Disraeli, Benjamin, later 1st Earl of Beaconsfield, 140, 200, 202–3, 206, 209, 236, 254, 278, 312, 321–2

Disruption of the Scottish Church, 138, 327–32

Don Pacifico case. See Pacifico, Don.

Donoughmore, Richard Hely-Hutchinson, 1st Earl of, 33

Douglas, Lord Alexander Hamilton, later 10th Duke of Hamilton, 31

Douglas, Sir Howard, 3rd Baronet, 168

Downing Street, 237, 263

Drayton Manor, 194

Dresden, 51, 52, 56, 57, 60, 61, 76

Dresden, Battle of, 51–2

Drouyn de l'Huys, Édouard, 287

Drummond, Henry, 307

Drummond, Sir William, 24, 32

'Duke's bench', 193

Dudley, John William Ward, 1st Earl of Dudley, 108, 110

Dundas, Sir James Whitley Deans, Admiral, 214, 232, 244, 252, 264

East India Company, 126

East Retford (Absorption) Bill (1828), 109–10

Ecclesiastical Titles Bill, 199–202

Education Bill, 289

Egypt, 213, 237, 279, 322

Elbe, 48, 50, 60, 75

Ellenborough, Edward Law, 1st Earl of 314

Enquiry into the Principles of Beauty in Greek Architecture, 107

Enrico, Don, Duke of Seville, 156, 162

Ephesus, 25

Erfurth, 60

Estcourt, James Bucknall Bucknall, Major-General, 284

Evans, Sir George de Lacy, General, 268, 313

Everett, Edward, 141, 179

Ferdinand, King of Sicily, 47

Ferns, H. S., 177

Finlay, George, 196

Fitzwilliam, William Wentworth, 2nd Earl Fitzwilliam, 133–4

Fontainebleau, Treaty of, 92

Foreign Enlistment Acts, 132, 151, 277, 278, 288

Fouché, Joseph, Duke of Otranto, 93

Fox, Charles James, 20, 192

Fox, Henry Stephen, 167, 169

France, 34, 48, 54, 60, 67, 68, 70, 72, 74, 87, 113, 118, 119, 127, 139, 141–65 *passim*, 191, 196, and chapters 16–25 *passim*

Francis Joseph I, Emperor of Austria, II and last Holy Roman Emperor, 46, 48–9, 51–3, 55, 59–60, 61, 64–6, 72, 79, 88, 90, 92, 115

Francisco, Don, Francisco de Asis de Borbōn, duque, de Cadiz, 156–7, 162–3

Frankfort, 50, 51, 61, 64, 65, 69, 72, 76, 84, 85, 89

Frankfort proposals, 70

Frederick William III, King of Prussia, 49, 55, 66

Free trade, 127, 200, 202

Freyburg, 79, 82, 84

Gallipoli, 239, 240, 243, 252

Gash, Professor Norman, 137, 141, 142

General Assembly of the Church of Scotland, 327, 328, 330, 331, 332

Gentz, Chevalier Friedrich von, 66

George III, King of Great Britain and Ireland, 36

George IV, King of Great Britain and Ireland, 106, 108, 121, 144. See also Prince of Wales and Prince Regent.

Gera, 60, 100

Germany, 47, 60, 70

Ghent, Treaty of, 167

Gight, Castle of, 17, 18

Giles, James, 124, 135

Gladstone, William Ewart, 13, 129, 138, 143, 195, 198, 203, 206, 209, 216, 220–2, 224, 226, 248, 255–6, 264, 272, 274–6, 281, 288, 294, 296, 299, 301–4, 306–7, 311, 316, 318, 320, 324

Gladstone, Catherine, 306

Globe, 194, 195

Gordon (House of), 21

Gordon Alexander, 4th Duke of, 20

Gordon, the Hon. Sir Alexander, Lt.-Col., 18, 31, 33, 34–9 *passim*, 40, 96–7, 132, 192

Gordon, the Hon. Alexander, General, 97, 132, 240, 258, 262–3, 264, 267, 268, 269, 284, 312, 313, 314, 317, 319, 323, 324

Gordon, Alexander, Penelope and John, Charles and Isobella, children of 3rd Earl of Aberdeen, 16

Gordon, Lady Alice, 31, 53, 100, 103–10, 127, 195

Gordon, Lady Alicia, 19, 29, 39, 106–7, 191
Gordon, the Hon. Sir Arthur, later Lord Stanmore, 13–14, 21, 39, 44, 68, 86, 95, 99, 127, 132, 136, 186–7, 199–201, 219, 231, 234, 248, 253, 255, 261, 264, 266–7, 272, 281, 289–92, 297, 302–9, 312, 317–20, 323–5, 332
Gordon, Caroline, the Hon. Mrs Alexander, 313
Gordon, Lady Caroline, 31, 53, 100
Gordon, the Hon. Sir Charles, Colonel, 18, 31, 33, 34, 98, 129
Gordon, Rev. the Hon. Douglas, 97, 323
Gordon, Lady Frances, 97, 128, 325
Gordon, Lord George, 16
Gordon, the Hon. Harriet, 238
Gordon, the Hon. James, 189
Gordon, Lady Jane, 25, 31, 52, 99–102, 104
Gordon, Jane, Duchess of, 20
Gordon, the Hon. John, Admiral, 18, 31, 33–4, 98, 106, 185, 309, 323, 325
Gordon, the Hon. Sir Robert, 18, 26, 33, 35, 43, 62, 114–15, 116, 119, 121, 191
Gordon, the Hon. William, Admiral, 18, 31, 33, 98, 137, 140, 190, 256
Gourdon, Bertrand de, 15
Government of India Bill, 220
Graham, Sir James Robert George, Baronet, 159, 183, 199–203, 205–6, 208–9, 221–3, 226, 244, 239, 241–2, 252, 255–6, 261, 263–6, 272, 274–5, 278, 281, 286, 291, 297, 303–4, 307, 309, 317–18, 320, 325
Grantham, Thomas Philip de Grey, 3rd Baron Grantham, 19
Granville, Granville Leveson-Gower, 1st Earl of Granville, 20, 210, 221
Greece, 24–5, 107, 108, 111–17, 142, 148, 191, 195, 276
Grenville, William Wyndham, Baron Grenville, 29, 30, 36
Greville, Charles, Cavendish Fulke, 217, 221, 224, 231, 240, 242, 262, 278, 280
Grey, Charles, 2nd Earl Grey, Viscount Howick and Baron Grey, 20, 121, 125, 126
Grey, Sir George, 2nd Baronet, 248, 290, 294, 296, 297
Grey, Sir Henry George, Viscount Howick, later 3rd Earl Grey, 183–4, 240, 245, 246
Guizot, François Pierre Guillaume, 118, 124, 143, 144, 145, 146, 147, 148, 150, 154, 155, 156, 157, 158,
159, 160, 161, 162, 163, 164, 175, 180, 184, 193, 194, 196, 320
Gully, James Manby, M.D., 255, 257
Gurney, Hudson, 20, 186, 321

Haddington, Thomas Hamilton, 9th Earl of, 19, 129, 134, 140
Haddo, George Gordon, Lord, 14, 17, 18
Haddo, Lady (wife of George Gordon, Lord Haddo), 14, 17, 19, 133, 134, 135, 136, 137, 187
Haddo, George John James, Lord, later 5th Earl of Aberdeen, 97, 128, 133, 134, 135, 136, 137, 187, 189, 190, 191, 255, 256–7, 309, 310, 313, 317, 319, 322–3, 325
Haddo, Mary, Lady, later Countess of Aberdeen, 133–6, 137, 189, 190, 191, 195, 197, 225, 238, 255, 256, 257, 268–9, 276, 278–9, 281, 287, 305, 306, 307, 308, 309, 317, 319, 323, 324, 325
Haddo House, 16, 17, 28, 30–1, 40, 44, 97–9, 100, 101, 124, 128, 134, 136, 155, 185, 187, 188, 192, 194, 221, 222, 260, 262, 308, 319, 321, 323
Hall, Sir Benjamin, 1st Baron Llanover, 290
Hall, Sir John, M.D., 311
Hamilton, Lord Claud, 95, 102, 136, 303, 312, 313, 323
Hamilton, Lady Harriet, later wife of Admiral Baillie-Hamilton, 185
Hamilton, James, Viscount, 38, 95
Hamilton, James, Viscount, 2nd Marquess of, and 1st Duke of Abercorn, 95, 102, 125, 192–3, 303, 323
Hamilton, Lady Maria, 25, 39, 41–2, 44–5, 47, 50, 52–3, 57–9, 61, 63–4, 69, 75–6, 78, 80–3, 95, 258
Hamilton, Sir William, 192
Hamilton, Emma, Lady, 192
Hanau, 64–5
Hanover, 46, 54, 71
Hansard, 106, 121
Hanson, Miss Catherine, later Countess of Aberdeen, 16
Hardenberg, Karl August, Prince von, 71
Hardinge, Sir Henry, 1st Viscount Hardinge, Field-Marshal, 282
Harrow School, 19, 192, 209
Harrowby, Dudley Ryder, 1st Earl of Harrowby and Viscount Sandon, 31, 40, 43, 44, 58, 79, 91, 95
Harrowby, Lady, wife of 1st Earl of, 31, 43, 44
Hawkesbury, Charles Jenkinson, 1st

Earl of Liverpool and 1st Baron Hawkesbury, 31
Hayter, Sir William Goodenough, 1st Baronet, 295
Herbert, the Hon. Sidney, later 1st Baron Herbert of Lea, 183, 203, 205–6, 209, 226, 241–2, 248, 254, 272, 277–8, 282, 285–6, 288, 290, 299, 304–5, 307, 311, 316, 319
Herkless, J. L., 213
Herschel, Sir John Frederick William, 313
Heytesbury, William A'Court, 1st Baron Heytesbury, 113, 115
Hobhouse, Sir John Cam, 2nd Baronet and later Baron Broughton de Gryfford, 110, 129
Holland, 46, 54, 68, 70, 71, 72, 73, 78, 87, 119, 127
Holland, Sir Henry, 308, 323
Holland, Henry Richard Vassall Fox, 3rd Baron, 125
Holland, Elizabeth Vassall, Lady, 42, 43, 44, 76, 82
Holland House, 41
Holland, King of, arbitration of, 167, 168
Hong Kong, 149
Honiton, 136–7
Hope, John, 329, 330
Hudson's Bay Company, 172
Humboldt, Wilhelm, Baron von, 64
Huskisson, William, 109, 110, 121

Indian Mutiny, 319
Inkerman, Battle of, 267–8, 269, 272, 277
Ionian Islands, 117
Ireland, 34, 126
Isabella, Queen of Spain, 132, 151, 152, 153, 154, 155, 161
Italy, 46, 47, 48, 54, 60, 70, 73, 89, 90

Jamaican constitution, Bill to suspend, 132
Jarnac, Comte de, 98 (footnote), 155, 162, 163–4, 188, 189, 320
Joinville, François Ferdinand Philippe d'Orléans, Prince de, 158
Jones, Professor W. D., 142, 181–2
Jones-Parry, Professor E., 163–5
Josephine, Empress of France, 21–2
July Revolution (1830), 117, 118, 119, 125, 143

Kainardji, Treaty of (1774), 214
Karlsruhe, 81
Katzbach, 51–2
Kemble, John Philip, 25, 188, 320
Kempt, Sir James, General, 168

Kennedy, the Rt. Hon. P., 275, 288
Keying, Chinese Imperial Commissioner, 149
King of Rome, 60, 92, 97
Kinglake, Alexander William, 252
Knighton, Sir William, 1st Baronet, 39

La Harpe, Frédéric César, 14
La Plata, River Plate, 148, 176–8, 187
La Rothière, Battle of, 87, 88
Lacour, Monsieur de, 224
Lamb, Frederick James, later 3rd Viscount Melbourne and Baron Beauvale, 26, 45, 51
Langres, 84, 85
Lansdowne, Sir Henry Petty-Fitzmaurice, 3rd Marquess of, 41, 121, 203, 204, 205, 207, 210, 216, 217, 226, 232, 237, 275, 290, 303
Laon, Battle of, 90
Lawrence, Sir Thomas, 21, 25–6, 111
Layard, Sir Austen Henry, 254, 310, 314
Leipzig, 60, 61, 62, 63, 64, 69, 73
Leipzig, Battle of, 62–4
L'Estocq, General, 51
Leveson-Gower, George Granville, Lord Granville, 41
Lieven, Count, later Prince, 121, 124
Lieven, Dorothea von Benkendorff, Princess, 112, 121–2, 124–5, 126–7, 129, 131–2, 134, 137, 139, 140, 142, 144, 146, 147, 163, 179, 182, 185–6, 193–4, 217, 222, 236
Light Brigade, 249, 266
Lisbon, 39, 160
Liverpool, Robert Banks Jenkinson, Baron Hawkesbury, 2nd Earl of Liverpool, 33, 36–7, 54, 91–2, 108, 192
London Missionary Society, 144
London, Treaty of (1827), 113, 114, 115; (1840), 139, 184
Londonderry. See Stewart, Charles William.
Lothian and Tweeddale, Synod of, 330
Louis XVIII, King of France, 88, 92, 97, 115
Louis Napoleon. See Napoleon III.
Louis Philippe, King of the French, 118, 119, 143, 145, 147, 151, 152, 153, 154, 155, 156, 157, 158, 161, 162, 163, 164, 175, 193, 194
Luisa, Infanta of Spain, 155, 156, 157, 163
Lutzen, Battle of, 63, 67
Lyndhurst, John Singleton Copley, 1st Baron, 253
Lyons, Sir Edmund, 1st Baron Lyons

of Christchutch, Rear Admiral, 148, 244, 265

Macaulay, Thomas Babington, 1st Baron, 207
Macdonald, Jacques Étienne, Duc de Tarente, Marshal, 52
McLeod, Alexander, 166, 169, 170
Magicienne, HMS, 140
Mahmoud II, Sultan of Turkey, 107, 112, 113, 114, 115, 116, 138, 139
Maine, 167, 172, 175, 181, 182
Malakov, 315
Malmesbury, James Howard Harris, 3rd Earl of, 216
Malta, 214, 237, 239, 243, 315
Malvern, 256, 257
Maret, Hugues Bernard, Duc de Bassano, 70
Mari-Cristina I, Queen Regent of Spain, 152, 153, 154, 155, 156, 157, 160, 162
Maria da Gloria, Queen of Portugal, 151, 152
Maria Ludovica Beatrix, 59
Marie-Louise, Empress of France, 2nd consort of Napoleon I, 52, 59
Marienberg, 60, 61, 62
Maritime Rights, 70, 71, 72, 93
Marmion, 192
Marmora, Sea of, 115
Marochetti, Carlo, Baron, 306
Maroto, Rafael, General, 152
Masson, Fréderic, 59
Maule, Hon. Fox. *See* Panmure.
Mehemet Ali, Pasha of Egypt, 117, 138, 139
Melbourne, William Lamb, 2nd Viscount Melbourne, 26, 129, 133, 139, 140, 141, 153, 210, 317, 331
Melville, Henry Dundas, 1st Viscount Melville, 12, 20, 25, 27, 28–9, 30, 31, 32, 41, 320
Melville, Lady Jane, 19, 29
Menschikoff, Aleksandr Sergeevich, Prince, 214, 215, 216
Merfeldt, General Count, 68
Methlic, 328, 329, 330
Metternich, Clemens Lothar Wenzel von, Prince, 47–9, 51–7, 60, 62, 65, 67, 69–72, 74, 77–80, 84, 85, 90, 92, 114, 124, 320
Mexico, 175, 176, 187
Miguel, Dom, Pretender to the Portuguese throne, 152
Militia Bill (1852), 202; (1854), 278
Milman, Henry Hart, 187
Milton, William Thomas Spencer, Lord, succ. as 6th Earl Fitzwilliam (U.K.) and 5th Earl (Irish), 133

Milton, Countess, wife of 6th Earl, 133
Minto, Gilbert, Elliot, 2nd Earl of, 214, 275, 292
Molesworth, Sir William, 8th Baronet, 210, 290
Monfort, Colonel, 63
Montenegrin troubles, 212, 214
Montevideo, 176
Montpensier, Antoine Marie Philippe Louis d'Orléans, Duc de, 154, 155, 156, 157, 162, 163
Moore, Sir John, Lt.-General, 20
Morea, 25, 112, 113, 114, 117
Morning Chronicle, 22, 183, 224
Morning Post, 215, 233
Moscow, 47, 88
Murat, Caroline, Queen of Naples, wife of Joachim Murat, 54, 56
Murat, Joachim, King of Naples, Marshal, 47, 54, 56, 68, 72, 93
Murray, Sir George, General, 168
Mutual Right of Search, 181

Nanking, Treaty of (1842), 149
Napier, Sir Charles, K.C.B., Admiral 244, 256, 258, 269
Naples, 47, 57, 93, 139, 209
Napoleon I, 21–3, 25, 47–9, 51–4, 60–4, 67–8, 70, 72–3, 78–9, 87–8, 90–3, 96–7
Napeoleon III, Charles Louis Napoleon, 22, 202, 235–6, 277–8, 285, 287
National Gallery, 186
Navarino, Battle of, 108, 111, 113, 117
Neipperg, Adam Albrecht, Count von, General, 59
Nelson, Horatio, Viscount Nelson, Vice-Admiral, 192, 195, 233
Nesselrode, Karl Robert, Count, 55, 68, 70, 73, 80, 84, 86, 213, 216, 223, 225, 226, 235
Netherlands, 48, 90, 111, 119
Netherlands, King of, 119
Newcastle, Henry Pelham Clinton Fiennes Pelham, 5th Duke of, 198–9, 202–3, 207, 209, 237, 241–3, 246–8, 250, 252, 258–9, 265, 270–2, 274–5, 278, 280, 282, 284–6, 290, 293–4, 296–8, 301, 303, 308, 311, 314, 324
Nicholas, Czar I, Nikolai Pavlovich, 212, 213, 214, 215, 216, 217, 220, 222, 223, 224, 225, 226, 229, 230, 231, 232, 233, 235, 236, 237, 247, 253, 287
Nightingale, Florence, 262
Nogle, Matthew, 325
Norway, 46, 70

O'Connell, Daniel, 132

Ölmütz, 225, 226
Omar Pasha, Mihajl Latas, General, 229, 230
Order of the Garter, 247, 281, 282
Oregon, 166, 167, 172–5, 179, 181, 182
Orléans, Philippe II, Duc d', Regent of France 1715–1723, 155
Orloff, Aleksei Federovich, Prince, 235, 236
Orsini, Félice, 321
Otho I, King of Greece, 117, 148
Oudinot, Nicolas Charles, Duc de Reggio, Marshal, 52

Pacifico, Don David, 195–7
Pakenham, Sir Richard, 172, 173
Palmerston, Henry John Temple, 3rd Viscount (1784–1865): Aberdeen compared with, 14, 121–3; at Harrow, 19; contests Cambridge seat, 29; Secretary-at-War, 108; and Huskisson's resignation, 110; and Greece, 112–13, 116, 117, 195–9; joins Whigs, 121; Foreign Secretary, 121; Princess Lieven's mistrust of, 124; Foreign Secretary again, 132; attitude to Aberdeen's foreign secretaryship, 143; Queen Pomare appeals to, 144; Aberdeen's attitude to, 146, 196, 197, 264, 273, 274, 275, 321; French attitude to, 146, 161; and China, 149–50; and Spanish Marriages, 151–65 *passim*; Russell's Foreign Secretary, 161; and American, relations, 166, 167, 169, 170, 171, 175; and Argentina, 176; and Brazilian slave trade, 178–9; and slave trade treaty with France, 180–1; Professor Jones on, 181–2; Grey objects to, as Foreign Secretary, 183–4; and visit to France, 184; unsigned articles in *Globe*, 195; and Don Pacifico, 195–7; Queen insists on exclusion from government, 200; and Napoleon III, 202; presses Lansdowne to be Prime Minister, 205; Aberdeen's fears that he will lead opposition party, 206; seat in Cabinet proposed, 208–9; Home Secretary, 209–10; calls for fleet to be sent to the Dardanelles, 215; forces Aberdeen's hand, 216, 237; rift with Aberdeen, 217; on occupation of Principalities, 218; against modifying draft convention, 219; on Reform 221, 232–3, 242; on Czar's rejection of modifications to the Vienna Note, 222; and Ölmütz proposals, 225–6; Vienna Note, 228–9; Aberdeen recapitulates posi-

tion for, 229–30; at odds with Aberdeen about new treaties, 230–1; return to Cabinet, 234; urges Russell not to press on with Reform Bill, 240; and 242; confident about attack on Sebastopol, 252–3, 275, 283; Layard urges that he be Prime Minister, 254; Russell confides his wish for the Premiership to him, 275; blames Raglan, 284; 289; Arthur Gordon believes Palmerston should take Newcastle's place, 290; 292; at final Cabinet, 293; Russell bargaining for him, 295–6; reconciled with Russell, 296; to move adjournment, 297; 298; feeble speech in reply to Russell, 299; winds up, 301; alone agrees to serve under Russell, 303; invites Aberdeen to join him, 304; Peelites join him, 305; 306; his health, 309, 306; Russell takes office under him, 307; entertains Aberdeen, 308; 310; 312; performance as Prime Minister assessed, 314–16; 317; Aberdeen believes his Government too weak to last, 318; General Election triumph, 319; gives way to Derby, 321; Prime Minister again, 322; opposes Haddo's bill, 323
Palmerston, Lady. *See* Cowper.
Panmure, the Hon. Fox Maule, 2nd Baron Panmure and later 11th Earl of Dalhousie, 314
Paris, Louis Philippe Albert, Comte de, 320
Parker, C. S., 255
Paul, Pavel Petrovich, Czar of Russia, 22
Peace of Paris (1814), 93
Petro I, Dom, of Brazil, 151
Peel, Jonathan, General, 310, 312
Peel, Sir Robert, 2nd Baronet, 13, 19, 108, 111, 116, 118, 121, 124–6, 129–33, 139–42, 145, 148–9, 153–4, 156–9, 161, 166–7, 171, 173–5, 179, 182–4, 187, 190, 194–201, 204–6, 210, 320, 324, 331
Peel, Julia, Lady, 111, 197–8
Peel, Sir Robert, 3rd Baronet, 289
Peelites, 198–9, 200, 202, 203, 204, 206, 208, 209, 221, 248, 255, 271, 275, 290, 299, 303, 304, 305, 307, 311, 312, 318, 319, 321, 322, 331
Peninsula, 35, 67; the campaign, 36, 300
Perceval, Spencer, 37
Persia, 33, 139
Philip V, King of France, 154
Philip V, King of Spain, 153

Phipps, Sir Charles Beaumont, Colonel, 203
Piedmont, 73
Piscatory, Monsieur, 148
Pitt, William, the younger, 19, 20, 21, 25, 29, 30, 31, 44, 46, 192, 197, 204, 207, 238, 255
Pnyx, 24
Poland, 48, 60
Polk, James Knox, 172–4
Pomare IV, Aimata, Queen of the Society Islands, 144, 145, 147
Portland, William Henry Cavendish Bentinck, 3rd Duke of Portland, 31
Portugal, 34, 46, 127, 151–2
Potsdam, 50
Pottinger, Sir Henry, 1st Baronet, 149
Pozzo di Borgo, Carlo Andrea, Count, General, 78, 79
Prague, 48, 50, 51, 52
Prince of Wales, George, later George IV, 20, 27
Prince Regent (See George IV), 33, 46, 71, 72
Pritchard, the Rev. George, 144, 145, 147
Protection, 203; Protectionists, 202, 203
Prussia, 47, 48, 49, 50, 54, 55, 71, 72, 86, 113, 118, 139, 236
Prussia, Crown Prince of, 50, 56, 61, 64
Prussia, King of, 49, 53, 66
Pyrenees, 46, 47, 70, 96

Quadruple Alliance (1834), 151–2
Quebec, 168

Raglan, Fitzroy James Henry Somerset, 1st Baron Raglan 239, 244, 252–3, 257–9, 261–2, 265–70, 277, 279, 280, 282–7, 300, 314
Ranger's House, Blackheath, 189, 309
Redan, 315
Redcliffe, Lord Stratford de. See Canning, Sir Stratford.
Reform, 120, 121, 125–6, 133, 137, 204, 221, 232, 233, 234, 239, 242, 316, 322, and see Russell, Lord John; Reform Bills, 120, 125–6, 322; Reform Act, 137
Regency Act, 36
Reichenbach, Treaty of, 49
Reine Blanche, 145
Retribution, HMS, 235
Ridley, Jasper, 196, 202
Right of Search, 70, 166, 181
Robinson, Frederick John, later Viscount Goderich, then Earl of Ripon, 19, 108

Roebuck, John Arthur, 289–90, 292–6, 298–9, 302, 303, 307, 309–11, 313, 316
Rogers, Samuel, 186
Roman Catholics, petition for relief, 107, 108, and see 109, 120–1
Romilly, John, Colonel, 295
Rosas, Juan Manuel de, General, 176, 177
Rose, Hugh Henry, Colonel, later Field-Marshal and Baron, 214–15
Royal Society, 32
Russell, Lord John, 1st Earl Russell (1792–1878): Arthur Gordon refutes inaccuracies by, 14; moves repeal of Test and Corporation Acts, 109; sneers at Wellington's and Aberdeen's lack of bellicosity, 113; 122; 125; Aberdeen's wish to avoid his sweeping reform measures, 125; 139; Prime Minister, with Palmerston Foreign Secretary, 176, 184; his 'Edinburgh Letter', 183; 184; Aberdeen supports his Government, 191; calls Stanley, Gladstone, Disraeli and Aberdeen an 'unprincipled coalition', 195; 199; resigns early in 1851, 200; Queen sends for him and he invites Aberdeen and Graham to join him, 200; Ecclesiastical Titles Bill and Aberdeen, 200; offers to carry on conditionally, 201; demands Palmerston's resignation, 202; forced to resign, 202; Aberdeen more in agreement with him than Derby, 203; Aberdeen's crucial meeting with him, 205; refuses to be Foreign Secretary and lead in Commons, 206; offers to lead and sit without portfolio, 207; his place-hunting for Whigs, 208; Aberdeen's concern about his relations with Palmerston, 209–10; The Times contemptuously dismisses him, 210–11; rebuff's Czar's proposals and sends Stratford de Redcliffe to Constantinople, 213; 215; with others forces Aberdeen's hand, 216; desire to frighten Czar, 217; 219; raises reform measure, 221; disagreement about Vienna Note, 222; over-ruled, 223; threatens resignation, 224; accused by Aberdeen of wanting to supplant him, 225; for action after Olmütz, 226; chips away at proposed Note, 228; more warlike, 229; his reform bill splits Cabinet, 232; Aberdeen writes to about his conscience, 233; disagrees with Aberdeen's self-

castigation, 237; threatens resignation and demands dissolution, 239–40; resignation crisis, 241–2, 309–12; turns attention to conduct of war, 242; plans reform of system, 246; again threatens to resign, 247; Aberdeen refuses to agree to reshuffle, 248; 250; meeting at Pembroke Lodge, 252; in Commons debate on war, 254–5; optimistic after landing in Crimea, 260; Clarendon disgusted with, 262; Aberdeen nervous of his intentions, 264–5; campaign to oust Aberdeen in the open, 271; and resignation crisis, 271–92; visit to Louis Napoleon, 287; *The Times* criticizes resignation, 299; fails to form Government, 303; Aberdeen's true feelings about him revealed, 302; peace negotiator in Vienna, 307; 309; his vote on the motion, 312; 315; effect of his machinations on Aberdeen's career, 316; 321; Foreign Secretary, 322; perfunctory comment on Aberdeen's illness, 323; joins the Radicals on Scottish Church Bill, 331

Russell, Frances, Lady John, 207, 214, 224, 241, 248, 264, 287, 292

Russell, Lady Louisa Jane, 125, 303

Russell, Sir William Howard, 243, 250–1, 258, 266, 269

Russia, 32, 48, 49, 54, 55, 67, 71, 72, 74, 86, 107, 111–17 *passim*, 139, 196, and chapters 16–25 *passim*, 276, 277

St Aignan, Count de, 70, 73

St Arnaud, Armand Jacques Leroy de, Marshal, 249, 253, 259, 261, 262, 287

St Aulaire, Louis Clair de Beaupoil, Count de, 161

St John River, 168

St Petersburg, 212, 215, 220, 222, 235

Saxe-Coburg, Duke of, 160, 161

Saxe-Coburg, Prince Ferdinand of, 152

Saxe-Coburg, Prince Leopold, later Leopold I, King of the Belgians, 116, 117, 120, 132–3, 136, 147, 152, 154, 160, 162, 182, 210

Schwarzenberg, Felix, Prince zu, 40, 51, 52, 56, 60, 61, 62, 67, 73, 76, 86

Scott, Sir Walter, 25, 97, 192

Scottish Church affairs. *See* Disruption of the Scottish Church.

Scottish Entails, Bill on, 107

Scutari, 249, 262, 266, 269, 279, 285, 288, 315

Seaton, Sir John Colborne, 1st Baron Seaton, 168

Sebastopol, 235, 249, 251, 252, 253, 254, 256, 257, 258, 259, 260, 261, 262, 263, 264, 265, 266, 267, 268, 273, 279, 283, 286, 288, 292, 313, 315

Sebastopol Report, 310–12

Seymour, Sir George Hamilton, 212, 235

Sheridan, Richard Brinsley, 20, 25, 26

Sheridan, Elizabeth Linley, 25

Sicily, 32, 46, 47, 70, 72

Silesia, 49, 51

Silistria, 249, 252

Simpson, Sir James, General, 314

Sinclair, Sir Robert, 331

Sinope, Battle of, 231, 232, 233, 234, 235, 249

Slave Trade, 93, 170, 178–9, 180–1

Smith, Vernon, M.P., 275, 295

Soane, Sir John, 25

Spain, 34, 46, 48, 54, 68, 70, 72, 82, 90, 127, 142, 151–65 *passim*, 191

Spanish Marriages, 151–65

Spanish War of Succession, 153

Stanhope, Lady Hester, 19–20, 25

Stewart, Sir Charles William Stewart, later 3rd Marquess of Londonderry, 49, 50, 54–5, 57, 59, 62, 66–8,

Straits Convention, 230

Stralsund, 48, 50

Strangford, Percy Clinton Sydney, 6th Viscount Strangford and 1st Baron Penshurst, 217

Stratford de Redcliffe. *See* Canning, Sir Stratford.

Strathbogie, 329

Strelitz, 50

Stuart, Lord Dudley Coutts, 254

Sutherland, Countess of, Harriet Elizabeth Georgiana, 188

Sweden, 46, 48, 55, 276

Switzerland, 48, 60, 72, 78, 82, 84, 89, 90, 191

Tahiti, 144–78

Talavera, Battle of, 34

Talleyrand, Charles Maurice Talleyrand-Périgord, 54, 78, 92, 119, 120, 151

Tangier, 145, 155

Taymouth Castle, 133

Tenedos, 115

Teplitz, 51, 52, 53, 54, 55, 60, 61, 69

Test and Corporation Acts, 109, 121

Texas, 173, 174, 176, 181

Thiers, Louis Adolphe, 139, 146, 184

Thrasher, 140

Times, The, 13–14, 20, 138, 142, 210–

11, 243, 252, 260, 262, 268, 278, 279–80, 287–8, 298–300, 312, 315, 317, 328
Thistle, Order of the, 32
Thouars, Admiral du Petit, 144, 145
Thuycidides, 186
Tiverton, 180, 184
Trapani, Count of, 156, 157
Treaty of General Alliance, 54, 68, 74, 77, 78, 79, 85
Treaty of Paris (1814), 93, (1856), 313–14
Treaty of Union (1709), 15
Triple Alliance, 151
Turkey, 111–17 *passim*, 139, and chapters 16–25 *passim*
Tyler, John, 166, 173
Tyrol, 46, 60

United States of America, 40, 139, chapter 14 *passim* (pp. 166–84)
Unkiar Skelessi, Treaty of (1833), 139
Uruguay, 176, 177
Utrecht, Treaty of (1713), 153–4

Valetta, 243
Valley of Death, 249, 250
Van Buren, Martin, 169
Vandamme, Dominique, Comte d'Unebourg, General, 52
Varna, 114, 249–51, 257, 259–60, 269
Venus, HMS, 144
Versailles, Treaty of (1783), 172
Veto Act, 327, 330
Victoria, Queen, 40, 154–5, 162, 182, 184, 195–6, 200–2, 204, 207, 209–10, 222–3, 225, 227, 229, 233, 240–1, 247, 252–3, 255–7, 260, 263, 266, 272, 274–6, 278, 282, 287, 295–9, 303–6, 309, 313, 315, 317, 319–20, 323–4
Vienna, 25, 41, 48, 59, 86, 90, 107, 191, 218–19, 220, 229, 231, 235, 236, 277, 286, 287, 289, 313
Vienna Conference, 219, 220, 223, 313
Vienna, Congress of, 86, 90, 107, 119, 120
Vienna Notes, then, 220, 222, 223, 225, 228, 235, 325
Vienna, Treaty of (1815), 163

Walpole, Sir Spencer, 205

Warspite, HMS, 168
Waterloo, Battle of, 96, 239, 244, 255, 316, 320
Webster, C. S., 71
Webster, Daniel, 166, 167, 172
Wellesley, Richard Colley, Marquis Wellesley, 36
Wellington, Arthur Wellesley, 1st Duke of, Field-Marshal, 13, 16, 34–7, 67, 79, 94, 96–7, 108–10, 112–14, 116–21, 126, 129–33, 141–2, 151, 158–9, 167–8, 187, 192, 201, 202, 203, 210, 244, 246, 300, 320
Wessenberg, Herr, 78
Westminster Abbey, 326
Westminster Hall, 106
Westmorland, John Fane, 11th Earl, 231
Weymouth, 37
Whitbread, Samuel, 20, 37
White Sea, 263
White's Club, 31
Whittington, the Rev. George Downing, 20, 32
'Who? Who? Ministry', 203
Whyte, Rev. James, 328, 329
Wilberforce, Samuel, Bishop of Oxford and of Winchester, 281, 325
Wilberforce, William 25
Wilkins, William, 31
William IV, King of Great Britain and Ireland, 132, 192
Wilson, Sir Robert Thomas, Major-General, 68, 73
Wimbledon, 19, 29
Windsor Castle, 121, 227, 274, 281, 294, 296, 302, 305, 306
Wood, Sir Charles, later 1st Viscount Halifax, 208, 210, 274, 289, 294–5
Wreford, Mr, Purveyor-General, 311
Würtemberg, 68

Yarmouth, 48
York, Frederick Augustus, Duke of, Field-Marshal, 33
Yorke, Sir Joseph Sydney, Admiral, 33
Young, Sir John, 300
Ystadt, 48, 50
Ythan, 17, 98, 124

Zwickau, 60, 63